NEW PERSPECTIVES ON THE HASKALAH

THE LITTMAN LIBRARY OF JEWISH CIVILIZATION

Dedicated to the memory of

Louis Thomas Sidney Littman

who founded the Littman Library for the love of God and as an act of charity in memory of his father

Joseph Aaron Littman

and to the memory of

Robert Joseph Littman

who continued what his father Louis had begun

יהא זכרם ברוך

'Get wisdom, get understanding:
Forsake her not and she shall preserve thee'

PROV. 4: 5

The Littman Library of Jewish Civilization is a registered UK charity
Registered charity no. 1000784

NEW PERSPECTIVES ON THE HASKALAH

◆

Edited by

SHMUEL FEINER

and

DAVID SORKIN

London

The Littman Library of Jewish Civilization

in association with Liverpool University Press

The Littman Library of Jewish Civilization
Registered office: 4th floor, 7–10 Chandos Street, London W1G 9DQ

in association with Liverpool University Press
4 Cambridge Street, Liverpool L69 7ZU, UK
www.liverpooluniversitypress.co.uk/littman

Managing Editor: Connie Webber

Distributed in North America by
Oxford University Press Inc., 198 Madison Avenue,
New York, NY 10016, USA

First published in hardback 2001
First published in paperback 2004

Catalogue records for this book are available from the British Library and the Library of Congress

ISBN 978-1-904113-26-3

Publishing co-ordinator: Janet Moth
Proof-reading: Bonnie Blackburn
Index: Sarah Ereira
Designed by Pete Russell, Faringdon, Oxon.
Typeset by Footnote Graphics, Warminster, Wilts.

Printed and bound in Great Britain by
CPI Group (UK) Ltd., Croydon, CR0 4YY

Preface

THE editors would like to thank the Oxford Centre for Hebrew and Jewish Studies for sponsoring as a Marc Rich Seminar the conference on which this volume is based. The beautiful setting of Yarnton Manor, its fine accommodation and its helpful and experienced staff allowed us the rare opportunity to experience the true meaning of the phrase 'a community of scholars'. We would especially like to acknowledge the achievement of the Centre's founder and first president, David Patterson: his dream of making Yarnton Manor a home to scholars and scholarship has been realized.

The Braun Chair for the History of the Jews in Prussia at Bar Ilan University recognized the importance of this project and provided financial support for editing the volume.

The Center for Jewish Studies at the University of Wisconsin-Madison, and its tireless secretary Anita Lightfoot, offered clerical assistance.

The Littman Library of Jewish Civilization has been everything for which the editors could have wished. Connie Webber has shown unflagging enthusiasm. Janet Moth has been an outstanding editor, expertly handling problems of all dimensions (from murky prose to the nightmare of transliteration).

Contents

Note on Transliteration

THE transliteration of Hebrew in this book reflects a consideration of the type of book it is, in terms of its content, purpose, and readership. The system adopted therefore reflects a broad approach to transcription rather than the narrower approaches found in the *Encyclopaedia Judaica* or other systems developed for text-based or linguistic studies. The aim has been to reflect the pronunciation prescribed for modern Hebrew rather than the spelling or Hebrew word structure, and to do so using conventions that are generally familiar to the English-speaking reader.

In accordance with this approach, no attempt is made to indicate the distinctions between *alef* and *ayin*, *tet* and *taf*, *kaf* and *kuf*, *sin* and *samekh*, since these are not relevant to pronunciation; likewise, the *dagesh* is not indicated except where it affects pronunciation. Following the principle of using conventions familiar to the majority of readers, however, transcriptions that are well established have been retained even when they are not fully consistent with the transliteration system adopted. Likewise, the distinction between *ḥet* and *khaf* has been retained, using *ḥ* for the former and *kh* for the latter: the associated forms are generally familiar, even if the distinction is not actually borne out in pronunciation; for the same reason, the final *heh* is also indicated. The *sheva na* is indicated by an *e*—*lomedim*—except, again, when established convention dictates otherwise. The *yod* is represented by an *i* when it occurs as a vowel (*bereshit*), by a *y* when it occurs as a consonant (*yesodot*), and by *yi* when it occurs as both (*yisra'el*).

Since no distinction is made between *alef* and *ayin* they are indicated by an apostrophe only in intervocalic positions where a failure to do so could lead an English-speaking reader to pronounce the vowel-cluster as a diphthong—as, for example, in *ha'ir*—or otherwise mispronounce the word.

As in Hebrew, no capital letters are used except in the titles of published works (for example, *Shulḥan arukh*).

Thanks are due to Jonathan Webber of the Oxford Centre for Hebrew and Jewish Studies for his help in elucidating the principles to be adopted.

Introduction

SHMUEL FEINER and DAVID SORKIN

IN a recent article Robert Darnton criticized the state of contemporary research on the Enlightenment as 'inflationary', noting that it 'has blown up to such a size that it would not be recognized by the men who first created it'. In view of the diversification of Enlightenment studies, seen for example in the multiplicity of conferences and publications on such subjects as the Josephine Enlightenment, the pietistic Enlightenment, and the religious Enlightenment, Darnton observed that 'the Enlightenment is beginning to be everything and therefore nothing'.[1]

The editors of this volume endorse Darnton's suggestion that Enlightenment studies ought to be deflated and that, first and foremost, the Enlightenment should be restored to history as a concrete trend fixed in time and place whose ramifications and transformations can be ascertained. They also agree that it is important to examine the milieu of the intellectuals who initiated the Enlightenment and who idealistically attempted to reform the world according to a rationalist, liberal agenda. In order to comprehend fully the significance of the Enlightenment, one must examine the enlighteners' rhetoric, describe their vision of a reformed world, study their strategies, reconstruct the social settings in which they worked, and analyse the objections their adversaries raised and the confrontations that ensued.

By reducing the Enlightenment to its French focus or even limiting it to eighteenth-century Europe, however, we may be losing the forest for the trees. In order to avoid overlooking less well known aspects of the Enlightenment, or homogenizing those that are known, it is advisable to think not about 'one' Enlightenment but rather about 'varieties' of Enlightenment. The essays in this volume address a subject which scholars of the Enlightenment have tended to neglect: the Haskalah, or Jewish Enlightenment. The Haskalah provides an interesting example of one of the Enlightenments of eighteenth- to nineteenth-century Europe which also constituted a unique chapter in the social history of European Jewry. It encompasses over 120 years (from around the 1770s to the 1890s), and a large number of Jewish communities, from London in the west, to Copenhagen in the north, to Vilna and St Petersburg in the east.

It should also come as no surprise that Darnton's call for deflation applies to the study of the Haskalah itself. Much scholarship in the past concentrated on the Haskalah's intimate relationship to Jewish modernization: scholars examined the role of the Haskalah in the processes of political emancipation and the integration of Jews into the larger society (in the older scholarship this was called 'assimilation'; in more recent work 'acculturation'). Whether the Haskalah was a primary factor or

[1] 'George Washington's False Teeth', *New York Review of Books*, 27 Mar. 1997, pp. 34–8.

an epiphenomenon in the ensemble of historical factors—whether it was cause or effect, syndrome or symptom—was a burning issue in the work of historians and sociologists.[2] In this, the study of the Haskalah resembled that of the French Enlightenment: because the latter was dominated by the question of its impact on the French Revolution, it often did not receive the attention it deserved as an independent phenomenon. Once disengaged from the Revolution, however, the French Enlightenment could begin to be examined through less partisan eyes.[3] Thus, as long as historians saw the modernization of the Jews as an integral aspect of the contemporary struggle in which they themselves were engaged, the scholarship was ineluctably partisan and the Haskalah was viewed through the lens of one or another ideological position.[4] A different approach became possible once the modernization of European Jewry came to be viewed as a series of processes that awaited adequate analysis and explanation, the Haskalah being one of the foremost among them.

This volume attempts to offer just such a deflationary approach, and to restore

[2] This has been the main focus of discussion at least since Graetz. See Heinrich Graetz, *Geschichte der Juden* (1853–75), repr., in 6 vols. (Munich, 1985). For the standard works see Jacob Katz, *Tradition and Crisis: Jewish Society at the End of the Middle Ages*, trans. Bernard Dov Cooperman (New York, 1993) (the Hebrew original, *Mesoret umashber*, appeared in 1958); Azriel Shohat, *Changing Eras: The Beginning of the Haskalah among German Jewry* (Heb.) (Jerusalem, 1960); Michael A. Meyer, *The Origins of the Modern Jew* (Detroit, 1967); David Sorkin, *The Transformation of German Jewry, 1780–1840* (New York, 1987); and Steven M. Lowenstein, *The Berlin Jewish Community: Enlightenment, Family and Crisis, 1770–1830* (New York and Oxford, 1994).

For east European Jewry see e.g. Michael Stanislawski, *Tsar Nicholas I and the Jews: The Transformation of Jewish Society in Russia, 1825–1855* (Philadelphia, Pa., 1983); Steven J. Zipperstein, *The Jews of Odessa: A Cultural History, 1794–1881* (Stanford, Calif., 1986); David E. Fishman, *Russia's First Modern Jews: The Jews of Shklov* (New York, 1995); and Immanuel Etkes (ed.), *Religion and Life: The Jewish Enlightenment in Eastern Europe* (Heb.) (Jerusalem, 1993), which contains an extensive bibliography.

For all of Europe see Jacob Katz (ed.), *Toward Modernity: The European Jewish Model* (New Brunswick, NJ, 1987).

Historians of literature have also contributed to this debate. For influential examples see Joseph Klausner, *History of Modern Hebrew Literature* (Heb.), 6 vols. (Jerusalem, 1952–4); Simon Halkin, *Modern Hebrew Literature: From the Enlightenment to the Birth of the State of Israel. Trends and Values* (New York, 1950); Moshe Pelli, *The Age of Haskalah: Studies in Hebrew Literature of the Enlightenment in Germany* (Leiden, 1979); and Shmuel Werses (ed.), *Trends and Forms in Haskalah Literature* (Heb.) (Jerusalem, 1990).

For the changing use of the terms 'assimilation' and 'acculturation' see Jonathan Frankel, 'Assimilation and the Jews in Nineteenth-Century Europe: Towards a New Historiography?', in Jonathan Frankel and Steven J. Zipperstein (eds.), *Assimilation and Community: The Jews in Nineteenth-Century Europe* (Cambridge, 1992), 1–37.

[3] See e.g. Roger Chartier, *The Cultural Origins of the French Revolution* (Durham, NC, 1991).

[4] For a Marxist view see e.g. Raphael Mahler, *A History of Modern Jewry* (London, 1971), and id., *Hasidism and the Jewish Enlightenment: Their Confrontation in Galicia and Poland in the First Half of the Nineteenth Century* (New York and Philadelphia, Pa., 1985); for the autonomist view see Simon Dubnow, *History of the Jews*, 5 vols. (1925–9; South Brunswick, NJ, 1967–73); for the Zionist view see Benzion Dinur, *At the Turn of the Generations* (Heb.) (Jerusalem, 1954). For a penetrating analysis of these historians see Frankel, 'Assimilation and the Jews in Nineteenth-Century Europe'.

to the Haskalah ambiguity and equivocality, detail and texture. It hopes to replace broad categories informed by later partisan debates and ideological positions with finer discriminations rooted in earlier situations. Above all, it hopes to replace simple dichotomies, such as Haskalah and Orthodoxy, modernizers and traditionalists, with more subtle and nuanced distinctions that capture the perceptions and convey the dilemmas of the historical figures themselves. In particular, where earlier scholarship stressed disjuncture, this volume emphasizes continuity: while it recognizes the innovative, if not revolutionary, character of the Haskalah, it also aspires to understand the relationship between 'tradition' and Haskalah as a spectrum of closely linked cultural options rather than as a single fateful choice between old and new, good and evil.

The volume also aims to revise our notion of the Haskalah by reconsidering major figures as well as studying secondary ones. Close study of major figures can alter our understanding of seemingly well-known works by locating them in the longer span of an individual's development, and by seeing them more clearly in the setting in which that person lived and thought.[5] Similarly, examinations of minor figures can cast the larger cultural trend in a new and sometimes surprising light.[6] In addition, groups that have hitherto received less attention, for example women and the Orthodox, or important subjects that have gone unexplored, open a new dimension in our understanding of the workings of the Haskalah.[7] If historical truth resides in the details, then this volume doggedly pursues details in order to offer new perspectives on the Haskalah.

The first three chapters proffer a fresh and innovative interpretation of several facets of the 'Berlin Haskalah'. The cultural developments of the first six decades of the eighteenth century, David Sorkin argues in Chapter 1, should not be treated as mere anticipations of the Haskalah but rather as constituting an 'early Haskalah' which aimed to broaden the curriculum of Ashkenazi Jewry.[8] Figures such as Solomon Hanau (1687–1746) and Asher Anshel Worms (1695–1769) aimed to revive the study of Hebrew language and grammar as well as biblical exegesis, while Israel Zamosc (1700–72) and Aaron Solomon Gumpertz (1723–69) aimed to renew the discipline of philosophy in Hebrew by harmonizing contemporary science and

[5] For some recent efforts see Michael Stanislawski, *For Whom Do I Toil? Judah Leib Gordon and the Crisis of Russian Jewry* (New York, 1988); David Sorkin, *Moses Mendelssohn and the Religious Enlightenment* (Berkeley and Los Angeles, 1996); Frances Malino, *A Jew in the French Revolution: The Life of Zalkind Hourwitz* (Oxford, 1996); and Shmuel Feiner, 'Mendelssohn and Mendelssohn's Disciples: A Re-examination', *Leo Baeck Institute Yearbook*, 40 (1995), 133–67.

[6] Two examples are Shmuel Feiner, 'Isaac Euchel: Entrepreneur of the Haskalah Movement in Germany' (Heb.), *Zion*, 52 (1987), 427–69, and Israel Bartal, 'Mordecai Aaron Gunzburg: A Lithuanian Maskil Faces Modernity', in Frances Malino and David Sorkin (eds.), *From East and West: Jews in a Changing Europe, 1750–1870* (Oxford, 1990), 126–47.

[7] For the role of historical consciousness, see e.g. Shmuel Feiner, *Haskalah and History: The Emergence of a Modern Jewish Historical Consciousness* (Heb.) (Jerusalem, 1995).

[8] Shmuel Feiner has analysed the early Haskalah in 'The Early Haskalah in Eighteenth-Century Judaism' (Heb.), *Tarbiz*, 62/2 (1998), 189–240.

philosophy with established but hitherto neglected patterns of Jewish thought. These thinkers aspired to a Hebrew-based curriculum capable of absorbing the best of contemporary culture. Sorkin argues that once we recognize the early Haskalah as an independent cultural trend we need to determine to what extent it influenced the Haskalah after 1770, and how far it remained a viable cultural option.

Naphtali Herz Wessely (1725–1805) was best known for his book *Divrei shalom ve'emet* (Words of Peace and Truth). Regarded as the formative text of the Haskalah, this book was a passionate response to Joseph II's Edict of Tolerance; in it, Wessely urged the Jews of the Habsburg empire to enrol their children in state schools where they would follow a balanced curriculum, studying Jewish religious subjects as well as languages, science, and the humanities in an orderly fashion. In Chapter 2, Edward Breuer departs from the usual portrayal of Wessely and depicts him as alienated from both traditional and modernist Jews, as well as from the other maskilim, at least during the later years of his life. He describes Wessely's indecision and frustration, in particular his sense that no one properly understood his vision of cultural renewal, and he shows how Wessely's alienation was compounded by his anxiety about the growing dimensions of religious heresy and by his disaffection from traditional circles. The chapter devotes special attention to an analysis of Wessely's early writings, revealing that his major interests were twofold: the revival of biblical Hebrew as an essential tool for a more precise understanding of rabbinic literature, and an affirmation of the credibility of the Oral Torah that was being criticized by European scholars.

In discussing Haskalah ethical literature, Chapter 3 highlights the way in which the Haskalah movement was poised between Jewish tradition and European culture. Harris Bor shows that moral improvement was a fundamental concern of the Haskalah: since moral education was meant to serve as a link between the aims of the Enlightenment and Jewish tradition, ethical literature was an index to the balance between the modern and the traditional. Bor illustrates the importance of comparative study: by comparing the texts and motifs of the Enlightenment on issues such as the immortality of the soul and civic education with the ethical ideas of such maskilim as Isaac Satanow (1732–1804), Wessely, Menahem Mendel Lefin (1749–1826), and Judah Leib Ben Ze'ev (1764–1811), he reveals the extent to which the Haskalah drew upon the educational methods of German reformist educators like Johann Heinrich Campe and Johann Bernhard Basedow.

David Ruderman's innovative essay (Chapter 4) sheds light on a largely unexplored facet of English Jewish history, reopening the issue of whether there was a Haskalah in England. Historians generally contend that the modernization of England's Jews was not ideological but was shaped by the irresistible pull of English society; in this view, the creative work of diverse Anglo-Jewish thinkers is seen as a specifically Jewish phenomenon, a response to English openness and tolerance. In contrast, Ruderman points to a number of thinkers who were in contact with English intellectuals and were influenced by such important trends as Lockian philosophy, millenarianism, Newtonianism, deism, and atheism. His discovery of this English Jewish intellectual current prior to the Berlin Haskalah, and apparently unrelated to the work of other maskilim, certainly provides students of the Haskalah with food for thought.

While there are differences of opinion about whether a Haskalah even existed in England, there is no doubt that it reached its peak among nineteenth-century east European Jewry. The historical conditions of a dense population of Jews, traditional in their culture and religious observance, who modernized at a relatively late date, explain the curious fact of the belated Enlightenment in this society. Nancy Sinkoff (Chapter 5) transports us to early nineteenth-century Galicia where we meet Menahem Mendel Lefin of Satanow, a fascinating maskil, who was a link between the German and the east European Haskalah. Because he often wrote in Yiddish he has usually been seen as a populist who advanced the maskilim's criticism of east European Jewish life and culture. He attacked the intoxication with mysticism, became involved in the literary battle against hasidism, and proposed the maskilim as leaders who could heal the ills of Jewish society. In contrast to the view of Lefin as a populist, which was rooted in earlier scholarship's nationalist bias, Sinkoff notes his sophisticated use of literary strategies aimed at different audiences according to the language of the text (he wrote in Yiddish, Hebrew, and French). She illustrates these strategies in her analysis of a text written for his fellow Jews, an adaptation and translation of a travel story in the New World meant as a tool of social criticism and anti-hasidic polemics, and also in a text written for a wider audience, an anonymous French memorandum that Lefin submitted to the Polish Sejm in 1791.

Chapters 6 and 7 also deal with the maskilim's struggle against hasidim. With its insularity, mysticism, and cult of the *tsadik* or spiritual leader, hasidism was seen by the maskilim as their chief enemy. In Yehuda Friedlander's view, the maskilim aimed to delegitimize hasidism in order to enhance their own standing. In this enterprise they drew on their predecessors, the numerous rabbis who from the last third of the eighteenth century had opposed hasidism, prominent among whom was Jacob Emden (1697–1776). By showing how the Galician maskil Judah Leib Mieses (1798–1831) selectively wove Emden's anti-hasidic polemic into his satires, Friedlander reveals the literary strategies of the Haskalah and illustrates how the maskilim, in their attack on the hasidic enemy, exploited Emden as a religious authority. His textual analysis demonstrates how well versed in talmudic and rabbinic texts the maskilim had to be in order to weave the associations and allusions of rabbinic polemics into the fabric of their own writings.

In Chapter 7 Immanuel Etkes takes as his point of departure the widespread assumption that the maskilim opposed all forms of superstition, including magic and miracle-working, because they viewed it as a hallmark of hasidism and the ignorant masses. Etkes rejects the Haskalah's twin allegations that *tsadikim* engaged in magic and that magic was the sole province of the hasidim. These allegations were inaccurate—not all *tsadikim* practised magic, and it was in fact also a central element in the culture of the Lithuanian mitnagedim—but they were convenient grist to the propaganda mill. The maskilim were so apprehensive about the danger that hasidism posed to the future of Jewish society that they had no compunctions about exaggerating its evils. In Professor Etkes's view this exaggerated image, together with a tendency to ignore hasidism's genuine spiritual elements, also coloured later scholarship on the movement,

The intellectual passage from the culture of Torah scholars to the new world of the Haskalah was one of the fundamental experiences of the maskil. In Chapter 8 Shmuel Werses reconstructs the social experience of the east European maskilim, showing the high price the young man paid for his attraction to the Haskalah, since that attraction often entailed a clash with parents and in-laws, teachers and religious leaders. One way to escape this predicament was to acquire a rich patron; another route was to forge strong ties with other maskilim. Werses also reveals the critical role played by the 'forbidden' book: the young man's clandestine reading of non-canonical books, his conversion through such reading, and the subsequent trauma of discovery and punishment.

Tovah Cohen (Chapter 9) also combines history and literature, this time to analyse the depiction of women in nineteenth-century Haskalah literature. Her detailed discussion shows just how gender-specific this was: Haskalah literature was written by men for a male audience, and the maskilim were taken by surprise when women readers and writers began to appear in the 1860s. Cohen outlines the two extremes of the literary image of women: the idealized depiction of the goddess or angel on the one hand, and the critical depiction of the insensitive, crass, and domineering woman on the other, both images deriving from literary conventions. She also analyses the interplay of these conventions with the social experience and social agenda of the maskilim.

Joseph Salmon (Chapter 10) portrays a special group which has suffered from lack of attention—rabbis in Russia in the 1860s and 1870s who, with a measure of enlightenment, aspired to reform Jewish society. Salmon suggests that in this period the gap between maskilim and traditional Jews was not as wide as is usually thought. He cautions against a simple dualistic view of the relationship between Haskalah and tradition, describing a group of Lithuanian rabbis who were involved in demands for reform in the spirit of an Enlightenment which turned Zionist in the 1880s. Like the moderate maskilim in eastern Europe, these rabbis tried to fuse Enlightenment and tradition; in Salmon's view they can be regarded as the source of modern Orthodoxy in Israel and the United States.

In the final chapter Shmuel Feiner surveys the long historiographic tradition in search of a definition of the Haskalah. He advocates reducing the historical parameters of the Jewish Enlightenment so that it can be recognized as a trend in which modernizing intellectuals aspired to transform Jewish society. Despite the obvious diversity and dispersion of the Haskalah, and the difficulty in defining it precisely, he enumerates a number of essential criteria, elaborating on the self-consciousness of the maskilim and paying special attention to their militant rhetoric and awareness of belonging to an avant-garde, redemptive, and revolutionary movement. He also sketches a portrait of the typical maskil, surveys the history of the movement and its various centres, and elucidates the dualistic nature of its ideology, explaining its links to the processes of Jewish modernization and secularization. He concludes that the Haskalah was the intellectual option for modernization that triggered the Jewish *Kulturkampf* which, still alive today—especially in Israel—separates modernists and anti-modernists, Orthodox and secular Jews.

Haskalah studies have recently become a flourishing field among a young generation of historians and students of literature. The essays in this volume, which are based on an international conference held under the auspices of the Oxford Centre for Hebrew and Jewish Studies in the summer of 1994, obviously do not cover all of the new directions that have emerged from these efforts. Yet they are sufficiently representative to indicate many of the areas in which older views have been, or are being, revised as well as those calling for additional research. Whatever the ultimate outcome of this new wave of research, students of the Jewish past can no longer recount the familiar and comfortable story of the Haskalah that has long informed textbooks and popular histories, but must instead come to grips with a more ambiguous and challenging, if still provisional, account of it.

ONE

The Early Haskalah

DAVID SORKIN

HASKALAH scholarship has so overwhelmingly emphasized the period after 1770 that prior developments and their exponents have long been relegated to the respective statuses of anticipations and precursors.[1] Since the nature of a movement remains opaque if its antecedents are not properly understood, it is time for us to scrutinize anew the period 1720–1770. We must ask whether it contained mere anticipations or in fact constituted a cultural phase that warrants recognition. If we extend to the early Haskalah the sort of treatment which scholarship on the European Enlightenment has given to the 'early Enlightenment' or *Frühaufklärung*, we might then need to consider the possibility that it represented a cultural entity which is able to cast new light on the Haskalah after 1770.[2]

To examine the developments prior to 1770 it is necessary to stop reading backwards from the nineteenth and twentieth centuries—to forgo the usual questions about emancipation and assimilation, modernization and the reform of Jewish society—and instead to begin reading forwards from the eighteenth century, enquiring about the relationship of early eighteenth-century thinkers to the cultural configuration of their time. What were these thinkers attempting to do with the available culture of their own day? Which aspects of medieval and early modern Jewish thought did they accept and which trends of thought did they reject? What was their attitude to recent developments in European philosophy and science?

If we begin with these questions, it is apparent that the early Haskalah may be defined as an effort to revise baroque Judaism or the Ashkenazi culture of early

[1] For scholarship that emphasizes the Haskalah after 1770 see Jacob Katz, *Tradition and Crisis: Jewish Society at the End of the Middle Ages*, trans. Bernard Dov Cooperman (New York, 1993); Moshe Pelli, *The Age of Haskalah: Studies in Hebrew Literature of the Enlightenment in Germany* (Leiden, 1979); and Michael Graetz, 'The Jewish Enlightenment', in Michael Meyer (ed.), *German-Jewish History in Modern Times*, trans. William Templer, 4 vols. (New York, 1996–8), i. 261–380.

Azriel Shohat addressed the earlier period, but failed to draw clear distinctions between Haskalah and such phenomena as assimilation and the Jews' exit from the ghetto. See Shohat, *Changing Eras: The Beginning of the Haskalah among German Jewry* (Heb.) (Jerusalem, 1960). For this criticism see Immanuel Etkes, 'On the Question of the Precursors of the Haskalah in Eastern Europe', in id. (ed.), *Religion and Life: The Jewish Enlightenment in Eastern Europe* (Heb.) (Jerusalem, 1993), 25–6.

[2] Paul Hazard pushed back the dating of the Enlightenment in *La Crise de la conscience européenne* (Paris, 1935). For another notable example see Eduard Winter, *Frühaufklärung* (Berlin, 1966).

modern Europe. That Judaism had four defining characteristics. Talmud study was primary, with the method of study (*pilpul*) increasingly if not predominantly casuist. Kabbalah was cultivated to such an extent that it permeated the understanding of Judaism and became the main supporting discipline to Talmud. Medieval Jewish philosophy was ostracized, while medieval biblical exegesis, and the study of Hebrew language and grammar and of the Bible as an independent subject, suffered a neglect bordering on ostracism. Finally, a glaring cultural insularity had led to disdain for the study of foreign languages and science, rendering them not merely superfluous but highly suspect.[3]

The early Haskalah was first and foremost an attempt to broaden the curriculum of Ashkenazi Jewry by reviving knowledge of neglected strands of the textual tradition while also engaging with the larger culture. A literal interpretation of the Talmud was to replace casuistry as a method of study. Philosophy and biblical exegesis in Hebrew, alongside the study of Hebrew grammar and language, were to displace kabbalah as the major supporting disciplines. And the cultivation of science and knowledge of vernacular languages were to put an end to cultural insularity.

The early Haskalah aimed to renew established Jewish disciplines of thought. Its awareness of European culture, whether in the form of science, philosophy, or exegesis, should be seen not as a form of acculturation or *Bildung*, which was the wont of earlier scholars, but rather as an effort at harmonization, that is, the integration of current knowledge into a decidedly Jewish framework.[4] Thus the early maskilim used traditional literary genres and modes, especially commentary, to express their ideas.[5] The early Haskalah can be seen as an effort to fashion a broad Hebrew curriculum which incorporated, but kept subordinate, the best of current science and philosophy.

The early Haskalah was attractive to individuals drawn from three social groups: autodidacts whose reputations rested primarily on the acquisition of secular knowledge and its application to Jewish texts; physicians trained at German universities; and rabbis who studied science, Hebrew grammar and language, or vernacular languages.[6] While the early maskilim often worked in isolation, they sometimes had contact with other like-minded individuals.

[3] See David Sorkin, 'From Context to Comparison: The German Haskalah and Reform Catholicism', *Tel Aviver Jahrbuch für deutsche Geschichte*, 20 (1991), 27–8.

[4] For the earlier scholarship see J. Eschelbacher, 'Die Anfänge allgemeiner Bildung unter den deutschen Juden vor Mendelssohn', in *Festschrift zum siebzigston Geburtstage Martin Philippsons* (Leipzig, 1916), 168–77. For the importance of harmonization in early modern European thought see Richard H. Popkin, 'Scepticism, Theology and the Scientific Revolution in the Seventeenth Century', in Imre Lakatos and Alan Musgrave (eds.), *Problems in the Philosophy of Science* (Amsterdam, 1968), 1–28. For Jewish thought and science see David B. Ruderman, *Jewish Thought and Scientific Discovery in Early Modern Europe* (New Haven, 1995).

[5] For the parameters of the early Haskalah see Isaac Eisenstein-Barzilay, 'The Background of the Berlin Haskalah', in Joseph Blau (ed.), *Essays on Jewish Life and Thought* (New York, 1959), 185–7. Using old modes of expression for new contents was characteristic of the early Enlightenment in general. See Winter, *Frühaufklärung*, 5.

[6] Sorkin, 'From Context to Comparison', 30–1.

More constant than personal contact was the influence of books: the early maskilim nourished their vision by reading medieval works of exegesis, grammar, and philosophy as well as the works of other maskilim. They drew particular inspiration from the 'Prague school'—dating from Judah Loew b. Bezalel (the Maharal; 1525–1609)—which not only criticized the extant Ashkenazi curriculum but also idealized the Sephardi curriculum as an alternative.[7]

A brief overview of the works of five individuals will give a sense of the scope and contours of the early Haskalah.

SOLOMON HANAU

Rabbi Solomon Zalman b. Judah Loeb Hakohen Hanau (1687–1746) was an autodidact who contributed to the revival of the study of Hebrew grammar as well as making important claims for the role of grammar in biblical exegesis. He wrote a series of studies over three decades which offered a systematic introduction to grammar.[8] At first he followed the categories and analysis provided by the medieval grammarians, yet with the growth of his own knowledge through teaching and study he felt emboldened to criticize his medieval predecessors.[9] Complaining that the discipline suffered from a timid reiteration of the views of medieval scholars, he claimed that his most popular grammatical work, *Tsohar hateivah* (1733), was based on his own understanding of Hebrew grammar.[10]

[7] A detailed study of the Prague school and its impact is greatly to be desired. The school included the Maharal's immediate students and disciples as well as other figures who might be said to be within its orbit. Its importance was pointed out by H. H. Ben-Sasson, 'Concepts and Reality in Jewish History in the Late Middle Ages' (Heb.), *Tarbiz*, 29 (1960), 309. Some of the sources are anthologized in Simcha Asaf, *Sources for the History of Jewish Education* (Heb.), 4 vols. (Tel Aviv, 1954), vol. i, pp. xviii–xxvi. The Prague school's importance has been reiterated by Morris Faierstein in his edition and translation of Isaac Wetzlar, *Libes briv*, Brown Judaic Studies 308 (Atlanta, Ga., 1996), 40–1, and Mordechai Breuer, 'The Early Modern Period', in Meyer (ed.), *German-Jewish History in Modern Times*, i. 211–24.

[8] The works on grammar were *Binyan shelomo* [Solomon's Building] (Frankfurt, 1708); *Sha'arei torah* [Gates of Torah] (Hamburg, 1718); *Yesod hanikud* [Foundation of Vocalization] (Amsterdam, 1730); and *Tsohar hateivah* [Window of the Word/Ark] (Berlin, 1733). The first criticized a popular prayer-book published locally, and thus brought him into conflict with the authorities in his home town of Frankfurt, which he was eventually forced to leave. A subsequent contribution to the prayer-book controversy, *Sha'arei tefilah* [Gates of Prayer] (Jessnitz, 1725), eventually led to a polemic with the arch-polemicist of the age, Jacob Emden: see Emden, *Luaḥ eresh* [Tablet of Expression] (Altona, 1769). Hanau subsequently wandered between a number of different central European cities, including Fürth, Hanover, Berlin, and Copenhagen. For an illuminating discussion of Hanau see Edward Breuer, *The Limits of Enlightenment: Jews, Germans and the Eighteenth-Century Study of Scripture* (Cambridge, Mass., 1996), 132–6.

[9] For an example for his second book see *Sha'arei torah*, 8*b*–9*a*, where Hanau criticized medieval scholars for not fully understanding the rules governing the 'minor vowels', and provided them himself.

[10] Hanau makes this point in *Tsohar hateivah*, 2*b*. In fact, that work used large portions of his previous ones, but also reordered them by omitting some chapters and adding new materials. *Tsohar hateivah* uses five sections of the 1718 grammar (*Sha'arei torah*), but adds two new ones ('Mikra' and 'Melitsah').

Just as Hanau's understanding of grammar developed over time so did his claims for it. His 1708 grammar abounds with criticisms of the current curriculum. It bewails those who devote their time to *pilpul* and, since they neglect the study of grammar, 'are unable to read a single verse [of the Bible] without making a mistake'.[11] Moreover, it argues, the ignorance of grammar results in a misreading of the liturgy, which renders some prayers ludicrous but others, especially the prayer for the dead (Kaddish), ineffective.[12] Hanau also asserted that grammar was a key to understanding certain homilies (*derash*) which are grounded in grammatical irregularities: 'everything that is found in the books of Scripture which does not accord with the grammatical rules of the language is the basis for a homiletical or esoteric interpretation'.[13] In this connection he criticized the medieval exegete Isaac Abrabanel (1437–1508), who had suggested that grammatical defects in the book of Jeremiah were the result of the prophet's youth and insufficient command of the language; if anything was difficult to interpret or understand in Scripture, said Hanau, the fault lay not with the text but the exegete.

In his grammar of 1718 Hanau argued that 'this lofty wisdom [grammar] is the wisdom of the Torah', and that 'the whole body of the Torah depends upon it'.[14] He also argued that with 'a proper understanding of the letters, vocalization and accents . . . no other commentary would be required' to understand the Bible, though he added the important caveat that such an understanding would only occur with the coming of redemption.[15]

In his 1733 grammar he escalated these claims: grammar was not only the key to the plain meaning of the Bible but also the foundation of Midrash and the Oral Law; in addition, he asserted its centrality as a discipline throughout the ages:

I myself chose the discipline [*ḥokhmah*] of grammar, since it is a major portion of the Torah, and I realized that this discipline was hidden away and neglected. No one enquired into or examined it. Yet it is blessed and its reason blessed. [Grammar] makes possible the correct reading of our pleasant Torah. . . . It elucidates all verses of the Scripture through its roots and applications, vocalizations and accents. . . . [It also elucidates] every profound homily [*drush*] according to the words . . . of Midrash Aggadah. That which they derived homiletically [*darshu*] from the verses of Scripture is elucidated by it [grammar] . . . so that it serves as an important proof of the existence of the Oral Law. It clarifies [the work] of all the commentators on the Torah such as Rashi, Ibn Ezra, Kimhi . . . the scholars of the ages held fast

[11] *Binyan shelomo*, second introduction ('Daltei habinyan' [Doors of the Building]), unpaginated. Here are some representative comments on the neglect of grammar and the deficiencies of the curriculum: 'all this occurs because of an insufficient knowledge of the grammar of the Bible, and there are many other sorts of mistakes like these'; 'they sent this form of knowledge/discipline into exile, they abandoned this source of living water'; 'this one studies the *turim* [commentaries of Jacob b. Asher (17th cent.)] and the *posekim* [halakhic authorities], this one wanders in the sea of the Talmud, and grammar is left solitary'.

[12] Ibid. Hanau points to the example of the Kaddish at the end of the second introduction.

[13] Third introduction, 'Ḥatser habinyan' [Courtyard of the Building].

[14] *Sha'arei torah*, introduction (unpaginated).

[15] Ibid. 77*b*–78*a*.

to it [grammar] . . . as did the men of the Assembly from whom we received the traditions [*mesorot*] . . . the Sages of the Talmud . . . and the *geonim* after the close of the Talmud, Hai Gaon, Sa'adya, etc. And now in our time we have repudiated this discipline.[16]

These claims were too far-reaching to be widely accepted, yet Hanau did find a receptive audience among other members of the early Haskalah: he served as a tutor to the 10-year-old Naphtali Herz Wessely during his stay in Copenhagen, and clearly aroused Wessely's lifelong interest in the connection between grammar and exegesis;[17] Gumpertz also read at least one of Hanau's books, and in his autobiography he mentioned it as playing an important role in his interest in grammatical studies.[18]

ASHER ANSHEL WORMS

One of the university-trained physicians who tried to expand the curriculum of Ashkenazi Jewry in the service of traditional piety was Asher Anshel Worms (1695–1769), the community doctor in Frankfurt am Main who had been educated at Frankfurt an der Oder.

His first book, published in 1722 while he was still a student, was designed to introduce his fellow Jews to algebra, which he considered a basic form of knowledge: it claimed to '[open] the gates of understanding to the nation which walks in the dark and did not see the light in the knowledge of quantities'.[19] The introduction contains an involved parable that emphasizes how algebra is an important branch of knowledge which, having previously been neglected, now deserves to be cultivated.[20] The body of the work offers a succinct handbook of the discipline.

In his major work *Seyag letorah* (1766), Worms defended the foundations of Jewish belief by asserting the authenticity of the masoretic text. He boldly proclaimed his intention on the book's cover: the books of Scripture 'were written by the finger of God and are extant today among us complete, without any change or alteration, as if they were given today at Sinai, and were spoken and taught by the prophets of truth and justice'.[21] What preserved Scripture from any trace of corruption was the masoretic system:

mesora is the bulwark and bastion of the twenty-four holy books, safeguarding those books, in the verses and letters, vocalization and accents against any change or alteration, whether by addition or subtraction or the like, such changes as result from the damage and destruction brought by the passage of time and the tribulations and exile . . . of the people of Israel.[22]

16 *Tsohar hateivah*, 2*a*.
17 Breuer, *The Limits of Enlightenment*, 136–7.
18 Aaron Solomon Gumpertz, *Megaleh sod* [Revealer of Secrets] (1765; Lemberg, 1910), 4.
19 *Mafte'aḥ he'algebrah heḥadashah* [Key to the New Algebra] (Offenbach, 1722), cover.
20 Ibid. 1–4.
21 *Seyag letorah* [A Fence for the Torah] (Frankfurt am Main, 1766), title-page.
22 Ibid. 1*a*.

Once this system was in place no change or alteration could, or for that matter need, be contemplated: 'and without [the *mesorah*] no one will lift a finger to correct anything in the Bible'.[23] The masoretic system had preserved the Bible throughout Israel's long and troubled history: 'without the *mesorah* and its signs Torah would have been forgotten in the dispersion'.[24] Were it not for the masoretic system there would be many Pentateuchs rather than one, just as there were many versions of the Aramaic translation of the Bible (known as Onkelos) for which no equivalent system existed.[25]

By preserving the text of the Bible, the masoretic system had also sustained the people of Israel; the *mesorah* was the cement of the exile and a sign of Israel's chosenness:

> Is there another wise and sage nation like this great people of Israel which was chosen from among all the nations? . . . And this is the sign that God did not cease to love them despite their being in a land that is not their own . . . For all the day the word of God is in their mouths as it was given to the prophets without a change or alteration. The evidence that [the word of God] is found throughout Israel that is dispersed throughout all the lands . . . all in the same version without change or alteration, is [a phenomenon] which has not occurred to all other composed books of all the nations.[26]

Worms made such far-reaching claims for the masoretic system because of the attacks upon it, which came from opponents of three sorts. The worst adversaries were atheists such as Spinoza, 'who deride all those believers, whether circumcised or uncircumcised, who rely on the words written by the finger of God and do not depend on reason alone'. These men treated the Bible as a human rather than a divine text, thereby refusing to acknowledge that 'reason needs to submit to the words of the living God who is king of the universe'.[27]

The other opponents were, respectively, Jewish and Christian scholars. Worms devoted a large part of *Seyag letorah* to refuting the contentions of Elijah Bahur Levita (1469–1549), who had argued that the masoretic notations did not date from Sinai but rather from the post-talmudic scholars of Tiberias.[28] Following the defence offered by numerous Jewish scholars, Worms asserted the divine, Sinaitic origin of the notations—a position Moses Mendelssohn would also adopt.[29] Using the internal evidence of rabbinic sources, Worms reduced human agency in the Bible to transmission alone, arguing that the notational system had been given at Sinai and then communicated orally from one generation to the next. Chronologically the masoretic enterprise began with Ezra and the men of the Great Assembly,

23 *Seyag letorah*, 1766), 19*a*. 24 Ibid. 25 Ibid.

26 Ibid. 1*b*. 27 Ibid., introduction (unpaginated).

28 *Mesoret hamasoret* [The Tradition of the Tradition] (Venice, 1538). For a recent discussion of Levita's work see Breuer, *The Limits of Enlightenment*, 43–4.

29 One of the first to make this point was Azariah dei Rossi: see *Me'or einayim* [Enlightenment of the Eyes] (Mantua, 1574).

who had introduced the vocalization and the accents as part of their effort to purify the people of foreign ideas after the Babylonian exile;[30] these efforts were continued by others until their culmination with the Tiberian masoretes. In opposition to Levita, Worms asserted that 'the [Tiberian] masoretes were not the inventors of punctuation but the placers of the punctuation in the books of the masses as well as of the accents'.[31]

The second group of scholarly opponents were recent Christians who had begun to question the antiquity and authenticity of the masoretic system; Worms only mentions these scholars ('Capullus, Brian Walton, and Hiller') without analysing the differences between their views and those of Levita.[32]

In addition to defending the authenticity of the masoretic text, Worms's work was also a contribution to the revival of the literalist tradition of biblical study (*pashtanit*). In an afterword to *Seyag letorah* Worms uses the key example of the Decalogue to show how the accents serve as a central exegetical tool, revealing what has been spoken by God, continuously and without interruption, and thus how the first two commandments are different in nature from the rest. Worms asserts that, therefore, 'the literal [or plain] meaning is dependent upon the masoretic tradition'.[33]

Worms's defence of the masoretic tradition was not an isolated effort, but part and parcel of his attempt to extend the curriculum of Ashkenazi Jewry. He mentions in the introduction to *Seyag letorah* that he has written a number of other works on various fields of knowledge. Whether he wrote and published these works and they have been lost, remain unread in manuscript archives, or merely represent a wish-list of books he hoped to write remains to be ascertained. Be that as it may, the order in which he places them provides a map of his intellectual world. Worms locates everything associated with Scripture first, making it the foundation of all knowledge; next comes logic, which he deems a method necessary to all forms of knowledge. Metaphysics and the sciences follow, and in the latter he mentions the experimental method.[34] In other words, Worms built his curriculum on a pious basis by first securing the source of revelation. He then made logic the bridge to further knowledge.

ISAAC WETZLAR

One of the more surprising figures of the early Haskalah whose thought testifies to the vitality of the Prague school was Isaac Wetzlar (1680?–1751), a wealthy merchant who lived in Celle. Wetzlar had studied for four years in Prague at the

30 *Seyag letorah*, 9*b*.

31 Ibid. 10*b*.

32 Ibid. 20*b*. Worms mentions a Latin work he had written in which he refuted the views of these authors.

33 Afterword to *Seyag letorah*: 'Midrash hapeirushim', unpaginated [p. 4].

34 *Seyag letorah*, introduction [p. 2].

yeshiva of Rabbi Abraham Broda (d. 1717). He wrote an extended ethical epistle in Yiddish, *Libes briv*,[35] which was designed to diagnose the maladies that afflicted his fellow Jews and prolonged their 'exile'.[36] Wetzlar's critique of Ashkenazi Jewry was permeated with the Prague school's ideas and the Sephardi ideal: he thought the curriculum of Ashkenazi Jewry was fundamentally mistaken; he advocated the study of Hebrew language and grammar in order to ensure a correct understanding of the liturgy and the plain meaning of the Bible;[37] he complained that only a tiny minority of Jews comprehended the actual words of the liturgy as they prayed, and was abashed at his co-religionists' inability to distinguish between the rabbinic interpretation, or midrash, and the plain meaning of the Bible. To replace the sterile intellectual exercise of casuistry he suggested the study of ethical works, or *musar*, such as Bahya ibn Pakuda's *Ḥovot halevavot* and Joseph Albo's *Sefer ha'ikarim* since these promoted correct behaviour and fear of God.[38]

His programme entailed a reordering of the curriculum following the Sephardi model. Students should begin with Pentateuch and learn the exact meaning of the individual words. Such study would also teach the meaning of the liturgy. Students should then proceed to Mishnah and ethical works. Only then should they study Talmud, and they should do so for its practical application. The method of *pilpul* should be secondary and used only sparingly, as a heuristic exercise to sharpen the mind, as he himself had done in Prague.[39] Wetzlar invoked the authority of prominent figures of the Prague school such as Sheftel Horowitz (?1590–?1660) and Ephraim of Luntshits (1550–1619) as well as other figures such as Hakham Tsevi Ashkenazi (1660–1718) and his son Jacob Emden, and Shabbetai b. Joseph Bass (1641–1718).

In his comparison of Sephardim and Ashkenazim Wetzlar linked the curriculum to economic well-being. He thought the economic decline of his day (and there was a discernible worsening of German Jewry's economic situation in the first half of the eighteenth century) was the product of a misguided curriculum that resulted in moral failings. Were the community to be placed on the right track it would, like its Sephardi brethren, begin to prosper.[40]

Wetzlar also evinced a sense of inferiority and embarrassment towards Christians. He had met Christians who had heard from Jews the most ludicrous accounts of the Bible and the principles of Judaism. These Jews did not know the difference between midrash and the Bible's plain meaning, and were entirely incapable of coherently defining, let alone defending, their faith.[41] Wetzlar thought their know-

[35] Wetzlar, *Libes briv*, ed. Faierstein, 98. See also Faierstein's introduction (pp. 4, 40–1). For an earlier discussion of Wetzlar see Shohat, *Changing Eras*, 131–3, 201–7.

[36] For the pervasive theme of the exile see *Libes briv*, 57–9, 61–2, 90–1, 96, 110, 117, 122.

[37] On grammar see ibid. 69, 81, 91–2.

[38] Ibid. 66, 69, 76, 83, 96, 102–10. Bahya b. Joseph ibn Pakuda, *Ḥovot halevavot* [Duties of the Heart] (11th cent.); Joseph Albo, *Sefer ha'ikarim* [Book of Principles] (15th cent.).

[39] *Libes briv*, 66, 68, 97.

[40] Ibid. 66, 81, 88.

[41] Ibid. 65, 79, 97, 110. See also the introduction, pp. 38–40.

ledge of the Bible could be improved by the curricular reform he advocated, while to clarify their beliefs he proposed they should be taught Maimonides' thirteen principles. He also complained that Christians who visited synagogues came away with an unfavourable impression of disorder; he may well have shared their view since, as we have seen, he thought that most worshippers did not understand the liturgy. As a corrective he advocated not only adequate teaching of the Bible as a means to make the liturgy understood, but also that the leaders of the congregation should insist on decorum.

Wetzlar's book abounds in coruscating criticism of contemporary Ashkenazi Jewry. He assigned primary responsibility for its sorry state to a failure of intellectual and moral leadership by the rabbis and communal leaders, but he also criticized the average householder. In this he followed the Maharal, but also the *musar* genre in which he wrote. For Wetzlar as for the Maharal, there was an indissoluble link between curricular reform and social criticism: a reordering of the curriculum was the remedy for the arrogance of rabbis, the unethical behaviour of lay leaders, and the ritual and ethical laxity of householders, as well as for general ignorance and indirection.[42] In keeping with the *musar* tradition, Wetzlar had complete confidence in the ability of proper knowledge to repair all damage.

Yet Wetzlar's work was characteristic of the early Haskalah in another way: it remained an unpublished manuscript. While this was probably read by a limited circle, Wetzlar's ideas, especially his social criticism, did not reach the public domain.

ISRAEL ZAMOSC

Israel b. Moses Halevi of Zamosc (1700–72), an autodidact from Galicia who came to Berlin, attempted in his first work, *Netzaḥ yisra'el* (1741), to use science and the method of literal interpretation to argue against the casuistry that dominated the interpretation of Talmud and encouraged the neglect of the study of the Bible's plain meaning.[43]

In his second work, *Sefer ruaḥ ḥen*, he tried to renew the discipline of philosophy in Hebrew. He reissued a medieval commentary which has traditionally been ascribed to the translator Judah ibn Tibbon (*c.*1120–*c.*1190).[44] In commenting on this work Zamosc attempted to harmonize the thought of Maimonides, but also of Hebrew philosophy in general, with current philosophical and scientific

42 For this point in the Maharal see e.g. Byron L. Sherwin, *Mystical Theology and Social Dissent: The Life and Works of Judah Loew of Prague* (Rutherford, NJ, 1982), 172–80.

43 *Sefer netsaḥ yisra'el* [Book of the Eternal Israel] (Frankfurt an der Oder, 1741; repr. Brooklyn, NY, 1991). For a recent discussion of the book see Jay Harris, *How Do We Know This? Midrash and the Fragmentation of Modern Judaism* (Albany, NY, 1995), 138–41.

44 *Sefer ruaḥ ḥen* [Book of the Spirit of Grace] (1744; edn. cited Warsaw, 1826; repr. Jerusalem, 1969). Scholars now generally hold that the commentary was written by the 13th-cent. Maimonidean philosopher Jacob Anatoli.

knowledge. Such harmonization did not entail a categorical rejection of the old, but was instead a complex process in which new ideas could be accepted, rejected, or deferred for future consideration.

Zamosc was unequivocal in accepting new ideas which rested on the evidence of experimental science. In his eyes the experimental method offered incontrovertible proof that was qualitatively different from other sources of scientific knowledge. The experiments he cited were primarily those associated with the air pump and the microscope, and he introduced knowledge derived from them in order to correct the medieval conception that informed Jewish philosophical literature.[45] The experiments with the air pump, for example, had taught that each substance has a weight of its own in relation to the earth, something which the 'ancients' did not understand.[46] In another case Zamosc used the new views established by the science of dioptrics to reject Aristotle's theory of the 'fifth' essence of the heavens, which had been at odds with the views of the Bible and the Sages, in order to espouse views closer to the original Jewish sources.[47] Such examples of obsolete ancient knowledge occurred so often in the medieval commentary that Zamosc eventually grew exasperated: 'the ancient commentators . . . did not know anything of this knowledge; therefore I do not see the value in detaining myself at every point at which they erred, for these [points] are numerous'.[48] In contrast, in those cases in which the current scientific debate rested on non-experimental knowledge which he deemed less certain, religio-philosophical concerns restrained, or at least influenced, his acceptance or rejection of new ideas. Zamosc recognized that scientific theory seemed to lean in the direction of the astronomical views of Copernicus rather than of Tycho Brahe, yet because Copernicus's views had the 'odour' of heresy, while Brahe's were closer to those of the Torah and the Sages, Zamosc advocated the views of the latter.[49]

In other cases Zamosc opted to retain ancient views which had the imprimatur of the older Jewish literature. Although contemporary chemistry proposed a theory of five rather than four elements, he elected to stick with the older theory of four because it agreed with the accepted views of Jewish literature—at least until such time as the new view received the sanction of tradition: 'once it is [accepted as] tradition we will accept it'.[50] In the many cases in which experimental science played no role, for example logic, the nature of the intellect, or the relationship between form and matter in creation, Zamosc simply espoused the ideas of the Sages and the philosophers.[51]

[45] For his discussion of the air pump, see *Sefer ruaḥ ḥen*, 5*b*–6*a*, 17*b*–19*a*; for the microscope, see pp. 3*b*–4*a*. For a recent and perceptive discussion of these passages see Ruderman, *Jewish Thought*, 332–4, 341–3. [46] *Sefer ruaḥ ḥen*, 19*a*. [47] Ibid. 2*a*–*b*. [48] Ibid. 20*a*. [49] Ibid. 2*b*.

[50] Ibid. 3*a*, 17*a*–*b*. The quotation appears on p. 17*b*. In this instance Zamosc cited the Zohar and *Sefer yetsirah*.

[51] For examples see the discussions of the nature of intelligence (p. 8*a*); the relationship between form and matter (p. 11*a*); the nature of prophecy (pp. 12*a*–13*a*); the nature of truth in those spheres not governed by logic (pp. 15*a*–17*a*); the rules of logic (pp. 26*b*–30*a*).

There were also significant instances in Zamosc's commentary in which not only did science and tradition concur, but where natural and supernatural causes also happily coexisted. In a discussion of heat transfer between the 'four elements' he explained the causes of precipitation, and especially the relationship between temperature and the size of raindrops, using the evidence of rain in the tropics to support his views. He also quoted the Sages as being in agreement with these scientific views,[52] and went on to argue that not all the causes of precipitation were natural: 'Yet rain and snow do not always fall as a result of the [natural] reasons already enumerated. For the Lord our God sometimes seeks the well-being of the earth. It is his duty as the superintendent [*mashgiaḥ*] to bring rain, either as a punishment or in order to satisfy the earth.'[53] In the same spirit, he argued at the very end of the book that the only language appropriate to praise or to describe God was the language of tradition extending from Moses to the prayer-book:

> Know that all of the efforts the philosophers made in explaining these matters were designed to bridle the speech of people who were quick to utter arbitrary titles and praise for God such as one person uses for another. . . . Yet these human categories are vanity; the praises of mankind are false. In application to God, the exalted transcends all accident, change and nomenclature. . . . We are not able or authorized to speak any praise before God except . . . those titles that were permitted to us by Moses having spoken them, and the Great Assembly [having spoken them] with him, and which they [subsequently] fixed in prayer.[54]

Zamosc's commentary offered a harmonization in which he reasserted the vitality of tradition and belief by demonstrating their compatibility with contemporary scientific and philosophical knowledge. Most significant in his work was his ability to use current scientific knowledge to renew the discipline of Hebrew philosophical thought without altering its basic design.

AARON SOLOMON GUMPERTZ

The self-imposed limits of the early Haskalah can be seen in the work of Aaron Solomon Gumpertz (1723–69), a university-educated physician. The scion of a Berlin family of scholars as well as court Jews, Gumpertz received a traditional Jewish education as well as a doctorate in medicine from the University of Frankfurt an der Oder (1751).[55] He found his way into the intellectual circles of the Berlin Enlightenment, including its associational life,[56] and was befriended by two

52 Ibid. 20*b*–21*a*.

53 Ibid. 21*a*.

54 In the edition I have used (Warsaw, 1826) there is a gap in the pagination from p. 30*a* to p. 33*a*. Were the pages numbered consecutively, the quoted passage would appear on pp. 31*b*–32*a*.

55 On Gumpertz see Alexander Altmann, *Moses Mendelssohn: A Biographical Study* (Tuscaloosa, Ala., 1973), 23–5; D. Kaufmann and Max Freudenthal, *Die Familie Gumperz* (Frankfurt am Main, 1907), 164–200.

56 He was a member of the Kaffeehausgesellschaft and the Montagsklub. He became acquainted with Lessing in those circles, and introduced him to Mendelssohn. See Kaufmann and Freudenthal, *Die Familie Gumperz*, 186–9.

members of the Royal Academy of Sciences, the marquis D'Argens and Maupertuis, both of whom he served at various times as a secretary.[57] Gumpertz was one of the few figures of the early Haskalah to write an autobiography, however brief. In addition, he wrote on other subjects central to the intellectual renewal of Judaism.[58]

In his autobiography Gumpertz asserted that his dedication to knowledge had shaped his life and set him apart from other people. His mother had decided before his birth that he would be a man of learning, and during his childhood she forbade him to play with other children.[59] An only child blessed with all the advantages of well-chosen tutors and his father's extensive private library, he devoted himself to his studies, which were conducted in a fully pious spirit.[60]

The first station of Gumpertz's intellectual odyssey was the study of languages, including Latin, French, English, and Greek, but above all Hebrew, which he called the 'divine language'. He systematically studied not only language and grammar but also biblical prose and poetry, as well as the old and the new grammarians, in which connection he recommended Solomon Hanau's *Sha'arei zimra* (Gates of Song). Gumpertz was especially interested in the intricacies of Hebrew prosody, and he tried to gain a thorough understanding of how it differed from that of other languages. Yet he felt that he was alone in this endeavour, for few of the grammarians had devoted themselves to it and the subject had virtually no current students: 'there was no one to support or aid me'.[61]

Gumpertz's discussion of Hebrew language study was an occasion to criticize some of the contemporary educational practices often targeted by the early Haskalah. He bemoaned the fact that children were not taught the Hebrew language properly so that they could understand the Bible; for this they needed a thorough grounding in vocabulary and grammar. He thought the practice of employing Yiddish-speaking tutors for students whose first language was German was a large part of the problem. Yet he did not lay the blame at the tutors' doorstep, since their intentions were 'good and true'; rather, he blamed his countrymen for continuing to hire such tutors instead of finding ones who were better qualified.[62]

Gumpertz's reserve is notable. His unwillingness to question the motives of the Yiddish-speaking tutors, let alone to castigate them, contrasts sharply with the

[57] He dedicated his dissertation to Maupertuis; see Kaufmann and Freudenthal, *Die Familie Gumperz*, 172–3, 179–82.

[58] He was also known as Aaron ben Zalman Emmerich: see Gumpertz, *Megalah sod*. The Lemberg 1910 edition which I am using has pagination in both arabic and Hebrew numerals. Page citations are according to the arabic numerals. To my knowledge the only other autobiography by a figure of the early Haskalah is Jacob Emden's *Megilat sefer* [Scroll of the Book] (Altona, 1740).

[59] *Megaleh sod*, introduction, p. 3.

[60] Michael Graetz asserts that there is a conscious tension in the autobiography between 'the traditional Jewish ideal of education' and the 'new Jewish identity' of the Haskalah. I find no textual evidence to support this claim. See Graetz, 'The Jewish Enlightenment', 325–6.

[61] *Megaleh sod*, 4.

[62] Ibid.

treatment the maskilim would accord them towards the end of the century when the stereotype of the boorish and intellectually inferior, if not morally depraved, *melamed* became commonplace. This reserve is further evident in the fact that he explicitly renounced any ambitions of leadership, rejecting suggestions that he was trying to determine how others should educate their children: 'who am I to lead other people in my path?'[63] This position would also be in stark contrast with that of the later Haskalah: in 1782, for example, Naphtali Herz Wessely boldly delineated a new curriculum for all Jewish children. Whatever personal reasons Gumpertz may have had for his reserve, it was entirely typical of the early Haskalah's concern with intellectual renewal rather than social reform or political leadership.

The next station of Gumpertz's intellectual odyssey was his realization that the study of languages could not be an end in itself but should instead serve as the means to the study of 'deep and hidden truths'.[64] He consequently undertook a study of all branches of the sciences. Significantly, he first became aware of science's importance through reading Hebrew texts such as the writings of Maimonides and Joseph Delmedigo (1591–1655).

Gumpertz's study of science was intellectually invigorating but personally demoralizing. What was he to do with his knowledge? Of what use could it be in his life? His answer to these questions was informed with piety. The merchant's calling, which was the obvious choice for a Jew of his station, was not appealing because 'the ways of cunning escaped me'.[65] Remembering the words of the Sages, that it is required of a father to teach his son a profession, he finally decided on medicine, asserting that many illustrious predecessors, such as Nahmanides, Maimonides, and Gersonides (Levi b. Gershom), had been doctors. Moreover, he deemed the work of medicine itself 'the work of God, great and awesome, from respect and love of wonders'.[66]

Gumpertz's autobiography serves as the introduction to a work in two parts: the body of the book comprises his own commentary on Abraham Ibn Ezra's commentary on the Five Scrolls (Ecclesiastes, Ruth, Song of Songs, Esther, and Lamentations); the appendix is his 'Treatise on Science' ('Ma'amar hamada'). Taken as a whole, the book offers a personal vindication of the intellectual pursuits of exegesis and science exemplified in both its main text and its appendix. Ibn Ezra's commentary on the Scrolls was ideally suited to Gumpertz's project to reclaim and revive the literalist tradition of biblical exegesis: for Ibn Ezra, 'the plain meaning of the text was [the] primary concern'.[67] Yet Gumpertz also realized that there were complications: although recognized as one of the leading literalist

[63] Ibid.
[64] Ibid. 5.
[65] Ibid. 6.
[66] Ibid. Gumpertz describes in detail the various branches of medicine and writes that 'in the end it is incumbent on the doctor to recognize and understand the laws of medicines, their natures, types and activities' (ibid. 7).
[67] Ibid. 25 (Gumpertz's introduction to Lamentations).

exegetes, Ibn Ezra was also concerned with midrash and esoteric knowledge. In his own commentary Gumpertz aimed to reawaken interest in Ibn Ezra's careful grammatical exegesis while taking issue with the midrash and allegory.

In the case of the Song of Songs, for example, Ibn Ezra had argued that in addition to being an erotic poem it was also an allegory of the history of Israel, which had hidden content as well as messianic import ('from the days of Abraham our father to the days of the Messiah'). He therefore wrote a tripartite commentary, which treated philological issues in the first part, the plain meaning in the second, and in the third explored the midrashic, allegorical, and esoteric meanings. Gumpertz argued against this approach, emphasizing instead the need to establish the plain meaning of the text. In commenting on the phrase 'will kiss me with kisses' (1: 2), for instance, Ibn Ezra had noticed the unusual construction of the verb and in the third part of his commentary had asserted that, in the allegory of Israel's relationship to God, it represented the Torah and the commandments. Gumpertz followed Ibn Ezra's discussion of the grammatical issue and affirmed that it could serve as the basis for a midrash, much as had Hanau, but that was all he was willing to acknowledge; he entirely avoided Ibn Ezra's esoteric reading.[68] He took a similar approach in other passages, reiterating Ibn Ezra's grammatical insights while avoiding his allegorical or esoteric readings.[69]

The 'Treatise on Science' exculpates the sciences from all charges of impiety by delineating their method and surveying their contents. Gumpertz found such an exculpation necessary because in his own day the sciences were neglected: the few scholars who studied them were subjected to abuse, and the range of sciences they studied was pitifully narrow. At the same time, those who opposed the study of science did so from jealousy and ignorance. Recalling the controversy over the study of Greek philosophy in the Middle Ages, Gumpertz asserted that all those who had pursued logic and philosophy had done so 'for the sake of heaven',[70] and cited earlier scholars of note who studied science and saw no contradiction between this and pious studies.

Gumpertz also transcended these arguments about motivation with a vindication that combined the scientific revolution with sensationalist epistemology. Echoing Israel Zamosc, with whom he was acquainted, Gumpertz argued that in the contemporary world science was above suspicion, no longer impinging on belief, since the experimental method had made natural and divine science separate and distinct. The natural or phenomenal world was apprehended through the senses and was thus to be studied empirically, using the experimental method:

[68] *Megaleh sod*, 9. For Ibn Ezra I have used the *Sefer torat elohim: Ḥumash* [Book of the Law of God: Pentateuch], 5 vols. (Warsaw, 1879–80), iii. 282–331.

[69] For additional examples of Gumpertz deflecting Ibn Ezra's esoteric or allegorical readings, see his comments on the phrase 'your oils are fragrant' and the verb *turak* in S. of S. 1: 3 (*Megaleh sod*, 9). For both, Ibn Ezra carefully dissects the grammar which serves as the basis for an esoteric interpretation, whereas Gumpertz discusses only the plain meaning.

[70] *Megaleh sod*, 31.

Recent generations have a distinct advantage over earlier ones in that [contemporaries] enquire into each and every matter in its own right, and especially in the study of nature they choose a different method, that of experimentation, demonstration, and analysis, and they conduct their activities and many experiments with ingenuity by using instruments designed expressly for this purpose of testing their hypotheses in regard to nature.[71]

Gumpertz argued that in the past physics and metaphysics had been studied together and thus ran the risk of being confused; the method of experimentation has removed any such risk. He cited the example of the pneumatic pump, which had led to a new understanding of the vacuum and the weight of air. Earlier scholars had mistakenly formulated the principle that nature always fills a vacuum. Experimentation with the pneumatic pump had shown, by contrast, that air has a specific weight like all other substances, and that this was a crucial property necessary to understanding its behaviour.[72]

The conclusion Gumpertz drew is that no ideas about nature could be advanced without experiment: the experimental method had attained unquestioned authority in the study of the natural world. Yet this method had no purchase on 'divine matters' ('beliefs and opinions'), for these were not subject to the senses.[73] The experimental method, he argued, had nothing in common with the 'enquiry into matters which are beyond nature, namely, the divine wisdom which is built either on explanation and opinion alone or on tradition transmitted from person to person. In divine wisdom there is no room for analysis and experiment because its elements are not subject to the senses.'[74] Rather, the subject-matter of the divine sciences could be studied using the method of logic, that is, inferences and syllogisms which lead to 'proofs'.[75] Divine science comprised three subjects: the world, the soul, and God. In studying the soul, one had to examine its properties and differentiate them from natural ones. Thus the central issues were the powers of perception and reason, the soul's immortality, and its connection to the corporeal body. In the study of God one was concerned with the foundation of being, omnipotence, and omniscience, with the origins of good and evil, and with the 'proofs of providence, both general and particular'.[76]

In the study of the divine sciences Gumpertz thought that unaided human reason was severely limited: these sciences comprised 'the depths and secrets of knowledge which human reason of its own accord is unable to grasp'.[77] Reason alone could attain no certain knowledge: 'Enquiry based on human reason into sublime matters is neither certain nor absolute.' Yet it could help man in his greater aim: 'it does serve as a basis and aid in understanding Torah'.[78] One also

[71] Ibid. 34–5.

[72] Ibid. 35. Gumpertz does not mention Galileo, Berti, or Torricelli, who conducted the experiments. For a lucid, if brief, discussion of this aspect of Gumpertz's thought, see Ruderman, *Jewish Thought*, 334–5, 343–4.

[73] *Megaleh sod*, 35. The Hebrew for the experimental method is *habeḥinah vehanisayon*.

[74] Ibid. [75] Ibid. 43–4. [76] Ibid. 44–5. [77] Ibid. 33. [78] Ibid. 34.

had to rely on tradition in order to attain the ultimate goal of 'fear of God' and 'love of Him'.[79] While affirming the validity of logic and philosophy, then, Gumpertz limited their reach by fully subordinating them to pious ends.

The bulk of the 'Treatise on Science' was a conspectus of the sciences in which Gumpertz surveyed arithmetic, geometry and algebra, geology and zoology, botany and anatomy, and physics and astronomy.[80] He demonstrated the connections between them—for example, the use of mathematics to measure motion in physics.[81] He also emphasized the importance of the experimental method and of scientific instruments, discussing the use of the thermometer in measuring temperature and the importance of the air pump for understanding the effect of the properties of air on the weather.[82]

Besides having a detailed knowledge of eighteenth-century science, Gumpertz also showed an awareness of philosophical developments such as the idea of a natural religion. He in fact used the relationship between the natural world and the senses to make an important, if rudimentary, argument for a natural religion common to all mankind. The 'rational precepts'—the prohibitions on theft, murder, and adultery, for example—which came to be embodied in the Noahide laws also belonged to nature and the realm of the senses and were thus universally accessible without reference to the higher, divine sciences. Indeed, Abraham himself first gained knowledge of the natural world through science before attaining to higher wisdom.[83] The basic moral principles were, then, part and parcel of the natural world and open to human reason.

In the 'Treatise on Science' Gumpertz exhibited the reserve already evident in his autobiography in two significant ways. First, he insisted that scientific education should reinforce rather than imperil faith: it should be introduced only after belief itself had been firmly established. Only a few disciplines such as geometry and arithmetic should be taught early on; the other sciences should not be studied until the age of 30, after a solid foundation of divine studies had been laid.[84] Second, he sought mutual toleration between students of rabbinics and students of science. He had no quarrel with those who wished to devote themselves exclusively to the study of halakhah: 'The man who does not desire to enquire into these matters, and who prefers to follow the path of the shepherds and to spend his years in talmudic studies of the laws and judgements . . . he too is blessed.'[85] Gumpertz only asked that in turn such authorities should tolerate the scientific studies of others—'do not let my soul loathe the sciences and their students without studying them assiduously, as if they strive in vain and their effort will beget confusion, God forbid!'[86]—and cited the illustrious line of scholars who were outstanding for their

[79] *Megaleh sod*, 45.

[80] Ibid. 36–43. Gumpertz's knowledge of astronomy also extended to calculating the calendar. From 1745 to 1752 he supplied such calculations for a calendar published in Berlin: see Kaufmann and Freudenthal, *Die Familie Gumperz*, 181.

[81] *Megaleh sod*, 42. [82] Ibid. [83] Ibid. 32–3. [84] Ibid. 35–6. [85] Ibid. 45. [86] Ibid.

knowledge of science as well as halakhah.[87] Gumpertz was typical of the early Haskalah in his primary concern with intellectual renewal. He entered a plea for the expansion of the curriculum by affirming the religious validity of science and logic. At the same time, he upheld the sanctity of traditional halakhic studies. He was also typical of the early Haskalah in the modesty of his ambitions. His intentions were in marked contrast to the politicized position of the 1780s when, for example, Wessely would assail the *talmid ḥakham*, or traditional scholar, who rejected or ignored secular studies.

*

The early Haskalah can be defined as an effort to revise baroque Judaism in order to create a broad Hebrew curriculum which, as a result of including hitherto neglected internal disciplines, was able to integrate contemporary knowledge into inherited Jewish thinking through the method of harmonization. Solomon Hanau aimed to revive the study of grammar, which he thought essential to understanding the Bible and the liturgy but also regarded as the foundation of the Oral Law. Asher Anshel Worms defended the masoretic system as the safeguard of the Bible and of Israel's election. Isaac Wetzlar advocated a thorough overhaul of the curriculum. Israel Zamosc endeavoured to renew the discipline of philosophy in Hebrew and to harmonize it with experimental science. Aaron Gumpertz tried to rehabilitate the plain tradition of biblical exegesis and to vindicate the study of science. In addition, the young Moses Mendelssohn (1729–86) can be counted among the members of the early Haskalah. An autodidact who benefited from contact with Zamosc and Gumpertz, his earliest Hebrew works (*Kohelet musar* and *Milot hahigayon*) were commentaries in which he attempted to renew the tradition of philosophy in Hebrew through harmonization with the thought of Christian Wolff.[88]

In its criticism of contemporary Ashkenazi culture and its intellectual agenda, the early Haskalah constituted an identifiable cultural tendency of the first six decades of the eighteenth century. The early Haskalah was first and foremost an attempt to renew the intellectual traditions of Ashkenazi Jewry: it was not a full-fledged cultural movement as it lacked an organization and the ability to mobilize adherents, whether in the form of a dense network of contacts and correspondence or of institutions such as journals, academies, and associations. It was also distinctly unpolitical: Gumpertz's reserve rested on his renunciation of all pretence to leadership

[87] He lists, among others, Sa'adya Gaon, Bahya Ibn Pakuda, Maimonides, Levi ben Gershom (= Gersonides), Joseph Albo, Isaac b. Moses Arama, Isaac Abarbanel, Moses Isserles, and Joseph Delmedigo. He then adds: 'if they did not speak unjustly [against the sciences], why are we inflamed with anger against them [the sciences] and [why do we] quickly oppose them?' (ibid. 46).

[88] For an account of Mendelssohn's thought along these lines, including analyses of *Kohelet musar* (?1758) and *Biur milot hahigayon* [Logical Terms] (Berlin, 1765), see David Sorkin, *Moses Mendelssohn and the Religious Enlightenment* (Berkeley and Los Angeles, 1996). For all biographical details see Altmann, *Moses Mendelssohn*.

and Wetzlar's bold manuscript remained unpublished. The early maskilim neither envisaged wide-ranging efforts at social or political reform nor did they have presumptions to leadership of any kind.

Yet if we recognize the early Haskalah as a cultural tendency in its own right, two sorts of question emerge. First, did the early Haskalah's effort to broaden the curriculum have a significant impact on the Haskalah after 1770? Did the early Haskalah set the intellectual agenda of the later movement? To what extent and in what way did the later Haskalah alter or radicalize that early vision, or at what point did efforts at social reform, acculturation, or emancipation overwhelm it? Second, did the early Haskalah endure as a cultural option? Is it possible that the early Haskalah became a viable alternative for those figures who eschewed the outlook of the later movement?[89]

These questions and others like them can be posed once we cease to see the cultural developments of the early eighteenth century as mere anticipations and instead recognize the existence of the early Haskalah as an intellectual force in its own right.

[89] Shmuel Feiner has recently advanced the argument that the early Haskalah was both a cultural configuration that arose in the 18th cent. and a viable cultural option in later periods. See his 'The Dragon in the Beehive: Y. L. Margoliot and the Paradox of the Early Haskalah' (Heb.), *Zion*, 63 (1998), 39–74.

TWO

Naphtali Herz Wessely and the Cultural Dislocations of an Eighteenth-Century Maskil

EDWARD BREUER

I

IN the autumn of 1804 a 22-year-old resident of Hamburg named Moses b. Mendel Frankfurt (1782–1861) sought out a recent arrival from Berlin, the ageing and venerable Naphtali Herz Wessely (1725–1805). Approaching his eightieth birthday, Wessely had moved from Berlin to spend what would be the last year of his life in the care of his daughter. The author of more than half a dozen books and countless essays and poems, he was widely recognized as one of the main catalysts of the Haskalah, second in stature only to Moses Mendelssohn. The young Frankfurt came from a family that had long admired both these early Jewish Enlightenment figures, and Wessely's move to Hamburg naturally attracted his attention. Some years later, when Frankfurt had occasion to discuss Wessely in his own writings, he recalled his encounters with the Berlin maskil with warm admiration.[1]

As one might expect, Frankfurt's depiction of Wessely and his contribution to the linguistic and cultural enlightenment of European Jewry was highly appreciative. Writing for a nineteenth-century audience that was only vaguely familiar with the lives and accomplishments of the early Enlightenment figures, he began by sketching Wessely's life in broad strokes: his birth in Hamburg, his moves to Amsterdam and Copenhagen, and, in 1774, his relocation to Berlin. He highlighted Wessely's literary and scholarly contribution, stressing his talents in the fields of poetry and Hebrew language, and noting how his writings differed—qualitatively

[1] Frankfurt, also known as Frankfurter, and later by the name of Moses Mendelson of Hamburg, refers to this meeting in his posthumously published *Penei tevel* [Face of the World] (Amsterdam, 1872), 239–41. See also his introduction to *Metsi'at ha'arets haḥadashah* [Discovery of the New Land] (Altona, 1807), unpaginated [pp. vii–viii]. Frankfurt pointed in his writing to the many ties his family had with the Berlin Haskalah. He reported that both his father and uncle were acquainted with Mendelssohn and Wessely, and that his nephew, R. Samson Raphael Hirsch, was in possession of Wessely's unpublished manuscripts; see *Penei tevel*, 227–34. See also Yehezkel Duckesz, *Ḥakhmei A H V* [Sages of Altona, Hamburg, and Wandsbeck] (Hamburg, 1905), 120–1, and id., 'Zur Genealogie Samson Raphael Hirschs', *Jahrbuch der Jüdisch-Literarischen Gesellschaft*, 17 (1926), 122–3, which includes the will of Frankfurt's father and its explicit reference to the 'unimpeachable' character of Wessely's writings.

as well as substantively—from those of Mendelssohn. The most noteworthy aspect of this presentation, however, was the fact that it managed to avoid the uncritical and gauzy hagiography of many contemporary writings about the early maskilim. Frankfurt's biographical essay, in fact, was striking in its depiction of Wessely as an isolated and misunderstood figure with few friends or supporters, increasingly ignored by the members of the Jewish community in Berlin. In Frankfurt's account, the unfortunate situation appeared to have been precipitated in part by Wessely's castigation of his fellow Jews for their sinful deprivations and petty jealousies, which only managed to gain him their enmity. At odds with his German co-religionists, Wessely's years in Berlin were described as singularly unhappy, an assessment that Frankfurt poignantly attributed to Wessely himself: 'He lived for many years in Berlin, in poverty and privation, impeded and abandoned by members of his community, as I heard from his own mouth: "the traditionalists distrusted me for being a modernizer, and the modernizers distrusted me for being a traditionalist".'[2]

This account must of course be regarded with some caution, but its unexpected shading of Wessely's life points suggestively to some salient features of his character. Despite all his accomplishments and the general acclaim he received from the maskilim, the overwrought quality and baroque density of Wessely's writing must have discouraged all but the most determined readers. The problem, however, went beyond a poor sense of style and lack of appreciation for literary brevity and clarity. Taken together, Wessely's published works seem to indicate a somewhat myopic individual who sometimes lost sight of the sensibilities of those around him. Wessely was nothing if not an impassioned writer, and he often became so absorbed by the project at hand that he lost any reasonable measure of its significance. Accomplished as Wessely was in his scholarly work, and important as he was to the early maskilim, there was clearly something in his disposition that many found wearisome and alienating.

Wessely's isolated position was most notably evident in the controversy occasioned by his *Divrei shalom ve'emet* (1782). Writing in response to Joseph II of Austria's Edict of Tolerance, Wessely seized upon the educational reforms proposed by this Habsburg emperor and enthusiastically called on Jewish communities in Europe to change fundamentally the way in which their children were educated. His epistle, brimming with fervour and unqualified conviction, proposed two sweeping reforms: the introduction of a solid general education, especially the teaching of European vernaculars, and the need to improve the teaching of Hebrew, Bible, rabbinics, and Jewish ethics. Almost as soon as *Divrei shalom ve'emet* was published, it was criticized and denounced as a threat to traditional Judaism. Despite his protestations and partial recantations, Wessely had effectively strained his long-standing

[2] *Penei tevel*, 241. In translating the last line, which in Hebrew reads 'hayeshanim yeḥashduni lemeḥadesh, vehaḥadashim yeḥashduni leyashan', I have taken considerable licence to avoid the opaque and awkward use of 'old' and 'new'.

relationship with the cultural-religious world of the European rabbinate, a strain partly born of the naivety and self-assured forcefulness with which he presented his argument. However inevitable the resistance on the part of the rabbinic leadership may have been, there was undoubtedly something in Wessely's assertive and sometimes polemical tone that could only have exacerbated their swift reaction to his arguments.

If Wessely found himself alienated from traditionalists, he was only partially cheered by the fact that other maskilim hailed his epistle as a cogent articulation of their ideals. In reality, Wessely's exuberant piety and deep rabbinic learning, and his apparently limited exposure to European culture, set him noticeably apart from those who applauded *Divrei shalom ve'emet*, largely a younger and less conservative group of maskilim. A well-known contemporary anecdote recounting a sharp exchange between Wessely and Isaac Euchel, a one-time student of Kant and an active organizer of the Haskalah in Königsberg, presumed a generational clash in which Wessely represented the 'supernaturalism' and uncritical thinking of traditional Jewry.[3] Those who applauded his call for educational reform, to be sure, conferred a certain heroic status upon him. Still, Wessely continued to embrace a religious sensibility that most younger maskilim found neither compelling nor attractive, a reality that fostered no small degree of friction between them. Wessely, moreover, continued to write and teach in an idiom and literary context that fewer and fewer maskilim could understand, further contributing to a mutual alienation.

My aim in this chapter is to examine this sense of alienation by looking afresh at Wessely's relationship to both the prevailing rabbinic culture of central Europe and the emerging circle of maskilim. Wessely's expansive *œuvre* had a complex relationship to both traditional and enlightened cultures, including a deeply felt disappointment with the splintering of late eighteenth-century Jewish culture. Although one cannot do justice to the scope of this work in the confines of a single chapter, I want to consider the variegated nature of his scholarship as a whole. Going beyond the many apparent discontinuities that characterize his work, I will seek to locate Wessely's thinking in an underlying set of cultural realities, and to measure his manifest frustrations against his own expectations and motivations. In so far as Wessely's sense of isolation emanated from the realization that his vision

[3] See Alexander Altmann, *Moses Mendelssohn: A Biographical Study* (Tuscaloosa, Ala., 1973), 366 and the sources cited on p. 818 n. 133. The anecdote, as recorded by David Friedländer and translated by Altmann, reads as follows: 'One day a venerable old man joined the unusually large evening party. He was a friend of the family, though a zealous supernaturalist. He was an excellent poet and happened to be occupied with a commentary on the Genesis story in Hebrew, and being deeply immersed in the subject, he spoke with great eloquence. This scholar, whose name was W[essely] was attacked by another man of younger age E[uchel], a great admirer of Mendelssohn, who took pride in calling himself his disciple. [Euchel] started arguing with [Wessely] in a lively fashion, and the difference between their respective viewpoints did not seem to permit any reconciliation.' Although the substance of this disagreement is nowhere made explicit, the juxtaposition of 'zealous supernaturalist' to a 'disciple' of Mendelssohn was clearly intended to underscore both a generational and a cultural gap between Wessely and others.

for Jewish cultural renewal had been widely misunderstood, it is our task to consider how he himself saw his writings and how he wished others to see them. By highlighting the significant dissonance that weaves its way through his work, one can go beyond the important task of biographical reassessment to an analysis of the cultural transformations and dislocations that buffeted his generation.

II

Wessely's first published work, though not the first fruit of his literary activity, was a two-volume book entitled *Gan na'ul*, which was published in 1765–6 while he was living in Amsterdam.[4] Printed as the first part of a series of studies on Hebrew language and literary style, *Gan na'ul* was an investigation of the apparent synonymity of Hebrew verbs and nouns. In his introduction, Wessely explained his choice of title—taken from the scriptural verse 'A garden locked is my own, my bride' (Song of Songs 4: 12)—by saying that his work would concentrate on synonyms for the Hebrew *ḥokhmah*, a supernal wisdom that was inaccessible to all but God.[5] Like the verse referred to in the title, however, this work resonates with other intentions and meanings of which Wessely was fully aware. His interest in synonymity was part of a lifelong campaign to revive the study and literary use of Hebrew, especially biblical Hebrew, by demonstrating its subtlety, richness, and capacity for sublime poetics. Since Wessely bemoaned the perceived pedagogic and cultural neglect of Hebrew, it was hardly coincidental that Song of Songs 4: 12 also served as a rabbinic springboard for the statement that the ancient Israelites merited redemption from Egypt because they had preserved their language.[6] This eighteenth-century writer evidently wished to usher the way back to the locked garden of linguistic delights.

Beyond these primary aims, *Gan na'ul* is peppered with comments that point to a secondary, though important, set of concerns. Time and again, Wessely insisted that a careful analysis of Hebrew roots would not only yield an appreciation of the qualities of Hebrew *qua* language, but would also effectively reaffirm the veracity of rabbinic and midrashic exegesis. The biblical text, he wrote, 'succinctly includes all of the Oral Law'.[7] This was possible because the rabbinic Sages of late antiquity 'knew the principles of the language, and understood the purity of its refined expressions; they built their statements and *midrashim* on the trusted principles which were made known to them'.[8] Statements of this kind represent a strategic grafting

[4] *Gan na'ul* [A Locked Garden], 2 vols. (Amsterdam, 1765–6). In his introduction (i. 11*a*), Wessely wrote that he had already completed *Gan na'ul* and other related writings in 1758. Later, in his introduction to *Ḥokhmat shelomoh* (see n. 14 below), he indicated that his first literary production was his translation of the extra-canonical Wisdom of Solomon, after which he penned *Gan na'ul*. Wessely also speaks in the introduction to *Gan na'ul* (i. 4*a*). of 'our commentary on *Avot*'; much of his early literary activity therefore appears to have taken place in the decade before the publication of this work.

[5] *Gan na'ul*, i. 21*b*.

[6] *Midrash shir hashirim* [Midrash on Song of Songs], 4: 12.

[7] *Gan na'ul*, i. 55*b*.

[8] Ibid. 20*a*; see also pp. 8*b*, 10*a*.

of traditionalist concerns on to a new-found linguistic revival. Surrounded by a traditional culture that upheld the primacy of rabbinic learning and largely eschewed serious language study, Wessely was indicating that an appreciation of biblical language and text had value beyond its own intrinsic importance, for it offered a perhaps unexpected insight into rabbinic literature as well. Sensitive to the resistance he was likely to encounter, Wessely was attempting to buttress his case by suggesting that a precise understanding of talmudic or midrashic literature necessitated a thorough mastery of the language of Scripture.

More importantly, his numerous comments on this point were accompanied by an unmistakable defensiveness towards those who would deny the authenticity and integrity of rabbinic traditions. If Wessely drew attention to the fact that the Sages of late antiquity were in full command of the biblical text, it was not only to uphold them as a cultural model, but to affirm that their interpretations of Scripture, and hence their teachings, stood on the most solid textual grounds.

> When these matters become clear to us, then we understand with our discerning eye the hidden words of our Sages—the masters of the legal traditions who received the explanations of the commandments and teachings; how their words agree with the perfect *peshat* [plain sense] such that each and every phrase written in the Torah will be reliable testimony to their tradition that they receive from mouth to mouth.[9]

Elsewhere Wessely made it clear that the effort to secure the reliability of rabbinic traditions was needed so that 'fools and those with a pretence to wisdom will acknowledge that truth was revealed to our forefathers and predecessors'.[10] These critics are described in harsh terms that betray a deep-seated hostility born of anxious concern. Affirming once again the correctness of rabbinic traditions, Wessely wrote that 'if they are unreasonable in the minds of fools and those wise in their own eyes who show pride in their own intellect, and who, in their foolishness, argue with truth—behold they walk in darkness'.[11] And although Wessely later reserved some of his harshest invective for those who would deny Sinaitic revelation entirely,[12] there was little doubt that his particular concerns were primarily focused on criticism levelled against rabbinic Judaism.

Wessely's comments on the usefulness of a work like *Gan na'ul* for the study of rabbinic literature underscore two salient points. First, he evidently perceived a need for a work defending the rabbinic traditions of late antiquity, and saw this work on language as providing such a defence. Second, from passages such as those cited above it appears that the perceived threat or challenge occasioning this defence was contemporary and actual, and that it emanated from non-Jewish European quarters. There is a certain hostility and anxiety in Wessely's tone that, even

[9] Ibid. 3*b*. [10] Ibid. 10*a*. [11] Ibid. 4*a*; cf. Isa. 5: 21 and Eccles. 2: 14.

[12] *Gan na'ul*, i. 48*b*: 'Behold men of wisdom from among the gentile nations who ridicule us and speak perversely about the commandments and the ordinances and the laws; they do this because they do not believe that the Torah is a divine text, and that these ordinances are from the mouth of the Almighty. They attribute all to the doings of man.'

allowing for his overwrought and affected rhetorical habit, seems to indicate a degree of immediacy rather than a mere use of stock historical tropes.

A decade after the publication of *Gan na'ul* and a year after his relocation (via Hamburg) to Berlin, the 50-year-old Wessely began what would be his most intensive period of literary activity. The first two works he published in Berlin, a commentary on the tractate *Avot*[13] and an original Hebrew version of the apocryphal Wisdom of Solomon,[14] underscored his sustained interest in Hebrew as well as in biblical and rabbinic literature. In both works Wessely positioned himself as a retriever and protector of lost Jewish traditions, seeking to reclaim linguistic subtlety and lost texts, and to redress what he saw as a failure to appreciate fully the refined social and ethical sensibilities of biblical kings and rabbinic sages. Moreover, beyond his lengthy introductions and verbose writings there hovers a keen sensitivity, if not embarrassment, in the face of the cultural gains of eighteenth-century Europe. As in other early writings of the maskilim, there is a determined if unstated attempt to demonstrate that Jewish texts and traditions are no less sophisticated or profound than those of non-Jewish European provenance.

Towards the end of the 1770s Wessely returned to some of the ideas expressed in *Gan na'ul* and developed them as a central concern. Four years after his move to Berlin, Moses Mendelssohn and Solomon Dubno (1738–1813) announced their intention to publish a new German translation of the Pentateuch accompanied by a Hebrew commentary (known as the *Biur*). Recognizing this project as a perfect contribution to his own vision of Jewish cultural revival, Wessely applauded it with a brief epistle and poem that he penned under the title 'Mehalel re'a'.[15] A year or so later, when it became apparent to Mendelssohn that he would need help to bring the proposed commentary to completion, Wessely's reputation as a man of Hebrew letters and considerable learning made him a natural choice.[16] Given his enthusiasm for this project and his long-standing interest in Leviticus and the rabbinic *Sifra*, Wessely was only too eager to participate by contributing a commentary on Leviticus.[17]

13 *Yein levanon* [Wine of Lebanon] (Berlin, 1775).

14 *Ḥokhmat shelomoh* [Wisdom of Solomon] (Berlin, 1780). While the commentary on *Avot* was in all likelihood composed in the early 1770s, *Ḥokhmat shelomoh* and its appended commentary *Ruaḥ ḥen* appear to have been written much earlier and left in manuscript. After moving from Amsterdam to Hamburg in the late 1760s, Wessely apparently found a publisher for it: the title-page of a Hamburg 1770 edition of Abraham Ibn Ezra's *Yesod mora* [Foundation of Awe] also served as the title-page for *Ḥokhmat shelomoh*. In the end, however, Ibn Ezra's work was published alone, and Wessely had to wait another decade before *Ḥokhmat shelomoh* was published.

15 'Mehalel re'a' [In Praise of a Friend] was originally published in the Exodus volume of *Sefer netivot hashalom* [Paths of Peace] and as part of the introduction of many subsequent editions; see Moses Mendelssohn, *Gesammelte Schriften Jubiläumsausgabe*, vols. i–iii(1), vii, xi, xiv, xvi, ed F. Bamberger *et al.* (Berlin, 1929–38); repr. and continued under the editorship of A. Altmann (Stuttgart, 1971–), xv(1). 8–14. Cited below as *GSJ*.

16 For Mendelssohn's description of Wessely's participation in the Bible project, see *GSJ* xiv. 247.

17 In a letter to Mendelssohn in 1775 David Wagenaar, who had known Wessely from his days in Amsterdam, sent regards to Wessely and specifically praised him for his knowledge and mastery of

Like his earlier writings, Wessely's ode to Mendelssohn laments the decline of the study of Hebrew and Scripture, emphasizing the difference between Hebrew and other languages: while 'profane languages' were human conventions, and so contained human imprecision and error, Hebrew was God-given and holy, and therefore pure, free of error, and intellectually rigorous. With a marked degree of linguistic sophistication, generations of Jews were able to plumb Hebrew texts with profit, including 'the breadth of the *halakhot* and the depth of the laws, for upon [the proper understanding of Hebrew words] were based the words of the Oral Law'.[18] Wessely went on to complain about the state of contemporary education, accusing schoolteachers of filling young minds with *derashot* (rabbinic interpretations) without first ensuring that all students had a rudimentary knowledge of Hebrew and Scripture. The fundamental problem, in Wessely's mind, was quite simply: 'The Rabbi did not know that all the *derashot* of our Sages were founded upon the holy mountains of the *peshat*. And whoever is ignorant of the *peshat* of the verse cannot understand the depth of the *derashah* based upon it.'[19]

Wessely repeated this theme in his introduction to the Leviticus volume of the *Biur*.[20] He began by acknowledging the difficulty of writing a commentary on Leviticus, especially in light of the vast amount of rabbinic material apparently derived from its verses. Recognizing the manifold exegetical challenges that arose from a simultaneous embrace of both the textual plain sense and its rabbinic interpretation, Wessely presented his approach to these problems in terms that explicitly drew upon *Gan na'ul*:

'I have made the Lord God my refuge' [Ps. 73: 28] . . . 'He will guide me with His counsel' [Ps. 73: 24], and in His kindness he will lead me in two ways [Gen. 19: 19; Job 13: 20]. First, that I may not turn away from the trusted path [Job 23: 11] of our forefathers' tradition, and second, that I should not falter from the path of clear *peshat* acceptable to one's intelligence, [so that the two] 'may come together equally . . .' [Exod. 26: 24].

And if the way to effect a bridge between the *peshat* and the midrash—which appear to be far from one another—is narrow, I said there is hope only if God favours me to understand

Leviticus and *Sifra*: see *GSJ* xix. 207. This early interest in this section of the Pentateuch is corroborated by an interesting passage in Frankfurt, *Penei tevel*, 240, which recounts the same conversation(s) between the author and Wessely mentioned above:

R. Naphtali [Wessely] told me a wonderful thing about this [commentary on Leviticus], and these are his words: 'Know my son, that when I was a youth in the yeshiva of my master and teacher R. Jonathan Eibeschütz, I took it upon myself to write my commentary on *Torat kohanim*. This became known to my teacher, and he called me and said "Naphtali, show me what you have written." I was fearful and ashamed to raise my head against our teacher, for his dread and fear was upon all his students. The rabbi raised his voice and said "I beseech you to read it." And so I read before him, and he sat on the chair with his arms on the armrests. After I had read a number of sections, he stood up from his chair, raised his hands, and said "Your words are as if given from Sinai." '

18 'Mehalel re'a', in *GSJ* xv(1). 8.

19 Ibid. 9.

20 Wessely's commentary originally appeared in autumn 1781 as the third volume of *Sefer netivot hashalom*; see the photographic reproduction in *GSJ* xvii (the introduction appears on pp. 3–6).

clearly the meaning of the roots [*hora'at hashorashim*]; if we reflect upon them, it will become clear that the words of the Midrash are nothing but the depths of the *peshat*, and matters far apart will be made close.[21]

Once again, Wessely insisted that a linguistically vigorous appreciation of the biblical text lay at the roots of the rabbinic interpretations of Scripture. Despite the inherent hermeneutical difficulties, one of his reasons for pursuing this commentary was to 'strengthen the tradition of our forefathers against those who speak arrogantly upon their words, to demonstrate that their tradition is determined from the *peshat* of the verses'.[22] A few lines later, apologizing for any errors that may have crept into his work, Wessely noted that his writing was particularly susceptible to error due to the fact that he was working on his own: 'I sit alone, and in all this I have no mentor or teacher, neither colleague nor student.'[23] In his own mind, at least, Wessely appeared self-consciously aware of the relative marginality of his interests.

Even a cursory examination of the body of Wessely's commentary on Leviticus affirms the degree to which he was profoundly committed to the goals set out in the introduction. More than in any other volume of Mendelssohn's *Biur*, there is here an enormous quantity of rabbinic literature, in many instances accompanied by discussion that highlights Wessely's preoccupation with the relationship of rabbinic interpretation to Scripture.[24] His sensitivity to this issue carried over to his evaluation and handling of medieval exegesis, as when he censured Ibn Ezra for ignoring rabbinic interpretations[25] or approvingly cited an earlier commentary that provided some textual basis for a halakhic midrash.[26]

[21] *GSJ* xvii. 4. [22] Ibid. 6. [23] Ibid.

[24] Wessely, it should be noted, did not always feel the need—or make the effort—to supply exegetical justifications for the rabbinic references he had cited. See e.g. *Biur* on Lev. 4: 17, 5: 4, 6: 19, 7: 5, 11: 12, 35, 14: 15, 19: 26, 22: 7, 25: 46, and 27: 10, where he juxtaposed *derash* to *peshat* without offering any explanation or analysis of the former.

[25] See e.g. *Biur* on Lev. 3: 1, 4: 8, 5: 1, 22, 24, 7: 33, 14: 8, and 16: 6. Conversely, when Rashbam (R. Samuel b. Meir, a 12th-cent. commentator) begins his commentary on the biblical chapters on plagues and impurities by expressing a lack of interest in actively seeking textual justification for rabbinical exegesis, Wessely is quick to respond:

> Rashbam wrote: '[With regard to] all the passages [involving] the plagues of man, of clothing, or of houses . . . there is no worth in following the plain sense of Scripture, nor in familiarity with the ways of the land [*derekh erets*]. Rather, the essence [of scriptural meaning] is the Midrash of the Sages, their statutes, and their traditions received from earlier scholars.' His words are truth. Nevertheless, it is proper for us to explain the scriptural *peshat*, and to render the verses in a way agreeable with the approach of the rabbinic tradition. (*Biur* on Lev. 13: 2)

Wessely certainly agreed that rabbinic exegesis captured the essence of Scripture, but he refused to accept the notion that the laws relating to disease (*tsara'at*) could not be readily explained in light of the scriptural text. He effectively rejected Rashbam's willingness to separate the study of *peshat* and rabbinic interpretation, for such an approach undermined his desire to defend the exegetical veracity of talmudic and midrashic literature.

[26] See e.g. *Biur* on Lev. 3: 4, 9, 7: 25, 25: 14.

More importantly, it is clear that Wessely applied considerable energy and originality to articulating the textual and philological underpinnings of rabbinic interpretation: his commentary is studded with examples of this kind of exegetical scholarship. To cite but one passage, we can turn to Leviticus 16 and the scriptural prescription for the priestly ritual on the Day of Atonement. Central to the High Priest's expiatory role in cleansing the nation of its sins was the ceremonial casting of lots upon two he-goats, which culminated in the 'release' of one of the animals into the desert: 'The goat upon which the lot fell for Azazel shall be set alive [*yo'omad ḥai*] before the Lord to make atonement over him, to send him away [*leshalaḥ oto*] for Azazel into the wilderness' (Lev. 16: 10). The verse, as the rabbinic midrash recognized, contained an ambiguous formulation: was the goat to be sent into the wilderness to live or to die? The rabbinic solution lay in the words *yo'omad ḥai*—the goat was alive only in the sense of standing before God, as opposed to its 'sending', which was apparently to its death.[27] Wessely was cognizant of the fact that as an interpretation of the plain sense of Scripture this inferential rabbinic reading was not particularly compelling. And although he faithfully cited the rabbinic solution, he indicated that he would return to this problem further on.

Wessely's handling of these texts turned on another textual problem he encountered in verses 21–2 of this same chapter:

And Aaron shall lay both his hands upon the head of the live goat . . . and shall send him away by the hand of an appointed man into the wilderness.

And the goat shall bear upon it all their iniquities unto a land which is cut off, and he shall send [*veshilaḥ*] the goat in the wilderness [*bamidbar*].

Why, Wessely wondered, did verse 22 include the phrase 'and he shall send the goat in the wilderness' since the subject of the verse—the 'appointed man' of verse 21—had already been dispatched with the goat to the wilderness? How could verse 22 indicate that the goat was to be sent to the wilderness, since he was presumably already there? On the other hand, if the verse was translated in its most straightforward sense as 'upon the wilderness', that is, 'letting the goat go', then it should really have read 'veshilaḥ . . . al penei hamidbar' instead of the simple 'veshilaḥ . . . bamidbar'.[28] Wessely's exegetical solution was to read the verse not as an indication of where to send the goat, but referring to the rabbinical explanation of *yo'omad ḥai*, as a directive to kill it: to 'let him go' or 'dispatch' him from life. Drawing upon his study of synonyms, Wessely went on to suggest that this reading was indicated by the word *shilaḥ* itself: 'For this is one of the meanings of this root, a complete letting go from life unto death. Because [of this meaning] a sword is also called a *shelaḥ*, as in "made weapons [*shelaḥ*] in abundance [2 Chr. 32: 5]" and "they shall perish by the sword [*beshelaḥ*]" [Job 36: 12].' Thus the plain sense of Leviticus 16: 22, based on an analysis of Hebrew roots, was offered as philological

[27] Sifra, 'Aḥarei mot', 2. 6.

[28] Wessely buttressed this point with a parallel in Lev. 14: 7.

support for the rabbinic reading of *yo'omad ḥai*.[29] Even where Wessely did not have recourse to this kind of linguistic analysis, he consistently sought to articulate the plain sense of Scripture in a way that called attention to the careful and sensible nature of rabbinic exegesis.[30]

The sheer bulk and scholarly sophistication of *Gan na'ul* and of the commentary on Leviticus lent weight to Wessely's declared concerns. Clearly, he saw his work not as an expression of new linguistic and textual approaches that simply remained within the confines of traditional Judaism, but as supporting a neglected body of learning that could serve to bolster traditional strictures and defend rabbinic Judaism. For Jews like Wessely who had already mastered a number of European languages and were familiar with the cultural landscape of the eighteenth century, the anti-rabbinic animus of contemporary culture, especially in the various European Enlightenments, was everywhere evident. In Wessely's mind, the need to defend Jewish traditions had become paramount.

Given this sensitivity to the integrity of Jewish textual traditions, one can begin to appreciate the complexities of Wessely's relationship to the prevailing rabbinic culture of eighteenth-century Europe. In one respect, his writing was openly critical of the cultural-pedagogic norms that reinforced the widespread neglect of the proper study of language and texts. He tried to provide a corrective to this perceived deficiency and to serve as an example of what could, and should, be done in response. Still, the fact that Wessely marshalled this interest in Hebrew and Scripture in defence of rabbinic traditions rendered his work acceptable, and undoubtedly accounted for the enthusiastic approbations he received from rabbis otherwise not given to such gestures. But here too there were cultural differences setting Wessely off from his rabbinic contemporaries, for his modest involvement in the world of European letters exposed him to incipient challenges to traditional Judaism that others simply could not appreciate. The marked sense of religious defensiveness which characterized his publications in the 1760s and 1770s stood in contrast to the rather stock defensive conventions employed by the existing rabbinic leadership. In more ways than one, Wessely waged a struggle against cultural forces others did not see, a fact that significantly shaped his own perceived place in the emerging cultural matrix of late eighteenth-century German Jewry.

III

The 1780s brought momentous developments for Wessely, as they did for the Haskalah and the Jewish communities of central Europe. It was in this decade that Wessely attempted to articulate further his attitudes towards European culture

[29] For similar examples, see *Biur* on Lev. 1: 1, 4, 12: 3, 18: 6 (cf. 18: 22, 20: 13), and 26: 3. Although Wessely did not refer to the German translation, Mendelssohn's choice of the verb 'schicken' for *shilaḥ*—like the English 'dispatch'—may also have been intended to preserve the multiple meanings of the Hebrew text.

[30] See e.g. *Biur* on Lev. 6: 13, 14: 47, 19: 35, 22: 4 (cf. 22: 6), 25: 13, and 26: 3 (cf. 26: 12).

and balance them against his concerns for the preservation of rabbinic Judaism. The appearance of his *Divrei shalom ve'emet* was clearly an expression of this effort, but its subsequent reception also engendered a much broader—and, for the first time, a publicly divisive—consideration of these issues. Wessely stood at the centre of this debate, and the events of the next few years profoundly changed his relationship with both the European rabbinic leadership and the maskilic circles of Berlin and Königsberg.

This is not the place to rehearse in detail the controversies of 1782–5 and the traditionalist reaction to his letters, but a number of observations are in order. However one evaluates Wessely's protestations that he had in effect said nothing new or heretical, it is evident that his writings had struck a raw nerve. In the eyes of many communal rabbis and leaders, *Divrei shalom ve'emet* had unleashed an attack on the long-established educational—and, by extension, religious—norms of the Jewish communities. The fact that he called for change in so public a manner, in a pamphlet devoted exclusively to the question of pedagogic and cultural reform, and in response to European developments, evidently presented itself as a flagrant challenge to those in positions of communal authority. Neither lay leader nor rabbi, Wessely's political presumptuousness made many such leaders bristle. That he also appeared to give the cultural predilections of eighteenth-century Europe primacy over those of Ashkenazi Jewry was no less threatening. Finally, the fact that this was the same individual who had been applauded as a defender of rabbinic Judaism made his challenge all the more threatening: since he was legitimated by the conservative sensibilities expressed in his earlier writings, the real danger of his current work was perniciously camouflaged.[31]

The rejection of Wessely by some influential rabbis was to some degree motivated by the very same reasons that led young adherents of the nascent Haskalah to hail his efforts. For them, Wessely was something of a hero: he was the first to offer publicly a cogent and articulate vision of how Jewish cultural norms needed to be changed. Moreover, the fact that he was a rabbinically learned and respected individual of his generation was not irrelevant: as the cultural tensions between traditionalists and maskilim grew, so too did Wessely's strategic usefulness as a spokesman.

Given the prominence of Wessely's relationship with these young maskilim, it is highly significant that at this very juncture he also began to express increased frustration and anxiety with regard to the Haskalah. Sometime in the late autumn or early winter of 1782 the maskilim of Königsberg announced their decision to publish a Hebrew journal under the title *Hame'asef*. Not surprisingly, the editors wrote to Wessely, praising him in the overwrought language of the Haskalah,

[31] On the general question of the rabbinic reaction to *Divrei shalom ve'emet*, see Moshe Samet, 'M. Mendelssohn, N. H. Wessely, and the Rabbis of their Generation', in A. Gilboa, B. Mevorach, *et al.* (eds.), *Research into the History of the Jewish People and the Land of Israel* (Heb.), vol. i (Haifa, 1970), 244–53.

requesting his permission to include some unpublished poems, and inviting him to submit others. In their eyes, Wessely was an individual of exemplary literary talents, a figure second only to Mendelssohn.[32]

In his response of January 1783 Wessely applauded the efforts of this group and expressed his sense of kinship with their endeavour. Within two paragraphs, however, he struck a different note, voicing concern about how certain individuals might come to distort the writings of these maskilim:

Know that your work is the work of heaven, and 'your springs will gush forth amidst the assembled congregation' [Prov. 5: 14, 16]. Be very careful with your words, so that no one will derive falsehood from them. For many are those who 'plan evil' [Prov. 12: 20] among us, and from a conspicuously well built sanctuary they make spider webs and say 'they are new ropes' [Judg. 16: 11–12]—but the yoke of Torah and commandments has never rested upon them; and about sweet waters drawn from 'wells which the chieftains dug' [Num. 21: 18], they say 'they are bitter' [Exod. 15: 23].[33]

Those with a more tenuous commitment to traditional Judaism, Wessely feared, might exploit the writings appearing in *Hame'asef* for their own ends. Warning this group from Königsberg to be vigilant against such dissenters, Wessely went on to offer advice, reiterating a now familiar theme in his writings:

Given your intention to make known the purity of our holy language, don't confine your study of language to speaking and writing purely, in the manner one teaches profane languages; rather, your [study] should extend to the vast sea of the Torah's wisdom, because through proper knowledge of [Hebrew] you will enable the nation to understand the pure passages of the Torah . . . and the true tradition in the hands of the Sages of the Mishnah and Talmud, whose foundations lay in the majestic holiness of the language and the refined expression 'glorious in sanctity' [Exod. 15: 6].[34]

In terms echoing *Gan na'ul* and his commentary on Leviticus, Wessely insisted that Hebrew should be seen as a tool to be utilized for a better understanding of rabbinic literature. Still smarting from the controversy over *Divrei shalom ve'emet*, he indignantly added that he had made this very point in the two letters written in 1782, 'which some of our Jewish brethren opposed, because they failed to appreciate the precious objective that we intended'.[35]

Wessely's concerns here were directed at a certain 'secularist' element within the Haskalah that would seem to have expressed greater interest in Hebrew as a cultural artefact than as a means to an increased religious and textual sophistication. But as the comment regarding *Divrei shalom ve'emet* indicates, he was equally sensitive to the cultural predilections of conservative-minded traditionalists. Indeed, after emphasizing the importance of language study, Wessely turned his criticism against those who would dismiss the revival of a textual and linguistically oriented study of Scripture:

[32] This letter was included in the prospectus for the journal, entitled *Naḥal habesor* [River of Tidings], which is printed with the first volume of *Hame'asef* (1784): see pp. 4–6.

[33] Ibid. 7.

[34] Ibid. 8.

[35] Ibid.

> Do not heed the words of those who scoff,[36] who denigrate all those who delve into Holy Scripture and the commentaries found in our hands, stating that there is nothing for us to add. They belittle themselves, all in order to be excused from the toil of Torah study and making sense of [Scripture] through its examination . . . this represents an exceedingly negative trait of laziness.[37]

In this passage, Wessely was not talking about Enlightenment-minded Deists who ridiculed and impugned Scripture, nor Jews who had drifted from the fold, but traditionalists who upheld the talmudic and halakhic focus of Ashkenazi culture and discouraged serious study of Bible.[38]

This letter to the *me'asfim*, then, is striking in weaving together two preoccupations which, from Wessely's perspective, ultimately coalesced into one problem. On the one hand, he was concerned that there were maskilim whose interest in Hebrew language and literature did not extend to Scripture and rabbinic texts. On the other hand, he criticized those who remained staunchly committed to traditional rabbinic study but who eschewed the revival of Hebrew and biblical exegesis. Both, in the end, denied him a long-standing goal that he had consistently articulated from his earliest writings: to use Hebrew in appreciation and defence of the rabbinic tradition. The letter of 1783 thus draws attention to the fact that, as a new cultural configuration began to emerge among Prussian Jews, Wessely appeared to be increasingly disappointed by both sides. The changes, instigated in no small part by Wessely himself, were beginning to manifest themselves in ways that frustrated him.

Less than two years later, in 1785, Wessely used the fourth and final public letter that followed the publication of *Divrei shalom ve'emet* to express these frustrations yet again. He now had the opportunity to reflect on the actual changes that shaped Jewish education in the wake of Joseph II's Edict of Tolerance and the vocal support he himself had offered. What he found greatly disturbed him. Many Jewish communities, to be sure, had established an *école normale* or its equivalent in compliance with the Habsburg decrees, but from Wessely's perspective they had also missed the point: 'It pains me to say', he wrote, 'that the emperor's law has been established, but that of the Torah has been abandoned.' His vision of Jewish education was that Jewish children

> should learn pure German through the perspicacity of the Torah; 'how good is a thing rightly timed' [Prov. 15: 23], such as the publication of a German translation, impeccably written and explaining scriptural verses according to their *peshat* and following the traditions of our forefathers. Since not all German words make it into this translation, they can learn the rest of the language from the history books and travelogues of gentile scholars, which they may read for a half hour a day; one comes and illuminates the other, for through

[36] Cf. Exod. 5: 9, where the verse reads '[let them] not heed deceitful words'.

[37] *Naḥal habesor*, 8–9.

[38] See Mordechai Breuer, 'Keep your Sons Away from *Higayon*', in Y. Gilat and A. Stern (eds.), *Mikhtam ledavid: Memorial Book for Rabbi David Oks* (Heb.) (Ramat Gan, 1977), 242–61.

the clarity of the translation they will understand the glory and majesty [Ps. 96: 6] of Scripture's refined expressions, and through the study of Torah they will also learn pure German. And for all this they have opened their mouths against me in strife and contention [Isa. 58: 4].[39]

Whether or not this was an accurate clarification of his intentions in writing *Divrei shalom ve'emet*,[40] Wessely's stated expectations stood in sharp contrast with the realities he confronted:

See now what [these schools] do. They waste many hours teaching young people to read and write German and mathematics and the like, while the Torah is taught as it had been earlier, with stilted and confused language. I was informed that it had been decreed that one may not study from the aforementioned German translation until the age of 13. This was tantamount to decreeing that one should not study Scripture at all. For from this stilted study currently used, it will appear that there is no purity and glory in the sayings of the Torah. And when this youth turns 13, he will not desire it any longer.[41]

While Wessely had hoped that German could be learnt in conjunction with Torah study—whereby both subjects would be enhanced and enriched—the schools had essentially put in place a dual but separate curriculum. His desire to transform the ways in which Jews studied their texts and traditions went unfulfilled.

Wessely was disheartened by what appeared to be an early compromise between supporters of Jewish pedagogic reform and the traditionalist rabbinic leadership. Those who had praised *Divrei shalom ve'emet* were evidently far more concerned about establishing schools where Jewish children would receive German-language instruction than changing the ways in which these students acquired Hebrew language and text skills. The former, clearly, was a visible and tangible goal with significant socio-economic implications; the latter, though a central concern to Wessely, was really a more nuanced issue of cultural and intellectual import that was harder to implement and promote. The muted conservatism of traditionalists —communal leaders and rabbis alike—manifested itself in the concern for the continuance of the status quo with regard to Torah study. Whether or not they approved of the establishment of new Jewish schools that incorporated German and general studies, the fact that existing substantive patterns of Jewish education could be maintained allowed them to accept these changes without feeling that their cultural traditions were being challenged. In the end, the *de facto* compromise effected between traditionalist and reform-minded Jews bore little relation to Wessely's professed aims. The realities shaping the culture of eighteenth-century

[39] *Reḥovot* (Berlin, 1785), 72*b*.

[40] Wessely had earlier spoken (*Divrei shalom ve'emet*, ch. 7), of Mendelssohn's Bible translation as a means of teaching German to young Jews, but not in the same exclusive terms as articulated here. He had also stated earlier that Jewish children should spend half an hour a day learning to read and write in a vernacular, corresponding here to the time allotted for supplementary language acquisition: see *Rav tuv leveit yisra'el* [Blessings on the House of Israel] (Berlin, 1782), 18*a*.

[41] *Reḥovot*, 72*b*–73*a*.

German Jewry effectively denied him his vision of a broadly integrated and unified Jewish culture.

IV

Throughout the 1780s Wessely's writings also began to express an anxiety regarding aspects of contemporary European culture. His concern focused on Enlightenment rationalism and its apparent absorption by an Enlightenment-minded segment of the Jewish community. This particular problem, however, was not entirely new to his work, and there exists at least one noteworthy exchange of letters with Mendelssohn that serves as an important backdrop to Wessely's later thinking. Written in the late summer of 1768, at a time when the two men knew each other only from afar, these letters revolved around the recent publication of Mendelssohn's *Phädon* and Wessely's apparent interest in translating this German work into Hebrew.[42]

After hearing of Wessely's intentions indirectly, Mendelssohn wrote to him and expressed his frank surprise at Wessely's enthusiasm for this rescripted Platonic dialogue. Mendelssohn admitted that he had assumed that Wessely would be hostile to any work relying on philosophical argumentation where faith alone should suffice. This impression appeared to be based on Mendelssohn's familiarity with *Gan na'ul* and some of its strident criticisms of thinkers who would deny revelation and knowledge of God in the traditional theistic sense.[43] Mendelssohn, of course, was only too happy to admit his misjudgement, and he acknowledged that whatever hostility Wessely appeared to have towards rationalistic speculation was limited to philosophical systems that were antithetical to religion.

In his reply Wessely insisted—with a measure of embarrassed indignation—that Judaism had always recognized a realm of discourse circumscribed by human knowledge and intellect. He did not, then, object to a text that sought to prove or demonstrate matters of faith. Reiterating the centuries-old position claimed by conservative rationalists, Wessely stated that since both the tradition of Jewish beliefs and the independent workings of the mind emanated from the same divine source, there was little reason to fault anyone attempting to strengthen faith through reason. He went on to make another telling comment: not only did he not object to true and honest philosophizing, but he recognized that such proofs were useful in responding to those who erroneously believed that intellect and reason alone could lead to pure knowledge and insight. Wessely's hostility here was evident, and, like passages of his *Gan na'ul* discussed above, it contained a degree of defensive anxiety. He gave no indication as to the source of this kind of challenge, but one has the impression that he was referring to ideas emanating from the culture of contemporary Europe.

This issue surfaced again in *Rav tuv leveit yisra'el*, the epistle published shortly after the appearance of *Divrei shalom ve'emet* in which Wessely tried to deflect the

[42] See Altmann, *Moses Mendelssohn*, 189–91.

[43] See *Gan na'ul*, i. 47*b*–48*b*.

rush of criticism against his proposals. Wessely had used *Divrei shalom ve'emet* to insist that all Jewish boys should be given a basic education in subjects such as mathematics and geography. Such knowledge was both intrinsically valuable and also practically useful in securing a livelihood. In classical scholarly fashion, Wessely simultaneously cited talmudic passages that supported his position[44] and sought to deflect those that would be seen as warning against unnecessary exposure to worldly knowledge. In *Rav tuv leveit yisra'el* he took up a rabbinic text that expressed scepticism about the value, especially for one steeped in traditional learning, of something referred to as *ḥokhmah yevanit*—secular wisdom.[45] Wessely emphatically argued, in consonance with the position of numerous medieval writers, that *ḥokhmah yevanit* referred not to the didactic or natural sciences, but only to classical Greek philosophy:[46]

> And thus, you will not find in my first letter with regard to humanistic knowledge [*torat ha'adam*] any reference to philosophy . . . It is not necessary for one wise of heart, since he knows his God from his Torah and belief and the knowledge of the divine in his heart. For a simple individual of imperfect knowledge, [philosophy] may undermine the foundation of his belief . . . The Sages permitted the house of Rabban Gamliel to study *ḥokhmah yevanit* because they had dealings with the authorities . . . [But] R. Yishmael never stated that it is prohibited, for the wise man who cleaves to the Lord—it is permissible for him to know it, so that [gentile] thinkers shall not be boastful towards him, and so that he may know how to respond to men of iniquity . . . But far be it from me to familiarize children and students in these studies before the light of the Torah and of knowing belief could shield them.[47]

Although much of his comment here is articulated with reference to the specific issue of educational reform, his general stance towards the study of philosophy was one of cautious appreciation. For mature and reasonably sophisticated adults, the rationalistic endeavour could be a useful, though not indispensable, mode of enquiry.

Wessely continued to address the question of contemporary rationalism throughout his writings of the latter half of the 1780s, and one can discern a sense of heightened anxiety. In *Sefer hamidot*, which appeared sometime around 1787,[48]

[44] As e.g. his use of BT *Horayot* 10*a*.

[45] BT *Menaḥot* 99*b*.

[46] On this term, see Saul Lieberman, *Hellenism in Jewish Palestine* (New York, 1962), 100–15; Bernard Septimus, *Hispano-Jewish Culture in Transition: The Career and Controversies of Ramah* (Cambridge, Mass., 1982), 85–6.

[47] *Rav tuv leveit yisra'el*, 20*b*–21*a*.

[48] *Sefer hamidot vehu sefer musar haskel* [The Book of Ethics, a Book of Morals]: neither the title-page nor the body of this work gives any indication of the year of publication, and it has been variously dated. Julius Fürst, *Bibliotheca Judaica*, vol. ii (Leipzig, 1863), 508, lists the first publication as 1784, and numerous bibliographers and historians have repeated this dating. Wessely's first biographer, David Friedrichsfeld, *Zekher tsadik* [In Memory of a Righteous Individual] (Amsterdam, 1808), 38, dates the book at 1785, as does his most extensive biographer, Wolf Aloys Meisel, in *Leben und Wirken Naphtali Hartwig Wesselys* (Breslau, 1841), 153. In fact, it appears that the book was in all probability published in the latter half of 1786 or in 1787. In spring 1784, and again in early summer 1785, the

Wessely delivered his most negative pronouncement regarding the study of philosophy. His markedly critical tone was clearly informed by the work's ethical focus, particularly his concern with the intellectual vanity and conceit of secular or atheistic philosophy and its deleterious impact on ethical discipline.[49] To be sure, he reiterated the notion that although the Torah and Western philosophy appeared to represent two vastly different bodies of thought, they were, for the most part, teaching the same truths. Wessely explicitly underscored the universalism of these truths, suggesting that they were the property of all mankind well before the revelation at Sinai.[50] And yet, given that the Jewish prophets and Sages incorporated these very truths in their sacred literature, he posed what appeared to him to be a natural and uncomplicated question:

This being as it is, why should one hasten to rely upon the work of writers who wrote according to their own investigations, and who violated the bounds of humility and were not ashamed to apply their minds to bewildering and hidden things? . . . Rather, it is proper that he conduct himself with regard to these matters with the fear of God. It is better for him to remain where he is, secure and reliant upon the refined sayings of his God, rather than going with his staff through fiery flames in dark places [Isa. 29: 6, 15]. One who reads the works of thinkers should understand that he is reading the books of laymen; he should put the light of truth revealed in prophecy before himself, and with it, he can darken and overshadow the light of human intellect when its claims oppose the clear truth.[51]

Wessely was here inclined to discount any benefit that may be gained from the study of philosophical texts.

In other writings of this period, however, Wessely sounded a more moderate note, in consonance with his earlier letter to Mendelssohn. In 1787, almost two decades after he had first broached the idea, a Hebrew translation of Mendelssohn's *Phädon* finally appeared.[52] Although, in the end, Wessely was not himself the translator, the publishers—the maskilic Hevrat Hinukh Ne'arim (Society for the Education of Youth) in Berlin—invited him to contribute a preface, in which

letters written in the wake of the *Divrei shalom ve'emet* controversy referred to 'the book on ethics which we are engaged in writing', and '*Sefer hamidot* that we hope, God willing, to publish': see *Ein mishpat* [The Fountain of Judgement] (Berlin, 1784), 5*a*, and *Reḥovot* (Berlin, 1785), 7*b*. By the time his 'Ḥikur din' [Discourse on Final Judgement] appeared in *Hame'asef* in spring 1788, *Sefer hamidot* was being cited as if already published; see the Königsberg 1857 edition, pp. 3*b*, 7*b*, and 17*b*. The best evidence for the dating of this book appears in a preface to the Hebrew translation of Mendelssohn's *Phädon*, published in 1787; this preface, written by Wessely himself, refers to 'the book *Hamidot* that we are now publishing' (unpaginated: see p. 3). Given that Wessely here refers to Mendelssohn as deceased, this preface could not have been written any earlier than winter 1786. If Wessely actually wrote this preface some time in advance of its publication, then it is possible that *Sefer hamidot* was indeed published as early as 1786; in the absence of such evidence, it appears that in all probability this text was not published until 1787.

49 *Sefer hamidot*, 46*a*–*b*. 50 Ibid. 50*a*–*b*. 51 Ibid. 50*b*–51*a*.

52 *Pha'edon: Hu sefer hasharat hanefesh* [*Phaedon*; or On the Immortality of the Soul] (Berlin, 1787); the translator of the work was Isaiah Beer of Metz. On this Hebrew edition of *Phädon*, see Altmann, *Moses Mendelssohn*, 192.

he selectively praised the philosophical writings of gentile authors for buttressing the belief in fundamental religious ideas. These works, he wrote, offered

evidence to those who despise wisdom and morality, and reproof to those who abandon the Torah. For when they understand the doings of the early nations that did not know the Lord . . . and how even among them there emerged singular men of repute in all the wisdoms and sciences . . . who rose above the beliefs of the masses, and proclaimed the existence of God and His unity, the existence of the soul and its immortality, and the judgment and accounting for its deeds. Despite this, there are individuals who have inherited the Torah, filled with the paths of life and peace, who shamelessly raised their hand against its ideas and beliefs without justice and honest thinking, but rather, according to whatever they fancied.[53]

This passage closely resembles Wessely's letter to Mendelssohn two decades earlier, but there is one conspicuous difference: when Wessely referred to those who would deny fundamental religious truths, he was pointing at Jewish sceptics.

This same point is evident in a preface Wessely wrote two years later for a new edition of Sa'adya Gaon's *Sefer ha'emunot vehade'ot*.[54] In this instance, Wessely's discussion was framed not by non-Jewish philosophical speculation and its relation to the Torah, but by a text written by one of the outstanding Rabbanite leaders and thinkers of the geonic period. Underscoring the importance of publishing such a work, he offered a threefold typology of contemporary Jewish reactions to philosophical literature of this kind. The first group, comprised of those who despise philosophical investigations of any sort, would either refuse to read this treatise, or—if they came to read it—would fail to understand its import. A second group was made up of God-fearing Jews who had an appreciation of philosophical literature, and who could confidently and judiciously sift through such writings in order to distinguish between the true and the false. Given their confidence, the fact that such Jews read philosophical texts written by 'men of faith' would only serve to bolster their religious sensibilities. The third group represented an altogether different phenomenon:

For men of critical thinking who are 'turned away backwards' [Isa. 1: 4] and who have removed their hearts from the Lord, perhaps books like this will be of some benefit; if they see that evil thoughts that caused them to cast down 'truth on the ground' [Dan. 8: 12] are included in books written by great critical men who nevertheless did not move from fear and wisdom. Then their hearts shall surely be overthrown [Jer. 51: 58] and they shall be embarrassed by their pride and say 'perhaps that which we have trusted in is worthless, and the counsels of our minds upon which we have relied are vanity'. They will abandon their ways and will return to the Lord.[55]

[53] *Pha'edon*, unpaginated [pp. v–vi].

[54] [Book of Doctrines and Beliefs] (10th cent.; Berlin, 1789). This work, like many of the others published by Hevrat Hinukh Ne'arim, came with no rabbinic approbation. The fact that its place was here taken by Wessely's preface underscores the extent to which the Berlin Haskalah exercised its social and cultural independence.

[55] Ibid., unpaginated [p. i].

It was Wessely's hope, however naive, that the dissemination of Jewish philosophical literature could serve to rekindle the faith of those who had already rejected their religious traditions.

These writings from the latter half of the 1780s draw attention to the fact that Wessely was thoroughly convinced of the need for such literature in order to counter what he considered a reversible drift among some philosophically oriented Jews. Once again, what is important is the fact that contemporary challenges to traditional Jewish belief, which Wessely had earlier identified with the philosophical speculations of Christian Europe, were now specifically perceived as a problem within the Jewish community itself. The fact that Wessely's concern with the relationship of rationalism to Jewish belief was decades old and had always been articulated in cautious terms only served to reinforce his consternation regarding this shift.

V

Taken together, Wessely's writings yield a sense of double alienation. Although one can never entirely dismiss the fact that such expressions are significantly coloured by personality and character, it is evident that his frustration was a manifestation of something more historically significant. The personal dislocation that informs so much of his writing says much about Wessely as a transitional figure caught between two worlds, but it also illuminates the complex cultural and intellectual developments of the late eighteenth century.

On the one hand, his alienation from traditionalists went beyond the controversy generated by the publication of *Divrei shalom ve'emet*. Rather, it must be understood in the context of his other writings, both before and after 1782, which were consistently tinged with feelings of apprehension regarding the preservation of traditional Judaism. His concern for the integrity of rabbinic literature and his attempt to assert the fundamental compatibility of philosophical speculation and Jewish belief were motivated by this very consideration. Wessely saw himself not just as a traditionalist bound by personal sentiment and practice, but as someone who perceived his tradition as being under attack and in dire need of defence. In his mind, at least, *Divrei shalom ve'emet* was very much part of this effort. He believed that one could appreciate the rigorous textual basis of rabbinic exegesis only if one first had a firm grasp of biblical Hebrew and scriptural philology and syntax. Since the existing pedagogic structures were simply not oriented towards this kind of textual study, Wessely's reforms were intended first and foremost as a means of systematizing the acquisition of language and text skills. The rabbis, scholars, and educators of central Europe, of course, were not exposed to the same set of European challenges. They therefore shared neither Wessely's anxieties nor the urgency of his reformist response. The controversy that followed the publication of *Divrei shalom ve'emet* made it painfully clear that Wessely's self-perception was at variance with the way in which others perceived him. His frustration was particularly acute because he came to realize that many traditionalists now viewed him as part of the very problem he so zealously sought to confront.

This alienation was poignantly compounded, on the other hand, by the fact that from the early 1780s, he also began to express his unease with the proclivities of some Enlightenment-minded Jews and his growing realization that here, too, Jewish traditions were being profoundly challenged. The sense that such heretical thinking sounded much like the kind of European rationalism he had so roundly criticized decades earlier clearly served to accentuate the visceral nature of his reaction. But beyond the substantial threat that such thinking represented, he had to deal with the fact that some of these objectionable ideas were being articulated by individuals who invariably supported his campaign to reform Jewish education. Aware of the way in which he was being perceived—or misperceived—by rabbinic and communal leaders, Wessely's denunciation of such rationalism was undoubtedly driven by a need to differentiate himself from those whose views he regarded as anathema.

Ultimately, Wessely's recognition of his own marginalization resulted from the confluence of these developments in the 1780s. At the very moment when he realized that his cultural and pedagogic values had alienated him from those of more cautious and conservative tendencies he was also becoming increasingly alienated from some of the maskilim who no longer shared his deeply rooted religious commitments. Separately, each set of concerns had an appreciable impact on Wessely's attitudes towards eighteenth-century German Jewish culture; together, they created a sense of alienation that cut deeply into his own sense of who he was.

It appears that Wessely's expressions of alienation were symptoms of the fact that his vision of a revitalized Judaism was at odds with the emerging realities of modern Jewish culture. As early as the 1780s, both traditionalists and maskilim implicitly acknowledged that the Haskalah's cultural ideals and values were coalescing as an entity distinguishable from the prevailing eighteenth-century Ashkenazi culture. Although from the perspective of modern Jewish historical writing this is a commonplace, Wessely himself did not recognize it as a contemporary reality. Indeed, the transformation of German Jewry from a largely homogeneous group into a variegated and distinct set of cultural entities was the opposite of what he had worked for. Throughout his writings, he never ceased to believe that his was a vision of a revitalized and strengthened Judaism, one thoroughly rabbinic and traditional in its beliefs, practices, and hermeneutics. He could as little conceive of the ideals of the Haskalah as something distinct from the substance of normative Judaism as he could imagine the survival of rabbinic traditions without renewed attention to language and text. Wessely did not seem to realize that his vision of a renewed Judaism used a set of European cultural values that threatened to subvert the authority of religious tradition. For all his impassioned efforts to reshape Jewish education and culture in accordance with the new political and social realities of contemporary Europe, it is not at all clear that he conceived of his endeavour as an internalization of European values. Contemporary Europe was certainly recognized as a catalyst enabling far-reaching changes in Jewish education and pedagogy, but to his mind these reforms ultimately represented a return to a pristine Jewish culture rather than a turn to a newly burgeoning European one.

Standing at the birth of the cultural and religious pluralism that is the touchstone of modern Jewish history, Wessely's vision was thoroughly monistic. More than any other quality of his thinking, this perspective clearly informed his early work and remained operative throughout. It was precisely because of his blindness to the nascent differentiation of Jewish cultures and its attendant tensions that Wessely never really came to terms with traditionalist suspicions and an incipient apostasy on the part of the maskilim. The unmistakable sense of dislocation that is evident in his writing is an expression of his failure to recognize the profound cultural and ideological divide that had opened within the Jewish communities of German-speaking Europe. But if Wessely's sense of alienation was manifested by his inability to come to terms with new realities, it was no less an embodiment of the dislocations that have come to define modern Jewish culture.

THREE

Enlightenment Values, Jewish Ethics: The Haskalah's Transformation of the Traditional Musar *Genre*

HARRIS BOR

MORAL education was a central component of the Haskalah programme. Naphtali Herz Wessely, in a public letter of 1782, had recommended the composition of 'new books about beliefs and opinions . . . in order to teach [the young] wisdom and ethics'.[1] Ethics formed an important element of suggestions for new school curricula, and the founding letter of *Hame'asef*, the Haskalah periodical, promised 'to gather from all branches of science and ethics [*musar*] articles and essays which will benefit and delight the soul which longs to sit in the shade of wisdom'.[2] In addition, the Haskalah produced numerous treatises and primers for children that dealt specifically with the question of ethics.[3]

The concern with moral improvement found throughout Haskalah literature highlights the movement's absorption of external criticisms of Jewish morality and its desire to encourage Jews to embrace the values of *Bildung* and Enlightenment. Moral education, however, served a further important function: it was a bridge, or an area of common ground, between the social goals of the German Enlightenment, the *Aufklärung*, and Jewish tradition. Besides holding a central place in Enlightenment thinking, moral literature was a ubiquitous commodity in Jewish society of the late eighteenth century, both high and low. For that reason the methods of moral education used by the maskilim can act as an example of how the Haskalah balanced modern and traditional forces.

Jewish ethical writing (*musar*) has a long history dating from the tenth century, with the writing of Sa'adya Gaon's *Sefer ha'emunot vehade'ot*, and continuing to the modern period. In contrast to Jewish legal writings, ethical literature displays a greater degree of flexibility in terms of both subject-matter and style. The moral

This chapter is based on my Ph.D. thesis 'Moral Education in the Age of the Jewish Enlightenment' (University of Cambridge, 1996).

[1] First pub. 1782; repr. in *Divrei shalom ve'emet* (Berlin, 1782), 13–14.

[2] *Hame'asef*, 1 (1783), 1–4, 11–14.

[3] On Jewish children's literature in general see Zohar Shavit, *Deutsch-jüdische Kinder- und Jugendliteratur von der Haskala bis 1945*, 2 vols. (Stuttgart, 1996).

genre seeks to provide a theoretical underpinning for halakhah by establishing a theological grounding for the religious life. The creative licence given to ethical works over halakhic writings meant that they were often used as a vehicle for moderate innovation, in one period encouraging a rational outlook and in another a mystical one.[4] A further function of *musar* was its role in dispensing social criticism. In the period prior to the Haskalah, *musar* literature is replete with attacks on religious and moral laxity. The Haskalah, in forming its own critique of Jewish life, acknowledged these earlier views yet moved beyond the suggestions for change found in them.[5] By focusing on the realm of *musar*, the maskilim were able to be innovative without trespassing on the hallowed ground of Jewish law. In line with the basic conservatism of the early Haskalah, enlightened ethical writings were not just forces of acculturation but also served to protect Judaism from the threat of rationalism.

Important in understanding the Haskalah's use of the *musar* genre are a number of ethical writings by moderate maskilim; while scholars have long been aware of this body of work, no one has as yet attempted an examination of its nature and purpose, as I hope to do here.[6] The earliest educational treatises such as Isaac Satanow's *Sefer hamidot* (1784), and Naphtali Herz Wessely's *Sefer hamidot* (?1786), as well as Menahem Mendel Lefin's *Ḥeshbon hanefesh* (1809), are clearly part of the *musar* tradition. Other writings operate within the tradition but innovate in terms of form and content: for instance, there exists a whole host of textbooks for Jewish children which treat the question of morality, but do so in the form of a Christian catechism. Included in this category are Judah Leib ben Ze'ev's *Yesodei hada'at* (1806) and Naphtali Herz Homberg's *Imrei shefer* (1802). In addition, letters and articles in the Haskalah periodical *Hame'asef* (1783–1811) adopt the language of *musar* but transform it to suit the style of the modern moral weekly. The history of ethical writing by maskilim follows the pattern of acculturation found generally. While the early works hark back to the Jewish ethical tradition, later writings, such as those found in the German Haskalah periodical *Sulamith*, openly adopt contemporary styles and notions.

In assessing these writings one must keep in mind that the Haskalah was not merely a reactive force but one which contained its own creative dynamic. The aim of this chapter is to demonstrate the manner in which it formulated a unique approach to religion and morality by bringing modern notions of self and society into the domain of traditional Jewish ethics. Writing on modern Jewish thought, Natan Rotenstreich observed that 'what strikes us as new is the insistence on the primacy of ethics in the sphere of faith; traditional religion is divested of its beliefs

[4] On the nature of *musar* literature see Isaiah Tishby and Joseph Dan, *Selected Ethical Literature* (Heb.) (Jerusalem, 1970), 1–22; Joseph Dan, 'Ethical Literature', *EJ* vi. 922–31; and id., *Ethical and Exegetical Literature* (Heb.) (Jerusalem, 1975), 11–12.

[5] David Sorkin, *The Transformation of German Jewry 1780–1840* (New York, 1987), 51.

[6] See Joseph Klausner, *History of Modern Hebrew Literature* (Heb.), 6 vols. (Jerusalem, 1952–4), iv. 175; N. R. Bersohn, 'Isaac Satanov, the Man and his Work: A Study in the Berlin Haskalah' (Ph.D. diss., Columbia, 1975), 5; Uriel Ophek, *Hebrew Children's Literature: Beginnings* (Heb.) (Tel Aviv, 1979), 59.

in transcendence, and pressed into the service of morality'.[7] While the association of religion with morality is most evident in nineteenth-century Judaism, it will be seen that, within the early Haskalah of the late eighteenth century, the first steps in this direction were already being taken. The maskilim shared in the process which led from the view of religion as providing a personal path to God, a *via mystica*, to one which stressed care of the self in terms of social improvement.[8] Central to this approach was the need to understand the individual psychologically, in terms of his practical functioning rather than in terms of his direct relationship or ontological unity with God.

In the Enlightenment period political, philosophical, religious, and scientific developments merged to shape a climate dedicated to a worldly morality based on rational principles: the state focused on the practical duties of citizens; philosophers sought a mathematical morality free from metaphysics; and the Church, as an arm of the modern state, turned away from dogma and towards society as a whole. While Moses Mendelssohn was undoubtedly an important source of knowledge of the wider society for the maskilim, they also seem to have been influenced to a significant degree by developments taking place in the realm of pedagogy.

One particularly influential group of educators was connected to the Philanthropin, a movement established in Germany by Johann Bernhard Basedow (1723–90), which asserted the futility of corporal punishment and the importance of physical education and natural science. Of these educators, Joachim Heinrich Campe (1746–1818) is considered to have had the most influence on modern Hebrew literature.[9] The Philanthropin movement provided a suitable model for emulation in that its proponents stressed modern language instruction, the sciences, and universal religion, all of which were major concerns of the Haskalah. More than this, however, their works could be seen as sharing in the Haskalah's religious conservatism: they had a religious underpinning and explicitly encouraged faith in God.

The literary activities of both the members of Philanthropin and of other popular thinkers brought to the maskilim's attention the major goals of enlightened education. There was a new awareness of a distinct realm of childhood, and educators of the age all took as their guide Rousseau's *Émile* (1762), the symbol for this new understanding. *Émile* describes the proper way to raise a child, in accordance with nature: he must not be coerced into good behaviour through fear of punishment, and he has a right to happiness, personal liberty, and freedom from guilt.

[7] *Jewish Philosophy in Modern Times: From Meldelssohn to Rosenzweig* (New York, 1968), 6.

[8] On the *via mystica* in medieval religious ethics see Joseph Dan, *Jewish Mysticism and Jewish Ethics* (Washington, DC, 1996), 115–31.

[9] Many of his works were translated into Hebrew. On Campe's influence on Jewish literature see Zohar Shavit, 'Literary Interference between German and Jewish Hebrew Children's Literature during the Enlightenment: The Case of Campe', *Poetics Today*, 13/1 (1992), 41–61; ead., 'From Friedländer's *Lesebuch* to the Jewish Campe: The Beginning of Hebrew Children's Literature in Germany', *Leo Baeck Institute Yearbook*, 33 (1988), 385–415.

Throughout the children's literature of the period runs the idea that young people could not be made to learn by rote, but that all their senses had first to be excited. Both Basedow and Campe responded to this need by making use of visual aids such as prints and drawings. One educator later claimed that nothing wearied children more than moralizing and preaching: 'They are not ripe for long sermons and exhortations. From this they cannot escape ennui. That which does not speak to the heart does not excite man to action.'[10] In Germany, as elsewhere in Europe, there was a surge of printed material designed specifically for children, including guidebooks, primers, moral works, stories, collections of fables, and journals. Examples of some of the moral works of the age include Basedow's *Elementarwerk* (1774), Campe's *Theophron* (1783), Salzmann's *Moralisches Elementarbuch* (1785), and Georg Schlosser's (1739–99) *Katechismus der Sittenlehre für das Landvolk*.

Much of this literature repudiates the educational tactics of the baroque period, which focused on the punishments a child would receive in this world and the next for his misbehaviour. In contrast to this approach, Salzmann attempts to rationalize the feeling of fear. In one tale a young boy undergoes the trauma of being lost in the woods, and later has the opportunity to discuss his experience with the curate, who uses the incident to teach a moral lesson: 'What you felt was fear. Fear is a sad thing, it makes people so foolish. They can neither see clearly nor hear distinctly when it becomes violent; and it seems as if all the accidents they thought of were just at hand.' Fear debilitates rather than saves: those who become scared 'make no effort and run directly into the fear they should shun'.[11] In contrast to the austere character of baroque education, Enlightenment treatments of ethical living saw an intimate connection between morality and happiness. For Basedow, *Tugend* (virtue) and *Glückseligkeit* (happiness) were twin sisters. He wrote that education should aim at producing 'an enlightened citizen, who strives to be of use to, and to achieve happiness for, himself and society as a whole'.[12] In a similar vein, Campe observed that 'every wise person who considers the ways of man, will testify to the fact that the good and happy are joined one to another, like a river and its source'.[13] This basic feature of late eighteenth-century pedagogical texts is mirrored in the Haskalah writings which seek to establish alternatives to the type of ethical literature popular in the Jewish baroque period.

While there was something of a renaissance of Aristotelian Jewish ethical thought in the early modern period, it was the mystical ethical approach which dominated

[10] J. C. A. Heinroth, *Erziehung und Selbstbildung* (1837), trans. A. Schloss as *On Education and Self-Formation* (London, 1838), 95.

[11] C. S. Salzmann, *Moralisches Elementarbuch* (Leipzig, 1785), trans. into English as *Elements of Morality for the Use of Young Persons* (Boston, Mass., 1850), 22.

[12] Johann Bernhard Basedow, *Praktische Philosophie*, cited in M. Jansen, *Religionsunterricht und Sittenlehre philanthropischer Pädagogen als Konsequenz ihrer theologisch-anthropologischen Standorte* (Duisburg, 1978), 138.

[13] Joachim Heinrich Campe, *Theophron* (Hamburg, 1783), 21. See also B. Rehle, *Aufklärung und Moral in der Kinder- und Jugendliteratur des 18. Jahrhunderts* (Frankfurt am Main, 1989), 93.

the popular culture of the eighteenth century.[14] Of the kabbalistic ethical works that circulated, the most important were the seventeenth-century treatises, Elijah de Vidas's *Reshit ḥokhmah* (Beginning of Wisdom, 1623) and Isaiah Halevi Horowitz's *Shenei luḥot haberit* (Two Tablets of the Law, 1717). Together with these writings should be mentioned the activity of the moral preachers whose job it was to rouse the people to repentance. The type of morality characteristic of these itinerants can be gleaned from a consideration of Tsevi Hirsh Koidonover's *Kav hayashar* (The Straight Measure, 1705) and Elijah Hakohen Ittamari's *Shevet musar* (The Rod of Chastisement, 1712). In addition to works written in Hebrew, Yiddish moral writings were circulated in great numbers. Not only were the works just mentioned translated into Yiddish, but ethical works were also written in that language and were read by both men and women.[15]

The response of this type of writing to religious laxity was to insist on greater Torah observance, along with an intensification of personal piety. The value of ritual was rooted in the belief that the performance of a divine command actually affected the metaphysical realms. Conversely, certain sins, such as that of harmful speech, were said to harm the Shekhinah itself. The *Kav hayashar* states that when one performs a bad deed 'all the angels that wish to exalt God flee from their place until the Creator Himself removes the pollution'.[16] The main focus of spiritual effort was the future world: one should refrain from too much worldly involvement and adopt a stoical attitude to one's own suffering. Ascetic penitential practices were common: the *Shenei luḥot haberit* states clearly that repentance implies 'sackcloth and fasts', and this view is shared in the other ethical works mentioned.[17]

This mode of spirituality focused more on the concept of fear of God than love of God, and defined this in terms of fear of God's punishment rather than awe at His majesty; *yirat ha'onesh* over *yirat haromemut*. The *Kav hayashar* and *Shevet musar* both dwell at great length on the punishment of the wicked in the world to come: 'Hell is large and wide and occupies tens of thousands of miles . . . The fire wherewith the wicked are burned is sixty times stronger than the fire on earth . . . There are coals that are as large as mountains and valleys. Rivers of pitch flow through hell and sulphur pours out of the depths of the abyss.'[18] The stress on fear in these works is carried over to their educational theories. Although parents were told to feel love for their children, it was recommended that they should not demonstrate this openly. In addition, they were advised not to spare the child

[14] For a bibliography of the baroque period see J. M. Davies, 'The Cultural and Intellectual History of Ashkenazi Jews 1500–1750', *Leo Baeck Institute Yearbook*, 38 (1993), 343–91. On the mystical ethical literature see Dan, *Jewish Mysticism*, 83–148.

[15] See Isaac Wetzlar, *Libes briv*, ed. and trans. Morris M. Faierstein (Atlanta, Ga., 1996), 96.

[16] Tsevi Hirsh Koidonover, *Kav hayashar* (Frankfurt, 1705; Jerusalem, 1993), 2.

[17] Isaiah Horowitz, *Shenei luḥot haberit*, abridged edn. (Frankfurt, 1717), 10*a*–*b*.

[18] Elijah Hakohen Ittamari, *Shevet musar* (Smyrna, 1712; Jerusalem, 1989), sect. 26; trans. in Israel Zinberg, *History of Jewish Literature*, vol. vi (New York, 1975), 168.

necessary punishment: 'You shall beat him with a rod and [as a consequence] deliver his soul from *she'ol*.'[19]

The ethical works of Satanow and Wessely represent the most conservative attempt at supplying an alternative ethical tradition to the one outlined above. In the introduction to *Sefer hamidot*, Wessely indicates his intention by setting his work in the context of earlier *musar* literature. *Musar* developed, he writes, at the point when the Jews were exiled to many lands: 'those versed in Talmud and Midrash arose and compiled specialized books on opinions and beliefs, on virtues and ethics . . . Each person wrote in his own way and to his own ability and according to his own wisdom.'[20] While Wessely respects these earlier writers, he asserts that their methods are not suitable for his own day. He wishes to write a book that relies neither on logic (*higayon*) or metaphysics (*metaphysica*), but one which 'accords with the rules of reason implanted in all of us'.[21]

A review article in *Hame'asef*, usually attributed to the maskil Saul Berlin (1740–94), similarly justifies itself in terms of the past as it traces the history of *musar* writing from its beginnings to the modern period. The writer regrets the degeneration of the *musar* genre in his own day: 'We have sunk lower and lower, and have forsaken the straight path'.[22] Blame for the poor quality of ethical writing is laid at the door of itinerant preachers, who are described as being insincere, greedy, and ignorant. Their discourses 'fail to benefit anyone who hears or reads them'.[23] The article points to Wessely's treatise and declares that 'anyone who reads his work will agree that if all the works of the itinerant preachers were placed on one side of the scale and Wessely's *Sefer hamidot* was placed on the other side, it would certainly outweigh all of them'.[24]

The maskilim turned the focus away from the asceticism characteristic of earlier *musar* literature towards a more positive spirituality: they stressed the disadvantages of renouncing the world in no uncertain terms. Lefin writes that only fools think that in order to break the animal soul one must also break the body.[25] Ben Ze'ev, in his *Yesodei hadat*, classifies as idolaters those who indulge in 'fasting, afflicting one's soul, [and who carry out] much praying and charity in order to impress others'.[26]

In place of fear of God's punishment the maskilim offered awe at God's majesty, making a traditional concept function as a vehicle for Enlightenment ideals. Fear of God, for the maskilim, involved appreciating the divine in nature,[27] and acting not through fear of punishment but through one's own sense of right and wrong.

[19] Elijah de Vidas, *Reshit ḥokhmah* (Mantua, 1623): 'Gidul banim' [Bringing up Children], 290*b*.

[20] Naphtali Herz Wessely, *Sefer hamidot vehu sefer musar haskel* (Berlin, *c*.1785/7), introduction.

[21] Ibid. [22] *Hame'asef*, 6 (1790), 363. [23] Ibid. 363, 370, and 374. [24] Ibid. 374.

[25] Menahem Mendel Lefin, *Ḥeshbon hanefesh* [Moral Accounting] (Lvov, 1809), art. 63.

[26] *Yesodei hadat* [Foundations of Religion] (Vienna, 1806), 196.

[27] Isaac Satanow, *Sefer hamidot* [Book of Ethics] (Berlin, 1784), 24*a*; Wessely, *Sefer hamidot*, sect. 2. 2. 6.

This move to autonomy is illustrated by their view of the evil inclination (*yetser hara*), which was not thought to be intrinsically bad, but rather a neutral force to be controlled and utilized. Wessely sought to adjust the traditional belief in an evil urge through an explanation of the biblical verse 'the desires of a man's heart [*yetser halev*] are evil from his youth' (Gen. 1: 91), pointing out that it did not imply that man was evil from birth, but only that a youngster is unable to channel the desires of the heart in a constructive direction.[28] Lefin only applies the term *yetser hara* to unusually powerful emotional pressures, arguing that, on the whole, the passions can be channelled to good ends. Associating the constructive use of the passions with the taming of wild beasts, he writes: 'the strength of an ox may be used for ploughing, the donkey for carrying burdens, and the speed of a horse for travel'.[29]

Another area in which the parallels between the moral concerns of the Haskalah and the *Aufklärung* are evident is in their respective theories of the mind and soul. The concern with self was something of an obsession in eighteenth-century Germany, and arose from the combination of pietist notions of *Bildung*, relative political freedom, and a mechanistic view of the world which asserted that man, like the universe, functioned in a consistent, observable fashion. Thus the human mind could be rationally understood, controlled, and directed. No longer was the soul a subject for discussion solely in the religious sphere; it was seen as an object of practical knowledge, one aligned to the science of medicine.[30] Questions of the nature of human understanding had been tackled by such thinkers as Leibniz, Wolff, Locke, and Condillac, and their views were absorbed by pedagogues and popular writers.

Basedow had dealt with the nature of the soul in his *Elementarwerk*, and in 1783 Campe had published his *Kleine Seelenlehre für Kinder* which aimed at transmitting an understanding of the soul to children. The work is divided into two sections: the first deals with the nature of the soul and the second with the desired virtues, reflecting the need to cultivate the former in order to attain the latter. Campe asks: 'How can one persistently use those terms unavoidable in moral lessons, such as reason, judgement, inclination, sentiment, sensation, passion and so on without having previously explained their signification?' Just as natural history must be studied before physics, so 'psychological lessons should introduce morality and religion'.[31]

In the eighteenth century there were three main theories of how the mind operates. Occasionalism, put forward by Malebranche and Descartes, asserted that there was no interaction at all between the body and the soul; events in the external

[28] *Sefer hamidot*, sect. 1. 4. 5.

[29] *Ḥeshbon hanefesh*, art 3.

[30] See C. Kerstig, *Die Genese der Pädagogik im 18. Jahrhundert. Campes 'Algemeine Revision' im Kontext der neuzeitlichen Wissenschaft* (Weinheim, 1992), 127; M. M. Davies, *Identity or History? Marcus Herz and the End of the Enlightenment* (Detroit, 1995), 122–34; Salzmann, *Moralisches Elementarbuch*, introduction.

[31] Joachim Heinrich Campe, *Kleine Seelenlehre für Kinder* (Berlin, 1783), trans. as *Elementary Dialogues for the Improvement of Youth* (London, 1792), pp. ii–iii.

world merely provided the occasion for God to arouse corresponding activities in the soul of man. The second view, known as *influxus physicus*, asserted that external reality directly affected the functioning of the soul, so that 'when I appear to kick a ball, I really am the cause of the ball's motion'.[32] The third model, that of pre-established harmony, was put forward by Leibniz and was adopted in large measure by Christian Wolff. This theory viewed the soul as a completely enclosed simple substance, a monad, whose functioning happened to accord with the world of objects. The relationship between the world and the soul could be described as that between two clocks wound up at the same time and allowed to run synchronically: despite the fact that the two appear to work together they are in fact entirely separate entities.[33]

So much for the relationship between body and mind. As far as the mind itself was concerned, eighteenth-century Germany saw a return to the form of thinking popular in antiquity and the Middle Ages known as faculty psychology: in this view, the mind is composed of a number of distinct entities, each in charge of a particular mental function. Christian Wolff, for example, in his writings on morality, divides the mind into higher and lower faculties: the lower faculties are only capable of unclear ideas, while the higher ones provide clear ideas which carefully distinguish between good and evil. In the lower part of the mind one finds sensation, imagination, memory, desire, repulsion, and attachment; the higher mind consists of understanding, reason, will, and freedom.[34]

Related to the theory of faculties is the manner in which external objects are perceived. Eighteenth-century theories of the soul are dominated by the notion of impressions, the indelible marks that external objects leave upon the brain. Mendelssohn was struck by this notion, seeing it as a given in all competing models of the soul.[35] Ernst Cassirer has in fact noted the popularity of the idea in the Enlightenment period: 'The assertion that every idea that we find in our minds is based on a previous impression and can only be explained on this basis is exalted to the rank of an indubitable principle.'[36]

John Locke was particularly influential in advancing the central role of

[32] Eric Watkins, 'The Development of Physical Influx in Early Eighteenth-Century Germany: Gottsched, Knutzen, and Crusius', *Review of Metaphysics*, 49 (1995), 296. Also on the theories of the relationship between body and soul in the period see E. O'Neil, 'Influxus Physicus', in S. Nadler (ed.), *Causation in Early Modern Philosophy: Cartesianism, Occasionalism, and Pre-established Harmony* (University Park, Pa., 1993), 27–55.

[33] A good account of Leibniz's views on monads and pre-established harmony can be found in D. Rutherford, 'Metaphysics: The Late Period', in N. Jolley (ed.), *The Cambridge Companion to Leibniz* (Cambridge, 1995), 124–75.

[34] Christian Wolff, *Vernunftige Gedancken von Gott, der Welt und der Seele des Menschen* (Frankfurt, 1733), ch. 3, no. 141 (pp. 227–32).

[35] Moses Mendelssohn, *Pha'edon: Hu sefer hanefesh* [*Phaedon*; or On the Immortality of the Soul], trans. into Heb. by Isaiah Beer of Metz (Berlin, 1787; 1797 edn. consulted), 3.

[36] *Philosophy of the Enlightenment*, trans. Fritz L. A. Koelln and James P. Pettegrave (Princeton, NJ, 1951), 98. See also Johann Bernhard Basedow, *Elementarwerk*, vol. i (Berlin and Dessau, 1774), 162.

impressions. In rejecting the concept that a person is born with innate ideas, he proposed two forms of knowledge, that acquired through the senses and that acquired through reflection: 'These two I say, external material things, as objects of sensation, and the operations of our minds within, reflection, are to be the only originals from whence all our ideas take their beginnings.'[37] This representational world is formed when objects create simple impressions on the mind via the senses; the mind then makes associations to form complex images. In terms of moral education these theories pointed to the need for practical reason, and a high degree of self-awareness and personal responsibility.

The works of Satanow, Wessely, and Lefin display this same interest, but their ideas are cast in traditional terms. In arriving at his view of the soul, Satanow looks both internally and externally. On the one hand he associates knowledge of the soul with that of *Anatomie* and remarks that 'Matters concerning the soul are very deep and there are many great people of our nation who do not understand anything [about them].'[38] On the other hand he felt that modern ideas had to be refracted through the prism of earlier Jewish traditions, and, like other maskilim, channelled the new understanding of the soul through medieval Jewish sources.

Satanow's view of the soul combines Enlightenment notions with ideas found in Maimonides and Judah Halevi's *Sefer hakuzari*, and also includes mythical and mystical conceptions. He refers specifically to such mystical works as the *Sefer yetsirah*, the Zohar, and the writings of Hayim Vital (1542–1620).[39] In accordance with the Aristotelian faculty psychology found in Maimonides' *Shemoneh perakim*, the soul is described as having five faculties: nutritive (*zan*), sensual (*margish*), appetitive (*mitorer*), imaginative (*medameh*), and intellectual (*sekhel*).[40] The components of the intellect also follow the Aristotelian scheme found in Maimonides: according to Satanow, it comprises the practical and theoretical faculties (the *koaḥ hama'asi* and the *koaḥ ha'iyuni*). The practical intellect is further divided into two parts: one which deals with ethical and political matters (the *koaḥ hamidoti*) and one which concerns itself with art and practical skills (the *koaḥ hamalkhuti*). To the Maimonidean model of the soul Satanow added concepts and terminology from Judah Halevi's work in order to distinguish further between the contemplation of real objects and the consideration of abstracted forms. He also adds two subdivisions to the theoretical intellect, the complex (*murkav*) and the simple (*pashut*): the complex contemplates an object in its totality, in terms of both form and matter, and the simple considers abstract notions.[41] In addition, Satanow uses two further

37 *An Essay Concerning Human Understanding*, ed. P. H. Nidditch (Oxford, 1975), bk. 2, ch. 1, sect. 4. See also Basedow, *Elementarwerk*, i. 170.

38 Satanow, *Sefer hamidot*, 17*b*.

39 See ibid. 11*a*, 17*a*.

40 Ibid. 7*a*. See *Shemoneh perakim* [Eight Chapters] (1168), ch. 1. On medieval views of the soul in general see H. A. Wolfson, 'The Internal Senses in Latin, Arabic, and Hebrew Philosophical Texts', in id., *Studies in the History of Philosophy and Religion* (Cambridge, Mass., 1973), 250–315.

41 Satanow, *Sefer hamidot*, 9*a*–10*b*; Cf. Judah Halevi, *Sefer hakuzari* [Book of the Kuzari] (11th cent.), ch. 5.

terms from the *Kuzari* to claim that the entire structure of the intellect exists twice over in the form of the internal (*penimi*) and the external (*ḥitsoni*) intellects. The internal intellect operates when, for example, an architect contemplates the abstract plan of the structure of a house, and the external intellect acts when an existing house is contemplated.[42]

Wessely's description of the nature of the soul is based essentially on the Platonic division into three parts corresponding to the three principal classes in a state.[43] In every society there are rulers who make decisions, ministers and army officers who implement them, and the populace which either accepts or rebels against the decisions that are made. In a sense the scheme of the soul found here lends support to the absolutist state model of the eighteenth century: 'If leaders are good then citizens do not rebel.'[44]

In the second part of his work Wessely deals with the rulers of the soul. These are the 'judges of the soul', namely, intellect (*sekhel*), reason (*binah*), and knowledge (*da'at*).[45] These judges, together with the essential qualities of wisdom (*ḥokhmah*) and fear (*yirah*), form the aspects of the soul (*penei hanefesh*). The structure of the psyche is thought to mirror the structure of the senses—the two work in harmony. Each one of the five aspects of the soul is thought to relate to the external senses (*penei haguf*). Intellect, for example, is thought to correspond to the sense of sight, understanding to hearing, wisdom to taste, and so on. The second level of the human psyche is composed of the motivating powers of the soul, such as might (*gevurah*), and the third level is comprised of the passions and emotions, such as love, hate, and jealousy.[46]

Lefin does not adopt as detailed a psychology of the faculties as the other two, but adheres to the ancient assumption that the psyche is comprised of two opposing units. One he terms the animal soul (*nefesh behemit*), and the other the rational soul (*nefesh sikhlit*). The animal soul responds to immediate stimuli only and is unable to take account of the future: 'It can only see that which is clear and to hand.'[47] In addition, 'it is engrossed in a profound sleep from which it is unable to arouse itself'.[48] In contrast to the animal soul, the rational soul is an active force which makes use of categories of thinking traditionally described as *ḥokhmah*, *binah*, and *da'at*. The rational soul is able to appreciate how certain distant events will affect the animal soul, and it urges the individual to stay clear of them.

The models of the soul that these Haskalah writers use are basically traditional; their novelty lies in the way in which they deal with questions of perception and epistemology. In line with Enlightenment thinkers more generally, the notion of

[42] Satanow, *Sefer hamidot*, 9*b*.

[43] Wessely, *Sefer hamidot*, sect. 1. 6. 2.

[44] Ibid., sect. 1. 6. 5. It was widely believed that a strong government would keep social order and replace, in a time of weakening belief, the notions of revelation and fear of God. See T. C. W. Blanning, *Reform and Revolution in Mainz, 1743–1803* (London, 1974), 16–17.

[45] Wessely, *Sefer hamidot*, sect. 1. 2. 4.

[46] Ibid., sect. 2. 1. 1–2.

[47] *Ḥeshbon hanefesh*, art. 8.

[48] Ibid., art. 2.

impressions becomes vital to ethical improvement. Wessely, echoing Locke and his followers, referred to the mind as 'an internal slate upon which a person writes'.[49] What is more, Locke's notion that ideas are known either through the senses or through reflection has its parallel in Wessely's statement that, 'in the case of all powers of the soul, they do not operate to a small or great extent until [either] the senses bring an external matter into the soul or before the intellect brings to bear upon it a particular matter'.[50] Later writers continued to display an interest in impressions. Moses Bock, in his primer for Jewish children, describes the way in which objects are perceived by being registered in the memory (*demut* in Hebrew, *Vorstellung* in German): if one sees a rose and smells its scent, its image lingers on even after the flower has gone.[51] This view implies that even a slight emotion is not entirely forgotten. Lefin held that, although an impression may be lost from the animal soul, 'there remains after it a small impression in the memory, and when this emotion is experienced for a second time, it attaches itself to the first impression . . . and so it is regarding all previous impressions'.[52]

The relevance of the notion of impressions to ethical improvement lies in the fact that these imprints stimulate the mind to action by arousing desire. This naturally leads one to the question of the relative strength of the intellectual and imaginative faculties. In Enlightenment thought it was believed that a mind dominated too much by the imagination would become unbalanced.[53] Campe writes that 'no faculty of the soul should be exercised in preference, or get the start on any other, but, on the contrary, all should be improved in due proportion at the same instant'. A true balancing of the inner forces leads to a sense of equanimity and contentment.[54]

In line with Enlightenment thought, the maskilim appreciated that the passions played a major role in decision-making: 'The power of the heart is a thousand times stronger than that of the mind.'[55] The fact that material desires arise first in man makes the desire for material gain the strongest, whereas spiritual longing remains only 'second nature'.[56] It is for this reason that a young man tends towards sins that involve physical pleasure: 'a fine garment or beautiful shoes are more dear to him than all the pearls of wisdom'.[57] The intellect makes little impression on the soul without a great deal of effort. Wessely argues that we know through the intellect that a fish must be in water in order to survive, yet we cannot really fully

[49] Wessely, *Sefer hamidot*, sect. 2. 2. 1.
[50] Ibid., sect. 1. 4. 4.
[51] Moses ben Zvi Bock, *Moda'ah leyaldei benei yisra'el uleda'at beḥokhmah umusar vehu reshit halimud belashon ivri, ashkenazit, vesefardit* [Announcement to Jewish Children . . .] (Berlin, 1812), pt. 3, sect. 5, pp. 129–30.
[52] *Ḥeshbon hanefesh*, art. 53.
[53] Immanuel Kant, *Anthropologie in pragmatischer Hinsicht* (1798), trans. Victor Lyle Dowdell as *Anthropology from a Pragmatic Point of View* (Carbondale, Ill., 1978), 49–50. See also H. Böhme and G. Böhme, 'The Battle of Reason with the Imagination', in J. Schmidt (ed.), *What is Enlightenment? Eighteenth-Century Answers and Twentieth-Century Questions* (Berkeley, Calif., 1996), 426–53.
[54] Campe, *Kleine Seelenlehre für Kinder*, p. iii; Heinroth, *Education and Self-Formation*, 173.
[55] Wessely, *Sefer hamidot*, sect. 1. 5. 1.
[56] Ibid., sect. 1. 4. 6.
[57] Ibid., sect. 1. 5. 7.

understand this need since we cannot experience what it is to be a fish out of water. The worth of spiritual values is only appreciated by the mind, 'which considers the truth of God, the righteousness of His ways, and the goodness of His attributes'.[58]

The negative effects of an overdeveloped imagination pointed out by Enlightenment thinkers helped to explain the dangers of superstitious beliefs. Satanow demonstrates the power of the imagination to deceive by likening those who indulge in such practices to people attempting to see into the future by looking into pools of spilt oil.[59] In a similar vein, Bock criticizes the 'super-pious' (*mitḥasdim*) for their superstition and their inability to follow reason. Instead they are led solely by their imagination: they believe in such a ridiculous phenomenon as ghosts, when it is obvious that 'the dead do not understand a thing'. In order to avoid the pitfalls of fancy, 'one must train oneself, from youth, to follow correct ways so that imagination does not lead one from the straight path'.[60]

So far it has been seen that the maskilim used medieval ideas to encourage Enlightenment ideals. However, it should be pointed out that, like conservative *Aufklärer* in general, the maskilim were well aware of the dangers of the new moral and psychological theories. It was feared that the study of the soul would become separated from religion and lead to a rejection of the beliefs in immortality and reward and punishment. It was further claimed that a rational approach to morality could eventually lead to the moral breakdown of society.[61] Of course, these concerns were not without some justification.

In France the years 1746 to 1754 saw the publication of a number of works which viewed man as little more than a machine. These included Maupertuis's *Essai de cosmologie* and *Système de la nature*, La Mettrie's *L'Homme machine* and *Système d'Épicure*, and Buffon's first volumes of *Histoire naturelle générale et particulière*.[62] The authors of these works did not envisage any real distinction between the mind of man and those of animals, and they suggested, to various extents, that life originated from matter by spontaneous generation, and that mankind developed out of lower forms of life. Other thinkers asserted in a similar vein that there was little difference between human and animal souls: Guillaume-Hyacinthe Bougeant saw animal souls as being human souls in purgatory, while Charles Bonnet, René-Antoine de Réaumur, and Charles-Georges Leroy believed that animals, like humans, could be perfected through education. In Germany these ideas had only limited appeal,

[58] Ibid., sect. 1. 5. 3.

[59] Satanow, *Sefer hamidot*, 8*a*.

[60] Bock, *Moda'ah leyaldei benei yisra'el*, pt. 3, sect. 5, p. 137.

[61] See the discussion of the Wednesday Society about the pros and cons of spreading Enlightenment to the masses: J. Schmidt, 'The Question of Enlightenment: Kant, Mendelssohn, and the Mittwochsgesellschaft', *Journal of the History of Ideas*, 50 (1989), 269–91.

[62] On the history of psychology in the period see J. Jaynes and W. Woodward, 'In the Shadow of the Enlightenment, I: Reimarus against the Epicurians', *Journal of the History of the Behavioral Sciences*, 10/1 (1974), 9. See also O. Finger, *Von der Materialität der Seele, Beitrag zur Geschichte des Materialismus im Deutschland der 2. Hälfte des XVIII. Jahrhunderts* (Berlin, 1961), and T. H. Leahey, *A History of Psychology* (London, 1987), 125–7.

but they were taken up by 'sensationalists' such as Dietrich Tiedemann, Karl Franz von Irwing, Christian Lossius, and Ernst Platner.[63]

Conservative responses to such potentially destructive views are found throughout the writings of moderate *Aufklärer*. Mendelssohn, in his *Phädon*, presented a philosophical defence of immortality: the Hebrew translation refers to this belief as a *yesod hatorah*, a basic doctrine of religion.[64] Similarly, Campe attempted to demonstrate the existence of the soul through reason and experience,[65] and Basedow's thought revolved around three central ideas: God, virtue, and immortality.[66] Hermann Samuel Reimarus (1694–1768), in his book on logic, the *Vernunftlehre* (1756), aimed to defend the religious belief in the uniqueness of human beings by defining human souls as having greater clarity of thought and reasoning than animal souls.[67]

The maskilim were equally concerned to stress the distinction between man and animals, and to assert the lofty nature of the human soul. Wessely contributed an article to *Hame'asef* entitled 'Ḥikur din' (Discourse on Final Judgement);[68] its aim was comparable to that of Mendelssohn in *Phädon*, namely to defend belief in the immortality of the soul and in reward and punishment after death. A major difference between Wessely's and Mendelssohn's projects, however, was that while Mendelssohn drew from the world of philosophy, Wessely took his inspiration exclusively from rabbinic writings. The need to protect the belief in the divine nature of human soul had a clear impact on the Haskalah's ethical programme. Wessely begins his *Sefer hamidot* on similar lines to Reimarus above, by stressing that, unlike animals, man is a social being who does not concern himself simply with the pleasures of the moment but with future goods, and the desire to attain ever greater perfection. While the animal soul 'can only think and act in relation to the world' the human soul aspires towards the spiritual.[69] Bock asserts that man's physical constitution 'is almost the same as that of the other animals'. What distinguishes him is the fact that he contains a living soul (*nishmat ruaḥ ḥayim*), 'which entered through his nostrils'. The existence of the soul can be ascertained 'even though it is not visible'. This is achieved through an awareness of its actions, namely, 'thinking and feeling [*denken und empfinden*]'.[70]

The need to avoid a purely mechanistic view of the soul is clear in Satanow's works. In both *Sefer hamidot* and his commentary on Halevi's *Kuzari* he expresses a certain fear of materialistic views, saying that such ideas threaten the 'foundations of the Torah'. He goes on to state that knowledge of the soul cannot be grasped

[63] It must be noted, however, that these thinkers were not materialists. They adhered to fundamental religious principles. See M. Kuehn, *Scottish Common Sense in Germany, 1768–1800* (Montreal, 1987), 45–6.

[64] *Pha'edon: Hu sefer hasharat hanefesh*, 1a.

[65] Campe, *Kleine Seelenlehre für Kinder*, 187.

[66] Jansen, *Religionsunterricht*, 141.

[67] Jaynes and Woodward, 'In the Shadow of the Enlightenment', 8.

[68] *Hame'asef*, 4 (1788), 97–111, 145–65.

[69] Wessely, *Sefer hamidot*, sects. 1. 1. 2, 1. 1. 3.

[70] Bock, *Moda'ah leyaldei benei yisra'el*, pt. 3, sect. 5, pp. 129–30.

clearly, and so 'tradition in this matter is better than research'.[71] Furthermore, there was a general awareness that reason was a dangerous tool in the hands of the masses: in the ethical works discussed in this chapter, as well as in many of the catechetical writings, Torah is seen as being vital to the ethical path. Satanow writes that only the Torah provides access to knowledge which is above rational understanding: 'The Torah knows better than the intellect what is good for the soul.' It follows, therefore, that 'the will that chooses its actions according to the Torah . . . is better than one that chooses them by applying his own reason [*sekhel*]'.[72] This theme continues throughout *Sefer hamidot*: 'One cannot know all that is in the heavens and upon earth until one has entered into the palace of the King.'[73]

Related to the defence of belief in a spiritual soul is the defence of religious ethics over those based on reason. In the writings of the maskilim, the fear associated with the split of ethics from religion comes out most strongly in an article entitled 'Ethical Rebuke' ('Tokhaḥat musar') by Tsevi Hirsh Glogau.[74] It recounts how a student had chanced upon a hedonistic work and through it had been led to doubt. The work asserted that 'man was created to pursue pleasure' and that 'the righteous and the wicked have one fate'. Love of women and wine are viewed as the highest ideals, and life in the world to come is denied: 'There is no life except the immediate.' The writer describes the disintegration of society that inevitably results from such a view: 'And now my good son come and see the true faith. It is commanded that we love the Creator and our neighbour as ourselves . . . Not for the life of this world were we created . . . The spirit will return to the God that has given it, in order to bask in the light of His glory, [a light] which is impossible to comprehend while we are still alive.'[75]

The idea that one needs to have a true knowledge of the soul in order to act ethically presented the maskilim with a way to justify revelation while accepting the basic principles of rational self-knowledge. The crux of the argument lay in the belief that only the Torah contains a true understanding of the soul. Satanow asserts that 'each commandment of God relates to a particular faculty of the soul'; for instance, laws of forbidden foods and of having to eat unleavened bread on Passover contribute to the perfection of the faculty of digestion (*zan*). Furthermore, laws against forbidden relations aid in the refinement of the sense faculty, and laws against coveting another's property cultivate one's imaginative faculty.[76] An understanding of the soul's operation, he believed, lies above reason and is seen as being synonymous with knowledge of 'the One who spoke and the world came into being'.[77] Wessely points out that no one can fully understand the workings of the human soul: 'Who can count the multitude of faculties and emotions of the soul and their counterparts? Even if someone could enumerate all the faculties of the soul, who could say in which situation one should apply this virtue and in

71 See Satanow's commentary on *Sefer hakuzari* (Berlin, 1795), 94*a*.

72 Satanow, *Sefer hamidot*, 27*b*.

73 Ibid. 34*a*.

74 *Hame'asef*, 8 (1809), 195–200.

75 Ibid. 198.

76 Satanow, *Sefer hamidot*, 13*b*–14*a*.

77 Ibid. 17*a*.

which situation its opposite?'[78] The commandments are viewed as being inextricably bound to the ethical life; they accord with the nature of the human psyche: 'They act on all facets of the human soul . . . whether through those commandments that are comprehensible to man, or commandments that are not comprehensible to man, whether commandments incumbent upon all peoples, or those incumbent upon Israel alone.'[79]

Such an argument highlights the manner in which the maskilim reshaped Jewish tradition. Through the desire to both embrace Enlightenment and preserve the Jewish religion they were forced in effect to shape their perception of religion around the ideals of Enlightenment. Medieval Jewish philosophy provided them with a multivalent tradition from which they could respond to their own ideological needs as well as to the changes in external culture. Of great importance in this respect is the medieval tradition of giving reasons for the commandments (*ta'amei hamitsvot*), which in a sense legitimized the view that the purpose of the Torah lay in ethical improvement rather than in pure obedience to God. The early modern emphasis on fear of God was replaced with this medieval approach. It must be noted, however, that despite the fact that the moderate maskilim defended Jewish tradition they were still involved in a process which led to a conception of religion as social morality. The personal path to God characteristic of earlier ethical literature was being replaced with the notion that practical ethical improvement is the goal of religious law.

Looking at the later development of the Haskalah's moral educational programme, one observes that the connection between religion and morality becomes increasingly explicit. This is true especially for articles found in *Sulamith*, where it is argued that it is not so much the Torah which leads to morality but religion in general: 'Morality and religion! You powerfully assist blossoming reason in its striving for wisdom, in its search for truth and light.'[80] As a result of this development the uniqueness of Judaism is called into question, and as the relationship between religion and morality became blurred it was left to thinkers of the nineteenth and twentieth centuries to clarify the uniqueness of Jewish morality in order to distinguish it from a purely rational morality.

Returning, however, to the early Haskalah, *musar* can be seen to have acted as both a force for acculturation and one that precipitated a drawing inwards. In some respects it served as a way of bringing Jews into alignment with the values of Christians, yet in others it ensured the very opposite. What the balancing of these concerns led to was a distinctive religious approach which viewed Jewish law as being intimately connected with moral improvement, and which demanded a self-awareness based on rational principles and an understanding of the science of human psychology. The turn to the self seen in the ethical approach of the mas-

[78] Wessely, *Sefer hamidot*, sect. 1. 3. 2.

[79] Ibid., sect. 1. 3. 4.

[80] Joseph Wolf, 'Über das Wesen, der Charakter und die Nothwendigkeit der Religion', *Sulamith*, 1 (1806), 314–15.

kilim is both a reflection of the more general modern movement inwards and of the developing self-consciousness of the Haskalah in particular. Fuelled by a desire to revamp Jewish society, the Haskalah aimed to provide individuals with the tools necessary to allow them to take an active role in shaping a spiritual life in harmony with both the ideals of Enlightenment and Jewish tradition, which, in the eyes of the maskilim, were considered to be fully compatible.

FOUR

Was there a 'Haskalah' in England? Reconsidering an Old Question

DAVID B. RUDERMAN

As early as 1893 the historian Lucien Wolf, in his inaugural address at the opening meeting of the Jewish Historical Society of England, articulated in the form of a rhetorical question what appeared to be a common notion about the history of Anglo-Jewry in his day: 'Where are your great men? . . . Where is your Maimonides, your Jehuda Halevi, your Isaac Abarbanel?' Feeling the acute need to justify the foundation of an organization devoted exclusively to the study of Anglo-Jewish history, Wolf could find no better answer than to admit that English Jews had never produced such prolific and seminal Jewish thinkers. The significance of Anglo-Jewish history was to be found elsewhere:

> The answer to these questions is, of course, simple. We have not produced any such men, and even if we had, it would be no proof that our history was more important than the histories of the French and German communities which, in this respect, are almost in the same case with ourselves. The truth is that this criticism belongs to a primitive order of historical science. Biography does not cover the whole domain of history. The true function of the historian is to reconstruct the lives, not of personalities but of communities and nations out of the largest possible accumulation of social facts and individual experiences.[1]

Wolf's protestation regarding the emphasis on biography over communal history based on the 'accumulation of social facts and individual experiences' might be translated into a more contemporary historical idiom to mean an excessive preoccupation with intellectual history, one focusing on the intellectual elites of the past, at the expense of an understanding of the social and political forces of Jewish communal life. Clearly, for Wolf, the historian's gaze on the latter rather than the former was not only legitimate but underscored the importance of Anglo-Jewry's past. That French and German Jewries were similarly deficient in their lack of intellectual giants was surely a more questionable assumption—Rashi or Moses Mendelssohn come quickly to mind—nevertheless, Wolf was more persuasive in

This chapter is a slightly modified version of my Hebrew article originally published in *Zion*, 62 (1997) 109–31.

[1] Lucien Wolf, 'A Plea for Anglo-Jewish History', *Transactions of the Jewish Historical Society of England*, 1 (1893–4), 1.

arguing that the real significance of England's Jewish past rested primarily on social and political rather than intellectual grounds.

Focusing on the modern era of Anglo-Jewish history, Simeon Singer, writing only a few years later, similarly underscored the lack of a serious intellectual legacy among English Jews. In this case, he made an unfavourable comparison between the intellectual ambience of German Jewry in the age of Moses Mendelssohn and that of England:

> The Mendelssohnian Revival in Germany during the last quarter of the eighteenth century had no counterpart in England. The smallness of the Jewish population, their comparatively recent settlement in this country, the character of their pursuits, which ran almost exclusively in commercial channels, the low state of education, both secular and religious, alike within and outside the Jewish community, may help to explain the absence among them at that period of men, I will not say like Moses Mendelssohn himself—for genius is always an incalculable phenomenon in regard alike to time, place, and circumstances—but of men of the type of the Meassephim.[2]

In more recent times, Cecil Roth cautiously challenged this standard assessment of Anglo-Jewish thought of the late eighteenth century.[3] His use of the term 'Haskalah' made this task of reconstruction difficult from the outset. By Haskalah he did not mean the movement for spreading European culture among Jews of Germany or eastern Europe; rather, he meant more generally 'the movement for the revitalization and modernization of Hebrew culture'. Roth admitted that, in England as well as in Holland, 'the lines of this process were blurred' because of the presence of an influential Sephardi element with strong interests in Hebrew and general culture long before the time of Mendelssohn.[4] Nevertheless, he felt justified in offering a survey of Jewish writers in England in the late eighteenth and early nineteenth centuries, almost all Ashkenazi Jews, who wrote primarily in Hebrew and shared common cultural and pedagogic concerns with the Jewish Enlightenment movement of central and eastern Europe. Offering little more than a biographical and bibliographical survey of a handful of Jewish intellectuals and their writings, and providing only scanty evidence regarding the points of substantial intellectual contact with the Continental Enlightenment, Roth remained considerably vague about the nature of this so-called 'Haskalah' in England and its relative significance either for Anglo-Jewish history in particular or for the history of modern Jewish thought in general. At the very least, however, he had offered a preliminary description of a limited literary harvest among Anglo-Jewry that still required more intense examination with respect to its connections with Jewish intellectual currents elsewhere and with English culture in general.

Roth's useful survey made little impact on subsequent historical writing. Todd

[2] Simeon Singer, 'Early Translations and Translators of the Jewish Liturgy in England', *Transactions of the Jewish Historical Society of England*, 3 (1896–8), 58–9.

[3] 'The Haskalah in England', in H. J. Zimmels, J. Rabbinowitz, and I. Finestein (eds.), *Essays Presented to Chief Rabbi Israel Brodie on the Occasion of his Seventieth Birthday* (London, 1967), 365–76.

[4] Ibid. 365.

Endelman's pioneering study of the Jews of Georgian England published in 1979 mentioned in passing Roth's 'Haskalah in England', but vigorously dismissed its conclusions out of hand.[5] In a later book, and in a more focused essay appearing as late as 1987, Endelman reiterated his negative reaction to Roth's claim that there had been a Jewish enlightenment in England and reasserted with strong conviction and authority the position intimated by Lucien Wolf almost a hundred years earlier that English Jewish history in the modern era was significant primarily for its new lines of social behaviour rather than for its new lines of thinking.[6] Given the importance of Endelman's influential and sophisticated treatment of this period, his consistent stance deserves a full hearing before I offer my own view.

In *The Jews of Georgian England* Endelman firmly maintained that there were no seminal figures—lay or rabbinic—who contributed to the development of modern Jewish thought or continued the scholarship of rabbinic Judaism. Moreover, those who left the Jewish fold rarely articulated their motives for doing so. Unlike their counterparts in France and Germany, the Jewish elite of England never created an ideology (the Haskalah) to justify and promote the modernization of Jewish life: 'Well-to-do Jews who embraced the English way of life felt no need to appeal to a set of ideas to justify their actions. They showed little interest in an intellectual reconciliation of English culture and Jewish tradition . . . Their unarticulated ideal was that of upper-class gentility.'[7] Regarding the beginnings of Reform Judaism in England, Endelman similarly maintained that the reformers

> were more concerned with the social consequences of enlightenment . . . than they were with the intellectual reconciliation of Judaism and European culture. If true, this would also explain why they treated German maskilim as a homogeneous coterie and ignored or remained ignorant of the profound differences between the radicals, the moderates, and Mendelssohn himself . . . Indeed, these Anglo-Jewish moderates would have found the ideas of the German radicals, such as David Friedländer and Lazarus Bendavid, totally unacceptable.[8]

In his later essay, written in response to an invitation by Jacob Katz to reflect on Anglo-Jewish modernization from the comparative perspective of the German experience, Endelman was even more emphatic: 'The ideological programs created by the Haskalah and later by Reform Judaism had little impact on the course of Anglo-Jewish history, primarily because they were inappropriate to the English context.'[9] The modern transformation, Endelman maintained, was strictly a local development, the result of a specific social setting and not imported from foreign trends. Referring to Roth's article, Endelman discounted the significance of its data. The individuals Roth discussed were not communal leaders, did not create

[5] *The Jews of Georgian England 1714–1830* (Philadelphia, Pa., 1979), pp. x, 8, 121, 149–52, 156–7, 159. Endelman refers specifically to Roth's essay in the footnote on p. 149.

[6] Todd Endelman, *Radical Assimilation in English Jewish History 1656–1945* (Bloomington, Ind., 1990), 28–30, 47; id., 'The Englishness of Jewish Modernity in England', in Jacob Katz (ed.), *Toward Modernity: The European Jewish Model* (New Brunswick, NJ, 1987), 225–46.

[7] *The Jews of Georgian England*, 121.

[8] Ibid. 156.

[9] 'Englishness', 226.

institutions to modernize Judaism, and did not constitute a cohesive circle of intellectuals committed to the transformation of the fundamental structure of Judaism. Endelman finally returned to the general characterization of the unintellectual character of Anglo-Jewish history:

> By comparison with the German Jewish middle class, well-to-do English Jews in the eighteenth and nineteenth centuries were ill-educated and intellectually unsophisticated. They took little interest in the intellectual life of their country nor did they make a significant contribution to English letters or Jewish scholarship . . . This indifference to the world of ideas stemmed primarily from the character of Jewish integration into English society rather than, presumably, from any innate lack of intelligence . . . Like the aristocratic and gentry circles which they sought to emulate, they shunned theoretical systems and philosophical abstractions, preferring instead an empirical, piecemeal approach to gaining acceptance in the larger society.[10]

From Wolf to Endelman, it would seem that the verdict regarding the mental landscape of Anglo-Jewry, especially during the period of the Enlightenment, was unequivocal. Roth's tentative probings notwithstanding, Endelman's portrait of a social world inhabited by assimilated aristocracy, middle-class businessmen, pickpockets, and pugilists appears to leave little room for Jewish intellectuals, of either the traditional or the secular bent. The recent appearance of David Katz's informative synthesis of English Jewry between 1485 and 1850 does little to challenge this evaluation.[11]

As a relative newcomer to the study of Anglo-Jewish history I have no reason to contest the general outline of the socio-cultural development of the Jewish community in the modern period so effectively and persuasively constructed by Endelman and others. Nevertheless, I am not convinced that Roth's fascinating inventory of Jewish intellectual life should be discounted so quickly. His essay, while conceptually flawed and superficially argued, does constitute a standing invitation to future historians to re-examine the evidence for an intellectual life among English Jews in the eighteenth century and beyond. Neither Roth nor Endelman ever bothered to examine extensively the writings Roth briefly describes. Without making any extravagant claims about the collective importance of this body of material, I would like to revisit the conclusions reached by Roth and refuted by Endelman by looking more carefully at four intellectuals who figure prominently in the essay and one who does not, although Roth treated him elsewhere.[12] All of them were active around the last quarter of the eighteenth century and, although they hardly represent a cohesive circle, were probably well aware of each other's reflections about Judaism. Moreover, given the relatively modest size of London Jewry in this era, they most probably encountered each other socially, although the evidence for close ties is generally not yet available.

[10] Ibid. 230–1.

[11] David Katz, *Jews in the History of England 1485–1850* (Oxford, 1994).

[12] I refer to Dr Samuel Falk and to Roth's essay in his *Essays and Portraits of Anglo-Jewish History* (London, 1962), 139–64.

I initially became interested in Jewish intellectual life in eighteenth-century England through my previous investigations of the dialogue between modern science and Jewish thought in the writings of several Anglo-Jewish thinkers, beginning with the first rabbi of the Sephardi Bevis Marks synagogue, David Nieto (1654–1728). Through an examination of Nieto's works I concluded that he had sufficiently acclimatized himself to English culture to be aware of the new merger between science and religion preached by the Latitudinarian clergy, especially through the widely publicized Boyle lectures in London in the early eighteenth century. I speculated that Nieto had learned of the well-known clergyman Samuel Clarke's creative use of Newtonian science to bolster the claims of Christianity, and that he adapted Clarke's formulations in presenting his own defence of traditional Judaism. Nieto's creative articulation of the Jewish faith made little immediate impact on his students and followers;[13] his most accomplished disciple, Jacob Sarmento, even left the synagogue and abandoned Judaism altogether.[14] But Newtonianism, that cluster of scientific, religious, and political ideas that left its powerful mark on the culture of England as well as on that of the Continent, profoundly affected the thinking of several other Jewish figures in England several generations after Nieto, particularly that of Mordechai Gumpel Schnaber Levison and Jacob Hart.[15]

Having looked at English Jewish thought solely through the lens of Newtonianism, I now chose to venture beyond Jewish discussions of science and religion to examine more broadly the activity of Jewish self-reflection in this dominant centre of creative thinking in early modern Europe. Given the vibrant nature of English culture in this period—its literature, its press, its theatre, its theological and philosophical ruminations, and more, it is hard to imagine that Jews were totally oblivious to the mental world that surrounded them.[16] Moreover, given the relative openness of English society to differing opinions, even radical ideas, on politics and religion, Jews could feel less inhibited about expressing heterodox ideas even about their own religious faith. As Frank Manuel puts it: 'Only in England had the separation of church and state proceeded so far that disputants could engage in open theological debate without jeopardizing their personal liberty, interpret Biblical texts loosely, and discuss miracles and the psychology of religion with impunity.'[17]

[13] David Ruderman, *Jewish Thought and Scientific Discovery in Early Modern Europe* (New Haven, 1995), 310–31.

[14] On Sarmento and the impact of Newtonianism on his thinking, see M. Goldish, 'Newtonian, Converso, and Deist: The Lives of Jacob (Henrique) de Castro Sarmento', *Science in Context*, 10 (1997), 651–75.

[15] For a general overview of Newtonianism, see B. J. Teeter Dobbs and M. C. Jacob, *Newton and the Culture of Newtonianism* (Atlantic Highlands, NJ, 1995). I have already treated Levison in *Jewish Thought*, 332–68, but see also below. On Jacob Hart see below and Ruderman, 'Newtonianism and Jewish Thought in England: The Case of Eliakim ben Abraham Hart', *Science in Context*, 10 (1997), 677–92.

[16] I have avoided a general bibliography here since the literature is obviously vast, beginning with the classic survey by L. Stephan, *History of English Thought in the Eighteenth Century*, 2 vols. (New York, 1962).

[17] *The Eighteenth Century Confronts the Gods* (Cambridge, Mass., 1959), 57.

Endelman's categorical statement regarding English Jewry's indifference to the world of ideas needs some revision, at least regarding the late eighteenth century. Endelman is correct that English Jews never suffered from 'any innate lack of intelligence'. On the contrary, in the stimulating cultural environment of eighteenth-century London, even assimilated Jews who stood on the margins of Jewish and English culture were at least potentially susceptible to the enchanting intellectual breezes ventilating the most stuffy corners of their religious life. It is my contention that a complete examination of the five thinkers I discuss below will suggest a fascinating relationship between English and Jewish thought. Despite the limited nature of this encounter, it is significant because of its specifically English character, informed by intellectual currents primarily located on English soil, and situated in a relatively tolerant social climate between Jews and Christians which was also unique to England.

Jewish thought, as exemplified by my sample of English Jews, includes the following themes: Deism and atheism; Lockian psychology and its impact on religious faith; physico-theology and Newtonian physics; prophecy, miracles, and the excesses of enthusiasm; pagan mythology, Euhemerism, and comparative religion; mysticism, magic, and masonry; millenarianism, and Christian Hebraism, as well as the traditional field of Jewish–Christian polemics. It is also uniquely English with respect to the social setting of Jewish self-reflection. Jewish thinkers not only articulated their thinking through engagement with books and authors; they openly entered into social encounters with non-Jewish intellectuals, and even engaged in public discussion and debate, both spoken and written. Such social interactions had previously existed in Amsterdam in the seventeenth century and in Mendelssohn's Berlin of the late eighteenth century, but Jews in England were more open about such social liaisons and public debates, even than those in such 'semi-neutral'[18] environments as the Netherlands or Germany.

Endelman was right in arguing that the Haskalah movement in Germany and eastern Europe had a minimal and inconsequential effect on Jewish intellectual life in England. Roth's use of the term 'Haskalah' was indeed misleading in implying that what English Jews were thinking about was imported from the Continent. It was a native growth, stimulated by English sources and independent of—in some cases, prior to—the Berlin Haskalah and the later intellectual developments of eastern Europe. England, of course, was not totally cut off intellectually from developments in the heartland of European Jewry—intellectuals and their books often migrated from east to west and from west to east. Nevertheless, one should not assume that English Jews required either the cultural image or the philosophical ideas of Mendelssohn and his followers to precipitate their own ruminations on Judaism and on culture in general. They did not.

Endelman is also right in pointing out that the handful of Jewish thinkers in England never constituted a movement with clear political and pedagogic objectives.

[18] The term is that of Jacob Katz. See his *Out of the Ghetto* (Cambridge, Mass, 1973), ch. 4.

There was never an organized programme of intellectual life like that of the *me'asfim* in Germany or that of later maskilim in Galicia or Russia. But this difference was not merely the result of dissimilarities between the German and English Jewish communities; it was also deeply rooted in the idiosyncratic nature of English intellectual life in the eighteenth century. While the full-fledged movements of *éclaircissement* and *Aufklärung* were under way and winning intellectual and political victories in France and Germany respectively, an 'Enlightenment' movement was unknown in England. Even the widely discussed cluster of ideas known as Deism hardly constituted an organized school of thought.[19] English Jews with intellectual pretensions were, in this respect, like their English Christian counterparts: they were highly individualistic, unsystematic, eclectic in their interests, and they reflected on a variety of practical, moral, religious, and political issues.

Endelman's position requires revision, however, in seemingly equating the lack of a Haskalah movement in England with a general Jewish indifference to English ideas or, to use his own words, with the reconciliation of Judaism with European culture. There was no Haskalah, but there did exist a Jewish intellectual life of some significance for modern Jewish history. Endelman is also misled by Roth in reducing this mental world to a mere literary phenomenon on the part of a handful of Jews who wrote in Hebrew. While some of the thinkers discussed below did write primarily in Hebrew, they were essentially bilingual; they read, wrote, and even published works in English; in fact David Levi's entire literary output was in English. The unique intellectual ambience of English Jewry was thus shaped through a cognitive process of translating a traditional Hebraic culture into a modern English one. It was also shaped in an environment where some Jews not only read and wrote Hebrew and English, but also Spanish, Portuguese, Latin, and German. Endelman also underestimates the radical nature of English Jewish self-reflection. As I shall show, several Jewish thinkers held fully articulated Deistic positions on religion, as radical and as corrosive to traditional Jewish faith as those of David Friedländer (1750–1834) or Lazarus Bendavid (1762–1832), if not more so, and this was independent of, and often earlier than, their counterparts in Germany.

The thinkers discussed in the rest of this chapter are Mordechai Gumpel Schnaber (1741–97), also known as George Levison; Eliakim b. Abraham (1745–1814), known as Jacob Hart; Abraham b. Naphtali Tang (d. 1792), also known as Abraham Abrahams; David Levi (1742–1801); and Samuel Jacob Hayim Falk (*c.*1710–1782). Of the five, Falk was the oldest and stands out from the rest because of his eccentricity, but, for reasons I shall elaborate below, he should be considered as a part of the same cultural ambience as the other four. All five were either born in London (Tang, Hart, and Levi) or lived there for many years (Falk and Levison). It would also be fair to say that each man's intellectual agenda was shaped primarily by the English environment in which he lived. This is not the place for extended

[19] On this, see e.g. E. C. Mossner, 'Deism', *Encyclopedia of Philosophy* (New York and London, 1967), ii. 327, 331.

treatments: I have already discussed Hart and Levison elsewhere[20] and am in the process of writing on Tang and Levi, whose work has been well summarized by Richard Popkin.[21] For Falk, I rely primarily on the extensive bibliography on him, especially the recent work of Michal Oron and Marsha Keith Schuchard.[22] My purpose here is merely to indicate the salient features of their intellectual projects which as a whole comprise a significant dimension of Jewish cultural life in late eighteenth-century England and a unique Anglo-Jewish contribution to modern Jewish thought in general.

MORDECHAI GUMPEL SCHNABER LEVISON

Levison was perhaps the most wide-ranging figure in this group, both in terms of his broad intellectual interests and his variegated social and professional relationships in England, Sweden, and Germany. While he primarily wrote in Hebrew, he also published many works in English, German, and French. So far my own study of Levison has focused on two of his major works: *Ma'amar hatorah vehaḥokhmah* (On the Torah and Wisdom), published in London in 1771, and *Shelosh-esreh yesodei hatorah* (Foundations of the Torah), a commentary on Maimonides' thirteen principles of faith, probably published in Altona in 1792.[23]

Levison arrived in London sometime in 1771 from Berlin, where he had received a traditional rabbinic education from the distinguished talmudist David Fränkel. He was drawn to London by the remarkable opportunity for a young foreign-born Jew to study at the famous medical school of the surgeon and physio-

[20] See n. 15 above.

[21] Richard Popkin, 'David Levi: Anglo-Jewish Theologian', *Jewish Quarterly Review*, NS 87 (1996), 79–101, who cites earlier references to Levi. See the extended treatment of this and the entire subject in D. Ruderman, *Jewish Enlightenment in an English Key: Anglo-Jewry's Construction of Modern Jewish Thought* (Princeton, NJ, 2000).

[22] Michal Oron, 'Mysticism and Magic in London in the Eighteenth Century: Samuel Falk, the Ba'al Shem Tov of London', in R. Tzur and T. Rozen (eds.), *The Book of Israel Levine* (Heb.) (Tel Aviv, 1995), 7–20, where earlier references are cited; id., 'Dr Samuel Falk and the Eibeschütz–Emden Controversy', in K. E. Grözinger and Joseph Dan (eds.), *Mysticism, Magic, and Kabbalah in Ashkenazi Judaism* (Berlin, 1995), 243–56; Marsha Keith Schuchard, 'Yeats and the "Unknown Superiors": Swedenborg, Falk and Cagliostro', in M. M. Roberts and H. Ormsby-Lennon (eds.), *Secret Texts: The Literature of Secret Societies* (New York, 1995), 114–68, where she refers to her forthcoming books on the subject. For another recent synopsis of Falk's activity, see Katz, *Jews in the History of England*, 300–3.

[23] Ruderman, *Jewish Thought*, 332–68. What follows is based primarily on this chapter, where full references to primary texts are given. A list of Levison's writings can be found on p. 345 n. 40. Many of the biographical details of Levison's life are collected in H. J. Schoeps, 'Gumpertz Levison. Leben und Werk eines gelehrten Abenteurers des 18. Jahrhunderts', *Zeitschrift für Religions- und Geistesgeschichte*, 4 (1952), 150–61, repr. in his *Studien zur unbekannten Religions- und Geistesgeschichte* (Berlin, 1963), 216–27; the article has been published in French as 'La Vie et l'œuvre de Gumpertz Levison', *Revue d'histoire de la médicine hébraïque*, 27 (1955), 133–43. See also H. M. Graupe, 'Mordechai Gumpel (Levison)', *Bulletin des Leo Baeck Instituts*, 5 (1962), 1–12.

logist John Hunter.[24] Upon completion of his medical studies in 1776 he received an appointment as a physician at the General Medical Asylum of the duke of Portland. In addition to his first Hebrew work, *Ma'amar hatorah*, he published two English medical texts during this period that reveal his indebtedness to his mentor Hunter and his equally famous medical brother William. Some years later, he was awarded a medical degree from the University of Aberdeen in Scotland.[25]

Levison's professional success soon led him in a rather remarkable and bizarre direction. In London he met a young medical student from Sweden, Auguste Nordeskjold, who was soon to become a well-known physician in his own right. In 1783 Auguste's brother Carl Frederik published in Stockholm a collection of hermetic and kabbalistic writings compiled by none other than Emanuel Swedenborg, the famous mystic, magician, and messianic thinker. Apparently through his contacts with the Nordeskjold brothers, Levison joined the Swedenborgian society in London, which would later claim as a member the poet William Blake.[26] Levison shared a keen interest in alchemy with his new friends, and even assisted Auguste in translating his *A Plain System of Alchymy* into English. Despite the more scientific and empiricist direction of his own published writing, Levison's connection with the Swedenborgians suggests at the very least a possible link with their most illustrious Jewish master, Samuel Falk. The Nordeskjolds apparently sang the praises of their Jewish friend to the royal court in Sweden. Levison was subsequently invited by Gustave III to Stockholm, where in 1780 he served as professor of medicine and laid plans for an alchemical laboratory and an entire institute of medicine. His short-lived fame came to an abrupt end with his return to London, the deterioration of his relations with members of the Jewish community there, and his relocation to Hamburg where he re-established his medical practice, which he ran until his death in 1797.

The primary theological concern of his principal Hebrew works is the relationship between science and religion. Despite his putative framework for discussion —Maimonides' thirteen principles—for Levison the issue was faith in general, not necessarily Judaism alone. He certainly did not hide his Jewish commitments; after all, he wrote in Hebrew with a wide range of citations from biblical, rabbinic, and kabbalistic sources. But like his contemporary Abraham Tang, with whom he is invariably compared, he was more interested in treating religion as a general cultural phenomenon, where belief in one God, providence, or prophecy constituted general categories of religious experience accessible to all humankind. Levison's two major sources in his discussion were the sensationalist epistemology of John Locke and the physico-theology of Carl Linnaeus, reflecting respectively the formative intel-

24 On the Hunters, see W. F. Bynum and R. Porter (eds.), *William Hunter and the Eighteenth-Century Medical World* (Cambridge, 1985).

25 See K. E. Collins, 'Jewish Medical Students and Graduates of Scotland, 1739–1862', *Transactions of the Jewish Historical Society of England*, 27 (1978–80), 79.

26 I have gleaned this new information from Schuchard, 'Yeats and the "Unknown Superiors"', 133.

lectual environments—London and Stockholm—of his own professional career. Levison was also enamoured of Isaac Newton, and was probably the first to present Newton's laws of motion to a Hebrew readership.

For Levison the disciple of Locke, Jewish faith rested on the single foundational principle of knowing God, a knowledge based solely on human sensation and cogitation as practised in the scientific laboratory. The primary evidence of God's existence was an intimate knowledge of how the world functions, specifically, the remarkable system of balance and compensation operating throughout the universe. Drawing freely on the writings of Linnaeus and the English tradition of physico-theology, Levison elaborated for his readers the 'great chain of being', a naturalistic understanding of divine providence based on the maintenance of equilibrium in nature, while virtually ignoring traditional notions of heaven and hell or revelation that fitted uneasily into his universal understanding of religion and the cosmos. The implications of Levison's ideas were radical indeed: he offered flimsy support for ceremonial observance or for the particularity of Jewish existence; his credo was universal at its core. Despite his sharp denunciation of Spinozism, his arguments in favour of Mosaic chronology based on the well-known works of Martini and Bochart, and his defence of Hebrew as the original language, Levison's allegiance to traditional faith and praxis was tenuous at best. He virtually transformed a Maimonidean theology of the twelfth century into a conventional Deism of the eighteenth.

JACOB HART

Hart was equally well attuned to the primary issues of religion and science discussed in his English environment, but his absorption of these issues and his Jewish slant on them took quite another direction to Levison's.[27] Hart was born in London in 1745. He earned his living as a jeweller, which allowed him to pursue his intellectual interests in fairly comfortable circumstances. He also was a prominent lay leader in various settings of the Ashkenazi community of London, as a trustee of the Hambro synagogue, a prominent member of the Denmark Court synagogue, and a generous benefactor to other communal institutions. At his funeral in 1814 three coaches were sent to the synagogue to accompany his body, doubling the cost. He also clearly had contact with several other contemporary Jewish thinkers. David Levi, although he himself wrote only in English, was responsible for publishing and selling the first volumes of Hart's planned series of ten Hebrew works, while Hart was in close contact with Elijah Pinhas Hurwitz (1765–1821), the author of the remarkably popular compendium *Sefer haberit* (Book of the Covenant), which

[27] What follows is based primarily on Ruderman, 'Newtonianism', where full references are cited. The only other scholars to have studied Hart and his work are A. Barnett and S. Brodetsky, in 'Eliakim ben Abraham (Jacob Hart): An Anglo-Jewish Scholar of the Eighteenth Century', *Transactions of the Jewish Historical Society of England*, 14 (1940), 207–23.

contains several citations from Hart's writings.[28] The name Eliakim b. Abraham also appears in a list of subscribers to *Midrash pinḥas* (1795), a homiletical work by the preacher of the Sha'arei Zion synagogue, Pinhas b. Samuel, who had succeeded Rabbi Moses Minsk (1750–1831) in that position. Abraham Tang was also probably connected with this synagogue, and, while there is no evidence that Hart knew him, their affiliation with Sha'arei Zion suggests a common social setting for their intellectual achievements.[29]

Hart began his literary career in 1794 with the publication of the first of his projected series of Hebrew books entitled *Milḥamot adonai*.[30] It was clearly his most original work, and was thoroughly rooted in the English milieu of the eighteenth century. It was followed by the publication of *Binah la'itim*, a commentary on the prophecies of Daniel explicitly linking them to the revolutionary era in which Hart was living. His other works appeared more sporadically. In 1799, with the support of a number of distinguished Jewish families in London, he published a condensation of part of the kabbalistic ruminations of Joseph Delmedigo, the scientific and kabbalistic writer of the seventeenth century. He succeeded in printing only two more volumes of the series, both published in Germany and dealing with kabbalistic matters. One additional work on Hebrew grammar—apparently unrelated to the series—was also published in Germany.

Hart's first work is clearly of the greatest historical interest in its announced intention to wage war on the enemies of the Jewish people of his day: the pagan chronologists who challenged the biblical account of the world's origins, together with Aristotle, Descartes, and the students of Newton, although not Newton himself. Hart's preoccupation with Chinese chronology and pagan hieroglyphics reveals a common universe of discourse with both Levison and, especially, Abraham Tang, who address similar issues in their own work. His attack on Aristotle constitutes no more than a conventional foil to indicate how the ancient sage had become increasingly obsolete in the light of new scientific theories and discoveries ranging from those of Boerhaave and Van Helmont to Brahe and Copernicus. Descartes is credited with attacking the physics of Aristotle, but is accused of constructing a mechanical universe where the direct hand of God is invisible. Hart lumped together the enemies of religious faith: Locke, Bayle, Spinoza, Hobbes, and Hume. He also attacked the Deists Voltaire, Bolingbroke, and Paine, enlisting the refutation of Joseph Priestley to his cause. He further impugned Descartes's science by citing Newton's critiques.

Hart's most interesting discussion is reserved for Newton, who initially receives gushing praise for his remarkable achievements in geometry, algebra, and optics. What was especially appealing to Hart was Newton's piety and his involvement in

[28] On Hurwitz and his work, see N. Rosenblum, 'The First Hebrew Encyclopedia: Its Author and its Development' (Heb.), *Proceedings of the American Academy for Jewish Research*, 55 (1988), 15–65.

[29] On the Sha'arei Zion congregation, see Cecil Roth, 'The Lesser London Synagogues of the Eighteenth Century', *Miscellanies of the Jewish Historical Society of England*, 3 (1937), 2–4.

[30] *Sefer milḥamot adonai* [Book of the Wars of the Lord] (London, 1794), 12*a*.

biblical prophecy: 'He taught people not to destroy even a small part of prophecy because of [the findings of] human investigation . . . The words of the prophets were very dear in his eyes, for even though he was constantly preoccupied with investigation and experiments, it did not prevent him from writing a commentary on the book of Daniel.'[31] Hart's own commentary on the same book could hardly have been coincidental. Moreover, that remarkable confluence of science and mysticism, natural investigation and messianic prophecy, is surely the key to understanding Hart's positive image of Newton, and also explains his retrieval of his Jewish ancestor, Joseph Delmedigo. It is also worth noting that Hart's attraction to the mystical side of Delmedigo's writing stands in sharp contrast to the efforts of later nineteenth-century maskilim to present Delmedigo's scientific and rational side alone.[32]

Hart's bitterness towards Newton was directed, not at Newton himself, but squarely at the camp of his radical supporters, who used his physical laws, especially gravitation, to undermine the notion of divine providence and purposeful creation. To substantiate his charge that they misused Newtonian physics to undermine religious faith, he cited the massive but relatively obscure critique of Robert Greene, a fellow of Clare College Cambridge and a scholar associated with the Tory camp, who had undertaken a thorough assault on the growing alliance between Newtonian natural philosophy and Latitudinarian theology.[33] For Greene, as for Hart, the growing vogue for natural philosophy associated with Newton imperilled the revealed doctrines of Christianity and Judaism. Hart also made use of William Whiston, a prominent Newtonian and Latitudinarian theologian. He initially referred to him in favourable terms, praising his defence of biblical over Chinese chronology, but he was less comfortable with his naturalistic explanations of the origins of the biblical flood based on Newton's universal law of gravity. For Hart, Whiston had severely diminished the role of divine providence by implying that the world was subject to random naturalistic forces and not to God alone.[34] By siding with a High Church man like Greene while excoriating the Deists and atheists and expressing reservations about the latitudinarian Whiston, Hart understood perfectly the complexity of the issues Newtonianism had raised for Jewish faith in eighteenth-century England. He was prepared to chart a more conservative course to distance himself from the radical camp of Newtonians while leaving himself room to appreciate the new science as a resource for traditional religious faith. This position was clearly at odds with that of Levison, and, as we shall see, of Tang as well. But it did make him a natural ally of David Levi, whose traditionalism also placed him at odds with the Deists and Latitudinarians. Levi singled out an almost

[31] Ibid.

[32] On this, see Ruderman, *Jewish Thought*, 118–52.

[33] On Greene, see esp. J. Gascoigne, *Cambridge in the Age of Enlightenment: Science, Religion, and Politics from the Restoration to the French Revolution* (Cambridge, 1989), 167–74.

[34] On Whiston, see esp. J. Force, *William Whiston: Honest Newtonian* (Cambridge and New York, 1985).

identical pantheon of enemies of religious faith, from Voltaire to Bolingbroke and Hume. When Hart alluded to both Priestley and Paine in the same passage, he was probably thinking of his friend's dual assault on these vaunted intellectuals of the Western world. And Levi's responsibility for publishing Hart's treatise surely made him a silent partner in clarifying a traditional Jewish position among the competing strands of Newtonianism current in eighteenth-century England.

ABRAHAM B. NAPHTALI TANG

Tang was, ironically, the least noticed intellectual of the five figures discussed here, but probably the most scholarly and original thinker. His relative obscurity is attributable to the fact that despite his many Hebrew compositions, which include hundreds of pages in manuscript, he succeeded in publishing only one book: an English commentary on the *Pirkei avot* (The Ethics of the Fathers).[35] Furthermore, his most original work, the *Beḥinat ha'adam*, on the existence of God and the ways in which we can know Him and acknowledge the divine presence, was unknown to both Cecil Roth and to the only scholar who devoted an essay to his work, S. B. Leperer.[36] Given his wide-ranging interests, the complexity of his thought, and the novelty of his thinking, especially about comparative religion and ancient history, he deserves a fuller treatment than I am able to give here.[37] More than the other four thinkers, Tang illuminates the profundity and originality of English Jewish thought in the eighteenth century. Whether he was typical or not, he fully demonstrated the remarkable potential for creative thinking among Jews which was unleashed by the stimulating debates over religion, science, and politics in early modern England.

The biographical details on Abraham Tang are scanty.[38] He was the grandson of Abraham b. Moses Taussig Neungreschel (hence the acronym Tang), *dayan* of the lesser rabbinical court of Prague, who died in 1699. His son Naphtali left Prague

[35] Shmuel Feiner has recently brought to my attention another printed work of Tang which he signed only as 'A Primitive Ebrew', entitled *A Discourse Addressed to the Minority* (London, 1770). This unusual pamphlet suggests a more public image of Tang than I first imagined. It also suggests the strong possibility that he wrote other works in English that are still to be identified. I discuss this work in my larger study, *Jewish Enlightenment in an English Key*. My thanks to Dr Feiner for this fascinating discovery.

[36] See Roth, 'The Haskalah in England', 368–72; S. B. Leperer, 'Abraham ben Naphtali Tang: A Precursor of the Anglo-Jewish Haskalah', *Transactions of the Jewish Historical Society of England*, 24 (1974), 82–8. There are three extant manuscripts of *Beḥinat adam* [Examination of Man]: St Petersburg RNL Heb. II A22 (no. 63945 in the catalogue of the Institute for Microfilmed Hebrew Manuscripts, University and National Library, Jerusalem) and Frankfurt am Main 8*59, cat. no. 63 (Jerusalem no. 25906) contain only pt. 1 in differing orders; Cincinnati Hebrew Union College 728/1 (Jerusalem no. 35913) contains the beginning of pt. 2 of the composition. The Cincinnati manuscript also contains the unfinished work entitled *Kol sinai*.

[37] See Ruderman, *Jewish Enlightenment in an English Key*.

[38] See Roth, 'The Haskalah in England'; Leperer, 'Tang'.

and settled in London, where he married the daughter of Rabbi Nathan Apta of Opatow, rabbi of the Hambro synagogue. Naphtali composed several rabbinic works which were not published, including an expansive commentary on *Pirkei avot* called *Ets avot* (Tree of the Fathers).[39] That Abraham his son elected to write his own commentary on this rabbinic collection of ethical maxims might be seen as an effort to please his father.[40] In another unfinished Hebrew work called *Kol sinai* (The Voice of Sinai), a kind of commentary on the basic *halakhot* (as enumerated by Maimonides), Abraham explicitly mentions a connection with his father. He claims that he began work on *Kol sinai* while he was writing *Beḥinat ha'adam*, because his father complained: 'I had taught nothing there of the laws, and that all my heart was devoted to non-Jewish learning. He was not pacified until I wrote this small work on the law according to Moses called *Kol sinai*.'[41] Apparently Naphtali knew his son well, since even in this allegedly 'traditional' project, Abraham also proved incapable of turning his attention away from non-Jewish sources.

The other biographical detail about Tang worthy of note is his relationship with Moses Minsk, who was appointed preacher and teacher of a small congregation that first appeared in London in 1770, called Hevrat Sha'arei Zion. Our only information about its membership is derived from a collection of Minsk's sermons published in London in 1772 under the title *Sefer even shoham*. Minsk's successor Pinhas b. Samuel published his own sermon collection in 1795. From the list of subscribers to both volumes it is possible to gain some sense of the community with which Tang was probably affiliated. Among the subscribers is a certain Leib b. Naphtali Tang, probably Abraham's brother.[42]

Among the many texts Minsk discusses in his published sermons is the enigmatic story of the first-century Palestinian rabbi Joshua b. Hananiah, and his strange encounter with the sages of Athens in that city where he had been sent by invitation of the Roman emperor.[43] That Tang actually heard Minsk's sermon or studied the text with him is suggested by a remarkable composition he penned in honour of his teacher on the very same passage. In Tang's hands, however, the text served no moral or homiletical purpose; rather, it offered a lesson in political science. In Tang's view the learned rabbi had worked surreptitiously on behalf of the Roman government to undermine a political faction in Athens which threatened the stability of Roman rule. Whether Minsk would have accepted his learned student's explanation of Rabbi Hananiah's behaviour is doubtful.[44]

[39] Naphtali's works are found in manuscript in the library of Jews College, MSS 9, 31, and 32.

[40] The translation was entitled *The Sentences and Proverbs of the Ancient Fathers . . . Written originally in Ebrew . . . by . . . R. Jehudah the Holy . . . now translated into the English language . . . By a primitive Ebrew* (London, 1772).

[41] MS Cincinnati HUC 728/2 fos. 11–12.

[42] See Roth, 'Lesser London Synagogues', 2–4; Leperer, 'Tang', 83.

[43] Moses Minsk, *Sefer even shoham* [Book of the Shoham Stone] (London, 1772), 15*a*–21*a*, on BT *Bekhorot* 9*b*.

[44] Tang, 'Sabei debei atunah' [The Sages of the Athens Academy], MS Jews College 35 (Jerusalem no. 4698); also completed in 1772, the same year as Minsk's sermons were published.

This bare outline of Abraham Tang's life hardly prepares the modern reader for the remarkable ruminations of this obscure writer on a variety of historical, psychological, literary, political, and theological topics. Along with the variety and magnitude of this output comes a sense of incompleteness, of existential uncertainty, possibly the result of inner turmoil, or of wrestling with the notion of Jewish identity in an increasingly sceptical and secularized environment. The boldness and originality of Tang's vision of God and humanity is thus tempered by a lack of clarity, a pronounced lack of integration exacerbated by the fact that neither his major work nor most of his other writings were ever finished, let alone published (although Tang's own radical positions may have contributed to the latter failure). In addition to *Beḥinat ha'adam*, 'Besabei ta'amei', his commentary on *Pirkei avot*, and *Kol sinai*, Tang wrote an incomplete commentary on the book of Ecclesiastes which includes a unique handbook of pagan mythology as a kind of introduction to its second part,[45] and a Hebrew translation of William Congreve's *Mourning Bride*.[46] These works demonstrate his wide erudition; they also display his linguistic ability and sensitivity to language. In his guide to pagan mythology he took pride in offering texts in their original Latin or Greek with Hebrew and English translations. Tang also had some artistic pretensions. His manuscripts were copied in a clear penmanship that emulates the perfection of the printed page; in addition, he occasionally included colourful charts and diagrams, and often used footnotes to expand on points made in the body of his text.

Tang was preoccupied in *Beḥinat ha'adam* with demonstrating that God exists and that this was a universal belief shared by all peoples, past and present. Relying on the vast taxonomies of writers such as Samuel Bochart and Edward Stillingfleet, he demonstrated how pagan philosophers and native Africans and Americans all acknowledged the one God. Most remarkable is his use of Voltaire's philosophical dictionary to make his point. Given the notoriety Voltaire had acquired through his biting critique of Judaism and the Jewish community and his blatantly Deistic positions which challenged the very foundation of Christian revelation, he was not an author that most Jews of good conscience could cite, except to refute or condemn.[47] But Tang had no such inhibitions. He translated two long sections from Voltaire's dictionary—the entries for 'Chinese Catechism' and 'Dieu'—which underscore Voltaire's bold Deistic faith and his antipathy towards organized religion. Tang integrated both sections in his text without comment; only in the first case did he even identify Voltaire by name. Even more audacious was his citation from Voltaire's entry on circumcision regarding the pagan origin of the ritual, which he inserted,

45 MS Jews College 7 (Jerusalem no. 4676), dated 1773.

46 On this see J. Schirmann, 'The First Hebrew Translation from English Literature: Congreve's *Mourning Bride*', *Scripta Hierosolymitana*, 19 (1967), 3–15.

47 On Voltaire and the Jews, see W. Klemperer, *Voltaire und die Juden* (Berlin, 1894); Léon Poliakov, *Histoire de l'antisémitisme de Voltaire à Wagner* (Paris, 1968), 103–17; Arthur Hertzberg, *The French Enlightenment and the Jews* (New York and Philadelphia, Pa., 1968), 280–308; A. Arkush, 'Voltaire on Judaism and Christianity', *Association for Jewish Studies Review*, 18 (1993), 223–43.

of all places, in *Kol sinai*, a work meant to demonstrate his piety and to pacify his traditional father! Tang mentioned Voltaire by name on one more occasion, in the summary of *Beḥinat ha'adam*. There he singles out for scorn Spinoza, whom he dismisses out of hand. He also mentions Voltaire in the same breath, calling him 'the sweetener and deceiver'.[48] The French philosopher, according to Tang, constituted a danger not so much for his fundamental ideas on religion but for what could be derived from them by his more radical followers. Tang did not clarify this ambivalence towards Voltaire, but it is clear from this reference and from his other long citations that he appreciated the philosopher's positions, regardless of the obvious dangers implicit in them. This appreciation stands in sharp contrast not only to the negative comments of Hart and Levi, but also the views of the overwhelming majority of Jews, who saw him and his assaults on Judaism as a grave danger to their community and faith.

Like Voltaire, Tang heaped scorn on small-minded clergy, ignorant rabbis who focused only on the minutiae of talmudic law. In contrast to what he saw as their shallowness and irrationality, Tang championed the cause of reason, experiment, and investigation, which he called a natural human urge. In a discussion heavily influenced by the discourse of Locke (and paralleling similar discussions in Levison's work), Tang asserted that faith without reason was meaningless; that the Torah never required Jews to suspend their intellect in accepting irrational dogma; and that prophecy was inauthentic when it contradicted reason. He reserved particular scorn for the kabbalists, whom he viewed as enthusiasts falsely following their inner voices of irrationality and foolishness.

Although he never cited Newton directly, Tang was familiar with the new sciences of his day and their impact on demonstrating God's existence. Like Levison, he was a strong advocate of physico-theology, waxing eloquent about the harmony of the water and plant cycle, and describing in minute detail the activity of beehives and the creation of honey. Espousing throughout a strong belief in a world directed by a divine hand, he openly criticized the randomness of a cosmos based on materialist Cartesian or atomistic foundations. He also provided a detailed analysis of the anatomy of the ear and eye, accompanied by charts and precise information based on the latest medical authorities. These sections suggest strongly that Tang also had a medical education.

Finally, Tang stands out from his contemporaries by virtue of his fascination with ancient history and mythology and his attempt to understand the mentality of the rabbis by comparing them with their ancient Classical and Near Eastern contemporaries. In this enterprise, he appears to be of two minds. On the one hand, for example, in his treatment of the parable of the Athenian sages, he adopts a Euhemeristic approach,[49] ignoring possible allegorical interpretations and favouring instead a strictly one-dimensional political explanation. On the other hand, he

[48] *Beḥinat ha'adam*, MS Frankfurt 8*59, fo. 198*a*.

[49] On this, see esp. Manuel, *The Eighteenth Century Confronts the Gods*, 103–13.

was capable of viewing the stories of the ancient world as mythopoeic creations that imparted religious value and universal truth. It was important for Jews to know mythology, Tang contended, not only because Moses and the rabbis were familiar with it, not only because the myths could be correlated with the Bible and could be understood to reveal the truth of one God, but also because of the poetic and literary value of these heroic stories. Tang understood that the ancient myths—both gentile and Jewish—effectively conveyed religious teachings. It was absurd to dismiss this legacy as meaningless; moreover, a poetic reading of myth was also appropriate for the study of midrash. The riddles of the rabbis, like those of the Greeks and Egyptians, could be deciphered to reveal a spiritual message for the modern reader.

Tang's commitment to recovering a fundamental universal belief in one God, and in correlating that belief with the Jewish one, diminished the singularity of the Jewish tradition to vanishing point. Despite his plentiful use of Jewish sources, both rabbinic and medieval (he was especially fond of the late medieval commentaries of Abraham ibn Ezra), there is no compelling message in his writings that distinguishes Judaism from other religions and cultures. He was clearly a Deist by belief and a Jew by cultural inclination. His ultimate role as a Jewish interpreter was to underscore Judaism's universal message and its links with the rest of civilization. Tang's attraction to Voltaire's plain talk about religion was not accidental; it was genuine and deeply felt.[50]

DAVID LEVI

In turning to the remaining two thinkers considered in this chapter, David Levi and Samuel Falk, we should note from the outset a significant difference between them and the previous three. Both had public profiles that made them well known to Jewish and Christian communities.[51] Levi's many publications in English and his public stand on issues affecting the welfare of the Jewish community in England elevated him to a kind of spokesman for Jewish interests in the London community. His fearless published rebukes of such luminaries as Joseph Priestley and Tom Paine could not help but enhance his public stature in his own city and even beyond. Yet, notwithstanding his remarkable record of publications, his wide mastery of English sources, and his exegetical dexterity in reading the Bible, Levi was no intellectual in the manner of Levison or Tang. He was primarily an educator and public apologist: his extant writing is exclusively directed to a general audience of religious leaders and their followings, and it was written to be read by assimilated Jews and curious Christians, not necessarily intellectuals.

Falk, on the other hand, gained even more notoriety, not for his intellect or

[50] Fuller information on Tang's thought is given in Ruderman, *Jewish Enlightenment in an English Key*.

[51] See ibid. for a fuller examination of Tang's public profile in the light of new evidence for his political activity.

writings, but because of his alleged magical and mystical abilities as a *ba'al shem*. But to dismiss him as a kind of comic freak performing alchemical experiments in his laboratory on London Bridge would be to ignore a vital component of the dynamic culture of Jewish life in London in the eighteenth century that enabled both rationalists like Tang and magicians like Falk to flourish. Despite the fact that Falk did not publish his reflections on Judaism, the shadow he cast over his contemporaries was so great it eclipsed those of all of his English co-religionists. Even more ironic is the fact that, at least in the eighteenth century, this *ba'al shem* of London was more familiar in the Christian world than even the founder of hasidism himself, the Ba'al Shem Tov. John Copley's famous portrait of Falk, often misidentified as of the great hasidic master, provides some indication of Falk's remarkable stature.[52]

Levi's phenomenal career flourished despite the relative poverty under which he laboured, first as a shoemaker and then as a hatmaker.[53] From the time of his first publication in 1782, *A Succinct Account of the Rites and Ceremonies of the Jews*, until the end of the century, he flooded the market with English tomes educating an illiterate Jewish public in the principles of traditional Judaism, and defending the integrity and honour of his religion before Deists and Christian millenarians alike. In addition to his account of Jewish ceremonies, he produced translations of the Sephardi and Ashkenazi prayer-books, a Hebrew grammar and encyclopaedia of key terms and personalities, the massive three-volume *Dissertations on the Prophecies of the Old Testament*, two responses to Joseph Priestley's attempt to proselytize the Jews, Jewish responses to the messianic pretensions of Richard Brothers and to Tom Paine's *Age of Reason*, and more. His publications elicited a considerable response from his Christian contemporaries, and his articulate responses to Priestley and Paine were especially well regarded. He enjoyed a certain social standing in the Christian literary community, particularly among a group of writers who gathered at the home of the bookseller George Lackington. He even merited a moving obituary in the pages of the *Gentleman's Magazine* penned by his loyal friend the Huguenot Henry Lemoine.[54]

As I have indicated, Levi's purpose was to explicate Judaism to a relatively unsophisticated readership of Jews and Christians. Thus his arguments lack subtlety and are generally conventional. His apologetic interpretations of the Hebrew Bible follow traditional lines essentially laid out by medieval exegetes, especially Isaac Abrabanel. He had little opportunity or inclination to offer novel interpretations of Jewish faith such as those of Levison or Tang. Indeed, despite his vast erudition, he was a theological conservative who chose to cite Christian authors either to bolster a traditional Jewish position or to refute a Christian or Deist one. These authors in-

[52] The portrait is reproduced in the *Encyclopedia Judaica* (Jerusalem, 1971), vi. 1160.

[53] On Levi, his life, publications, and previous work on him, see Popkin, 'David Levi'. David Katz succinctly summarizes his life in *Jews in the History of England*, 295–300.

[54] This is often quoted, and is also reproduced in Popkin, 'David Levi'.

cluded Samuel Bochart, Jacques Basnage, Humphrey Prideaux, Ralph Cudworth, Josiah Mede, Isaac Newton on biblical prophecy, Robert Lowth, John Hutchinson, Pierre Jurieu, William Warburton, and many more. He also referred often but disparagingly to Voltaire, Bolingbroke, Hume, Locke, Spinoza, and Hobbes.[55] It is unclear whether he had actually read these authors in depth or whether their names were simply invoked as a rallying cry against the enemies of organized religion. On the other hand, he understood Paine well, and underscored his indebtedness to Voltaire, whom he also must have read.

In short, Levi functioned as the consummate public intellectual and polemicist ready to defend the honour of Judaism at every turn, to educate assimilated Jews in a language they could understand, and to correct proudly and bombastically the misrepresentations of the Bible by contemporary Christians manipulating the Hebrew text for their own theological purposes. While he wrote in English, he knew Hebrew and particularly traditional biblical exegesis well and was a gifted translator of Hebrew liturgy. He was particularly astute in using his mastery of Hebrew grammar and syntax as a sword with which to bludgeon his Christian opponents and to ridicule their tendentious reading of Scripture. Walking gingerly and shrewdly among the minefields placed by millenarian Christians on the one hand and by radical Deists on the other, he seemed to relish picking a fight. He argued rationally and historically against the former, and with a traditional and triumphalist orthodoxy against the latter. He could attack the Catholics to score points with his Protestant allies and brazenly vilify the Unitarian Priestley for his rejection of the Trinity which disqualified him, claimed Levi, from representing authentic Christianity.[56]

Richard Popkin has shown that, even after Levi's death in 1801, he was seen as a standard authority and cited with approval by many Christian authors such as Abbé Grégoire, Hannah Adams, and Elias Boudinot. Popkin compares him to Menasseh b. Israel (1604–57), the Amsterdam writer and publisher who made Jewish learning and belief accessible and available to both Christians and Jews. However, the brashness and temerity of Levi's polemical style distinguished him both from Menasseh and from Moses Mendelssohn, another figure to whom Levi is compared, but whose style was to move quietly and strategically in Christian elite society, careful not to offend either his Christian associates or the more traditionalist rabbinic establishment. While upholding a consistent orthodoxy, Levi hardly appears to have been a cautious individual. He dismissed without further thought the admonitions of his fellow Jews to avoid a public confrontation with the likes of Joseph Priestley. He appeared to be uninhibited about speaking his mind

[55] All of these authors are cited frequently in the notes to Levi's volumes, especially his *Dissertations* and *Lingua Sacra*. I deal with these works and their sources in greater detail in *Jewish Enlightenment in an English Key*.

[56] I refer in this last point to Levi's *Letters to Dr Priestley in Answer to his Letters to the Jews* (London, 1794), 111.

freely.[57] This difference in style is rooted, I would suggest, in the distinctive ambience of English society. Levi's defiant stance is a significant indicator of the relatively high levels of tolerance English society would allow itself with respect to its Jewish minority.[58] It also suggests the confidence and security an English Jew could feel about the stability of his position and that of his community in modern England many years before legal emancipation had been effected. Levi even felt entitled to speak on matters transcending specifically Jewish concerns. In his attack on Paine he presumed to speak not only for Judaism but for organized religion in general. In this sense, he functioned uniquely in the European Jewish world in insinuating himself into the public social arena to a degree unprecedented before the nineteenth century.

SAMUEL FALK

Falk would seemingly have had little in common with David Levi, let alone Hart, Tang, and Levison. He epitomized the kind of ignorance and superstition, and the exploitative and mercenary character, so repulsive to Deists like Tang. But despite his image as an uneducated rabbi and charlatan which was fostered especially by Rabbi Jacob Emden, who viewed him as a radical Shabbatean, the notorious Dr Falk displayed a certain genius in projecting an image that gained him both fame and fortune. Overcoming the suspicions of the organized Jewish community, he won the support of the powerful Goldsmid family, and generously assigned his burgeoning funds—perhaps accumulated through gambling—to support the rabbinate and Jewish charities. From the site of his private synagogue and home in Wellclose Square, he fostered a remarkable network of admirers and supporters who sought out his magical powers and enhanced his mystical aura among some of the most fascinating and influential figures in the Christian world. If Tang might have disapproved of his activities, he did not dare voice his feelings in public while there were many others who were charmed by them.[59]

Falk was born in Galicia, grew up in Fürth, moved to Westphalia, fled the city after being accused of witchcraft, and arrived in London, where he spent the remaining forty years of his life, in 1742. His early years are documented in the diary of his personal valet Tsevi Hirsch Kalischer (1795–1874). The diary offers rare glimpses of Falk's magical activities, his personal life, his failed relationship with his wife, his alchemical experiments, and more. Falk also left a diary that begins in 1772, and contains inventories of household items, descriptions of dreams, magical formulas, and a listing of some of his social contacts.[60]

57 This lack of inhibition about entering public debate seems to have characterized the behaviour of Abraham Tang as well.

58 On this see Endelman, *Georgian England*, 13–85.

59 On Falk, see Oron, 'Mysticism and Magic', and 'Samuel Falk'; Schuchard, 'Yeats and the "Unknown Superiors"', and the earlier work they cite.

60 This diary is fully discussed in Oron, 'Mysticism and Magic', and id., 'Samuel Falk'.

Despite mention of several unusual Christian guests in his home in these Hebrew documents—particularly the international adventurer Theodore De Stein and the king of Poland, Prince Adam Czartoryski—there is little reason to assume from this alone that he was any more than a minor celebrity. But these enticing notices are apparently the mere tip of the iceberg. According to Marsha K. Schuchard's research on the Swedenborgians, the figure of Falk was legendary among Jewish and Christian freemasons, and, especially in the last years of his life, he apparently played a significant role in an ambitious effort to develop a new form of Judaeo-Christian freemasonry which did not pressurize its members to convert to Christianity.[61] When Emanuel Swedenborg himself arrived in London in 1744 he visited Falk in his mansion in Wellclose Square, and for the next thirty years he remained on intimate terms with him. Swedenborg studied Hebrew and kabbalah and was obsessed with messianic fantasies which he recorded in his writing, including a reference to an arcane Hebrew parchment received 'from Heaven' in Falk's neighbourhood. According to Schuchard, a notice by Falk in his diary to 'Emanuel, a servant of the King of France' probably refers to Swedenborg. As Swedenborg's reputation grew throughout Europe through his masonic contacts and publications, Falk's fame was also enhanced within these same circles.[62] By the 1770s Swedenborg and Falk had both assumed the exalted status of 'Unknown Superiors' in the Strict Observance masonic lodges. By the time William Blake had joined the Swedenborgian circle in London, Falk shared centre-stage with Swedenborg and his associate Giuseppe Balsamo Cagliostro as one of the three Unknown Superiors of the masonic-Rosicrucian society. His mysterious profile was recorded well into the nineteenth century, and was even known to W. B. Yeats, who published an edition of Blake's poems at the end of the nineteenth century.[63] Schuchard's unravelling of the complex tradition of the Unknown Superiors involving 'secret Jewish adepts, masonic political intrigue, and mystical millenarianism' testifies, in the mind of 'illuminated' historians, as she puts it, 'to the perennial vitality of the Jewish visionary tradition that nourishes and regenerates both Rabbinic and Christian orthodoxies'.[64] Be that as it may, the centrality of a kabbalistic magus from London in this bizarre and mind-boggling encounter between Jews and Christians in eighteenth-century Europe casts an entirely different light on the intellectual and social relations between Jews and Christians in London and beyond. To dismiss these mystical fantasies as unrelated to the more 'rational' streams of Jewish and Christian thought in England or Germany is to miss the complex web of relations between Enlightenment thought, social tolerance, and the continued fascination with the occult that still prevailed in Europe well into the nineteenth century. To cite only one example, Gotthold Ephraim Lessing, Mendelssohn's associate, had been initiated into the Swedish rite of masons as

[61] Schuchard, 'Yeats and the "Unknown Superiors"', 117; see my fuller evaluation of her position in *Jewish Enlightenment in an English Key*.

[62] Schuchard, 'Yeats', 140–1.

[63] Ibid. 114–15, 145–6, 148–9.

[64] Ibid. 156.

early as 1771. In 1778, at the height of speculation in Germany over Falk's role in freemasonry, he published his masonic dialogues, provocatively entitled *Ernst und Falk*. Lessing seemed to portray Falk by his reputation in the Swedish rite as an inspired kabbalist and political manipulator.[65] Were Mendelssohn and Falk thus connected in some way through the writing of Lessing? Such speculations await further scrutiny by Schuchard and others.

*

Falk may have been the outsider in the group of five intellectual figures described in this chapter. But as we have seen, Levison was also connected with the Swedenborgians in England and Sweden, Hart was clearly fascinated with kabbalah and messianic prophecy, and David Levi dabbled as well in messianic prognostications. Only Tang had no use for such mad enthusiasts. In other words, despite the profound differences in the substance and style of their Jewish reflections, all five men shared a common universe of discourse shaped by the special ambience of late eighteenth-century England.

How significant, in the final analysis, are the reflections of these and similar thinkers in reconstructing the cultural and social history of Anglo-Jewry in the modern era? In the case of Levi and Falk, their public impact on Jewish and Christian society is beyond doubt. Hart and Levison, on the other hand, left only a limited impression through their Hebrew publications, and Tang, perhaps England's most profound Jewish thinker in the eighteenth century, seemingly had almost negligible influence. But as the case of Tang illustrates, the historical importance of critical thinkers in any era cannot merely be reduced to their impact on other thinkers or readers. Tang's discourses on Judaism, Deism, and pagan mythology are important to the historian in suggesting the range of possibilities through which Jews were capable of conceptualizing their religion and culture in the last quarter of the eighteenth century. Viewed comparatively with the thinking of Tang's four contemporaries, they suggest real and vital engagement with English ideas, hardly indifference, among a small but not insignificant group of English Jews. Lucien Wolf could not easily find a Maimonides or a Halevi on English soil, but he could have discovered several fascinating examples of Jewish self-reflection in early modern England had he bothered to look.

[65] Ibid. 145.

FIVE

Strategy and Ruse in the Haskalah of Mendel Lefin of Satanow

NANCY SINKOFF

I

STANDARD historiography depicts Mendel Lefin of Satanow (1749–1826), the east European maskil who spent time in Berlin among Mendelssohn's circle in the 1780s and returned to Poland and Galicia to spread the message of the Haskalah, as a populist. Born in Satanow, Podolia in 1749, Lefin lived in Berlin from 1780 to 1784, then returned to Poland, where he settled in Mikolajow, Podolia, and participated in the debates of the last Polish parliament (the Four Year Sejm of 1788–92). In the first decade of the nineteenth century he lived in Russia on the estate of Joshua Zeitlin, the generous patron of many east European maskilim; at the end of his long life, he moved to Austrian Galicia, living first in Brody (1808–17) and then in Tarnopol, where he died in 1826.[1] Prolific from the 1790s until his death, Lefin penned works which cover a broad spectrum of maskilic concerns: biblical translations (into Yiddish), philosophical speculations, programmes for the moral and cultural reform of the Jewish community, dissemination of medical and scientific information, and translations of German literature.

Implicit in the image of Lefin as a populist is the view that his Haskalah, or programme for enlightening the Jews of eastern Europe, was 'nationalist' in that it was directed towards the Jewish masses.[2] N. M. Gelber, for example, concluded that

Research for this chapter was supported by the IIE Fulbright Foundation, the Memorial Foundation for Jewish Culture, and the Interuniversity Program in Jewish Studies.

[1] General biographical information about Lefin can be found in the following sources: Samuel Joseph Fuenn, *Kiryah ne'emanah* [Faithful City] (Vilna, 1860), 271–3; Joseph Klausner, *History of Modern Hebrew Literature* (Heb.), 6 vols. (Jerusalem, 1952–4), i. 201–22; Raphael Mahler, *Chronicles of Jewish History* (Heb.), vol. i, bk. 4 (Rehavia, 1956), 71–2; Israel Weinlös, 'Mendel Lefin of Satanow: A Biographical Study from Manuscript Material' (Yiddish), *YIVO Bleter*, 1 (1931), 334–57, and id., 'Menachem Mendel Lefin of Satanow' (Heb.), *Ha'olam*, 13/39–42 (1925), 778–9, 799–800, 819–20, 839–40; Israel Zinberg, *A History of Jewish Literature*, vol. vi (New York, 1975), 275.

[2] The use of the terms 'nationalist' and 'nationalism' for the late 18th and early 19th cents. is extremely problematic, although very widespread. For example, though Isaac Eisenstein-Barzilay makes the distinction between modern Jewish nationalism (the will for political, economic, and cultural autonomy) and the nationalism (a 'consciousness of uniqueness', or a 'deep consciousness of their

'his books were widely dissiminated; they reached a broad audience and had a great "cultural-national" impact on the Jewish community', and depicted Lefin himself as one who 'endeavored that the circle of enlightened Jews in Brody should not be isolated from the people, but rather they should be intimately connected to the everyday life of the masses'.[3] Historians such as Raphael Mahler and Israel Weinlös contrasted Lefin to Herz Homberg (1749–1841), the German maskil who as supervisor of Joseph II's schools in Galicia was viewed with deep suspicion by east European Jewry, and to other Berlin maskilim whom they believed to be anti-nationalist and assimilationist. They saw 'explicit democratic justifications'[4] in Lefin's utilitarian use of Yiddish to disseminate the ideas of the Haskalah. Lefin, Weinlös wrote, 'tried to approach the masses and to be endeared to them. He loved his people, the simple people, [with] a real love and, in contradistinction to [Homberg], he was one of the first to "descend" towards this people to speak with it in its language [Yiddish] and in its spirit.'[5]

Lefin's populist image is the result of a naive reading of his published materials, virtual neglect of manuscript materials,[6] and a bias in modern Jewish historiography which, up to the 1960s, viewed the Jewish past in polarities, pitting the allegedly open, corrosive West against the closed, authentic East and searching for members of the intelligentsia who were committed to the 'people'. In this reading, the maskilim of western Europe were damned as assimilationists for their use of German and embrace of Western, non-Jewish culture and, together with their east European peers, censured for their identification with and support of the gentile state.[7]

common past and future destiny') of the maskilim he still refers to both historical phenomena as 'nationalism'. Despite Eisenstein-Barzilay's clarity about the difference between these two types of 'nationalism' I believe the term is obfuscating, inherently carrying the layered meaning of the later (late 19th- and 20th-cent.) political, economic, and cultural nationalism. Its use is anachronistic for the late 18th cent. and should be avoided. See Isaac Eisenstein-Barzilay, 'The Enlightenment and the Jews: A Study in Haskalah and Nationalism' (Ph.D. diss., Columbia University, 1955), pp. xi and xii, and id., 'National and Anti-National Trends in the Berlin Haskalah', *Jewish Social Studies*, 21/3 (July 1959), 165–92, esp. p. 173.

[3] *Arim ve'imahot beyisra'el* ['Cities and Mothers of Israel'], vol. vi: *Brody*, ed. Y. L. Maimon (Jerusalem, 1955), 179 and 224.

[4] Mahler, *Chronicles*, 79. See also Weinlös, 'Mendel Lefin of Satanow: A Biographical Study', 344. Despite Max Erik's venomous opinions about Weinlös's Zionism, he, too, regarded Lefin's Hebrew style as democratic. See Erik, *Studies in the History of the Haskalah* (Yiddish) (Minsk, 1934), 147, and Meir Weiner, *The History of Yiddish Literature in the Nineteenth Century* (Yiddish) (Kiev, 1940), 7, on the democratic element in modern Yiddish literature generally.

[5] 'Mendel Lefin of Satanow', 819.

[6] On the importance of manuscript materials for the history of the Haskalah see Shmuel Werses, 'The Joseph Perl Archives in Jerusalem and their Wanderings' (Heb.), *Ha'universitah*, 19/1 (Mar. 1974), 38.

[7] On the etatism of Galicia's maskilim see Raphael Mahler, *Hasidism and the Jewish Enlightenment: Their Confrontation in Galicia and Poland in the First Half of the Nineteenth Century* (New York and Philadelphia, Pa., 1985), 121–5, 221–9. Mahler's critique of the Haskalah as being etatist is only partly incorrect; the maskilim of Galicia in the generation after Lefin were oriented towards Vienna and the absolutist Austrian state. But Lefin was oriented towards Poland and, in particular, towards his magnate patron. Moreover, Mahler's negative assessment of the political loyalty of the maskilim—to

Nationalist historians praised the early Haskalah for its Hebraism, but depicted the late Berlin Haskalah as a force for communal and national disintegration.[8] They saw Lefin's criticism of the radicalization of the Berlin Haskalah[9] and his decision to write in Yiddish as proof that he was more sympathetic to the Jewish masses than were his Berlin compatriots.

Lefin may have written in a popular style, but we should not confuse the medium of his Haskalah with its message, and retrospectively project a 'nationalist' vision on to him. When he employed popular literary forms he did so precisely because of his critical perspective on east European Jewish life. His turn to Yiddish, to mishnaic Hebrew, and to popular literature all resulted from the perspective he shared with other maskilim that the Jews of eastern Europe, through their own ignorance and failings, had become intoxicated with mysticism and were desperately in need of enlightened leadership. Lefin made no secret of his belief that east European Jewry needed the guidance of maskilim like himself in the battle against hasidism.[10] He recognized that, without the creation of an accessible and comprehensible literature, the message of the Haskalah would be lost to them.

Lefin was not a simple popularizer; indeed, his writing is characterized by an extraordinary range of literary strategies. Here was a member of the east European Jewish intelligentsia consciously creating different texts for different audiences in a multiplicity of languages—Hebrew, Yiddish, French, German, and Judaeo-German (German written in Hebrew characters).[11] Two of Lefin's works, *Masaot hayam* and *Essai d'un plan de réforme*, allow us to observe his method.

whichever 'vertical' authority, Polish or Austrian—is an anachronistic criticism based on his own belief in the need for an autonomous Jewish political culture for the self-emancipation of the Jewish people. On modern Jewish politics and the maskilim see Eli Lederhendler, *The Road to Modern Jewish Politics* (New York, 1989); for the classic discussion of the 'royal alliance' see Yosef Hayim Yerushalmi, *The Lisbon Massacre of 1506 and the Royal Image in the Shebet yehudah*, HUCA Supplements, 1 (1976).

[8] See Jonathan Frankel, 'Assimilation and the Jews in Nineteenth-Century Europe: Towards a New Historiography?', in Jonathan Frankel and Steven J. Zipperstein (eds.), *Assimilation and Community: The Jews in Nineteenth-Century Europe* (Cambridge, 1992), 1–37. See also Michael F. Stanislawski's broad critique of the historiographic assumption in modern Jewish history in which the authenticity of eastern European Jewry is contrasted with the assimilationism of Western Jewry: *For Whom Do I Toil? Judah Leib Gordon and the Crisis of Russian Jewry* (New York, 1988), 5.

[9] For Lefin's critique of *Hame'asef* see [Mendel Lefin], *Essai d'un plan de réforme ayant pour objet d'éclairer la Nation Juive en Pologne et de redresser par là ses mœurs* (Warsaw [1791]), in Artur Eisenbach, Jerzy Michalski, Emanuel Rostworowski, and Janusz Woliński (eds), *Materiały do Dziejów Sejmu Czteroletniego* [Materials on the History of the Four Year Sejm], vol. vi (Wroclaw, Warsaw, and Krakow, 1969), sects. 45–7 and n. 9 (pp. 413 and 420).

[10] See e.g. his famous rebuke of Nachman Krochmal's alleged philosophical retreat from the responsibility of engaging and enlightening the Jewish masses: Meir Letteris (ed.), *Mikhtavim* [Letters] (Lemberg, 1827), 33–5.

[11] For subtle analyses of Lefin's Yiddish translation of Proverbs see Chone Shmeruk, 'Regarding Several Principles of Mendel Lefin's Translation of Proverbs', in id., *Yiddish Literature in Poland: Historical Research and Insights* (Heb.) (Jerusalem, 1981), 165–83; on his *Ḥeshbon hanefesh* [Moral Accounting], see Hillel Levine, 'Between Hasidism and Haskalah: On a Disguised Anti-Hasidic Polemic', in

II

Throughout the nineteenth century, east European maskilim answered Naphtali Herz Wessely's clarion call in *Divrei shalom ve'emet* (1782) that 'the forms of the lands and the oceans (geography)' should be an obligatory element of the secular curriculum.[12] For example, Lefin's disciple Joseph Perl (1773–1839) encouraged the study of natural science and geography in *Luaḥ halev*, the second section of his calendars (the *Luḥot*) which appeared in 1814–16; Samson Halevi Bloch (1784–1845) penned *Shevilei olam*, the first general geography in Hebrew, in the 1820s; and Mordecai Aaron Guenzburg (1795–1846), the noted Lithuanian maskil, devoted considerable energy to spreading historical and geographical information among Russian Jewry through translations of German histories and of non-Jewish travel accounts.[13]

One of the vehicles favoured by maskilim for disseminating geographical knowledge was the translation and adaptation of the writings of Joachim Heinrich Campe (1746–1818), a leader of the German Philanthropin movement and a correspondent of Moses Mendelssohn. Campe's philosophical and pedagogical writings emphasized belief in divine providence, the immortality of the soul, reward and punishment, and the possibility of improving one's life through good deeds. Campe sought to base his new educational system on a 'realistic' approach which eschewed fixed texts, workbooks, and rhetorical exercises that were divorced from the actual lives of the students.[14] Jews who translated Campe's work into Hebrew and Yiddish, however, often removed the texts from their Philanthropin framework in order to use them as a means of teaching geography to the Jews of eastern Europe.[15] At least five of Campe's books were translated into Hebrew and Yiddish and Lefin himself translated and adapted at least two of Campe's *Reisebeschreibungen* in his *Masaot hayam*; however, little scholarly attention has been paid to this work, which was published in Zolkiew in 1818.[16]

Immanuel Etkes and Joseph Salmon (eds.), *Chapters in the History of Jewish Society in the Middle Ages and the Modern Period* (Heb.) (Jerusalem, 1980), 182–91.

12 *Divrei shalom ve'emet* [Words of Peace and Truth], 2nd edn. (Vienna, 1826), 3, 13.

13 On Perl's under-studied *Luḥot*, see Mahler, *Hasidism and the Jewish Enlightenment*, 149, 167. On Bloch, see Klausner, *History of Modern Hebrew Literature*, ii. 354. On Guenzburg see Israel Bartal, 'Mordechai Aaron Guenzburg: A Lithuanian Maskil Faces Modernity', in Frances Malino and David Sorkin (eds.), *From East and West: Jews in a Changing Europe 1750–1870* (Oxford, 1990), 126–47.

14 Ernst A. Simon, 'Pedagogic Philanthropism and Jewish Education', in Moshe Davis (ed.), *Jubilee Volume in Honor of Mordecai Kaplan* (Heb. section) (New York, 1953), 149–87.

15 In the 1810 issue of *Hame'asef*, Moses Mendelsohn of Hamburg's translation of Campe's *Entdeckung von Amerika* was praised for the benefit it would bring to 'the dear people of Poland, who will not read [gentile] books'. Quoted in Tsemah Tsamriyon, '*Hame'asef*': *The First Modern Periodical in Hebrew* (Heb.) (Tel Aviv, 1988), 83.

16 *Masaot hayam* [Sea Journeys] (Zolkiew, 1818; 3rd edn., containing pp. 37–52, Lemberg, 1859), contains translations of two travelogues by Joachim Heinrich Campe, which originally appeared in Campe's *Sammlung interessanter und durchgängiger zweckmässig abgefasster Reisebeschreibungen für die Jugend* (Reutlingen, 1786–93). Citations from *Masaot hayam* are from the 1818 edn. up to p. 36, and

In broad outline, the first journey included in *Masaot hayam* tells of the travails of a group of British sailors who, after departing from the Chinese port of Macao, become shipwrecked on the island of Pelew.[17] From the earliest moments, it is clear that the trip will be a difficult one, and the story describes how the sailors are ultimately saved by their own ingenuity, the generosity of the natives they encounter on Pelew, and, most of all, God's providence.[18] In an introduction to *Masaot hayam* which remained in manuscript, Lefin informs his readers that he intended his translation to remind those who had fallen into dire straits, like the sailors of Campe's tales, of God's eternal vigilance: 'But one who is drunk with misfortunes is likely to forget the divine providence of the Holy One, blessed is He, [and he is likely] to despair of his life and to lose all expectation and hope forever.'[19] He emphasizes continuity with traditional rabbinic views of God's soteriological power and of divine reward and punishment, beliefs which were consonant with the Philanthropin ideology, based as it was on notions of natural religion. Lefin urged his readers to take Campe's descriptions of extraordinary human suffering ultimately redeemed by a compassionate God as succour during their own misfortunes. Moreover, he urged those who had been saved from danger to spread the story of their salvation as widely as possible. This desire to emphasize God's providence does not seem particularly innovative or subversive; yet he also included the following vague comment in his introduction: 'Moreover, sometimes one teaches, incidental to this [to publicizing God's salvific power], another kind of suggestion or stratagem [*taḥbulah*] unrelated to the original event.'[20]

Lefin used the word *taḥbulah* in all of his writings. Its origin lies in Proverbs 1: 5: 'A wise man will hear, and will increase learning; and a man of understanding shall attain to wise counsels [*taḥbulot*].' However, *taḥbulah* carries other meanings in different biblical contexts, and can indicate 'tactics', 'strategies', 'ruses', or 'evil

from the 1859 edn. for later page nos. On Jewish interest in Campe, see Zohar Shavit, 'From Friedländer's *Lesebuch* to the Jewish Campe: The Beginning of Hebrew Children's Literature in Germany', *Leo Baeck Institute Yearbook*, 33 (1988), 407; on Guenzburg's translation of Campe's *The Discovery of America*, see Bartal, 'Mordechai Aaron Guenzburg', 141–2; on the genre of travelogue in general see Moshe Pelli, 'The Literary Genre of the Travelogue in Hebrew Haskalah Literature: Shmuel Romanelli's *Masa be'arav*', *Modern Judaism*, 11 (1991), 241–60.

[17] The first journey is an adaptation of Campe's 'Ein Bericht von den Pelju-Inseln, nach den Aufzeichnungen des Kapitain Wilson aus dem Jahr 1783', published in his *Sammlung*, vol. ix, and based on the English version of the story, *The Shipwreck of the Antelope East India Packet, H. Wilson, Esq. Commander, on the Pelew Islands, situate in the West Part of the Pacific Ocean; in August 1783* (London, 1788), 'by one of the unfortunate officers'.

[18] *Masaot hayam*, 2*a*, 11*b*; cf. Campe, *Sammlung*, ix. 16.

[19] Joseph Perl Archive, Jewish National University Library Archive (JNULA), folder 124; this folder consists of one single page of text. Though there is no date on the document itself, the watermark on the paper is legible as 1806. Self- or external censorship may have been the reason why the introduction was not included in the published version of *Masaot hayam*, but Lefin himself gives no indication why the text remained in manuscript.

[20] Joseph Perl Archive, folder 124.

designs'.[21] In *Ḥeshbon hanefesh*, a detailed behaviourist guide to moral education and self-improvement modelled on the thirteen principles of conduct Benjamin Franklin had outlined in his *Autobiography*, Lefin uses the word to indicate both a benign method to guide behaviour and a conscious subterfuge to counter the spread of hasidism.[22] As we will see below, Lefin chose to use the word *taḥbulah* in his unpublished introduction to *Masaot hayam* precisely because of its complex, double-edged meaning.

To what kind of 'suggestion' or 'stratagem' was Lefin referring? First, *Masaot hayam* implicitly shared with other maskilic translations of Campe's work the conviction that east European Jewry should have a wider knowledge of the world.[23] Second, an obvious 'suggestion' inherent in Lefin's translation was the value of appreciating an experience, even if its source was non-Jewish, that affirmed the theological assumptions shared by all enlightened men. The tales told by non-Jews who believed in divine providence were worthy of being heard for their own sake, without any reference to their 'enhancement' of traditional learning.[24] Because Lefin intended his translation to be read by traditionally educated east European Jewish youth, he was careful to justify his 'suggestion' with proof-texts from the rabbinic tradition:

> It is not sufficient to listen to stories of triumph that occurred before us; rather, one must always pursue and honour the events of men come what may, either to listen to them or to read them. As the Sages wrote: 'Who is wise? The one who learns from every man',[25] and they said: 'whether from a non-Jew or from Israel or from a slave or from a handmaid, the Holy Spirit rests upon him according to his deeds'.[26]

Lefin's citation of rabbinic sayings was not only a strategy to give his work the imprimatur of tradition. It also reflected his sincere conviction that a rational Judaism could be open to the universal values inherent in the experiences and knowledge of enlightened gentiles.

This conviction is implicit in the tales Lefin selected for translation, choosing those in which the encounter between enlightened, 'civilized' Europeans and 'noble savages' figures prominently as a leitmotif. A central component of the eighteenth century's discourse on non-European peoples, the image of the 'noble savage' contrasted the natural purity of non-Western tribal society with the depravity and

[21] See also Prov. 11: 14, 12: 5, 20: 18, 24: 6, and Job 37: 12.

[22] Even Lefin's opponents, such as the maskil Tobias Feder, who ridiculed his Yiddish translation of Psalms, identified Lefin with the word *taḥbulah*: 'It [the debased translation of Proverbs into Yiddish] is the deed of R. Mendel Satanow and his stratagems [*taḥbulotav*].' Quoted from Yehuda Friedlander, 'Tuviyah Gutmann Feder: *Kol meḥatsetsim* (*Voice of the Archers*)' (Heb.), *Zehut* (May 1981), 290. On the anti-hasidism of *Ḥeshbon hanefesh*, see Levine, 'Between Hasidism and Haskalah'.

[23] Mahler, *Chronicles*, 79.

[24] See Immanuel Etkes, 'On the Question of the Precursors of the Haskalah in Eastern Europe', in id. (ed.), *Religion and Life: The Jewish Enlightenment in Eastern Europe* (Heb.) (Jerusalem, 1993), 25–44.

[25] Mishnah, *Pirkei avot* 4: 1.

[26] *Tana deveit eliyahu rabah*, 10: 1.

corruption of European civilization.[27] The 'savages' of Pelew, in Lefin's rendering, are described as 'proper and good men'.[28] Through their travail, the unfortunate Europeans learn (to their surprise) the important Enlightenment message that character, not pedigree, is the essence of mankind. In the second travel story included in *Masaot hayam*, which describes an ill-fated search for the North-East Passage,[29] a sailor affirms the Enlightenment's belief in man's universal nature: 'And this is a faithful testimony that God, may He be blessed, casts sparks of compassion in the heart of every man; he can be from any people that can feel pity and have compassion, one man for his brother, and can empathize with his pain.'[30] Although the natives encountered on Pelew are pagan, they, too, believe in the immortality of the soul and in the world to come. Raa Kook, a Pelewan native who is the very embodiment of the noble savage,[31] explains to Wilson, the British captain, 'In our land, too, it is true that the wicked remain in the earth and the righteous rise to the firmament and are illuminated in a great radiance.'[32] The first travelogue is full of anthropological descriptions and digressions about the people of

[27] For European representations of the New World, see Brian Fagan, *Clash of Cultures* (New York, 1983); Frank E. Manuel, *The Broken Staff: Judaism through Christian Eyes* (Cambridge, Mass., 1992); Stephen Greenblatt, *Marvelous Possessions: The Wonder of the New World* (Oxford, 1991); Howard Eilberg-Schwartz, *The Savage in Judaism* (Bloomington, Ind., 1990). The first encounter between the British and the natives of Pelew is characterized by mutual wonder. Later in the narrative, however, the British compare, to their dismay, their selfishness and suspicion to the generosity and compassion of the Pelewan natives. See *Masaot hayam*, 4*b*, 28*a*, 31*a*, and 31*b*.

[28] *Masaot hayam*, 4*a*; Campe, *Sammlung*, ix. 27: 'Er fügte hinzu, daß dieser König ein sehr guter Mann und sein Volk eine sehr freundliche Menschenart wäre' (He saw that this king was a very good man and that his people were a very friendly race of men).

[29] The travelogue is an adaptation of Campe's 'Jakob Heemskerks und Wilhelm Barenz nördliche Entdeckungsreise und merkwürdige Schicksale', which first appeared in vol. i of his *Sammlung*.

[30] *Masaot hayam*, 54*b*; cf. Campe, *Sammlung*, i. 106: 'Seht, ihr jungen Menschen, so giebt es, Gott sei Dank! unter allen Zonen und in allen Ständen Leute, denen die Pflichten der Menschlichkeit heilig sind, und die sie gern und ohne Eigennutz erfüllen! Solcher Beispiele muß man sich erinnern, so oft man schlechter Menschen lieblose und ungerechte Handlungen sieht, damit man nicht in Versuchung gerathe, um einiger solcher Menschen willen, die ganze Menschheit für böse und lieblos zu halten' (See, young men, how there are—thank God!—people in all regions and among all classes to whom the duties of mankind are sacred and who willingly and without self-interest fulfil them. One must remember these events in order not to be tempted, as often as one observes the unkind and unjust actions of evil men, to consider, based upon a few of this kind, all humanity as evil and unkind).

[31] For descriptions of the nobility of the Pelewan natives, see *Masaot hayam*, 18*a*, 60, 63. Raa Kook is described concisely in *The Shipwreck of the Antelope* as appearing to be 'above every species of meanness' (p. 28), a quality which is embellished by Campe: 'Dieser verständige und liebenswürdige Mann äusserte bei jeder Freundschaftsbezeugung, die man ihm erwies, die größte Erkenntlichkeit; er bemühete sich, die englischen Gebräuche und Sitten anzunehmen; und stöste durch sein ganzes Betragen Jedermann die höchste Achtung für die Geradheit und Güte seines Karakters ein' (This intelligent and kind man expressed the greatest gratitude for each sign of friendship that was shown to him; he strove to adopt English customs and morals and by his example pushed everyone to pay the greatest attention to the uprightness and goodness of his character). *Sammlung*, ix. 37–8.

[32] *Masaot hayam*, 70.

Pelew and how they compare physically and culturally to the hapless British.[33] But the differences between the two cultures are rarely a source of discord. The value of recognizing that which is universal in men is underscored by the cultural exchange that takes place at the end of the story; a British sailor decides to remain in the East Indies while Lee Boo, the King of Pelew's son, sails to England with the British once they have repaired their ship.[34] In parting from his son, the King of Pelew tells him to regard Wilson as a father, and urges the captain to instruct his son in all the customs suitable for a British citizen.

These paeans to universalism notwithstanding, Campe's text was still imbued with the belief in Western superiority which informed the eighteenth-century image of the noble savage. Europeans ardently projected a utopian nobility on to non-Western peoples, but saw them as childlike, and remained firmly convinced that their nobility was still inferior to the mature, though problematic, advances of civilized life.[35] Lee Boo is confronted with the limitations of his paradisal island upbringing when, on landing in England, he realizes the liability of being unable to read or write.[36]

Lefin was well aware of the cultural dissonance inherent in the tales. In fact, in the realm of metaphor, he appears to be comparing the 'noble savages' with east European Jewry and the British and their world with Western, non-Jewish culture, and depicting their encounter as the result of a tumultuous journey.[37] By the second decade of the nineteenth century, the image of the east European Jew as culturally backward was already well on its way to becoming an immutable stereotype among Germans, German Jews, and east European Jewish maskilim who moved in German cultural circles.[38] In *Masaot hayam*, the savages (or east European Jews)

[33] *Masaot hayam*, 4*a*, 7*b*, 9*b*, 15*b*. In fact, Lefin added two chapters to Campe's version of Wilson's voyage. These chapters comprise a quasi-anthropological exploration of the culture of the Pelewans and are devoted to 'their customs, crops, houses, utensils, weapons and how they built boats', and to their 'marriage, burial and religious customs, and to their virtues'. See *Masaot hayam*, 64–71.

[34] *Masaot hayam*, 29*a*; cf. Campe, *Sammlung*, ix. 170. This kind of cultural exchange was typical of the period. In 1774 a Tahitian native was brought back to London by Captain Thomas Furneaux. See Fagan, *Clash of Cultures*, 111.

[35] Fagan, *Clash of Cultures*, 90; Greenblatt, *Marvelous Possessions*, 9.

[36] *Masaot hayam*, 36*a*.

[37] Moshe Pelli suggestively ends his article on Shmuel Romanelli's *Masa be'arav* with a similar thought. He suggests that Romanelli's trip from Germany to Morocco may be seen metaphorically as a maskil's 'voyage to, and exposure of, the unenlightened segment of the Jewish people, not only in Morocco, but in other places closer to home' ('The Literary Genre of the Travelogue', 257). Note, too, that other east European Jews seemed to feel that their encounter with modernity was as turbulent as a ship's voyage on a tempestuous sea. See the letter to Mordecai Aaron Guenzburg cited in Bartal, 'Guenzburg', 126 and the letter by Samuel Joseph Fuenn cited in the introduction to *From Militant Haskalah to Conservative Maskil: A Selection of S. J. Fuenn's Writings*, ed. Shmuel Feiner (Heb.) (Jerusalem, 1993), 12, 17.

[38] Steven E. Aschheim, *Brothers and Strangers: The East European Jew in German and German Jewish Consciousness*, 1800–1823 (Madison, Wis., 1982), 3–32. See also Larry Wolff, *Inventing Eastern Europe: The Map of Civilization on the Mind of the Enlightenment* (Stanford, Calif., 1994), for an analysis of the creation of the construct of 'eastern Europe' in the minds of the *philosophes*.

are described as men in the fullest sense of the word, but men who are living within the confines of a parochial, island-bound world. Lefin compares the King of Pelew's surprise on meeting the white-skinned British and their Chinese deck-hands for the first time, and his concomitant realization that 'his little nation was [not] the only one in the world, and that the world [did not] only extend as far as what his eyes could see of the neighbouring islands', to the experience of the daughters of Lot in Genesis 19: 31 who, after the destruction of Sodom and Gomorrah, fear that their father is the only man left in the world.[39] In Lefin's mind, east European Jewry, too, lived in a circumscribed world, one in which non-Jewish learning was suspected of heresy.[40] He took it upon himself to journey to the west in order to acquire the knowledge necessary to enlighten his people, whose culture he believed was unnecessarily restricted. In *Masaot hayam*, Lee Boo, the 'noble savage' ever conscious of his people's shortcomings, travels to England in order to acquire knowledge and skills for their advancement. The obstacles he encounters, such as his illiteracy and his inability to ride a horse, spur his efforts at self-improvement 'for the benefit of his people'.[41] Lefin too, returned to his native Poland after his sojourn in Berlin armed with the knowledge that he believed would 'benefit' his 'backward' people.

Clearly, Lefin translated Campe's tales, which were well respected by his fellow maskilim, as a way of broadening the geographical and cultural horizons of Polish Jewry. The beliefs the tales embodied—in God's providence, divine reward and punishment, and the immortality of the soul—were not discordant with rabbinic Judaism, and Lefin hoped that his effort to expand Jewish life beyond the limits of the traditional curriculum would disarm suspicion.

Yet there is an even more covert message within *Masaot hayam*. Of the three editions published in the nineteenth century,[42] none contains a preface and, as mentioned above, Lefin's introduction remained in manuscript. Lefin opened the 1818 edition by alluding to Psalm 107: 23–4—'They that go down to the sea in ships [*yoredei hayam be'oniyot*], that do business in great waters; these saw the works of the Lord, and His wonders in the deep'—on the title-page, which reads, 'The Book Journeys By Sea, They are God's Deeds and Wonders Seen by Those who Went Down to the Seas [*yoredei hayamim*] in Dutch and British Boats [*be'oniyot*]'. A paraphrase of the psalm also appears in an abbreviated form in the translator's note of the anonymous 1823 edition, while the 1859 edition cites Psalm 107: 23–4

[39] *Masaot hayam*, 9*b*. This is a clear example of how Lefin Judaized Campe's text, which makes no mention of the scriptural typology; other examples of Judaization include Lefin's use of the names of Hebrew months and allusions to biblical language.

[40] See Lefin, *Likutei kelalim* [Collections of Rules], a pamphlet on the internal life of the Jewish community of Poland, which was published as the second appendix in N. M. Gelber, 'Mendel Lefin of Satanow's Proposals for the Improvement of Jewish Community Life Presented to the Great Polish Sejm (1788–1792)' (Heb.), in *The Abraham Weiss Jubilee Volume* (New York, 1964), 287–301. In para. 66 (p. 300), Lefin complains that 'the study of wisdom and science and the rest of the sciences is considered apostasy [among the Jews of Poland]'.

[41] *Masaot hayam*, 58, 64.

[42] Zolkiew, 1818; Vilna, 1823; Lemberg, 1859.

on the back of the title-page. On the one hand, Lefin's use of the psalm as an introduction to his translation served to make the work more palatable to a traditional audience; its simple meaning suited the contents of the story well.[43] But his choice was not merely literary; the decision to use this particular proof-text was part of his larger campaign against the mystification of traditional rabbinic Judaism.

A hasidic commentary on Psalm 107, which was popularly known as 'Commentary on Hodu' and attributed to the Ba'al Shem Tov, was first published as *Sefer ketan* in Zhitomir in 1805 and printed a second time in Leszczow in 1816.[44] The commentary on the psalm was well known among both hasidim and kabbalists in the late eighteenth and early nineteenth centuries, and was cited by the disciples of the Besht, including the Maggid of Mezhirech, Jacob Joseph of Polonnoye, Levi Isaac of Berdichev, Nahum of Chernobyl, and Samuel Shmelke Horowitz of Nikolsburg. The mystical interpretation of verses 23–6 glosses the verbs 'descend' and 'ascend' in the psalm to address the dilemma faced by human souls inextricably mired in sin.[45] In the most general terms, this problem is known in hasidic thought as *nefilat hatsadik*, in which the *tsadik*'s special responsibility to the sinful men of his generation requires that he, the leader of the generation, should descend to their base level in order to elevate them as he ascends to the divine.[46] This dangerous 'descent' of the 'higher souls' was the supreme test faced by the *tsadikim*; the successful 'ascent' or redemption of captive souls was predicated on taking that risk. Indebted to the ideas within Lurianic kabbalah which it transformed, the hasidic interpretation of the adventure of descent into *she'ol* led to the creation of the new ritual of reciting Psalm 107 on the Sabbath eve.[47]

The importance of Psalm 107 for mystical circles within central and east European Jewry was known to their opponents as well. Eleazer Fleckeles (1754–1826), a leading rabbinic figure in Prague, which was the centre of Frankism until the beginning of the nineteenth century, devoted the fourth part of his *Olat haḥodesh* to a lengthy sermon, *Ahavat david*, against Shabbateans and Frankists.[48] In the early

[43] Later in the century, the maskil Isaac Meir Dick also employed a paraphrase of the psalm in his popular Yiddish travelogues entitled *Pilei hashem* [Wonders of the Lord] (Vilna, 1856). See Zalman Reizen, 'Campe's "Entdeckung von Amerika", in Yiddish', *YIVO Bleter*, 5/1 (1933), 36 n. 11.

[44] Rivka Schatz-Uffenheimer, *Hasidism as Mysticism: Quietistic Elements in Eighteenth-century Hasidic Thought* (Princeton, NJ, 1993), 342. Menahem Mendel of Bar was also credited with penning *Perush al hodu* [Commentary on *Hodu*], an attribution Gershom Scholem believed to be more faithful to the historical record. See Moshe Rosman, *Founder of Hasidism: The Quest for the Historical Ba'al Shem Tov* (Berkeley, Calif., 1996), 122–3.

[45] Schatz-Uffenheimer, *Hasidism as Mysticism*, 347, 354.

[46] Isaiah Tishby and Joseph Dan, 'Hasidic Thought and Literature', in Avraham Rubinstein (ed.), *Chapters in the Doctrine and History of Hasidism* (Jerusalem, 1977), 263–4, 266. See also Schatz-Uffenheimer, *Hasidism as Mysticism*, 367–8 n. 43, on the psychological dimensions of the doctrine of the 'descent of the *tsadik*' in hasidic thought.

[47] Schatz-Uffenheimer, *Hasidism as Mysticism*, 367–8. In normative rabbinic practice, Psalm 107 was recited either on the eve or the morning of the first day of Passover (ibid. 344).

[48] *Ahavat david* [The Love of David] (Prague, 1800). On Fleckeles's battle against Shabbateanism, see Shmuel Werses, *Haskalah and Shabbateanism: The Story of a Controversy* (Jerusalem, 1988), 63–98.

pages of *Ahavat david*, Fleckeles uses the talmudic discussion of Psalm 107: 23–6 (*Baba batra* 73*b*), in which Rabbah bar Bar Hana relates a series of extraordinary sights that he encountered when travelling by ship as the springboard for his homily against the deviance of the kabbalists and Shabbateans. Fleckeles compares the water in the psalm to the 'water' of the Torah and states that only men who have sufficiently plumbed its depths, through immersion in the Talmud, and the halakhic authorities, are worthy. His sermon also plays on the well-known talmudic discussion of the four permissible forms of interpretation, simple (*peshat*), symbolic (*remez*), homiletic (*derash*), and esoteric (*sod*), in which the last mode of interpretation, the esoteric, was only to be studied after the first three forms had been mastered.[49] Punning on the acronym *pardes* (orchard) for the four modes of interpretation, Fleckeles referred to *sod*, the mode favoured by the Shabbateans and kabbalists, as the wine produced only at the end of the season. The kabbalists who have not mastered the Talmud and the halakhic authorities err like 'old drunkards', who become intoxicated on 'cellared wine' before they have drunk water. Steeped in kabbalah, they will emerge tottering and reeling, inebriated by the esoteric tradition, an allusion to Psalm 107: 27: 'They reel to and fro, and stagger like a drunken man, and are at their wit's end'.[50] The leitmotif of the sermon is that the Shabbateans bypass the traditional system of learning which permitted only those who had mastered the whole rabbinic corpus to turn to mysticism.[51]

Joseph Perl gives further evidence of the widespread knowledge of the hasidic interpretation of the psalm among both mitnagedim and maskilim in eastern Europe. On a small slip of paper, found buried in his archive, Perl had noted that in his opinion Psalm 107: 26 referred to *nefilat hatsadik*. Taking exception to Fleckeles's commentary, he wrote:

> In my limited opinion, it seems that the interpretation of 'they ascend to the Heavens, they go down again to the depths' (Psalm 107: 26) is that sometimes the *tsadik* descends to *katnut* [the 'minor' or 'imperfect' state in which profane activities are carried out] in order to raise up the evil ones (see their holy books); the meaning of 'they go down again to the depths' is that the *tsadik* needs to descend to the depths, meaning to *katnut*, in order to 'ascend to Heaven', to raise the evil ones to Heaven.[52]

Lefin was well acquainted with anti-Shabbatean rabbinic writings and frequently mentioned the writings of Jacob Emden (1697–1776), the great anti-Shabbatean polemicist, as a source for his own perspective on the links between the publication of the Zohar, the spread of Shabbateanism, and the emergence of hasidism.[53] The

[49] BT *Ḥagigah* 14*b*.

[50] Fleckeles, *Ahavat david*, 5*a*.

[51] Isaiah Tishby, *The Wisdom of the Zohar*, 3 vols. (Oxford, 1989), introduction, i. 40.

[52] Joseph Perl Archive, JNULA, folder 59. On *katnut*, see Tishby and Dan, 'Hasidic Thought and Literature', 266, and Gershom Scholem, '*Devekut*, or Communion with God', in id., *The Messianic Idea in Judaism* (New York, 1971), 219–22.

[53] See Joseph Perl Archive, folder 72, pp. 1*b* and 2*a*; Tishby, *The Wisdom of the Zohar*, i. 40; Werses, *Haskalah and Shabbateanism*, 103–6.

fact that both a prominent anti-Shabbatean, Eleazer Fleckeles, and Lefin's virulently anti-hasidic disciple Joseph Perl knew the mystical interpretation of Psalm 107 suggests that the Ba'al Shem Tov's commentary was also known to Lefin himself. It is highly probable that he deliberately appropriated verses 23–4 for his own purposes: by using the psalm and its paraphrase to open *Masaot hayam*, he was attempting to uproot the biblical text from the mystical matrix into which hasidism had placed it. This was not the first time he had used such a strategy. As Shmuel Werses has shown in his study of a manuscript bearing on Lefin's lost and unpublished *Maḥkimat peti* (Making Wise the Simple), Lefin made ironic and caustic use of the verse from Psalms that formed the title of his work. Alluding to Isaiah Horowitz's *Shenei luḥot haberit*, in which the mystic interprets Psalm 19: 8 as an attack on the study of philosophy and an endorsement of kabbalah, Lefin used the psalm to rebut the authority of the Zohar and to denigrate the spread of mysticism.[54]

It is therefore clear that Lefin's use of Psalm 107: 23–6 in *Masaot hayam* had compound meanings: using it as an epigraph gave his Hebrew translation of Campe's tales a traditional cast, while, by appropriating the Ba'al Shem Tov's use of the passage, he made a broad statement about the opposing world-views of hasidism and Haskalah. While the Ba'al Shem Tov and his disciples used the psalm to encode the biblical text with the religious significance specific to hasidism and its leaders, Lefin cast it as an invitation for traditional Jews to gain a broader appreciation of the non-Jewish world, which he believed shared with them such fundamental beliefs as the concept of divine providence. He read the psalm literally, that is as a *pashtan*, using its lyrical biblical poetry to introduce his translations of two treacherous sea-journeys undertaken by Europeans. Encapsulated in Lefin's use of the psalm is his conception of a Haskalah faithful to rational rabbinic Judaism, open to non-Jewish culture, and inimical to hasidism and other forms of Jewish mysticism. Although *Masaot hayam* appears superficially to be a simple, popular translation of the travails of some British sailors and a celebration of God's salvific power, it is in fact an example of Mendel Lefin's subtle use of a literary form to disseminate his programme of enlightenment.

III

In 1791 Lefin penned a French work entitled *Essai d'un plan de réforme ayant pour objet d'éclairer la Nation Juive en Pologne et de redresser par là ses mœurs*; he published it anonymously.[55] The pamphlet's intended audience was the group of Polish reformers engaged in the debates of the Four Year Sejm and, in particular, those on the Committee for Jewish Affairs who were involved with the 'Jewish question'.

54 Shmuel Werses, 'On the Tracks of the Pamphlet, "Making Wise the Simple"', in id. (ed.), *Trends and Forms in Haskalah Literature* (Heb.) (Jerusalem, 1990), 326.

55 In Eisenbach *et al.*, *Materialy do Dziejów Sejmu Czteroletniego*, 409–21. On dating the pamphlet, see Alexander Guterman, 'The Suggestions of the Jews of Poland for the Reforms of their Legal, Economic, Social and Cultural Status' (Heb.) (MA thesis, Jerusalem, 1975), 70.

The debates on the status of the Jews in Poland, which opened on 6 October 1788, focused on the issue of municipal citizenship, but grew to encompass discussion of Jewish attire, taxation, leaseholding on breweries and taverns, and communal autonomy. Lefin's pamphlet was part of the journalistic battle over the reform of Jewish life in Poland which raged throughout this unusually long session of the Sejm.[56] In the pamphlet's first forty-eight sections (of a total 160), Lefin outlined his theory of the development of Judaism, arguing that there were two parallel, if opposing, paths in Judaism's development which had shaped the current contours of Polish Jewish life. One was the rational tradition based on the teachings of Moses Maimonides. The other was the tradition of mysticism which had produced the kabbalistic text, the Zohar, which Lefin believed had spawned the hasidic movement of his own day. He argued that the staunch conservatism and low cultural level of his Polish Jewish brethren was caused by the kabbalah having too great a hold over them. Because he believed that religion was the core of Jewish life, all reform efforts had to begin with religious instruction.[57] Although he treated many of the same issues in his unpublished Hebrew pamphlet *Likutei kelalim*, in writing the *Essai* he directly addressed a gentile audience.

Lefin's interaction with the non-Jewish world is attested not only by his warm reception in the Mendelssohnian circle in Berlin, which included Gotthold Ephraim Lessing and Christoph Friedrich Nicolai, but in his almost lifelong relationship with Prince Adam Kazimierz Czartoryski (1734–1823). When Lefin returned to Poland in 1784 after leaving Berlin, he settled in Mikolajow, which was under the jurisdiction of Czartoryski, then General of Podolia, one of Poland's most powerful magnates and an enlightened Polish reformer. Czartoryski was to become Lefin's patron: he first hired him to tutor his sons in mathematics and philosophy, and later published his political and literary works.[58] It was Czartoryski who made possible the publication of Lefin's 1794 *Sefer refuat ha'am* (Book of Popular Healing) and who undoubtedly played a role in his writing the *Essai*.

Czartoryski's influence notwithstanding, Lefin had his own reasons for writing the French pamphlet. As he explained in an unpublished manuscript entitled 'Teshuvah', it was composed in response to deputy Hugo Kollataj's order and the

[56] See Artur Eisenbach, *The Emancipation of the Jews of Poland, 1780–1870*, ed. Antony Polonsky, trans. Janina Dorosz (London, 1991), 67–112.

[57] Gelber, 'Mendel Lefin of Satanow's Proposals', 273–4.

[58] Abraham Baer Gottlober mentions the story, no doubt apocryphal, of Lefin's chance meeting with Czartoryski, when the noble was visiting a crockery shop in Mikolajow and noticed Christian Wolff's mathematical text in the store. The store just happened to be run by Lefin's wife, who eagerly called her husband to meet the prince; the fortuitous meeting led to lifelong patronage. See Gottlober, 'Memoirs' (Heb.), *Hamagid*, 39 (1873), 356. In a letter written by Joseph Perl to his mentor on 19 Mar. 1826, Perl reprimands Lefin for failing to be in touch with a 'Sir Count Babaweski' who, upon finding out 'accidentally the other day that you live in Tarnopol, felt hurt that he did not know about your presence in Tarnopol. He has very high regard for you. Soon I will be at his place, and will give him all the information.' According to Weinlös, Count Babaweski was not the only Polish aristocrat who had high regard for Lefin. See Weinlös, 'Mendel Lefin of Satanow', 355.

Commission for National Education's[59] agreement (later slightly modified by Father Piattoli) that all Jewish men should shave their beards.[60] No matter how well intentioned non-Jewish reformers might be, Lefin wrote, they did not know what was best for the Jewish community:

The ministers of the 'Deputation' themselves, and so much more so the advisers themselves, are sincere men of truth and justice who sit to legislate for the betterment of the world, to inculcate love and peace in our country, to banish injustice, and to enlighten the people with knowledge beneficial for a man's life. Nevertheless, the wise men of the gentiles do not know what is good for us, and they can err due to the delusions of ill-intended writings that are in their possession, as they will, God forbid.[61]

In the *Essai* Lefin emphasized the centrality of religion for the Jewish community in order to convince the Polish authorities that they should not intervene in internal Jewish affairs. This commitment to the preservation of Jewish communal autonomy is echoed throughout his later Hebrew work *Likutei kelalim*, where he not only mentions Emperor Joseph II's Edict of Tolerance as an example of misguided benevolence, but also refers to a dispute he had with Moses Mendelssohn over the appropriate degree of involvement on the part of non-Jewish authorities in the internal life of the Jewish community.[62] According to Lefin, Mendelssohn believed the selection of Jewish communal representatives should be shouldered by the ruling authorities. This represented a transfer of power to non-Jews that Lefin could not brook. In contradistinction to Mendelssohn and to the Polish reformers who advocated abolition of Jewish communal organizations (the *kahal*), Lefin sought to reform what he perceived was the community's rotten core in order to preserve internal autonomy. He believed that Jews themselves should select

[59] This Commission, established in 1773 with former Jesuit funds, oversaw the reform of education throughout the Commonwealth, and was Europe's first modern ministry of education. See W. H. Zawadzki, *A Man of Honour: Adam Czartoryski as a Statesman of Russia and Poland, 1795–1831* (Oxford, 1993), 17.

[60] N. M. Gelber refers to this document as *Teshuvot be'inyanei hadat* [Responsa on Religious Matters], but the manuscript itself carries no such title. See Gelber, 'Mendel Lefin of Satanow's Proposals', 300. On the top of the first page is simply the word *teshuvah* (responsum). See Joseph Perl Archive, JNULA, folder 72, p. 1*a*. Kollataj's order read: 'All the Jews living or domiciled in the States of the Republic, with no exceptions, must shave off their beards and stop wearing the Jewish dress; they should dress as the Christians in the States of the Republic do.' Quoted in Eisenbach, *Emancipation*, 96.

[61] Joseph Perl Archive, JNULA, folder 72, p. 3*a*; published in Gelber, 'Mendel Lefin of Satanow's Proposals', 276.

[62] Lefin, *Likutei kelalim*, para. 2, cited in Gelber, 'Mendel Lefin of Satanow's Proposals', 287. Emperor Joseph II promulgated the Edict of Tolerance on 2 Jan. 1782, which promised religious tolerance in return for the abolition of Jewish communal autonomy. In particular, Lefin is alluding to those sections of the edict which baldly admit the emperor's goal to make the Jews 'useful' to the state by directing them into artisanal trades and away from commerce. Most Jews perceived the series of edicts, which outlawed the use of Hebrew and Yiddish for commercial records, abolished the autonomy of the rabbinic courts, and imposed conscription as well as Germanic surnames upon the Jewish community, as an attack on their traditional way of life.

their communal supervisors and base all their reforms on the internal edicts (*takanot*) culled from the communal registers of 'upright' Jewish communities, 'those renowned for their reason and justice (such as the reforms of the communities [*kehilot*] of Vilna and Grodno, etc.)'.[63]

In 'Teshuvah' Lefin not only clarified the reasons which compelled him to write the *Essai*, but also explicitly mentioned why he wrote in French and published anonymously.[64] Apparently the deputies of the Commission for National Education wanted to hear Lefin's opinion, no doubt on Czartoryski's recommendation, on the reform of Jewish life in Poland and wanted it to be presented in a way that would be received by the Sejm as a whole. In Lefin's account, they ordered him to write the pamphlet and to:

> Conceal the name of the writer and not even to use the language spoken by him as one of our nation so that the words of this publication would not be suspected as the opinion of one who is affected by the matter, causing [its readers] to shut their ears to the reasonableness of his words. Rather [I should] arrange the words according to the tradition of the [gentile] states alone, and to direct the opinions of the legislators to thank themselves for the truthful uprightness of these edicts.[65]

In making every effort to ensure that his pamphlet's content did not unmask the ruse, Lefin tells us that he was guided by a story in tractate *Me'ilah*,[66] where Reuben, the son of Istroboli, responded to the Roman government's three anti-Jewish decrees (violating the sabbath, proscribing circumcision, and compelling transgression of the laws governing sexual relations) by disguising himself as a Roman. Sitting unrecognized among them, Reuben posed three questions, each carefully framed to elicit a response which would force the Romans to lift the respective edict. Reuben's

[63] Lefin, *Likutei kelalim*, paras. 4, 34, cited in Gelber, 'Mendel Lefin of Satanow's Proposals', 287, 292. Vilna, the capital city of Lithuania, was the home to the *gaon* Rabbi Elijah, who was considered the leader of rationalist traditional Judaism and on whom the rabbinic struggle against hasidism in the 18th cent. centred. See Immanuel Etkes, 'The Vilna Gaon and the Haskalah: Image and Reality', in I. Etkes and Joseph Salmon (eds.), *Chapters in the History of Jewish Society in the Middle Ages and the Modern Period* (Heb.) (Jerusalem, 1980), 192–217.

[64] *Essai d'un plan* was not Lefin's only anonymous work: he published his Yiddish translation of Proverbs (1814) anonymously; moreover, an anonymous anti-hasidic Yiddish comedy, *Di genarte velt* [The Foolish World], which probably appeared in the second decade of the 19th cent. and whose author had connections to the Galician Haskalah, relied on Yiddish translations of Proverbs that are very close to those of Lefin; one Yiddish scholar believed that Lefin himself had written the book. See Chone Shmeruk, *Yiddish Literature: Chapters in its History* (Heb.) (Tel Aviv, 1978), 236–8, esp. n. 66.

[65] Joseph Perl Archive, JNULA, folder 72, p. 3*a*. Gelber argued that in this section of 'Teshuvah' Lefin was referring to an anonymous French work, 'Pensées sur la réforme des Juifs de Pologne', which was translated from the Hebrew and found in Hugo Kollataj's library. This assessment does not make sense, as will be shown below. Hillel Levine has also noted the inaccuracy of Gelber's attribution, and concludes that 'Lefin's comments in "Teshuvah" better fit the anonymous *Essai d'un plan* [than 'Pensées']', yet he does not fully prove his conviction. See Hillel Levine, 'Menachem Mendel Lefin: A Case Study of Judaism and Modernization' (Ph.D. diss., Harvard University, 1974), 176.

[66] See Joseph Perl Archive, JNULA, folder 72, p. 3*a*.

strategy was successful until, as the Talmud notes, 'they came to know that he was a Jew, and [the decrees] were reinstituted'.[67]

Lefin's unpublished 'Teshuvah' reveals more about his strategy in addressing a non-Jewish audience. Striving to deceive his readers even further, he remarks that he quoted 'as much as possible from their great writers on this [political] science, moreover, even from the books of the writers who are haters of Israel, so they would be obligated to say "yes" to the rightness of my words'.[68] A cursory glance at the *Essai* reveals at least one of those 'haters of Israel': on the last page Lefin cites Voltaire, arguably the eighteenth century's most dominant intellectual figure and a man known by his contemporaries, including the maskilim, as an enemy of the Jews.[69] In fact, the very title of Lefin's work may have been a deliberate allusion to Voltaire's *Essai sur les mœurs*, in which the French philosopher cavilled at alleged Jewish greed, misanthropy, and fanaticism. Although he quotes from Voltaire, Lefin argues against his belief in the fundamental incompatibility of Judaism and the modern state; to counter this view he gives prominence to the words of Montesquieu, the eighteenth-century French Enlightenment figure who was perceived as Voltaire's ideological opposite on the Jewish question. By citing Montesquieu on the title-page—'One must pay great attention to the disputes of theologians, but it is necessary to conceal it [that attention] as much as possible. . . . Religion is always the best guarantee that one can have of men's morals'—Lefin both threw down the gauntlet in his covert battle with the hasidim and suggested to his non-Jewish readers that aggressive reform of the Jewish community that disregarded their religious tradition would be an unmitigated disaster.[70]

[67] BT *Me'ilah* 17*a*. Given Lefin's own testimony as to why he deliberately disguised his origins and published *Essai d'un plan* anonymously, Alexander Guterman's conclusion ('Suggestions of the Jews of Poland', 71) that 'one should not suggest that the intention was to blur the Jewish identity of the author; the opposite is true' is quite surprising, particularly because Guterman had access to both Gelber's article and to folder 72 in the Joseph Perl Archive.

[68] Joseph Perl Archive, JNULA, folder 72, p. 3*a*.

[69] This is conclusive evidence that the comment in 'Teshuvah' about his anonymous pamphlet refers to the *Essai*. Lefin apparently thought his pamphlet was successful in amending some of the deputies' more destructive proposals. As he wrote regarding his tactics of concealment and ruse: 'And it stood me in good stead, thank God, that through the words of explanation in this part, the slanderous mouths were closed shut, one by one, as they read it.' On Voltaire's attitude towards the Jews, see Arthur Hertzberg, *The French Enlightenment and the Jews* (New York and Philadelphia, Pa., 1968), esp. pp. 10, 286–7, 290, 297; Manuel, *The Broken Staff*, 193–201. See also Shmuel Feiner, '"The Rebellion of the French and the Freedom of the Jews": The French Revolution in the Image of the Past of the East European Jewish Enlightenment', in Richard Cohen (ed.), *The French Revolution and its Historiography* (Heb.) (Jerusalem, 1991), 240, on Voltaire as the blemish on the image of the Revolution for enlightened Jews who advocated political emancipation.

[70] In the endnotes which clarify the text of the *Essai* Lefin cites Montesquieu again, using the Frenchman's condemnation of Tsar Peter I's compulsory shortening of the beards and restrictions on the clothing of the Muscovites to underscore his conviction that the contemporaneous Polish decree ordering Jewish men to shave their beards was tyrannical. See *Essai d'un plan*, in Eisenbach *et al.*, *Materiały do Dziejów Sejmu Czteroletniego*, 320 n. 14.

IV

Lefin's long life was characterized by the diversity of places he inhabited and the variety of cultural spheres he negotiated. He lived in traditional east European Jewish society, among the enlightened circles of maskilim in Berlin and Galicia, and had regular contact with distinguished members of the Polish nobility. The heterogeneity of his works bespeaks an ability to traverse these cultural realms with apparent ease. *Masaot hayam* and the *Essai* represent only part of his work, but they illustrate his remarkable talent for tailoring his writing to a specific audience. Although *Masaot hayam* was written for internal consumption and the *Essai* for non-Jewish readers, conscious subterfuge shaped the literary form of both. *Masaot hayam* attempted to broaden the geographic horizons of east European Jewry but also to usurp the hasidic movement's expropriation of the 'normative' rabbinic tradition through its mystical interpretation of the Bible. In the *Essai*, Lefin deliberately dissimulated in order to influence the hostile Polish deputies debating the reform of Jewish life in Poland at the Great Sejm, disguising his Jewishness through the work's anonymity, its language of composition, and its reliance on the writings of a well-known antagonist of the Jews. Ever conscious of the audiences he was addressing, Lefin was not someone who simply wrote in a popular style for the 'people', his fellow maskilim, or gentile readers. *Masaot hayam* and the *Essai* both exhibit his highly self-conscious and subtle sense of literary artifice.[71]

[71] On the maskilim's camouflage of European secular literature as Yiddish didactic literature see David Roskies, 'The Medium and the Message of the Maskilic Chapbook', *Jewish Social Studies*, 41 (1979), 275–90.

SIX

The Struggle of the Mitnagedim and Maskilim against Hasidism: Rabbi Jacob Emden and Judah Leib Mieses

YEHUDA FRIEDLANDER

IT is well known that the Haskalah shared a common source with the movements of the mitnagedim and the hasidim. In the words of Dov Sadan, 'beyond their superficial differences they draw nurture from common concealed roots; to be precise: from a single root, and they finally meet at the same pinnacle'.[1] Both the Haskalah and hasidism emerged from the *beit midrash* and the yeshiva, and even after they developed in different directions they clearly retained common spiritual elements. The impressive expertise in Torah literature displayed by the overwhelming majority of the maskilim, acquired in their pre-maskil days, served two purposes. First, they wanted to create a firm basis for the delegitimization of hasidism —in this respect their position closely resembled that of the rabbis who opposed hasidism, the mitnagedim. Their second goal was to lay an ideological foundation for the Haskalah as a legitimate movement within Judaism that was superior to other trends; one of the ways in which they did this was by engaging in an exegetical dispute concerning the sources in halakhic literature which were open to differing interpretations.The nature of the first goal has been examined by Shmuel Feiner, who has demonstrated the resemblance between the attitudes of the maskilim and mitnagedim to hasidism.[2] Both camps made strenuous efforts to delegitimize the movement, the mitnagedim because they regarded it as heresy, the maskilim because they saw it as anti-rational. But, beyond this common purpose, we should not lose sight of the maskilim's further objective: to establish themselves as more legitimate than the hasidim.

An example will serve to illustrate this point. The maskilim attacked the language of the hasidim, who were contemptuous of Hebrew grammar, as corrupt and distorted. Joseph Perl gave trenchant expression to this view in his satirical book

[1] 'Opening Essay, Article A: Testing the Framework', in *Avnei bedek* [Test Stones] (1947; Tel Aviv, 1962), 9–10.

[2] Shmuel Feiner, *Haskalah and History: The Emergence of a Modern Jewish Historical Consciousness* (Heb.) (Jerusalem, 1995), 130.

Megaleh temirin;[3] a later literary-satirical echo of this struggle appears in Shmuel Agnon's *Hakhnasat kalah*, in the encounter between Rabbi Yudel Hasid and his entourage and the maskil Heschel:

Said Heschel to the youngsters, My lads, take care to learn wisdom and style and grammar, for grammar is the foundation of the world.[4] Wherein is a man more than other living creatures? Surely in understanding, in speech and in writing; but if he is not precise and grammatical he might as well be a beast. As the beast in question lows [*go'eh*] without grammar, so he bellows [*po'eh*] without grammar.[5]

As the maskilim knew, an insistence on precision in language was not a new idea, but was anchored in the halakhah (for example in the laws governing the reading of the Shema). Jacob Emden, the halakhic authority and kabbalist,[6] was one leading figure who sharply criticized cantors who were not accurate in their use of Hebrew. He writes at length on this point in his prayer-book *Beit ya'akov*:

You desire to know? Merely examine our advocates, the congregational readers, who fulfil the obligation [of prayer] for the public and for those who are insufficiently proficient. Inspect their fluency in the Holy Tongue [Hebrew]. I will expand on this, openly. Once I heard a learned congregational reader (who sought to demonstrate his punctiliousness by his linguistic perspicacity as he led the prayers), who, when he came to the blessing of Hashkivenu ['Grant us to lie down', in the Ma'ariv service], said *ushemor tse'atenu* ['guard our excrement', instead of *ushemor tsetenu*, 'guard our going']. Then I said to him, 'You must fulfil [*tishmor*] what has crossed your lips' [Deut. 23: 24], 'and when you have squatted, you shall cover up your excrement [*tsetkha*]' [Deut. 23: 14].[7]

The use by the maskilim of the writings of the mitnagedim in their anti-hasidic polemics and satire was thus a deliberate tactic that enabled them to link their ideas with established traditions within Judaism.

This raises the question of what the maskilim really thought about the views of the rabbis who opposed hasidism. Were their interpretations intended to be a clarification of the halakhah, or were they, rather, contentious and satirical? Did the

[3] Joseph Perl (1773–1839) was a leading figure of the Haskalah movement in Galicia. His vigorous fight against the hasidic movement is depicted in *Megaleh temirin* [Revealer of Secrets] (Vienna, 1819) and another satirical work, *Bohen tsadik* [Who Tries the Righteous] (Prague, 1838).

[4] A satirical version of the aphorism 'the righteous is an everlasting foundation' (Prov. 10: 25).

[5] Shmuel Yosef Agnon, *Hakhnasat kalah*, trans. I. M. Lask as *The Bridal Canopy* (New York, 1987), 68. Version A of the Hebrew edition was published in 1930, and version B in 1931.

[6] Emden (pen-name Yavets, 1697–1776), was regarded as one of the most distinguished scholars of his generation; he was also familiar with sciences and languages. He wrote numerous polemical books in which he devoted himself to the campaign against the Shabbateans. His writings express his independence and his original and stormy temperament. Two of his best-known books are *Mitpaḥat sefarim* [A Scroll Wrapper; the title refers to Mishnah *Kelim* 28: 4], 2 pts. in 1 vol. (Altona, 1768; 2nd edn. Lvov, 1871), and *Torat hakenaot* [Law of Jealousies; the title refers to Num. 5: 29] (Amsterdam, 1752; 3rd edn. Lvov, 1870).

[7] *Beit ya'akov* [House of Jacob] (Altona, 1745–7; Lemberg, 1904), 314.

maskilim attack hasidism because it conflicted with their unique understanding of the rabbinic literature; or did they have other motives which led them to treat the works of the rabbis tendentiously?

I will approach these questions by examining how the satirist Judah Leib Mieses[8] understood Jacob Emden's writings on hasidism, and how he used them in his satire; I will also try to establish exactly who Emden was attacking in his polemic. Mieses's interpretation of Emden's views on mysticism and hasidism illuminates the satirist's overall approach to the many rabbinic writings which he used in his polemical and satirical work *Kinat ha'emet*. Mieses was not an isolated case; his struggle against hasidism and, by extension, Shabbateanism, was part of a protracted and far-reaching battle,[9] and his views were shared by many other maskilim. I shall therefore begin my analysis by looking at the historical context, which illuminates hidden levels of the literary text.

Jacob Emden's position on hasidism was equivocal, and to some extent unclear. Historians commonly use a passage of his 1768 work, *Mitpaḥat sefarim*, 2. 31*a*, to claim that he fiercely opposed hasidism. Simon Dubnow thought that Emden was here referring to the hasidism of the movement's founder, the Ba'al Shem Tov (1698–1760), which had not yet spread beyond the areas of Volhynia, Podolia, and eastern Galicia, and argues that Emden was responding to reports that reached him in the years 1750–60.[10] Benzion Dinur does not reject Dubnow's opinion,[11] but is more precise, arguing that Emden's use of the term 'hasidism' specifies the ascetic hasidism of the Shabbatean Judah Hasid,[12] whose followers included Jacob Joseph of Polonnoye and Dov Baer, the Maggid of Mezhirech, two disciples who developed the Ba'al Shem Tov's teachings.[13]

[8] Judah Leib Mieses (1798–1831), a leading member of the Galician Haskalah movement in the early 19th cent., attacked the hasidic sects in his generation, and other obscurantist beliefs in demons and superstitious views. His satirical book *Kinat ha'emet* [The Zeal for Truth] (Vienna, 1828) is written in the form of a dialogue between Maimonides and R. Solomon of Chelm (?1717–1781), the author of *Sefer mirkevet hamishneh* [Chariot of the Second-in-Command], 3 pts. (1: Frankfurt an der Oder, 1751; 2–3: Salonika, 1782); Mieses takes the role of annotator of this dialogue. See Yehuda Friedlander, 'Hasidism as the Image of Demonism: The Satiric Writings of Judah Leib Mises', in Jacob Neusner, Ernst S. Frerichs, and Nahum M. Sarna (eds.), *From Ancient Israel to Modern Judaism: Intellect in Quest of Understanding, in Honor of Marvin Fox*, vol. iii (Atlanta, Ga., 1989), 159–77.

[9] See Jacob Katz, 'On the Relationship between Shabbateanism and the Haskalah and Reform', in his *Halakhah in Straits* (Heb.) (Jerusalem, 1992), 261–78 (the article was first published in 1979). This subject is developed extensively in the comprehensive study by Shmuel Werses, *Haskalah and Shabbateanism: The Story of a Controversy* (Heb.) (Jerusalem, 1988); see also Rachel Elior, 'Nathan Adler and the Frankfurt Pietists: Pietist Groups in Eastern and Central Europe during the Eighteenth Century' (Heb.), *Zion*, 59 (1994), 31–64.

[10] Simon Dubnow, *A History of Hasidism* (Heb.) (1931; Tel Aviv, 1960), 77 n. 1.

[11] Benzion Dinur, *Historical Writings* (Heb.), vol. i (Jerusalem, 1955), 83.

[12] R. Judah Hehasid (?1660–1700), the Shabbatean, not to be confused with the 13th-cent. R. Judah b. Samuel Hehasid, the author of *Sefer ḥasidim*.

[13] Dinur, *Historical Writings*, 161–2. Cf. Gershom Scholem, 'The First Two Testimonies on the Relation between Hasidic Groups and the Ba'al Shem Tov' (Heb.), *Tarbiz*, 20 (1949), 228–40.

Ben Zion Katz agrees with Dubnow. He cites *Mitpaḥat sefarim*, 2. 31*a*, adding a parallel fragmentary quotation from *Ḥali ketem*, a sermon Emden published a year before his death, in which he repeats the ideas expressed in *Mitpaḥat sefarim*.[14] Katz understands from this that Emden opposed the hasidism that had emerged in his lifetime, that is, the hasidism of the Ba'al Shem Tov.

A completely different opinion was held by Abraham Bick, a descendant of Emden. Bick questions whether Emden really was a scathing critic of hasidism: 'It cannot be determined with certainty that his statements against "the new sect of hasidim" were made in opposition to the hasidism of the Ba'al Shem Tov. He may possibly have been referring to the remaining Shabbateans and Frankists.'[15] Bick reasons that, since Jacob Emden's son, Rabbi Meir, greatly respected the Ba'al Shem Tov,[16] and since the leading founders of hasidism wrote in praise of Emden's books,[17] if Emden had really fought against hasidism, its leaders would not have praised him. Notwithstanding the fact that Bick is an interested party, his remarks represent a distinctive interpretation of Emden's work. Indeed, a reading of *Ḥali ketem* in its entirety supports Bick's position more than Ben Zion Katz's. Emden's own reliance in *Ḥali ketem* on his *Mitpaḥat sefarim* confirms the hypothesis that he was not referring specifically to the hasidism of the Ba'al Shem Tov; I will develop this point in more detail below.

In contrast to Perl, who uses the hostile documentation method in *Megaleh*

[14] *Ḥali ketem* [Ornament of Fine Gold]: the title refers to Prov. 26: 12, 'as an earring of gold, and an ornament of fine gold, so is a wise reprover upon an obedient ear'. *Ḥali ketem* was printed in *Tefilat yesharim* [Prayer of the Upright] (Altona, 1775), 22*b*–28*a*. See p. 23*b*:

> And every day sects which spring from this cursed one are renewed. One of these consists of those who dance, clap their hands, strike their hands against each other, and [strike] with the middle finger in the middle of the Shemoneh Esreh prayer, and [engage in] other despicable acts which our forefathers and elders could not imagine, and they are almost in my eyes as Ba'al-worshippers. I have already mentioned them in my book the *Mitpaḥat*: see there, p. 31. There also remains in our place a sect of the destructive ones, people who are ignorant and empty of the revealed teachings in the Torah. They burst in to engage in the secrets of the Torah and the kabbalah; and they make use of [Holy] Names to dig up worthless treasures and a pit which though empty of the water of Torah [contains] serpents and scorpions [cf. Gen. 37: 24, 'and the pit was empty, there was no water in it'; BT *Shabat* 22*a*, 'There is no water in it, but there are serpents and scorpions in it'] . . . who are certainly a branch of the heretics . . . and filthy ones of the youth, the jackal Eibeschütz, who think to grasp the Tree of Life and the soul of the Torah. . . . Consequently, my brothers, extreme vigilance is required against these serpents and scorpions, lest desolation be drawn from the secret [knowledge]. (Cited in Ben Zion Katz, *Rabbinate, Hasidism, and Haskalah* (Heb.), vol. i (Tel Aviv, 1956), pt. 2, p. 186.)

On his use of the word 'secret' Emden goes on: 'Do not read "the desolation" [*hashod*, Isa. 51: 19], but rather "the secret" [*hasod*], i.e. the secret which is the hidden things of the Torah and the kabbalistic teachings from the time that the impudent ones of the generation made light of them and began to use the Names for their own benefit and use; [but] these have become a stumbling-block for them, and have caused desolation, which is [the meaning of] the text.'

[15] Abraham Bick [Shauli], *Rabbi Jacob Emden* (Heb.) (Jerusalem, 1975), 36.

[16] Ibid.

[17] Ibid. 37–9.

temirin,[18] Mieses employs the supportive documentation method in *Kinat ha'emet*, explicitly citing Emden eight times, and identifying completely with him in the process.[19] His first citation (p. 23), is of *Mitpaḥat sefarim*, 2. 31*a*; this passage, analysed below, appears in a note written by Mieses in his role as annotator to illustrate claims about the behaviour of the Ba'al Shem Tov and his disciples: that they immersed themselves in the ritual bath every day even in the winter; that they drew out to great length new prayers, 'recently composed by someone insane, whose mind is confused, a man of dreams, whose power of imagination exceeds that of his intellect'; and that they engaged in excessive study of the kabbalah.[20] Mieses's use of Emden's passage indicates that he took it to refer to the followers of the Ba'al Shem Tov; otherwise, it would not have been relevant to his own attack on these hasidim. In this, I do not believe that Mieses was intentionally misrepresenting Emden's meaning, for it may be assumed that the fine distinctions between the different sects of hasidism were insufficiently clear in those days, and that the 'exceptional' groups were perceived as a single body. Moreover, for Mieses, who rejected both hasidism and Shabbateanism, the distinctions between the two sects were immaterial.

In order to determine exactly who Emden was referring to I will now examine *Mitpaḥat sefarim*, 2. 31*a* in its entirety; I will then compare it to additional passages from Emden's writings.

But we, who dwell in houses of clay,[21] must know our duty in this place of darkness, and thereby be enabled to see the light of the upper world. An ignoramus cannot be pious [*ḥasid*], as I wrote at length at the beginning of the book *Hashevet*.[22] And also in this book, *Mitpaḥat*, we refute the stupid, stubborn ones who think to exert themselves to ascend in the Divine Chariot and enter the chambers of the King of the Universe, to enter the gate of divine mysteries, to the concealed treasures. And if they are not utter fools they are wild asses of simpletons, who are incapable of penetrating even the fifth material.[23] How are they untrue to themselves, that they will pass on further, where there is no matter, but only form, no darkness, but only light? For even with regard to their soul, which is entwined in their bosom, they are incapable of perceiving its essence, nature, and form, and they strive in vain to explore it. The receptacle of their comprehension will return empty. How will the one who searches in the exalted secrets not be ashamed and blush, [for] wisdom [is un-

18 For Perl's use of the method of hostile documentation, whereby an author's works are selectively quoted from to create a negative picture, see Shmuel Werses, 'The Satirical Methods of Joseph Perl', in id., *Story and Source: Studies in the Development of Hebrew Prose* (Heb.) (Ramat Gan, 1971), 21–8.

19 *Kinat ha'emet*, 23, 24, 25, 134, 135 (twice), 136, 137.

20 Ibid. 23–6. See also Yehuda Friedlander, *Hebrew Satire in Europe*, iii: *The Nineteenth Century* (Ramat Gan, 1994), 28–30, 86, 112.

21 i.e. our bodies; see Job 4: 19: 'How much less in them that dwell in houses of clay'.

22 The reference is to *Shevet legav kesilim: Kuntres shelishi mitokh sefer shimush* [A Rod for the Fool's Back: A Chapter from the Book of Service] (Amsterdam, 1758–62); the first part of the title refers to Prov. 26: 3. This statement is based on Mishnah *Pirkei avot* 2: 5: 'nor can an ignorant person be pious'.

23 The reference is to the 'fifth element' of the celestial spheres and bodies, which are eternal.

obtainable] to a fool,[24] if in the gate of the wise he will not open his mouth, to understand and to teach what Israel will do, as is proper regarding every action there, not fearing lest he be called 'guilty'. But now, every silly fool who has no knowledge, even of what is inevitable or impossible, and lacks all discernment, possessing neither comprehension nor wisdom, and is ev[en] ignorant of the Bible, and also Talmud and Mishnah, who has no understanding of the Holy Tongue, [nevertheless] is occupied with and studies the book of the Zohar. [He does this] without the knowledge [to distinguish] between good and evil, and is certainly incapable of directly reading the book of the Zohar and other kabbalistic works. He whispers and does not know what he whispers.[25] I writhed to hear that now a new sect of hasidim has recently come into existence in Volhynia and Podolia. And some of them have come to this state as well. They are occupied only with the book of the Zohar and the kabbalistic books. And they prolong their prayer for half the day, much more than the early pietists, who would tarry only one hour in prayer.[26] But in addition to this, according to what was related to me, they engage in strange and disgraceful movement in the Shemoneh Esreh prayer. They strike with their hands and sway to the sides, with their heads thrown back and their faces and eyes pointing upwards.This is contrary to what our Sages, of blessed memory, said, that the eyes must be [directed] downward and the heart upwards.[27] In *Tanḥuma*, it is stated that the eyes are to be [directed] upwards only during the Kedushah, and [then they must be] closed,[28] as it is written in the *Sulam*.[29] In a responsum, the Rama forbade any movement during prayer.[30] I have moved heaven and earth [lit. 'danced around a great deal'—an obvious comment on these movements] to find an explanation, to permit only some of these movements of the body, back and forth, for it is

[24] i.e. 'wisdom to a fool is as precious stones, neither of which he possesses', after Prov. 24: 7: 'Wisdom is as unobtainable to a fool as corals, he opens not his mouth in the gate.'

[25] After BT *Sotah* 22*a*: 'There is a popular saying, "The magician mumbles but he does not know what he says."' The Gemara provides various definitions for the term *am ha'arets*, an ignoramus.

[26] See Mishnah *Berakhot* 30*b*: 'The early pious men used to wait an hour before praying, so that they might concentrate their thoughts on their Father in Heaven.'

[27] See BT *Yevamot* 105*b*: 'A person who prays must direct his eyes below and his heart above.'

[28] See *Tanḥuma*, 'Tsav' 13: '"And with two, he flew" (Isa. 6: 2)—and with wings shall he fly[?]. Rather, based on this, [the Sages] of blessed memory instituted that man must rise on his feet when the reader recites "K[adosh], k[adosh], k[adosh], Hashem Tsevaot" [Holy, holy, holy is the Lord of Hosts]'; *Tur shulḥan arukh*: *Oraḥ ḥayim*, Laws of Prayer, 125: 'It is the practice of Sephardi Jews to cast their eyes down when they recite "K[adosh], k[adosh], k[adosh]", while those from Ashkenaz and France direct their eyes upward and raise their bodies up.' See *Beit yosef*, chapter entitled 'Venohagim', and *Hagahot bedek bayit*, based on the above passage in *Tanḥuma*.

[29] See Jacob Emden, 'Sulam beit el mutsav artsah verosho magia shemaimah' [The Ladder of Bethel is set up on the earth, and the top of it reaches to heaven], introduction to his *Beit ya'akov*, 29*a* (Lemberg edn., p. 12).

[30] Rama: R. Menahem Azariah of Fano (1548–1620), a *posek* (halakhic authority) and kabbalist. Known *inter alia* for the collection of responsa *She'elot uteshuvot harama* (Venice, 1600; Jerusalem, 1963). The reference here is to p. 113 (Jerusalem edn., p. 240). It is of interest that in 'Sulam beit el' Jacob Emden notes: 'In my humble opinion, it is not determined, and we have found, regarding our m[aster], R[abbi] J[acob b. Moses] [Moe]ll[in] [Maharil, 1365–1427; *Minhagei maharil* was first published in Sabionetta, 1556], the fact is, my master acted in this manner, as is attested by his pupils at the beginning of the Laws of Prayer, that he would move his body backward and forward. This was the case with an outstanding rabbi and hasid, and we certainly, undoubtedly, can rely upon his [practice].'

permitted only to arouse the essential powers and spirits, as it is written in our 'Ladder of Bethel',[31] The early ones made no uproar in their prayers. According to the book of the Zohar, this has been determined [*sumah*][32] that when they stood, they let down their wings.[33] While these [on the other hand] spread their wings to fly to heaven. And you may wonder, whether they would do so before a king of flesh and blood, who would cast them to the ground, so that all their limbs would be shattered, and all their bones would be broken in pieces.[34] In truth, if I would see one of great appearance[35] who does these things which our forefathers, of blessed memory, the true pietists, did not imagine, I would cut their thighs with iron instruments.[36]

This text clearly shows how Emden lashed out against those who were not knowledgeable in either the revealed or the hidden Torah, but who nevertheless sought to become expert in esoteric teachings. He attacked the phenomenon of Jews who were not scholars engaging in the study of the Zohar and kabbalistic works, adding to his condemnation his opinion of the 'new sect of hasidim', which he does not define but rather describes through its actions. In *Torat hakenaot*, first published in 1752, Emden writes explicitly: 'And from this evil sprouted a new sect of hasidim in Poland, which is a band named after Rabbi Judah Hasid,[37] all of which is built entirely on the collapsed foundation and worthless plaster of Shabbetai Tsevi, may the name of the wicked rot, even though it shows kindness to its companions.'[38]

Emden's statements in *Mitpaḥat sefarim* cannot be separated from the criticisms of hasidism expressed by Solomon of Chelm in his book *Mirkevet hamishneh* (1751) and by Israel of Zamosc in *Nezed hadema* (1773).[39] Together these three scholars represent the mainstream approach of eighteenth-century Ashkenazi mitnagedim to the various hasidic sects. The question of the exact identity of the 'hasidim'

[31] See above, n. 29.

[32] After 2 Sam. 13: 32: 'for by the appointment of Absalom this has been determined [*ketiv: simah; keri: somah*]'.

[33] After Ezek. 1: 24: 'when they stood, they let down their wings [and therefore were silent]'. See also Zohar, 'Shelaḥ', I: 173*a*: 'And in silence they remained standing without moving.'

[34] After Dan. 6: 25: 'and broke all their bones in pieces' (i.e. crushed them).

[35] After BT *Bava kama* 81*b*: 'Who is that man who wants to show off [lit. 'of great appearance'] in front of us?'

[36] i.e. I would excommunicate them, after BT *Bava kama* 81*b*: 'If you were not R. Judah ben Kenosa, I would have sawed your joints with an iron saw.' See Friedlander, *Hebrew Satire*, iii. 29–30, n. 63.

[37] See above, n. 12.

[38] Following BT *Ḥulin* 63*a*: 'R. Judah said: The *ḥasidah* is the white stork. And why is it called *ḥasidah*? Because it shows kindness [*ḥasidut*] to its companions.' See *Torat hakenaot*, 26 (Lvov edn., p. 55).

[39] For Solomon of Chelm, see above, n. 8. The introduction to *Sefer mirkevet hamishneh* includes criticism of the hasidim. See Yehuda Friedlander, *Hebrew Satire in Europe*, ii: *The Eighteenth and Nineteenth Centuries* (Heb.) (Ramat Gan, 1989), 19–23. Israel of Zamosc (?1700–72) was a talmudist and mathematician. The title *Nezed hadema* refers to a pottage containing ingredients of *terumah* (tithe), based on BT *Ḥulin* 34*b* and Mishnah *Tohorot* 2: 3: 'a dish mixed with *terumah*'. The various meanings of the term *Nezed hadema* are discussed in Friedlander, *Hebrew Satire*, ii. 19–21.

mentioned in *Mirkevet hamishneh* and *Nezed hadema* has been of great interest to researchers specializing in this period, who have discussed their verbal parallels and the similarity of their imagery.[40]

Mieses's second reference to Emden comes shortly after the first (p. 24): he notes generally that Emden claims in *Torat hakenaot* that the new sect of hasidim constitutes the 'remnant of Shabbetai Tsevi'.[41] Mieses does not explicitly identify the members of the new sect of hasidim.

The third citation (on p. 25) is from *Mitpaḥat sefarim*, 1. 6*b*:

> Who requires [me] to accept whatever can be conceived by a person as true and divine secrets? Even if he is wise and a great intellect in Israel, who will trust in him? Let him provide himself with securities and guarantees, so that he will not err in his imagination.[42]

Like the first citation, this also appears as a parenthetical comment by Mieses the annotator in the context of his discussion of the mad individual 'whose power of imagination exceeds that of his intellect'. Mieses uses Emden's attack to support his own criticism of the 'traditional authority of the Sages', in which he, as a maskil, was so interested.[43]

The fourth citation (on p. 134) is from *Mitpaḥat sefarim*, 2. 30*b*:

> Extreme vigilance is required now, so as not to be led astray by the fraudulent writings by the writers of iniquity and the writings of perverseness of Shabbetai Tsevi, may the name of the wicked rot, and his cursed disciples, which have become mingled within the books of the kabbalists, and especially the writings of R. Isaac Luria have been falsified by these despicable ones.[44]

Mieses uses this citation, framed (with slight changes) as a parenthetical comment by himself as annotator, to undermine the kabbalistic foundations of hasidism. He also puts the following words into the mouth of Solomon of Chelm:

> For first of all, it would be worthwhile for one of the educated [*mimaskilei*] of our people to write some books against the contents of the books of the new and the old kabbalah, especially against the Zohar, and to prove, in accordance with the Torah and intellect, how its words are deceitful and vain, and that they are all full of nonsense and heresy.[45]

The fifth and sixth times, Mieses cites, as parenthetical comments, passages from *Torat hakenaot* and *Mitpaḥat sefarim* which discuss the falsification of kabbalistic works, placing harsh words in the mouth of Solomon of Chelm regarding the distortion of the Zohar:

40 Suffice it to say that verbal similarity does not necessarily attest to the identity of the presumed subjects. See Friedlander, *Hebrew Satire*, ii. 15–35.

41 See also ibid. iii. 112, 131 n. 12*b*, and n. 38 above.

42 Lvov edn., p. 12; see Friedlander, *Hebrew Satire*, iii. 114, 132 n. 10d.

43 See Yehuda Friedlander, 'The Revolt against "Traditional Authority of the Sages" in Hebrew Satire in the Nineteenth Century' (Heb.), in Avigdor Shinan (ed.), *Proceedings of the Sixth World Congress of Jewish Studies*, vol. iii (Jerusalem, 1977), 363–76.

44 Lvov edn., p. 77; see Friedlander, *Hebrew Satire*, iii. 45 n. 128; Werses, *Haskalah and Shabbateanism*, 113.

45 *Kinat ha'emet*, 134; see Friedlander, *Hebrew Satire*, iii. 45.

One of these deceivers, whose name is R. Moses de Leon, wrote this book [the Zohar] at the beginning of the sixth millennium, attributing it to the *tanna* R. Simeon bar Yohai in the language of the Chaldaeans [i.e. Aramaic]; he undoubtedly did this intentionally, either so that the masses would think that it had been written during the time when the Israelites spoke and read this language fluently, and was therefore a very ancient composition; or so that most of the people would accept it as a book which no one could understand, and accordingly put it on a pedestal, for it is their way to wonder at and honour incomprehensible works and esoteric teachings.[46]

Mieses had to undermine the sanctity and credibility of the Zohar in order to weaken the link between Judaism and mysticism, and especially hasidism; the authority of Jacob Emden served to support this goal. The rabbinic polemic surrounding the Zohar and the struggle of the maskilim against the work were in harmony; it should be emphasized, however, that the motives of the maskilim and those of Emden were completely different. The former sought to destroy completely the authority and sanctity of the Zohar and other kabbalistic writings which could not be reconciled with European rationalism, while Emden sought to effect internal reform. As a true kabbalist he held the Zohar to be holy, and was consequently concerned about the falsifications which had been introduced into it.[47] Two passages from his writings are relevant. The first is from *Torat hakenaot*, 49*a*: '*Sefer razi'el* is also possessed by everyone, but is apparently a forgery.'[48] This is taken from an extensive discussion of the origins of the various books attributed to angels. Emden adopts a critical-rationalist approach: 'It is improbable that an angel would write a large book filled with wisdom such as this for any human, from the time of Adam to the present, or for anyone considered to be wise or discerning. Proof from what was must be taken for what is, for there is no shadow of anything new under the sun.' He continues:

Nevertheless, there are many books in the Zohar that came to the ancient ones from angels, such as *Sefer de'adam*, *Sefer deḥanokh*, *Sefer deshelomoh malka*[49] [that came] from Ashmodai,[50] and similar good things in the Zohar. *Sefer razi'el* is also possessed by everyone, but is apparently a forgery. . . . And this appears to belong to the category of impossible things.[51]

The second passage is from *Mitpaḥat sefarim*, I. 17*b*: 'This is not something new in compositions that—we find in most instances—are attributed to a great authority,

[46] *Kinat ha'emet*, 136; see Friedlander, *Hebrew Satire*, iii. 45–7.

[47] *Mitpaḥat sefarim*, I. 2*b* (Lvov edn., p. 2): 'But I have no doubts [about this] at all. Notwithstanding the praise [due] the book of the Zohar, it could not escape the introduction into it of things which have no basis.'

[48] Lvov edn., p. 100. *Sefer razi'el* is an ancient kabbalistic book: an old legend tells how the angel Razi'el gave it to Adam.

[49] Three ancient kabbalistic books, the first related to Adam and cited in the Zohar; the second, also cited in the Zohar, related to Enoch (Gen. 5: 24; there is a legend that Enoch became an angel); and the third related to King Solomon.

[50] Ashmodai is the king of the demons (see BT *Gitin* 68*a*).

[51] *Torat hakenaot*, 49*a* (Lvov edn., p. 100).

as happened with several commentaries which are falsely attributed to Rashi.'[52] It is noteworthy that, since the maskilim were calling for a critical approach to the sources, the entire subject of falsification served them well.

The seventh and eighth times, in the same context, Mieses once again cites *Mitpaḥat sefarim*, ii. 37*a*, para. 92, and also relies on an additional passage on p. 82*a*. The subject under discussion is the authorship of the Zohar, and Moses de Leon's role in its composition:[53]

However, the love of truth is more beloved to me than the love of any desired thing upon the earth, [or of] the foolishness which is done on earth. I will not deny the holy sayings [by the author of *Sefer yuḥasin*] regarding the reality of the composition of the Zohar, as it first appeared, which the wise and pious one, the author of *Sefer yuḥasin*, initially attributed to the rabbi, the kabbalist, Rabbi Isaac of Acre . . . I will present them here, all of them, in their entirety, as they were written, in order to subject them to examination, to investigate the incessant report[s], [to reveal the things that were deep in the hearts of the ones who reported this] if this is so, or if everything is foolishness, something which was fabricated in a transient spirit of falseness. The mind of the wise will hear, to judge between truth and falsehood, and to deduce [the truth].[54]

In these lines we see Emden taking the approach of a responsible religious leader. Real satire has an ethical base, and Emden was convinced that he had a mission to save Judaism from false sects who, in his view, merely pretended to represent authentic Judaism.

For Mieses the differences between the various mystical movements were irrelevant; in general, his satirical work emphasizes the struggle against the hasidism of the Ba'al Shem Tov, the heir of Shabbateanism and various mystical movements. However, in relying on Jacob Emden he blurs the distinction between the followers of Judah Hasid and those of the Besht and his disciples, and this has left its mark on the writings of historians, who have not taken account of how Emden confuses them in his own writings.

[52] Lvov edn., p. 40; cited in *Kinat ha'emet*, 135.

[53] Jacob Emden cites a story about Moses de Leon which appears in Abraham b. Samuel Zacuto, *Sefer yuḥasin* [Book of Pedigrees] (Constantinople, 1566), 143*b*. Cf. *Sefer yuḥasin hashalem* [Complete Book of Pedigrees], ed. Abraham Hayim Freimann (Frankfurt am Main, 1925), 95–6. Although Mieses quotes from *Mitpaḥat sefarim*, he attests that he saw a copy of the Constantinople edition in the library of Joseph Perl. Jacob Emden annotated a rare edition he possessed; these notes were published in *Sefer yuḥasin*, ed. Tsevi Filipowski (London and Edinburgh, 1857).

[54] *Mitpaḥat sefarim*, 2. 37*a*, para. 92 (Lvov edn., pp. 92–3); *Kinat ha'emet*, 136–7.

SEVEN

Magic and Miracle-Workers in the Literature of the Haskalah

IMMANUEL ETKES

THE Haskalah movement, following the lead of its parent, the European Enlightenment, declared all-out war on 'superstition'.[1] Motivated by the desire to reform Judaism and Jewish society according to the dictates of reason, the maskilim aspired to uproot superstition and to eradicate behaviour patterns they considered mere vestiges of ignorance and illusion. One of their prime targets was the belief in magic in all its manifestations.

This chapter will discuss the position of the Haskalah movement regarding magic and magicians (*ba'alei shem*), as revealed in the Haskalah literature of nineteenth-century eastern Europe. Haskalah authors, as we know, considered magic and hasidism to be two sides of the same coin and fought both with equal ferocity: I discuss the significance of this juxtaposition below. First, however, I will examine some pertinent excerpts from the literature and try to determine its influence on the way magic and *ba'alei shem* have been seen in the historiography of hasidism. Finally, I shall address the question: what does Haskalah literature's attitude to magic and *ba'alei shem* tell us of the inner world of the Haskalah?

I

An early critic of magic and *ba'alei shem*, anticipating Haskalah literature by a few decades, was Solomon Maimon (1753–1800), who wrote the following in his memoirs:

> A well-known kabbalist, R. Joel Ba'al Shem, earned much fame at the time by virtue of a few successful healings, achieved with the help of his medicinal knowledge and illusory trickery; he claimed, however, to have done all this through practical kabbalah and the power of the Ineffable Name. This gained him much renown in Poland.[2]

Maimon returns several times to the assertion that the *ba'alei shem* employed 'conventional medications' and that their so-called magical powers were mere illusions. His view represents the position of a devout rationalist, deeply troubled by the

[1] On the European Enlightenment's war against superstition in general and the belief in sorcery in particular see Paul Hazard, *The European Mind 1680–1715* (Harmondsworth, 1964), 185–212.

[2] Solomon Maimon, *Ḥayai* [My Life] (1792; Tel Aviv, 1953), 137.

fact that *ba'alei shem* successfully gained people's confidence. It was important, he believed, that his readers should have no doubt as to the real reason for the magicians' successes.

The equation of magic with the hasidic movement is a central motif in nineteenth-century Haskalah satire.[3] There is no more typical representative of the trend than Joseph Perl (1773–1839). As early as 1819, in the preface to his book *Megaleh temirin*, he describes a wonderful experience that befell the 'anthologizer and editor'. Portrayed by Perl as a typical hasid, this person relates the following tale:

When I journeyed from the Holy Community of Medzibezh to the Holy Community of Zuanitz and went astray by night . . . exhausted by the journey, I fainted away and fell upon a certain stone. There came an old man and woke me, and I was terrified of this old man . . . I asked him, Who are you? and he said, I am the guardian posted by the Besht to watch over the writings of R. Adam, which he enclosed in this stone. And since the Besht commanded me to stand here on guard, until some person should stray from the path in the dark . . . and give him one of the said writings, I am therefore awakening you and am full of joy that the time has come. . . . And I began to weep before him and implore him to give me all the writings, but he said that he was not permitted to do so. And forthwith he chanted a spell, and a small crack formed in the stone. . . . A piece of paper emerged through the crack, and the guard took the paper and the stone as immediately closed. The guard then took that paper and told me that, by the power of what was written thereon, I would be able to become invisible—that is, provided I kept it in my pocket, but specifically in my right pocket, for if I were to keep it in my left pocket the writing would be useless . . .[4]

Perl's anti-hasidic satire was based on the book *Shivḥei habesht* (1814)—in this particular case on the stories about Rabbi Adam Ba'al Shem. These stories purported to reveal the source of the Ba'al Shem Tov's knowledge as a *ba'al shem*: the 'writings' that Rabbi Adam gave the Besht contained esoteric magical lore. It is also related in *Shivḥei habesht* that the Besht sealed up Rabbi Adam's 'writings' in a stone on a nearby mountain.[5] The blurred borderlines between legend and reality exemplified in the above excerpt are a typical feature of hasidism as described by Perl. The magical elements in the Besht's person and biography, which the maskil sees as nothing but delusion or hallucination, are perfectly real for the hasid.

The hasid's uncritical acceptance of the legend about the Besht is just one side of the coin. The other is the hasidic conviction that even the contemporary leaders of hasidism were capable of performing miracles like those attributed to the Besht.

[3] On Haskalah satire and its role in the struggle against hasidism see Shmuel Werses, 'Hasidism in the Eyes of Haskalah Literature: From the Polemic of Galician Maskilim', in Immanuel Etkes (ed.), *Trends and Forms in Haskalah Literature* (Heb.) (Jerusalem, 1990), 91–109.

[4] Joseph Perl, *Megaleh temirin* [Revealer of Secrets] (Vienna, 1819), 1*b*.

[5] Dov Ber b. Shmuel of Linits, *Shivḥei habesht* [Praises of the Ba'al Shem Tov] (Kopys 1814–15); ed. Abraham Rubinstein (Jerusalem, 1992), 41–6, 59. On the stories of Rabbi Adam in *Shivḥei habesht* and their sources and purpose, see Chone Shmeruk, 'The Stories about R. Adam Ba'al Shem and their Formulations in the Versions of the Book *Shivḥei habesht*' (Heb.), *Zion*, 28 (1963), 86–105; Joseph Dan, *The Hasidic Story* (Heb.) (Jerusalem, 1975), 79–83.

Indeed, one of Perl's characters, Rabbi Zelig Letitshiber, says: 'And now all respond in unison and exclaim with awe . . . that the *tsadikim* can do everything their heart desires, and that they compel the Lord, praise be to Him, to do everything they wish, and that they perform wondrous deeds.'[6] The letters that make up Perl's book are full of stories of hasidim and their wives who appeal to the *tsadik* and avail themselves of his miraculous powers. While doing his best to demonstrate the ignorant simple-mindedness of the rank-and-file hasidim, Perl spares no effort to expose the avarice of their leaders, the *tsadikim*. To that end he repeatedly returns to the subject of the redemption money (*pidyon*) that the hasidim bring their leaders when they come to them for help.[7]

Underlying Perl's satire is the assumption that no one—at least, among his enlightened readers—doubts the ridiculous and contemptible nature of magic in general and of the belief in the magical powers of the hasidic leaders in particular. Hence the mere description of various instances of this belief among the hasidim should suffice to provoke derision and revulsion. Nevertheless, Perl did not make magic the focus of his critique of hasidism merely because he considered it a weak point where the enemy was most vulnerable to attack. He was in fact convinced that belief in the miracles performed by the Besht or the contemporary *tsadikim* was a major factor in the steady growth and spread of hasidism. It was therefore imperative to challenge such beliefs.[8]

While Perl's strong point was the indirect barb of parody, another Galician maskil preferred to mount a direct frontal attack. Judah Leib Mieses (1798–1831) indeed devoted a larger part of his *Kinat ha'emet* (1828) to a fierce assault on superstitious beliefs in demons and sorcery. Relying on the views of some of the greatest Jewish sages in the past, particularly Maimonides, Mieses argued that 'pure' Judaism rejected such beliefs, which were not only baseless but also at times dangerous. Many foolish practices, deleterious to the moral fibre of the Jewish people, were the outcome of such superstitions.

Mieses considered hasidism a misfortune that had befallen the Jewish people because of their belief in demons and sorcery, 'In so far as only people who believe in demons and sorcery . . . might ascribe any sanctity to the leaders and heads of this sect'. Like Perl and other maskilim, Mieses also argued that belief in the hasidic leaders' magical powers was basic to the existence of the despised movement. It was only a natural conclusion that those who wished 'for the eradication of this sect . . . from the Jewish people' must tackle the popular belief in demons and sorcery.[9]

Like most maskilim of this time, Mieses was convinced that these obscurantist beliefs were the outgrowths of ignorance and folly. People of learning and wisdom

[6] *Megaleh temirin*, letter 1 (p. 3*a*).

[7] Ibid. 5*b*, 11*a*, 13*b*, 33*a*–*b*, and *passim*.

[8] Ibid., e.g. letter 76 (p. 30).

[9] *Kinat ha'emet* [The Zeal for Truth] (Vienna, 1828), 6–8. On Mieses and his book see Yehuda Friedlander, *Hebrew Satire in Europe*, iii: *The Nineteenth Century* (Heb.) (Ramat Gan, 1994), and also Ch. 6 in the present volume.

would never tolerate them. In an attempt to illustrate this important principle, Mieses cited no less an example than the Besht himself.

There was once a person, of little knowledge, named Israel son of Eliezer, known among the masses as Ba'al Shem. His ancestors had been from the poorest and basest of the people living in a certain village in Poland (the home of darkness and ignorance), and therefore they could not afford to hire a teacher for him, to tutor him in his youth. . . . And even later, when the boy grew up, he did not mix with the wise of heart, nor did his feet cross their threshold, for his heart was void of sense and his mind quite incapable of understanding scholarly things. Therefore, even as an adult, he was ignorant, bereft of words of learning and knowledge, not understanding any passage of the Talmud, how much less so of the Bible . . .[10]

Thus the Besht's biography was presented as proof that poverty, ignorance, and stupidity went hand in hand to mould the character of the *ba'alei shem*. Where, then, did the Besht obtain the knowledge he needed to become a *ba'al shem*? Mieses's explanation is also no credit to the founder of hasidism: the Besht learned from the non-Jewish peasants among whom he lived how to pick medicinal herbs and how to use them. He took up sorcery after realizing that herbal healing would not earn him the fame he wanted. The model that he chose to emulate was that of the non-Jewish sorcerer.[11] In sum, the two main factors that shaped the Besht's career were poverty and ignorance on the one hand, and the non-Jewish subculture on the other. No wonder, therefore, that conclusions could be drawn from the person of the Besht as to the nature of his followers.

Views like those of Perl and Mieses were so deeply entrenched among the Galician maskilim that their colleagues and fellow-writers in Italy embraced them too.[12] A typical example is a letter written by Samuel David Luzzatto (1800–65) to his maskil friend Samuel Leib Goldenberg. The occasion for the correspondence was a rumour that the hasidic leader Rabbi Israel of Ruzhin (1797–1850) had settled in Galicia. This news inspired Luzzatto to set out his view of hasidic beliefs in the *tsadik*'s supernatural powers. His account begins as follows:

I know not whether to laugh or to weep at the rumour that you have conveyed, my friend, concerning that man named Israel, bearing the same name as his master Israel Ba'al Shem Tov, who has led the children of Israel astray this past generation in your country; that same Ba'al Shem Tov who received books of secrets and mysteries from R. Adam, who moved the king's palace through the power of Names and brought it to another city, that same Besht who moves mountains from their place and brings them near one another . . . that same Besht who found the frog in the desert in which was embodied a Jewish soul who had neglected [the commandment of] washing the hands, and redeemed that soul, which had already spent five centuries in the body of a frog; that same Besht who performs wonders and miracles too numerous for the mouth to tell or the ear to hear . . .[13]

[10] *Kinat ha'emet*, 22.

[11] Ibid. 23.

[12] Werses, 'Hasidism in the Eyes of Haskalah Literature', 93.

[13] *Kerem ḥemed*, 2 (1836), letter 24 (pp. 149–50). (*Kerem ḥemed* was an annual publication of the Galician Haskalah from 1833 to 1856.)

Like his colleagues of the Galician Haskalah, Samuel Luzzatto was familiar with Dov Ber of Linits's *Shivḥei habesht* and took advantage of his familiarity to ridicule the hasidim. The reference to some of the miracles ascribed to the Besht in the book reinforces the idea that belief in his magical powers (and those of the other leaders of hasidism) was a cornerstone of hasidic life. Like Perl, Luzzatto also thought this so contemptible and repulsive a belief that merely describing it would lend his words an overtone of irony and arouse an appropriate reaction in the reader.

Samuel David Luzzatto was so ensnared by Haskalah preconceptions that he unhesitatingly ascribed to Israel of Ruzhin the same predilections as the popular figure of the Besht. Had he taken the trouble to check his facts, he would have found that Rabbi Israel dissociated himself from the performance of miracles.[14] Luzzatto, however, together with the maskilim as a whole, automatically identified the hasidic leaders with the *ba'alei shem*, believing that he needed no supporting proof. Not content merely to ridicule the superstitions of the hasidim, he took issue with them directly. If the hasidim should respond to his criticisms, he mused, by asking: 'Why judge the *tsadikim* differently from biblical and talmudic figures who had also experienced wonders?', one should reply:

> How are their eyes besmeared, and they see not, their minds, and they cannot think, that they cannot distinguish between the holy and the profane, between the impure and the pure? Were the saints of old like these pretenders to sanctity? . . . Did they entreat the Lord on behalf of their brethren for their own personal gain? When they prayed for their companions, were they showered with gold and silver?[15]

Clearly Luzzatto, like his Galician colleagues, entertained no doubts: the primary basis for the hasidic leaders' pretensions to supernatural powers such as the ability to heal their followers and to render material help of various kinds was simply their desire to enrich themselves.

The literary assault of the Galician maskilim on hasidism, with its focus on ludicrous beliefs in the supernatural, was also taken up by representatives of the Russian Haskalah. Thus, Isaac Baer Levinsohn (1788–1860) wrote his satirical work *Emek refa'im* (1830) in the form of a confession by a supposed miracle-worker or hasidic *tsadik*. This character makes a clean breast of his misdeeds, admitting that all the 'wonders' he has performed were fraudulent. Levinsohn does not omit to mention that the wonder-worker's success in misleading the public was due to the nature of his audience:

> I therefore elected to settle in a very small town, where there were neither scholars nor scribes, neither wealthy men nor merchants, but people who were so poor that they were forever preoccupied with making a living and did not understand even the ways of the world,

[14] See David Assaf, *The Regal Way: The Life and Times of Rabbi Israel of Ruzhin* (Heb.) (Jerusalem, 1997), 68–9.

[15] *Kerem ḥemed*, letter 24 (n. 13).

let alone deceit and subterfuge. They were sincere believers in every lie and deception and vanity, consulted soothsayers and sorcerers, believed old crones and their magic spells . . .[16]

Thus Levinsohn shared the view of the Galician maskilim that poverty and ignorance were the soil that nurtured the belief in the miraculous powers of the *ba'alei shem*. Another important motif in the Haskalah attack on magic and its manifestations in hasidism was the extreme contrast between the magicians on the one hand and legitimate medicine on the other. For example, Levinsohn's wonder-worker declares, 'I would prove to them at all times that they should not believe in any physician or doctor at all, just come to me and give me their *pidyonot* that I should pray for them.'[17]

This was a central motif in the autobiography of the Lithuanian maskil Mordecai Aaron Guenzburg (1795–1846). Guenzburg renders a lively account of his contemporaries' superstitious beliefs. He himself fell victim to superstition when, having married at an early age, he discovered that he was sexually impotent. His mother-in-law, convinced that he had been bewitched, forced her young son-in-law to drink a 'remedy' concocted by an old witch to counteract the spell that had been cast on him. As a result, he fell ill with a fever and a bad cough. Nevertheless, relates Guenzburg, 'my mother-in-law would not agree to consult a doctor, only old women, by whose flame I had already been burned'.[18]

Guenzburg was cured of his ills by an elderly physician with many decades of medical experience. Needless to say, unlike the old crones with their nostrums, the old man summoned up his experience and medical knowledge, and in addition 'took no money for his fee, for he was a very wealthy man, and practised medicine for nothing but the love of humanity'. Moreover, he was also a scholar, well versed in languages, and in fact encouraged the young Guenzburg to set out on the path of Haskalah.[19] Throughout, Guenzburg contrasts the grotesqueries of magic and witchcraft with their respectable, useful counterpart—conventional medicine based on science. Living in Lithuania, he aimed his criticism not at hasidism but at the local mitnagedim, who he thought were unduly influenced by superstitions and witch-doctors. His action in consulting the wise doctor was considered unusual in Lithuanian Jewish society, and was even criticized.[20]

[16] Isaac Baer Levinsohn, *Yalkut ribal* [anthology of Levinsohn's works] (Warsaw, 1878), 121.

[17] Ibid. 125. Cf. Levinsohn's condemnation of the use of Holy Names for magical purposes in the guise of 'practical kabbalah' in his *Beit yehudah* [The House of Judah] (Vilna, 1858), 130–3.

[18] *Avi'ezer* (Vilna, 1864), 94–8.

[19] Ibid. 124.

[20] East European maskilim, eager to displace the *ba'alei shem* and popular healers and enhance the prestige of scientific medicine and its practitioners, also wrote and published medical literature. The two best-known examples are Moses Marcuse, *Ezer yisra'el* [The Help of Israel] (Paritzk, 1790), and Menahem Mendel Lefin, *Refu'at ha'am* [Book of Popular Healing] (Zolkiew, 1794). For Lefin's book see Joseph Klausner, *History of Modern Hebrew Literature* (Heb.), 6 vols. (Jerusalem, 1952–4), i. 226–30. A detailed discussion of Marcuse's volume, including a comparison with Lefin's work, may be found in Chone Shmeruk, *Yiddish Literature in Poland: Historical Research and Insights* (Heb.) (Jerusalem, 1981), 184–203.

Some echoes of Haskalah literature's anti-hasidic campaign are discernible in the works of Mendele Mokher Seforim (1835–1917), particularly in his *Ha'avot vehabanim* (1868), one of whose major characters is a hasidic *tsadik* who claims to be a wonder-worker and to heal all his followers' ills.[21] Mendele's picture of magic and magicians is painted with colours not used by his predecessors.[22] Nevertheless, despite some moderation in his polemical tone, Mendele does make his contribution to the image prevalent in Haskalah literature of the ignorant masses steeped in magical beliefs. Moreover, he reveals the non-Jewish roots of the magical practices common among Jews.[23] This equation of *ba'alei shem* with gentile magicians was not Mendele's innovation. Nevertheless, he characteristically placed the equation in a striking literary mould. The following excerpt, in which a woman is searching for her husband who has disappeared, is a case in point.

If you will hearken to me and heed my advice, said Hannah, I advise you to consult a gypsy woman, a witch. . . . Last year a woman came to me grieving, clad in sackcloth for the husband of her youth, who had abandoned her some years before, and she had consulted *ba'alei shem* and wonder-workers, to no avail. Not one of them passed through the village but she gave him money for redemption of the soul—but there was no salvation. And she came to the gypsy woman and implored her to heal her sorrow and bring her husband back. So she went out with her at evening with magic spells. . . . She placed a pot full of bones and the innards of unclean creatures on a fire, and made spells and cakes. . . . Then she said to the woman: Look into the pot. . . . All of a sudden she began to tremble, like a woman in travail, and screamed out with a loud voice. Fear not—said the witch—for what have you seen? Said the woman: I saw my husband rising from the ground. . . . Said the gypsy: May I not live to see redemption if you do not see your husband this very night! . . . And it came to pass, scarcely had the woman lain down in her bed . . . but lo! her beloved was knocking at the door . . . And she rose to let in her beloved, who rushed into the house helter-skelter, riding on a rake, holding a broom in his hand![24]

The butt of the ridicule in the passage is surely the *ba'alei shem* and those who believe in them. Not only is there no real difference between the magical practices of the *ba'alei shem* and those of a gypsy witch, the witch is in fact more powerful. This comparison, almost an equation, between the magical arts of the Jewish *ba'alei shem*

[21] *Ha'avot vehabanim* [Fathers and Sons], in Mendele Mokher Seforim, *Complete Works* (Heb.) (Tel Aviv, 1952), 28–31.

[22] As Shmuel Werses writes, 'However, unlike his predecessors and his contemporaries, [Mendele] does not intend to expose the deceptions of *ba'alei shem* and swindlers, and he does not concentrate on harsh accusations hurled at the leaders of the hasidic movement, who claim to be wonder-workers—except for his description of the false *tsadik* and his cronies in *Fathers and Sons*. His primary emphasis lies not on the practitioners of magic themselves . . . but mainly on the people who appeal to magic. . . . These acts of healing and wonders worked by magical arts are not seen here as exceptional, unusual cases . . . but portrayed as a common phenomenon in the life of the popular, uneducated classes.' Werses, 'The World of Folklore in Mendele's Works' (Heb.), *Dapim lemeḥkar basifrut*, 9 (1994), 8.

[23] Ibid. 12. Cf. Israel Bartal, 'Gentiles and Gentile Society in Hebrew and Yiddish Literature in Eastern Europe, 1856–1914' (Heb.) (Ph.D. diss., Jerusalem, 1981), 95.

[24] *Complete Works*, 24.

and the gentiles contradicts the common belief among Jews that the former derive their abilities from the kabbalah.

Of course, these excerpts from Haskalah literature do not exhaust that literature's attitude to magic in general and its hasidic manifestations in particular. Nevertheless, even these few passages are sufficiently representative. The Haskalah position may thus be summarized as follows:

1. Magic of all kinds is based on illusion and deception; it has no place in a society founded on reason and science.
2. Magical beliefs and practices are characteristic of the popular, ignorant classes.
3. There is no real difference between the magic of the *ba'alei shem* and that of their non-Jewish neighbours.
4. Magic is a central element in the hasidic movement. The masses of hasidim are steeped in superstition and their leaders are deluding them for their own personal interests.

II

As we know, the Haskalah was unable to stem the tide of hasidism, despite the war it waged against the movement through literature and other means. Haskalah literature may nevertheless be credited with some success: its constant emphasis on magic and *ba'alei shem* significantly affected the perceptions of the historians of hasidism.[25] Traces of this influence were visible in historical literature and in the minds of educated people until quite recently. A few examples will illustrate this.

One historian who applied a rational criterion to the evaluation of hasidism was Heinrich Graetz (1817–91). He chose to define and characterize the movement by presenting it as the polar opposite of the Haskalah, aptly expressing the self-perception of the Haskalah and its relationship with hasidism:

> It seems remarkable that, at the time when Mendelssohn declared rational thought to be the essence of Judaism, and founded, as it were, a widely extended order of enlightened men, another banner was unfurled, whose adherents announced the grossest superstition to be the fundamental principle of Judaism, and formed an order of wonder-seeking confederates.[26]

The 'wonders' of which Graetz was speaking were those that hasidism attributed to its founder and its leaders. Graetz thus accepted the thesis that the essence of hasidism was belief in the *tsadik*'s magical powers. Echoes of what we have read in Haskalah literature may also be heard in his account of the life of the Ba'al Shem

[25] The influence of Haskalah literature on the historiography of hasidism in areas other than those discussed here has been pointed out by Israel Bartal in his article 'From Distorted Reflection to Historical Fact: Haskalah Literature and the Study of the Hasidic Movement' (Heb.), *Mada'ei hayahadut*, 32 (1992), 7–17.

[26] Heinrich Graetz, *History of the Jews* (Philadelphia, Pa., 1956), v. 374–5.

Tov. For example, Graetz wrote that the Besht had learned his magical lore 'probably from the peasant women who gathered herbs on the mountain-tops and on the edges of the river. As they did not trust the healing power of nature, but added conjurations and invocations to good and evil spirits, Israel also accustomed himself to this method of cure.'[27] Nevertheless, historical perspective and a desire for objectivity rid Graetz of certain Haskalah misconceptions concerning the Besht and the new movement. For example, he did not repeat the canard that the Besht used magical remedies (*segulot*) to make money. He was also more restrained in his discussion of the Besht's ecstatic prayer and mystical experiences.[28] For all that, one cannot help sensing the continuity between Haskalah literature and Graetz's account of hasidism.

It was Eliezer Tsevi Zweifel (1815–88) who first broke with the Haskalah's traditional hostility to hasidism. In his *Shalom al yisra'el* (1868), Zweifel described hasidism as a legitimate phenomenon, alongside the Talmud and kabbalah. Moreover, he argued, hasidism was—or, at least at its inception had been—a religious revival movement.[29] But even Zweifel, who revealed both the spiritual-ideological and the social virtues of hasidism, maintained the negative Haskalah position *vis-à-vis* magic. This is particularly striking in view of his efforts to defend the Besht against the accusation of being a *ba'al shem*:

It is an error of those who think and write 'Besht' meaning wonder-worker and one who activates *segulot* and medicines by Holy Names. (1) For it is known that the Besht did not generally use Names save in prayers. (2) How could the Besht refer to himself and sign his name as a wonder-worker? (3) What point would there be to add the word *tov* [good]—is there a wonder-worker who is anything but good?[30]

Zweifel was trying to smooth over the magical elements in the Besht's character, both by arguing that the Besht had almost never used 'Names' and by denying the magical content of the epithet Ba'al Shem Tov. It is hard to say whether Zweifel was sincere or whether he was dissembling when he wrote, 'How could the Besht refer to himself . . . as a wonder-worker?' Whatever the case may be, the very formulation of the question, as well as the other arguments adduced, clearly imply that Zweifel was faithful to the traditional distaste of the Haskalah for anything to do with magic. Like other maskilim, previous and contemporary, he viewed healing through Holy Names and *segulot* as contemptible and repellent. It was inconceivable, therefore, that this could have been the occupation of the founder of a religious revival movement.

Some subsequent writers took a similar approach. While casting hasidism in a

[27] Ibid. 376. [28] Ibid. 387 ff.

[29] Abraham Rubinstein, introduction to Eliezer Tsevi Hakohen Zweifel, *Shalom al yisra'el* [Peace Upon Israel], 4 vols. (Zhitomir 1868, 1869, 1870, 1873); ed. A. Rubinstein (Jerusalem, 1973), i. 7–33; on this point see Shmuel Feiner, 'The Turning-Point in the Evaluation of Hasidism: Eliezer Zweifel and the Moderate Haskalah in Russia' (Heb.), *Zion*, 51 (1986), 167–210.

[30] Zweifel, *Shalom al yisra'el*, ii. 20.

positive light, they felt it necessary to belittle the prominence of the magical element in the figure of the Besht. One of these was Samuel Abba Horodezky (1871–1957), who tried to portray hasidism on the basis of his own familiarity with the movement's literature. Despite his rather detached point of view, he evinced some sympathy for the movement and its leaders. Unlike Zweifel, Horodezky was fully aware that the Besht was a 'genuine' *ba'al shem*, who actually used 'Names'. Nevertheless, he saw fit to differentiate between the Besht and other practitioners of the art: 'Hasidism knows how to elevate the Besht above the level of previous *ba'alei shem*. Although they too healed the sick with spells and charms and *segulot*, the Besht, in contrast, could detect sicknesses before they occurred and fended them off with his remedies.' At this point Horodezky refers to two cases described in *Shivḥei habesht*, in both of which the Besht called upon his ability to foretell the future in order to help the invalid.[31] Another sign of the Besht's superiority over other *ba'alei shem* is that 'the Besht objected to consulting sorcerers and magicians, as was the popular custom in those days. He himself sometimes ordered a doctor to be summoned.'[32] These distinctions between the Besht and other *ba'alei shem* illustrates how difficult it was for Horodezky to break the Haskalah's shackles of contempt for magic and magicians.

If this was the case with such authors as Zweifel and Horodezky, whose object was to defend hasidism, it was all the more so with a scholar and thinker like Saul Israel Hurwitz (1861–1927) who, in an essay entitled 'Hasidism and Haskalah' (1923),[33] wrote a reply in the spirit of Haskalah to those who had begun to speak favourably of hasidism. He was thinking of authors such as Y. L. Peretz and Micha Josef Berdyczewski and scholars like Samuel Horodezky, whose neo-hasidic romanticism, as he saw it, angered him. In his essay, he tried to draw up a balance sheet, comparing the good and evil that each of the two movements had caused the Jewish people. His point of departure in this comparative survey is that of a nationalist maskil. For him, the Haskalah movement had brought the Jews out of the darkness of the ghetto and paved the way for the emergence of Jewish nationalism. Hasidism, by contrast, had tried to block any positive step and was therefore a typical Diaspora phenomenon.

Among the many faults that Hurwitz attributed to hasidism was, naturally, its association with magic. The accusation was linked mainly to the Besht:

> It would seem that the gentile environment in which the Besht had grown up and lived influenced him to a considerable degree and obscured his spiritual nature. It was from that Haydamak-Wallachian environment that the Besht took his melodies, the *nigunim* . . . and, especially, the melancholy melodies of the peasant maids (together with whom he had picked medicinal herbs in the Carpathians). . . . From that very same environment he also derived a good many strange tendencies and superstitions. . . . He also liked to jest and

[31] Samuel Abba Horodezky, 'Rabbi Yisrael Besht' (Heb.), *He'atid*, bk. 2, 2nd edn. (Berlin and Vienna, 1923), 145.

[32] Ibid. 146.

[33] The article was published in Hebrew in *He'atid*, bk. 2, 2nd edn., 29–99.

curse with coarse expressions, like a bloodletting, spell-chanting sorcerer, a familiar type among the peasants. . . . Such was the Besht. This Besht, they say, left 'people' behind after him. It is easy to guess just who those 'people' were who had come to learn Torah from this sorcerer and *ba'al shem* . . . a few backward people, remnants of the Frankists, an ignorant, coarse riffraff, contemptible and vulgar, lickers of leftovers, believers in miracles and familiar spirits and all kinds of superstitions . . .[34]

In other words, neither the distance in time nor the nationalist viewpoint had weakened Hurwitz's animosity towards hasidism. Moreover, his attitude to the Besht and to his magical practices could have come from any essay by a Galician maskil of the first half of the nineteenth century.

It was Simon Dubnow (1860–1941) who laid the foundations for the critical historical treatment of hasidism. His influence on the scholarly study of the movement in the last few generations is inestimable. He was no less important in altering the popular image of hasidism. When one examines Dubnow's position in regard to magic and *ba'alei shem*, it turns out that he was well rooted in the Haskalah literature of the nineteenth century and the writings of the authors who followed its lead. Describing the background of the Besht's activities as the founder of hasidism, Dubnow wrote:

At that time the wonder-working kabbalists known as *ba'alei shem*—that is, those who worked wonders by combinations of Holy Names—were quite popular. They would wander around the cities and villages, healing all sorts of diseases and ills by means of spells, charms and other such *segulot* . . . As the masses believed that mental disorders were caused by a *dibuk* or evil spirit entering a person's body, some of the *ba'alei shem* were experts in that area and knew how to expel the *dibuk* from the invalid's body.[35]

To help his readers understand the cultural environment of the *ba'alei shem*'s actions, Dubnow related a story about demons who had allegedly occupied a Jewish home in Poznan towards the end of the seventeenth century. The story illustrated, he claimed, 'to what degree the belief in demons and spirits was widespread at the time'. Moreover, he asserted, such stories not only showed the kind of ideas that had become popular, but the very telling of the stories had a negative influence, for 'they were passed around by word of mouth, inspired religious hallucinations and spread superstitious beliefs among the people'.[36]

These passages clearly demonstrate Dubnow's view that the *ba'alei shem* constituted a typical folk phenomenon. Evidence of their popular, not to say vulgar, nature was their particular popularity among the masses and the fact that their activities were based on 'hallucinations' and 'superstitious beliefs'. Dubnow's sympathy for the Haskalah position is also obvious in his description of the *ba'alei shem* as intruding in matters that properly belonged to the medical profession: 'At a time when learned physicians were rare and in fact non-existent in the smaller towns

[34] Ibid. 36–7.

[35] *A History of Hasidism* (Heb.) (1931; Tel Aviv, 1960), 30.

[36] Ibid. 30–1.

and villages, the *ba'alei shem* took the doctors' place as healers of physical and mental sickness among the people, who were steeped in hallucinations and superstitious beliefs.'[37] Not content with having reiterated for his readers that the activities of the *ba'alei shem* relied on popular superstition, Dubnow also exposed the scoundrels' base motives: 'The *ba'alei shem* exerted considerable spiritual influence on the masses, who believed in their remedies and "miracles". Many exploited such superstitions for their own good, exacting payment.'[38]

In general, Dubnow's negative attitude to magic and *ba'alei shem* derived from a historiographical tradition that was deeply entrenched in Haskalah literature and ideology. He may nevertheless be counted among those scholars who were resolved to demonstrate the positive elements of hasidism. He maintained that hasidism constituted a challenge to the fossilized Judaism of the rabbinic establishment. How could one reconcile the fact that the Besht was a *ba'al shem* on the one hand, and the founder of a movement that played a positive role in Jewish history on the other? Dubnow found his solution ready made in the writings of Zweifel, Horodezky, and their colleagues. Like his predecessors, Dubnow made a distinction between the Besht and other *ba'alei shem*; more precisely, he distinguished between the corrupt, fraudulent *ba'alei shem* and 'the best of them', one of whom was the Besht. While he had also started out as a *ba'al shem*, he ultimately abandoned that vocation and focused his efforts on 'revealing a new Torah'. Moreover,

> the rumours that had spread about his miracles prepared people's minds for his teachings. And since he was not content to heal the body but also cared for the soul and became a religious and ethical guide for all those who sought his help, the masses sensed that this was no ordinary *ba'al shem*, but a *good*, benevolent *ba'al shem*, a guide and an educator. Hence the epithet Ba'al Shem Tov [the *good ba'al shem*] (and its abbreviated form, the Besht), which became the permanent nickname of the creator of hasidism.[39]

Dubnow's assertion concerning the transformation in the Besht's career, as well as his explanation of the origin of the nickname Ba'al Shem Tov, were sharply criticized by Gershom Scholem, who essentially offered three objections:

1. Of the *ba'alei shem* known to us, almost none made any attempt to expound religious beliefs and ideas.
2. The nickname Ba'al Shem Tov was not new; neither was it applied solely to the Besht.
3. We do not know of any proven transformation in the Besht's career; on the contrary, he continued to practise his magical arts all his life, and was even proud of them.[40]

Scholem's objections to the attempt to remove the magical sting from the Besht's personality were not confined to Dubnow. Among the other authors who provoked

[37] *A History of Hasidism*, 47. [38] Ibid. [39] Ibid. 47–8.

[40] Gershom Scholem, 'The Historical Figure of R. Israel Ba'al Shem Tov', in id., *Explications and Implications* (Heb.) (Tel Aviv, 1975), 292–3.

Scholem's criticism was Martin Buber, who claimed that the charms the Besht gave to those requesting his aid were not magic spells; rather, they served as a kind of symbol linking the helper to those being helped. Scholem firmly rejected this suggestion too, citing incontrovertible proof that the Besht gave out charms and in this respect was no different from any other *ba'al shem*.[41] Now that Scholem has extricated the Besht from the fetters of rationalist apologetics, proving him no different from *ba'alei shem* in general, the time has come to free *ba'alei shem* in general from the contemptible image imposed on them by Haskalah authors and the historians who followed them.[42] However, this topic is beyond the scope of the present discussion.[43]

III

What can one learn about the inner world of the Haskalah movement from the treatment of magic and *ba'alei shem* in Haskalah literature? Before answering this question, we must consider why the Haskalah aimed its attack on magic and its practitioners specifically at hasidism, for the belief that demonic powers could determine the fate of human beings and in the use of magic as protection against such powers was not confined to hasidim. It will be remembered that Mordecai Aaron Guenzberg consulted a witch to combat the spell that had made him impotent—and Guenzburg lived in Lithuania, stronghold of the mitnagedim. His case was by no means exceptional; there is copious evidence that magic was commonly used throughout traditional Jewish society in eastern Europe, including among the learned scholars of Lithuania. Here are some examples:

1. R. Nahman Reuben of Smorgon, a Lithuanian rabbi who studied in his youth at the Volozhin yeshiva, related that Isaac, the son of Hayim of Volozhin, wrote charms to heal two yeshiva students of epilepsy.[44]

[41] Ibid. 297–9.

[42] The author of the entry '*Ba'alei shem*' in Judah David Eisenstein (ed.), *A Jewish Treasury* (Heb.), vol. iii (New York, 1951), 137, adopts a tone very similar to that of Dubnow. Even such a scholar as Joseph Weiss adhered to the derogatory view of *ba'alei shem*. In his article 'The First Emergence of the Hasidic Way' (Heb.), *Zion*, 15 (1951), 53–5, he assigns the *ba'alei shem* to the lower echelons of the intelligentsia, citing, among other things, the allegation that R. Jacob Joseph of Polonnoye forged a passage of midrash in defence of *ba'alei shem*. However, this allegation was refuted by Hayim Lieberman in his book *The Tent of Rachel* (Heb.), vol. i (New York, 1980), 3–5. Neither, it seems, could Benzion Dinur dissociate himself from the conventional censure of *ba'alei shem*. This is most probably why he ignored the Besht's profession in his comprehensive and detailed article, 'The Beginnings of Hasidism and its Social and Messianic Foundations', in id., *At the Turn of the Generations* (Heb.) (Jerusalem, 1954), 83–227. As Dinur holds that the Besht played a major role by paving a new path to redemption, any reference to his despicable profession would be deleterious and it would therefore be better to ignore it,

[43] For a fuller discussion see Immanuel Etkes, 'The Role of Magic and *Ba'alei Shem* in Ashkenazi Society in the Late Seventeenth and Early Eighteenth Centuries (Heb.), *Zion*, 60 (1995), 69–104.

[44] Yizhak Yudelow, 'The Book *Ḥelkat re'uven*' (Heb.), *Alei sefer*, 14 (1987), 139–40.

2. Joseph Sundel of Salant (1786–1866), one of Hayim of Volozhin's closest disciples, who exerted a profound influence on Israel Salanter (1810–83, the founder of the *musar* movement) and was later consulted on halakhic matters by the *perushim*[45] of Jerusalem, possessed a manuscript list of 'Spells and Remedies [*segulot*]'. Among other things, these spells were supposed to help barren women, women in childbirth, epileptics and other unfortunates. We may assume that Joseph Sundel actually used these charms.[46]

3. Lithuanian scholars and rabbis were involved on several occasions in exorcizing a *dibuk*. According to traditions passed on by the disciples of Hayim of Volozhin, the Vilna Gaon himself was involved in two such cases.[47] Among the manuscripts of Samuel of Kelmy is a letter rendering a detailed account of an exorcism performed by the rabbi of Deliatitz in 1844.[48] Two other accounts of the exorcism of *dibukim* in Lithuania at the end of the nineteenth and beginning of the twentieth centuries are cited by Gedaliah Nigal.[49] In one case the exorcism was performed by Moses Hakohen of Stotzin. In the second case the presiding rabbi was Elhanan Wasserman, then a student at the Hafets Hayim's yeshiva in Radun and later a yeshiva principal in his own right.

These examples are surely sufficient to disprove the prevailing conception, resulting from the influence of Haskalah literature, that the practice of magic was specific to hasidism; the truth was quite different. We are therefore faced again with the question of why Haskalah literature persisted in this misrepresentation of the facts. The question becomes even more acute if we observe that hasidism may in fact have mitigated the influence of magic. Wherever hasidism gained ascendancy, the *tsadikim* inherited the function of the *ba'alei shem* in the sense that they became the new address for requests for help in material matters. At the same time, not all the *tsadikim* thought of themselves as wonder-workers.[50] Even those who considered themselves successors of the Besht as wonder-workers frequently exercised their powers through prayer rather than through charms and spells. On the other hand, it is a reasonable assumption that, in areas where hasidism made no headway, people continued to consult *ba'alei shem* of the old type, who unabashedly used the paraphernalia of magic.

The motives of the Haskalah movement's opposition to hasidism were no doubt

[45] *Perushim* ('separatists') was the name given to the disciples of the Vilna Gaon in Erets Yisra'el.

[46] Eliezer Rivlin, *The Tsadik Rabbi Joseph Sundel of Salant and his Masters* (Heb.) (Jerusalem, 1927), 65–8.

[47] Asher Hakohen Ashkenazi, *Keter rosh: Orehot hayim* [The Crown of the Head: Ways of Life] (Warsaw, 1914), p. 75, sects. 6, 8.

[48] National and Hebrew University Library, Jerusalem, MS 8° 3287. Deliatitz (Polish: Dolatycze) is a small town some thirty kilometres north-east of Novogrudok.

[49] *Dibuk Stories* (Heb.) (Jerusalem, 1983), 186–96.

[50] See Immanuel Etkes, 'R. Shneur Zalman of Lyady's Style of Hasidic Leadership' (Heb.), *Zion*, 50 (1985), 323–31.

deep-seated and more varied than the mere objection to magical elements. For the maskilim, hasidism was the most extreme manifestation of the multiple deficiencies of traditional life which they strove to 'mend' and change. In addition, they perceived the spread and upsurge of hasidism as a threat to the future of Jewish society. That being so, nothing was easier for the maskilim than to seize on the magical elements in hasidism in order to attack it. It had always been the contention of east European maskilim that the opposition to the Haskalah came from an obscurantist movement of the ignorant masses.[51] The prominence they ascribed to the role of magic in hasidism enabled them to prove decisively that these were the Haskalah movement's most bitter enemies. No wonder, then, that Haskalah authors portrayed magic as a central motif in hasidism, ignoring the spiritual elements that played such an important role in it.

The treatment of the magical arts in Haskalah literature has an additional and more profound significance. Indeed, beyond the desire to combat the 'enemy', the literary war against hasidism was crucial in shaping the Haskalah leaders' self-image. This idea has been stated with admirable clarity by Shmuel Werses:

> Indeed, hasidism inadvertently contributed to the strengthening and coalescence of Haskalah literature. . . . The slogans and self-awareness of the Haskalah were consolidated and more clearly formulated through its polemical portrayal of hasidism; moreover, the existence and success of the hasidic movement sometimes lent motivation and meaning to the objectives of the Haskalah.[52]

This penetrating observation is also relevant to the present analysis. Haskalah literature, by ridiculing magic and *ba'alei shem* and by identifying the phenomenon with hasidism, which provided the Haskalah movement with both an adversary and a kind of reverse mirror-image, was better able to express its own inner truth —its image of itself as having transcended the superstition of the magical arts. This was no trivial matter: after all, the writers of the Haskalah movement had been reared and educated in an environment where magic, in all its manifestations, played a role of crucial importance.

[51] See Isaac Baer Levinsohn, *Te'udah beyisra'el* [Testimony in Israel] (Vilna and Horodno, 1828), introduction, pp. 2–3.

[52] See Werses, 'Hasidism in the Eyes of Haskalah Literature', 91.

EIGHT

Portrait of the Maskil as a Young Man

SHMUEL WERSES

THE VISION OF THE HASKALAH AS EXPERIENCED BY THE YOUNG JEW

THE process of modernization that began to penetrate east European Jewish society at the end of the eighteenth century, and which reached its zenith during the nineteenth, stimulated the growth and development of the Haskalah movement there. As a historical phenomenon, the Haskalah has engaged the attention of scholars from a number of disciplines; in this chapter I will take a different approach, monitoring change as it occurred at the level of the individual, in the souls and minds of the young men who were attracted to the movement.

Evidence can be found in a variety of sources. The struggles and doubts of young men trying to realize the Haskalah's ideals are reflected in the biographical, autobiographical, and memoir-style compositions and epistolary literature of the period, and also in fictional form, in stories, novels, satire, and epic poetry. Certain motifs are repeated again and again in different contexts. There is, for example, the youth of the figures peopling this material, swept up by the idea of the Haskalah during their adolescence or the early years of marriage; here are described the stages of ideological transformation, the gradual transition from the traditional Jewish study system to the world of secular education, a change brought about mainly by the key texts of the Haskalah. Another motif is the role played by fellow students or by teachers who helped and encouraged the budding maskilim with persuasive conversation and books. These guides included mature maskilim, some of them respected and wealthy figures in the Jewish community, who advised young novices seeking a secular education or planning to travel to foreign parts, sometimes offering financial support. In this connection, we must note the phenomenon of the young men who drifted to the cities of Russia, or who travelled further afield to western Europe in order to continue their studies. The odds that they would go back to their homeland and their home town were slim. Optimistic writers picture them returning as bearers of authoritative, reforming influence, acquired as a result of the professional and intellectual status achieved during their absence from the community, but others show them settling abroad after having completed their advanced studies. The web of relationships between the young maskilim and their families constitutes another self-sustaining typological unit. The literature presents the various facets of this situation: the crisis engendered by a son's changed outlook, or the problems of a newly blossoming marital relationship undermined by the husband's ideological reversal.

The process whereby young men joined the Haskalah, affiliating themselves to its ideology and literature, had already taken place in western Europe, particularly Germany, during the last quarter of the eighteenth century, and there it had its own unique characteristics. Although some of these repeated themselves later in eastern Europe—in Russia, Lithuania, Galicia, and Poland—the circumstances, as expressed in the personalities of the young men and in their environmental and educational backgrounds, were different. The earlier Haskalah literature, created by the generation of the *me'asfim* and eminently suited to its time and place, was, in the nineteenth century, transplanted into and absorbed by a different social and political reality with all its unique problems. For example, the vision of the departure for the 'lands of the west', the 'promised land' of the young men of eastern Europe, had had no relevance for the young Jews of Germany, except in the sense of cultural and linguistic assimilation within their native country.

By the nineteenth century Moses Mendelssohn and his successors were already being mythologized, their works arousing admiration and even awe in the young maskilim of eastern Europe. In this they reflected another of the literature's stereotypes: the young Israelite striving for wisdom and knowledge in the era of modernization.

REFLECTIONS ON HASIDISM AND WISDOM

One of the questions facing the young Jew immersed in the world of the *beit midrash* and seeking new directions for his intellectual development, particularly during the early stages of the Haskalah movement in Russia, Lithuania, and Galicia, was the need to choose between the hasidic movement, which was flourishing among the masses, and the more elitist path of the Haskalah.[1]

The Hebrew fictional literature of the early nineteenth century presents a number of models of questioning and path-finding for young men in crisis, who were emerging from the atmosphere of traditional Torah study in order to join the tempting and magical world of hasidism. One such model, written from a hasidic perspective, was presented by Rabbi Nahman of Bratslav in his 'Ma'aseh beven rav' a story about a rabbi's son.[2] Written from the opposite viewpoint is Joseph Perl's satirical epistolary novel *Megaleh temirin* (Revealer of Secrets), in which the son

[1] See Shmuel Werses, 'Hasidism in the Eyes of Haskalah Literature: From the Polemic of Galician Maskilim', in id. (ed.), *Trends and Forms in Haskalah Literature* (Heb.) (Jerusalem, 1990), 103–6.

[2] In *Sipurei ma'asiyot* (Berdichev, 1815), pub. in Eng. as *The Tales*, ed. Arnold J. Band (New York, 1978), 131–8.

of a wealthy man, who has previously devoted himself to the study of Torah, is suddenly drawn into the world of hasidism and becomes devoted to *Shivḥei habesht*, a tract in praise of the founder of hasidism. In vain does his learned teacher labour to open his eyes and convince him that the words of the legendary book he so admires are totally worthless and untrustworthy. In a letter to his friend, he writes of his pupil's passionate and angry reaction.[3]

Though in many cases the attraction hasidism held for young men culminated in their enlistment and total immersion in the movement, in others their efforts to learn about hasidism, its ideals and its leaders, ended in disappointment and a great sobering, together with a decisive move in the direction of the Haskalah. We have, for example, the testimony of Solomon Judah Rapoport (Shir, 1790–1867), a friend of Perl and a leading figure of the Galician Haskalah during the same period (1815–20). In 1815 Rapoport sent a detailed letter 'to a young man, learned in Torah and from an excellent family, who has recently become a hasid, and he has his place among persons who call themselves hasidim'. Through carefully reasoned argument Rapoport attempts to clarify the spiritual background to this surprising move and to return his young friend to the right path, the world of Torah study and the teaching and rationalistic thinking of Maimonides.[4]

In contrast to the expressions of attraction and doubt which filled the souls of the young men of Galicia trying to choose between hasidism and Haskalah there were also cases of open clashes between young maskilim and their hasidic environment. Such a stubborn struggle is portrayed for us in the letter of Nahman Krochmal (Renak, 1785–1840) to his young admirer Avraham Goldberg, who lived in the Galician village of Mosty. In the midst of his encouraging words he recalls how Goldberg was hounded and intimidated by the zealous hasidim of that village: frightened by the threats, he agreed to hand over to his persecutors the Haskalah books in his possession to be burned. Shocked by these events, Krochmal attempts to encourage his friend to stand firm: 'Are you not a man, and who of thousands of young men of your age is like you? You are in the spring of your lifetime, and such fear does not suit you, being twenty years of age.'[5] The plight of Goldberg, caught between his loyalty to his hasidic environment and his striving, for all kinds of reasons, to enter the world of the Haskalah, is reflected in the allegorical satire 'Ḥasidut veḥokhmah' (Hasidism and Wisdom), by another Galician maskil, Isaac Erter (1791–1857), which was first published in 1836. In the introduction, written in the style of *The Dream* by the second-century Greek satirist Lucian, the young narrator tells of a dream in which the allegorical figures of Hasidism and Wisdom attempt to woo him. He finally chooses the path of Wisdom, with its promise of the

[3] *Megaleh temirin* (Vienna, 1819), letter 77; pub. in Eng. as *Revealer of Secrets*, ed. Dov Taylor (New York, 1997), 138–71.

[4] Rapoport, 'Ner mitsvah' [Lamp of the Commandment], in *Naḥalat yehudah* [The Inheritance of Judah] (Krakow, 1868), 1–26.

[5] The letter was first published in M. Letteris (ed.), *Mikhtavim* [Letters] (Zolkiew, 1827), 10–16. See also Nahman Krochmal, *Collected Writings*, ed. Shimon Ravidovitz (Berlin, 1924), 416–18.

future advantages of intellectual satisfaction, over the immediate worldly advantages of honour and wealth offered by Hasidism.[6]

Among the first to examine the attitude of young men to the hasidic movement at the time of its initial expansion was Solomon Maimon (1753–1800), who grew up in Lithuania, travelled to Germany, and there entered into the world of Jewish enlightenment and German philosophy. In his autobiography he testifies that 'Young men were leaving their parents, their wives and their children, and going, group after group, to wait upon these exalted "rabbis" and to listen to the words of the new doctrine from their lips.'[7] Maimon says that he did not have a clear concept of the hasidic movement and so, when he met 'a young man who had already joined this society', he questioned him, asking for information about joining, about hasidism's doctrine, and to see examples of its interpretation of the Torah.[8] The young man's replies excited Maimon's imagination so much that he decided to visit Dov Baer, the Maggid of Mezhirech, one of the movement's founders, to learn from this distinguished rabbi. However, Maimon, being of a rational and realistic bent, was disappointed in him, thinking he lacked originality and intuitive ability. Although he later stressed the essential bond between the hasidic movement and the young generation of the time, pointing out that hasidism 'put special effort into attracting young men',[9] it was the Haskalah that had the upper hand in fashioning Solomon Maimon's development and intellectual outlook.

Just as Maimon questioned Dov Baer of Mezhirech in the 1780s, so Samuel Joseph Fuenn (1818–90), one of the leaders of the Haskalah in the Lithuanian city of Vilna, did the same in his youth with regard to the Habad version of hasidism. Fuenn's hasidic family tried to convince him that there was actually no essential difference between hasidism and the study of faith based on Haskalah ideology. In his memoirs Fuenn describes his very moving private meeting with the local rabbi. They talked for about half an hour. The young maskil appealed, supposedly innocently, to the rabbi 'to open my eyes to the light of hasidism, so I may be able to distinguish, for a youth of my sort cannot make do with simple meanings'. He voiced his reservations strongly, but was not at all convinced by the rabbi's responses. He disappointedly summed up the effect of this fateful conversation on his beliefs and ideas: 'I came to him full of good hopes and I left him empty. I looked into my soul and I knew that those who insisted that my soul cannot deal with hasidism were right.'[10]

Throughout the area of Jewish settlement in Lithuania the hasidic movement, with its various factions, exerted a powerful attraction on the young man seeking a

[6] In Erter, *Hatsofeh leveit yisra'el* [The Watchman of the House of Israel] (Warsaw, 1883), ed. Yehuda Friedlander (Jerusalem, 1996), 87–91. See also Werses, 'Hasidism in the Eyes of Haskalah Literature', 106–7.

[7] Maimon, *Ḥayai* (1792), trans. I. L. Baruch as *My Life* (Jerusalem, 1942), 135.

[8] Ibid. 141–2.

[9] Ibid. 145–6.

[10] *From Militant Haskalah to Conservative Maskil: A Selection of S. J. Fuenn's Writings* (Heb.), ed. Shmuel Feiner (Jerusalem, 1993).

path of faith. Even Abraham Mapu (1808–67), one of the bastions of the Hebrew novel of the Haskalah, was caught in the grip of hasidism and its lifestyle when he was about 17. Although Mapu's father was tolerant, his mother expressed her strong opposition their son's connection with hasidic society: 'And she came into their meeting place and removed him from there with angry words and poured out her wrath upon him, and from that time on he did not return to them again.'[11] The young Mapu cut his ties with the hasidim; nor did he remain long in the camp of the rival students of Torah, and soon became a declared secular maskil *par excellence*.

Abraham Baer Gottlober (1810–99), who himself grew up in a hasidic environment, describes in his story *Hizaharu bevenei aniyim* the fate of a young man who studies Torah in a hasidic synagogue. He is followed by one of the zealots and the supervisor of studies, who catch him red-handed with Wessely's *Sefer hamidot*. Despite the threat to evict him from the synagogue and leave him penniless and homeless, the youngster has no intention of changing his behaviour or opinions, asserting with great conviction: 'Heaven forbid that I should turn my back on the road which I have taken, and on which I walk with confidence.'[12]

This experience of crisis, of the tense relations between hasidism and the Haskalah within the world of the young Jew in eastern Europe, continued in Byelorussia and in Lithuania into the second half of the nineteenth century, at a time when modern influences were beginning to seep into those countries. Thus the writer Judah Leib Levin (Yehalel, 1844–1925), a native of Minsk, tells of how at the age of 17 he married and went to live with his hasidic father-in-law in a small Russian town. There he discovered the Habad movement and diligently studied its doctrine and literature. At first, he relates, 'I feared God greatly, worshipped Him with joy, with a pure heart and in the right spirit, and at that time I was immensely happy in my soul.'[13] But this period passed. The young Judah Leib was attracted to the literature of the Haskalah and even began to write poetry. On a visit to his brother-in-law, a hasidic *tsadik* in Kobrin, he found himself engaging in tense and excited arguments, and a rift between the young sceptic and his disappointed family became inevitable. He did not repent, and severed himself totally from the spiritual world of hasidism, becoming the spokesman of radical Haskalah poetry and later the literary and journalistic figurehead of the Hibbat Zion movement.

Eliezer Ben-Yehuda (1858–1922), who was orphaned in his youth and grew up in a small town near Polotsk, diligently studied Talmud, but also Bible and Hebrew grammar. Here he describes his path to Haskalah in the midst of the hostile atmosphere surrounding him:

> And he strove with all his might to find books of the Haskalah—and because of the great love he bore for the Haskalah he did not know how to protect himself from the watching

[11] H. A. Medalia, 'Biography of Abraham Mapu' (Heb.), *Hamelits*, 11 (1869).

[12] Gottlober, *Hizaharu bivenei aniyim* [Take Care of the Children of the Poor] (Warsaw, 1877), 9. The story was published in *Haboker or* [Morning is Light], a magazine under Gottlober's editorship.

[13] Levin, *Sefer hazikhronot* [Memoirs] (Zhitomir, 1910), 8.

eye, and the people began gossiping about him and he became known in the town as a maskil. Then the hasidim avoided him and spoke badly of him to his uncle and to his cousin, and they tried to teach him the right path, but he would not take notice and went on his way.[14]

Another Hebrew writer, Abraham Shalom Friedberg (1838–1902), who had himself experienced the hostility of his community because of his enthusiasm for the Haskalah movement and its literature, describes in his reminiscences the sad fate of the young men who were persecuted for such attitudes, and the tale-bearing of some of their friends and acquaintances: 'These poor people, the young maskilim, were like doormats trampled by all. They were hounded by the pious and the fearful, who saw them as a blight on the House of Israel.'[15]

SUPPORT FROM BENEFACTORS

The phenomenon of openly declared maskilim, already past the various stages of the ideological struggle and well read in the literature of the Haskalah, who were guiding young men towards that world, repeats itself in various forms in the memoir-style literature.

In the figure of Judah Leib Mieses (1798–1831), who was active as a maskil and a Hebrew writer in Galicia in the 1820s, we have the image of the wealthy and generous patron.[16] He is described for us in an idealistic fashion by his friend Meir Letteris: 'He was a strong and courageous man of spirit, and knowledgeable in the Torah . . . and he was good to all men of maskilic bent. He was a lover of wisdom and struggled with all his might so that its bounteousness would flow outwards.'[17] In the same description we find praise for his expressions of support for and his encouragement of the young men on their journey towards learning. Letteris also admired Nahman Krochmal, who as a young man had himself moved to Zolkiew and found a teacher after his own heart, Baruch Zvi Neyh. Krochmal made much use of this teacher's library in his studies to become a maskil.[18]

The biography of Shneur Sachs (1816–92), a maskil who later applied himself to the study of medieval Hebrew poetry, highlights the significance of the role of the publicly respected benefactor in supplying Haskalah literature. Sachs, a native of the town of Kaidan in Lithuania, enjoyed the support of the leader of the community in Zhager, where he spent his adolescent years. It was in the home of that patron that, along with other works, he discovered *Kerem ḥemed*, the periodical that appeared in 1830s Vienna. He was so impressed by Erter's 'Ḥasidut veḥokh-

[14] In Nahum Sokolov, *Sefer zikaron lesofrei yisra'el haḥayim itanu hayom* [Memorial Book for Jewish Sages Alive Today] (Warsaw, 1888; 3rd edn. Tel Aviv, 1940), 141–3.

[15] Friedberg, *Sefer hazikhronot* [Book of Memoirs] (Warsaw, 1899), pt. 2, pp. 23–9.

[16] For information about Mieses see Joseph Klausner, *History of Modern Hebrew Literature* (Heb.), 6 vols. (Jerusalem, 1952–4), ii. 262–77; Y. Friedlander, *Hebrew Satire in Europe*, iii: *The Nineteenth Century* (Ramat Gan, 1994), 17–47.

[17] Letteris, *Zikaron basefer* [Memoirs] (Vienna, 1868), 115.

[18] Ibid. 42.

mah', published there, that he was inspired to leave home to go and meet the author personally, 'and not wishing to hurt his parents, he spun a web of lies, telling them that he was leaving in order to study at the yeshiva in Vilna'.[19]

One way for a patron to support the young and already knowledgeable maskil was to employ him as a tutor in his own household. In his memoirs Samuel Joseph Fuenn describes his employment as a teacher in the Vilna home of the wealthy Zvi Klatchko. This angered the Orthodox, who viewed the step as a public declaration by Fuenn, the young Torah scholar, of his defection to the Haskalah camp. This new standing was of great importance and intellectual significance to him.[20] A. S. Friedberg provides a similar testimony from a later period, describing how young men, hounded for their ideas, found shelter and a source of livelihood as tutors in wealthy homes; Friedberg had experienced this himself in his youth.[21]

At times the wealthy patron, free from the constraints of public opinion, not only encouraged the budding maskilim in their studies but also actively taught them the concepts of Haskalah and the rejection of the traditional environment and its conventions. Judah Leib Levin describes how, together with his friend the writer I. M. Wohlmann, he made clandestine visits to the home of David Lurie, the son of a wealthy maskil who was actively involved in the establishment of secular schools: 'and his home was a meeting place for sceptics'.[22] This pattern was repeated almost exactly in the path taken by the young Haim Selig Slonimski on his way to the world of Haskalah in his native city of Bialystok.[23] The memoirs of P. Yampolski provide a reliable testimony about one devoted patron and supporter of young men thirsting for secular knowledge in Russia during the second half of the nineteenth century. He has nothing but praise for the writer Ya'akov Shmuel Trachtman, employed as a clerk for the wealthy Brodsky, whose home in Odessa was a meeting-place and shelter for the maskilim, particularly the young ones.[24]

Many portraits of patrons and supporters of these young men exist in the fictional Hebrew writing of the Haskalah period. Shalom Jacob Abramowitz (Mendele Mokher Seforim, 1835–1917) depicts the relationship between patron and protégé in his novel *Ha'avot vehabanim* (Fathers and Sons). The young hero Shimeon flees the home of his hasidically devout parents, and finds a supporter and benefactor in the figure of the wealthy maskil Aryeh, who, unknown to him, is his uncle. During the years of Shimeon's stay Aryeh devotedly helps him with his studies, hiring a tutor to teach him 'knowledge and the language of the country'. Shimeon succeeds brilliantly, and the time eventually comes for him to realize the ideals of the Haskalah and serve the Jewish community.[25] Gottlober's *Hizaharu bivenei aniyim*

[19] Yafaz A. Goldblum, 'Jubilee: On the Seventieth Anniversary of the Life of Shneur Sachs' (Heb.), *Keneset yisra'el*, 1 (1886), cols. 833–6.

[20] *From Militant Haskalah to Conservative Maskil*, 87–8.

[21] Friedberg, *Sefer hazikhronot*, pt. 2, p. 29.

[22] Levin, *Sefer hazikhronot*, 10–11.

[23] Sokolov, *Sefer zikaron*, 78.

[24] Yampolski, 'Memoirs of my Youth', *Keneset yisra'el*, 1 (1886), col. 863. On Y. M. Trachtman, see G. Kressel, *Lexicon of Modern Hebrew Literature in Recent Times* (Heb.), vol. i (Merhavia, 1967), 44.

[25] *Ha'avot vehabanim* (Odessa, 1868), 119–22.

contains a similar sympathetic portrayal in the figure of the wealthy Yonadav, a native of Brody. A wise and intelligent man, Yonadav ridicules superstition and encourages the orphan Shmuel in his aspiration to enter the world of Haskalah, providing him with a teacher, Mordechai, who 'opened the eyes of the lad Shmuel . . . and from him he learned his wisdom and his knowledge of the Torah and the language and his great and expansive desire to fill his soul from the sweet rivers of wisdom'.[26] In the home of his benefactor Shmuel finds the books he needs to achieve his goal. As he progresses in his new studies, Yonadav sends him to the government rabbinical seminary at Zhitomir, describing to him his brilliant future and outlining his life's path as one of enlightenment. Shmuel completes his studies with great success, and finally wins the respected status of a modern, officially appointed rabbi in Keziv, the very city which had ostracized and rejected him as a youngster.[27] Even in a period of revision and questioning of the value of the Haskalah movement and its disappointing results in western Europe, Gottlober still nurtures the idealistic version of the young seeker of enlightenment in Russia who succeeds in fulfilling his mission for the sake of the community and who later also achieves respected public status.

In Judah Leib Gordon's story 'Hame'orav beda'at' (The Deranged, 1880),[28] the patron figure is the wealthy merchant Zvi Brodovski, steeped in the world of Haskalah from his youth despite the hostile attitude of his traditional environment rooted in the *beit midrash*. Brodovski is a successful importer of goods from England, and his home serves as a meeting-place for young seekers of secular knowledge. He encourages the 17-year-old hero and narrator and outlines his path of learning, trying, in a spirit of loyalty to the language and culture of the Jewish people, to offer guidance as well as inspiration. He also makes a number of practical suggestions, advising him to prepare for examinations on his own, without teachers, and providing him with the 'list of studies taught in the gymnasium' and a letter to the bookseller with instructions to supply his protégé with the books he will need.[29] Brodovski's mission is not completed even after the young man fulfils his expectations and passes the examinations successfully, gaining the longed-for certificate. He declares his willingness to go on supporting him as he travels abroad to continue his studies, and, not content with helping just one young man, establishes 'a society for the increase of secular knowledge and wisdom among the youth of our city'.[30]

Joseph Visner was a living example of such a patron. He is described in the memoirs of Abraham Baer Gottlober, who met Visner when he was still a boy and immediately fell under his spell. An intellectual and spiritual guide whose home served as a meeting-place for young maskilim, Visner lived in the city of Brody, Galicia, where he absorbed the environment of the Haskalah as it was created by the maskilim who had gathered there during the first half of the nineteenth century.

[26] *Hizaharu bivenei aniyim*, 29.
[27] Ibid. 31.
[28] In Gordon, *Collected Works: Prose* (Heb.) (Tel Aviv, 1960), 138–9.
[29] Ibid. 140.
[30] Ibid. 139.

Following his return to his native city of Dubno he cultivated the spirit of Haskalah there as well, attracting a circle of interested young men; all this was done, reports Gottlober, unobtrusively, in a spirit of devotion to the cause of enlightenment.[31] Visner acted as a spokesman for Moses Mendelssohn, transmitting the great thinker's ideas to the small Jewish towns of Russia almost forty years after his death; he explained Mendelssohn's interpretation of Maimonides' *Milot hahigayon* (Words of Logic) to Gottlober, and his influence on the young man was immense. As Gottlober wrote much later: 'I seemed to have suddenly entered a different world: for my eyes were opened and I saw new things, which had not entered my imagination until this time.' He goes on to describe his impressions of the episodes described in Isaac Euchel's classic biography of Mendelssohn which he was reading at that time, such as his dispute with Lavater or his friendship with the German writer Lessing.[32]

The home of Nahman Krochmal in Zolkiew served as a meeting-place for young maskilim. Meir Letteris, a native of the same town and Krochmal's student and ardent admirer, describes his role as a spiritual mentor and guide to young men of various ages taking their first steps on the path to the acquisition of secular knowledge: 'Then the young men, so anxious to stand in the temple of wisdom with the help of someone who was keeping watch at its doors, began to gather in the home of Nahman the wise, in order to hear wisdom from his lips.' The spiritual guidance that he offered was tailored to their level of understanding, their spiritual aspirations, and their immediate needs: 'And he gave them abundantly of his goodness—to each person as he wished and as he could achieve—through conversation and in books, in fable and proverb, the history of each people, the study of antiquity, engineering and algebra.' This guidance did indeed bear fruit, and transformed those who had need of it: 'And the young man who entered his home to hear sweet words from his mouth was a different person when he turned to leave, learning to love knowledge and thought.'[33]

In Abramowitz's *Ha'avot vehabanim* the authoritative leader of a group of young maskilim is David, a 25-year-old teacher who works in the public school in the town of Kesalon (literally 'town of fools') during the 1850s.[34] This moderate maskil serves as the spiritual mentor of the town's young men; his intention is 'to attract all the young men of Kesalon to develop their intelligence while it is still strong and to teach them sayings of wisdom'.[35] His home and the nearby woods serve as gathering-places for these young men, who meet him clandestinely, lest they offend the observant community in which they live.[36]

[31] Gottlober, 'Zikhronot miyemei ne'urai' [Memoirs of my Youth], in id., *Zikhronot umasaot*, ed. R. Goldberg, vol. i (Jerusalem, 1976), 79.

[32] Ibid. 81–2.

[33] Letteris, *Zikaron basefer*, 53.

[34] On the figure of David see Shmuel Werses, *Story and Source: Studies in the Development of Hebrew Prose* (Heb.) (Ramat Gan, 1971), 72.

[35] *Ha'avot vehabanim*, 8.

[36] Ibid.

It was not only the wealthy patrons who provided solid support for the young seekers of Haskalah by supplying the necessary material means, the teachers and the books. Guidance and intellectual inspiration were also supplied by Hebrew writers and men of letters who had themselves experienced a similar process in their youth. The biographer of Abraham Mapu describes his role as a spiritual mentor in the city of Kovno in flowery language: 'The young men in whom the spirit of knowledge had begun to vibrate gathered around him. And he showed them the path to walk and the track along which they would achieve understanding and knowledge.'[37]

The young Eliezer Ben-Yehuda, who later compiled the famous dictionary of the Hebrew language and is known as the reviver of Hebrew as a spoken language, also found himself a number of intellectual patrons and practical supporters on his way to the world of modernity. The maskil and writer Shmuel Naphtali Herz Jonas, whom he met while visiting the city, took an interest in his progress and decided to encourage and support him: 'And he exchanged words with him and found him knowledgeable, and drew him close and gave him a place in his home. . . . In the home of Jonas the lad found books of the Haskalah.'[38] When he was 13 Ben-Yehuda was sent to study in the city of Polotsk, and had the unusual experience of being encouraged and helped in the study of secular knowledge by the head of the yeshiva. This man, a hasid of the Habad sect, wanted 'to expose to him his secrets for he is a maskil, that is, he loves the Hebrew language and understands its grammar, and from time to time peruses Hebrew books'. He encouraged Ben-Yehuda to follow him in this path of moderate enlightenment, teaching him to study the Bible and read the fictional works of the Haskalah; he even secretly taught him grammar, using the famous *Talmud leshon ivri* (1796) by Judah Leib Ben Ze'ev.[39]

AMONG FRIENDS AND COLLEAGUES

In some instances it was the bonds of friendship which led to the path of Haskalah, when one young man looked up to a friend already involved in the movement. Such a relationship developed between the Galician writer Samson Bloch (1784–1845) and Nahman Krochmal, 'who was young and full of knowledge'. Their biographer, himself a maskil, describes in literary style the emotional transformation Krochmal brought about in his friend.[40] The powerful ties of friendship between two young men, both of whom possess a solid body of knowledge in Jewish studies and language and who converse on ideological matters, also existed between the young Samuel Joseph Fuenn and Mordechai Trivush, who was seven years his senior. In his memoirs, Fuenn describes the subjects of their conversations: 'We

[37] Medalia, 'Biography of Abraham Mapu'.

[38] Sokolov, *Sefer zikaron*, 189.

[39] Ibid. 188.

[40] Y. Meler, 'Biography of Rabbi Samson Bloch' (Heb.), *Kochavei yitshak*, 7 (1846), 44–5. See also Letteris, *Zikaron basefer*, 40.

offered one another every idea and thought regarding the understanding of the subjects of learning and studies, and by discussions of the language, of the interpretations of the Bible and the writings of the talmudic sages, criticism of new as well as old books . . .'.[41] These happy hours were a blessing for the two friends, both as part of their advanced studies and for the effect on their poetic and literary writings.

The strong influence that could be exerted by the experienced maskil on the young man still immersed in the world of tradition can also be seen in the life of Judah Leib Levin, as he relates in his autobiography. The expressions of scepticism to which he was exposed and which he absorbed in the home of David Lurie in Minsk shattered his faith in the Scriptures. However, the changes in his beliefs and opinions regarding the traditional literature which took place after he had begun to examine them from a critical viewpoint did not bring him a sense of happiness and satisfaction.[42]

Mapu's novel *Ayit tsavua* (The Hypocrite) depicts the expressions of friendship and comradeship that were meant to nurture and strengthen loyalty to the concept of the Haskalah and to its literature. Nehemiah, an aged maskil, nostalgically recalls his youth when the lofty Enlightenment ideals were being formulated. He and his good friend Yeroham would isolate themselves in the countryside, on the outskirts of the city, and devote themselves to poetry in the spirit of the Haskalah: 'We read the poems "Layesharim tehilah" [Praise to the Righteous] and "Shirei tiferet" [Songs of Glory], tastefully and with understanding and with the splendour of our voices, and the echo of the woods followed us; together we praised the seasons in poetry, and our poems were approved, since no man's eye beheld them.'[43]

After the 1850s the body of material available to young readers expanded with the development of the maskilic novel genre as created by Mapu. This change is reflected in Smolenskin's *Hato'eh bedarkhei haḥayim* (Wanderer in the Paths of Life). A young maskil well versed in Mapu's novels tries to interest the orphan Joseph, a constant wanderer, in them as well. In his efforts to convince and lure Joseph, he praises Mapu's novel *Ahavat tsiyon* (Love of Zion): 'You are not yet aware that no pleasure in the world equals that of reading a book filled with the spirit of knowledge.'[44] Despite Joseph's feeble response to these words of persuasion and promise, the dedicated maskil continues to praise and enthuse in a style that reflects a clear ideological trend in the world beyond the fiction. This is the reward awaiting readers of such novels: 'From the peaks of enduring mountains we shall look at the world . . . on those events and acts that take place before our eyes, and we shall cry out joyfully, "Hurrah! We have found wisdom! Our eyes have seen the secrets of Creation" .'[45] The well-read maskil even reproves Joseph for his

[41] *From Militant Haskalah to Conservative Maskil*, 85.
[42] Levin, *Sefer hazikhronot*, 11–12.
[43] *Ayit tsavua* (1857–64), in *Collected Works* (Heb.) (Tel Aviv, 1939), 282.
[44] Peretz Smolenskin (1842–85), *Hato'eh bedarkhei haḥayim*, 4 vols. (1869–71; Warsaw, 1910), i. 162.
[45] Ibid. 163.

lack of interest in this literature—'Why have you not read many books that would bring wisdom into our hearts?'—and promises the lad that from now on he will be both his literary and his ideological guide. Later, in the course of his wanderings, the young Joseph meets Gideon, who also guides him through the Haskalah literature, particularly its poetry. Gideon's activity is crowned with success, as Joseph admits: 'there are times when its spirit alights on me and I, too, find value and pleasure in those books'.[46]

Often the friend and mentor in these situations not only had to do the convincing but also choose the literature best suited to the potential convert's nature and religious background. In the novel *Hadat vehaḥayim* (Religion and Life) by Reuven Asher Braudes (1851–1902), Shraga the maskil, the son-in-law of the town squire, suggests his friend Shmuel should read *Alfei menasheh* (The Thousands of Manasseh) by Rabbi Manasseh of Ilya, and *Te'udah beyisra'el* (Instruction in Israel) by Isaac Baer Levinsohn, since Shmuel is still immersed in the world of Torah study. This is the perfect choice of books, explains Braudes, since they are ideally suited to the concepts familiar to a young man immersed in the world of the *beit midrash*.[47] Shmuel is indeed powerfully influenced by his diligent reading of these books; they transform his outlook: 'section upon section becomes confused and they confound his mind; many questions and queries, or problems and puzzles run riot in his head'. Yet considering the intellectual revolution inspired in him by these Haskalah writings, he is not at all happy with his situation. He even complains to the friend who brought him to this crisis: 'Have you any idea what you have stolen from me? My entire life! . . . a gloomy heart, a suffering soul, and a world that is covered in darkness.'[48] Shraga counters with his own rationalistic concept, according to which 'The foundation of man's life is intelligence . . . with his eyes he reads the books of the wisdom of his time. He will see that in each generation there is new knowledge . . . and he too will yearn for the paths of wisdom.'[49]

Within the fictional framework of Judah Leib Gordon's story 'Hame'orav beda'at', the young man who is the object of a friend's persuasion recalls in later years the conversations that he had with Meshulam, the intended son-in-law of the town squire. His testimony depicts again the typical situation with which we are familiar from the memoirs, autobiographical works, and letters of the period: the thrilling experience of studying in secret and living a double life, split between Torah and the Haskalah.[50]

READING HASKALAH LITERATURE IN SECRET

Scholars have already and justifiedly pointed out the central role of the book in the process of ideological change experienced by the young man on his path to Haskalah. It has also already been stated that literature is always a salient factor in the hero's

[46] Ibid. ii. 88. [47] Braudes, *Hadat vehaḥayim*, 2 vols., ed. G. Shaked (Jerusalem, 1974), i. 89.
[48] Ibid. [49] Ibid. 85. [50] Gordon, *Collected Works: Prose*, 133.

process of enlightenment: most descriptions of the awakening of enlightenment within the yeshiva community centre on books.[51]

The motif of a book triggering intellectual change in a young man's life plays a central role in *Avi'ezer*, the autobiography of Mordecai Aaron Guenzburg (Ramag, 1795–1846). Written in the 1840s and published posthumously in 1863, it reflects Jewish life in the small towns of Lithuania at the end of the first quarter of the nineteenth century;[52] it was one of those documents which ignited the imaginations of Jewish readers in Russia, even in the midst of the new realities that characterized the 1860s in that country. *Avi'ezer* expresses the aspirations and situation of young maskilim on the path to the Haskalah, and illustrates the influence of Moses Mendelssohn's writings in eastern Europe and the deep impression they made on young men there. Its hero praises Mendelssohn's *Phädon,* on the immortality of the soul, which he has read in Hebrew translation in his early youth, and points out, with great astonishment, 'By his book *Phädon*, Ben Menahem has made himself great in my eyes. To me it is as if there is no better person than he in all the community of the wise in the world.'[53] One experience for such students of Haskalah literature—and in this too they had the active help of a mentor—was the surprise awaiting them in Mendelssohn's new interpretation of the book of Ecclesiastes.

Among the books of medieval philosophy that left their stamp on the philosophical outlook of the new age of young Jewish men was Maimonides' *Moreh nevukhim* (Guide of the Perplexed), whose influence is marked throughout the development of the Haskalah movement.[54] It is therefore no wonder that the young Solomon Judah Rapoport heartily recommended it to a friend as a reliable guide to the desirable and balanced path between Torah and wisdom, giving him instructions on how to read and learn Maimonides' texts and seeing them as a fortifying factor in the ideological struggle against his adversaries—those who hated the Haskalah and progress.[55] Nahman Krochmal's ideological struggle as he moved in the direction of enlightenment in early nineteenth-century Galicia is also illustrated by his biographer Letteris in terms of forbidden books.[56]

With local and personal variations, such situations are repeated throughout the history of the Haskalah movement, including its later stages in the towns of Russia

[51] See Ben-Ami Feingold, 'Books and Literature as a Subject in Maskilic Literature', in *Testimony: Research on Hebrew Literature* (Heb.), vol. v (Tel Aviv, 1986), 85–100

[52] On *Avi'ezer* and its author see Werses, 'The Development of Autobiography in the Haskalah' (Heb.), in id., *Trends and Forms in Haskalah Literature*, 252–3; Israel Bartal, 'Mordechai Aaron Guenzburg: A Lithuanian Maskil Faces Modernity', in Frances Malino and David Sorkin (eds.), *From East and West: Jews in a Changing Europe, 1750–1870* (Oxford, 1990), 126–47.

[53] *Avi'ezer* (Vilna, 1864), 92, 115–16.

[54] On the influence of Maimonides on the literature of the Haskalah see Y. M. Lehman, 'Maimonides, Mendelssohn and the *Me'asfim*', *Leo Baeck Institute Year Book*, 20 (1975), 87–108; Yehuda Friedlander, 'The Place of Halakhah in Haskalah Literature: The Attitude to Maimonides as a Halakhic Authority' (Heb.), *Meḥkarei yerushalayim bemaḥshevet yisra'el*, 5 (1986), 349–62.

[55] Rapoport's letter is published in Krochmal, *Letters*, 45–6.

[56] Letteris, *Zikaron basefer*, 119.

and Lithuania, and the role of burners and destroyers of forbidden books was fulfilled not only by zealous members of the community, but also by the families of the young men themselves.

Even after the young maskil stopped hiding his desertion of the world of the *beit midrash* and made his new affiliation public, he still had the problem of obtaining the essential classic Haskalah texts. Gottlober was able to borrow a number of books from his friend in Zhitomir, who owned a rich library, including Luzzatto's and Wessely's poetry and the journal *Hame'asef.* There he also found well-known medieval religious and philosophical texts, such as *Moreh nevukhim* and Joseph Albo's *Sefer ha'ikarim* (Book of Principles). Even in his old age Gottlober recalled the kindness and generosity of his friend, and stated emotionally in his memoirs: 'I owe him thanks for ever, for having graced me with his books, and whatever my eyes requested he did not withhold from me.'[57] As well as his authentic personal list of the classic Haskalah literature that he read in his youth, Gottlober also gives a brief catalogue of the reading material, including poetry and philosophy, that constructs the world of the young Shmuel in *Hizaharu bivenei aniyim*:

> He also had as his guide the books *Moreh nevukhim*, *Or lanetiv* . . . And his ear took something from the books of Mendelssohn and Weisel. And G–d made precious to him the books *Kinat ha'emet*, *Teḥunat harabanim*, *Megaleh temirin*, *Te'udah beyisra'el*, *Hatorah vehafilosofiyah*. These were the books that opened the eyes of the young man and deepened his critical approach to the traditional Jewish reality in which he had been living up to that time.[58]

In the footnote to this list the storyteller adds his own experience of reading in the midst of the intolerant hasidic environment which constituted his world when he was young.[59]

As has been mentioned, Moses Mendelssohn and his writings continued to exert a powerful influence in Russia and Galicia long beyond his lifetime. In Mordecai David Brandstaedter's story *Hatsorer beigrilov* (The Oppressor from Grilow, 1870), the governor of the town of Grilow in Galicia, who was himself attracted to the world of Haskalah in his youth, and who now holds a high position in the Austrian government, acts as spiritual mentor for the 16-year-old Shmuel, prescribing the course of Haskalah texts for him to read, and is even lending them to him. He advises him as follows:

> When you read the Hebrew books of the new Jewish scholars and the Bible . . . study with the German translation. And beyond all those, study the Bible as interpreted and translated by the late Moshe, son of Menahem [Moses Mendelssohn]. Your eyes will be opened to his words that are sweeter than honey, and more to be desired than gold, yea, than much fine gold.[60]

[57] 'Zikhronot miyemei ne'urai', 124–5.

[58] *Hizaharu bivenei aniyim*, 17. *Kinat ha'emet* is by Judah Leib Mieses, *Teḥunat harabanim* by Joseph Karo, and *Hatorah vehafilosofiyah* by S. Reggio.

[59] Ibid. 18.

[60] In Brandstaedter, *Sipurim* [Stories], ed. B. E. Feingold (Jerusalem, 1974), 134.

The *beit midrash*, in which groups of young people devotedly studied Talmud, was also the place in which the threads of their affinity to the Haskalah movement were being spun through the clandestine reading of forbidden or suspect literature. In this story Brandstaedter describes this underground reading. Shmuel and his friend Nathan habitually hide in Shmuel's parents' attic: 'And not a soul in the house knew that under the huge thick books open on their table there were now hiding small books . . . over which they pored the entire day.' Instead of studying the various talmudic rulings, as is expected of them by their community, 'they now put all their efforts into things . . . such as the history of earth and sky, of the world and of man who dwells in it'.[61]

Another typical event in the exposure of the young maskil who was secretly reading forbidden literature was the revelation of his ideological identity through the discovery, and subsequent confiscation and destruction, of his personal box of books. Testimonies to such acts appear in the memoir-style autobiographical literature, in the biographical literature written shortly after the deaths of the authors involved, and in the fictional Haskalah literature which absorbed much from such events. Judah Leib Levin relates how, following the severance of ties between himself and the elders of his hasidic family, with whom he had lived when he stayed in Kobrin, 'I found out that they had searched my bag and removed all my writings, which they did not understand; and because they didn't understand, they assumed them to be works of profanity and burned them.'[62] Eliezer Ben-Yehuda also told his biographer about a box of books, the contents of which had been exposed by his hasidic hounders during his stay with members of his family in a small town. Once, in his absence, his hasidic uncle and cousin entered his room, 'and they smashed his box of books and searched and found Haskalah literature, and then the downfall of the lad was complete and his situation dreadful'.[63]

The experience of reading the forbidden Haskalah literature in secret is satirically reflected in Abramowitz's *Ha'avot vehabanim*, which depicts the search of the young Shimeon's bookshelves after he has fled his parents' hasidic home to acquire secular knowledge. His father and mother angrily and scornfully throw out all those books that they consider unfit, such as Mendelssohn's *Biur* and Erter's *Hatsofeh leveit yisra'el*.[64]

In 'Hame'orav beda'at' Judah Leib Gordon tells the story of young Russian Jews on the path to the world of secular learning and science during the second half of the nineteenth century. The point of view is that of the young man, who describes the cultural and intellectual change taking place within him in light of the persecution of Yermiyahu, a *beit midrash* student, punished for reading Levinsohn's well-known *Te'udah beyisra'el*. This does not deter the young man, but on the contrary, strengthens his resolve.[65]

61 Brandstaedter, *Sipurim*, 136.

62 Levin, *Sefer hazikhronot*, 17.

63 Ben-Yehuda, *Zikaron basefer* [Memoirs] (Warsaw, 1889), 188–94.

64 *Ha'avot vehabanim*, 23.

65 In *Collected Works: Prose*, 130.

A special focus on the reading of books as one of the decisive stages in the gradual, underground process of shifting from the *beit midrash* to the world of the Haskalah is found in the autobiography of Moses Leib Lilienblum (1833–1910). Here is a detailed catalogue of the books from that period—a sort of historical total of the maskil's corpus of secular and Torah literature, his and that of his era. What we have is a list of many books that encompass the spheres of literature and philosophy, with texts of a typical maskilic character. At the same time, the talmudic literature continues to serve him as a source of intellectual competition until the Haskalah literature finally gets the upper hand.[66] In the spirit of the critical attitude to the Haskalah movement and its literature that was prevalent at the time of publication of his autobiography (1876), Lilienblum sums up the balance of his enthusiastic reading during those years in which he consolidated his maskilic awareness:

It was not the Haskalah that I loved, for at that time I knew nothing about it, but I had had my fill of books of *pilpul* and of sermons, and I sought food for my soul in books, which were of a type new to me—and I imagined in my heart, that I loved those books themselves which were called 'books of the Haskalah'.[67]

In contrast to the expressions of tension and polarity that generally characterized the relationship between the young aspiring maskil, who was reading about and associating with the Haskalah in secret, and the traditional mitnagdic or hasidic environment of Torah study there are also some biographical models—for example the fathers of Guenzburg and Gottlober—that bear witness to the coexistence of these two intellectual worlds, whether by way of open and declared mutual affinity, or by way of a delicate balance of forced or voluntary tolerance on the part of the family or the community.

The impulse to read the Haskalah literature was sometimes also related to the young reader's aspiration to become a poet; indeed, the writing of poetry was identified with a bent for the Haskalah camp. This was one of the reasons for Lilienblum's intensive reading. As a young man he had already published some of his poetry in the Hebrew weeklies *Hamagid* and *Hakarmel*, and he identified passionately with *Shirei sefat kodesh* (Poems of the Holy Tongue) by Adam Hakohen-Levinson, and particularly with the poems of his son Micha Yosef Levinson (Michal). Lilienblum said: 'My reading of those poems helped me to put in my heart the style of the poetic language.'[68]

With the appearance of the weekly *Hamagid* at the end of the 1850s and then in the 1860s, in Russia, of the weeklies *Hakarmel* and *Hamelits*, the press joined books as another significant way to spread the Haskalah among young men.

[66] Lilienblum, *Ḥatot ne'urim* [Sins of my Youth], in *Autobiographical Writings* (Heb.), ed. S. Breiman (Jerusalem, 1970), 131.

[67] Ibid.

[68] Ibid. 121–3.

NINE

Reality and its Refraction in Descriptions of Women in Haskalah Fiction

TOVA COHEN

'O Hebrew woman, who can fathom your life?'

JUDAH LEIB GORDON
Kotso shel yod

THIS chapter will examine the relationship between the extra-literary reality of women's lives and the attitude towards them in European Jewish society of the nineteenth century, and the portrayal of female characters in the fiction of the Haskalah.[1]

Literature never directly reflects reality but at most refracts the given historical moment. The transition from the actual 'environment' of history to its literary counterpart involves fundamental changes resulting partly from the author's personality and partly from the inherent assumptions and requirements of the literary medium.[2] For the literary critic the social environment serves as a frame of reference for gauging the changes that have taken place in the 'literary environment'—the work itself. Once the historical reality has been defined, it is possible to identify the literary features of the fictional characters. As far as the prose works of the Haskalah are concerned, the refraction of reality can be examined from two points of view. One is the extent to which the maskil's socio-historical reality affected his fictional descriptions; the other is the manner in which literary models, genres, and traditions contributed to the portrait of his fictional characters.

[1] The scope of this chapter is limited to descriptions found in three genres of fiction: satire, romance, and the novel. Poetry is excluded on the assumption that it does not reflect extra-literary social reality to the same extent as the prose genres. This is in accordance with Simon Halkin's well-known definition: 'The prose of the Haskalah period tends to see the "real" Jew, while the poetry of the Haskalah tends to see the desirable Jew, the Jew envisioned as the ideal': *Trends and Forms in Modern Hebrew Literature* (Heb.) (Jerusalem, 1984), 56.

[2] According to Robert Alter, 'Literary Reflections of the Jewish Family', in D. Kraemer (ed.), *The Jewish Family: Metaphor and Memory* (New York and Oxford, 1989), 225–6.

THE MALE-ORIENTED CHARACTER OF HASKALAH LITERATURE

In considering the portrayal of female protagonists in the prose works of the Haskalah, the fact that this is male literature *par excellence* is highly significant. Not only was this literature male-authored, but it was addressed to a predominantly male readership (at least until the 1870s, as will be clarified below). Socially the maskil can be defined as a male member of the social class known as the *lomedim* (studying) circles. This definition, which has gender-related social and cultural overtones, largely accounts for the male bias permeating the descriptions of women in Haskalah literature.

The maskil had to be a *lamdan* (a scholar) because of the inherent connection between Haskalah and the Hebrew language. A good understanding of Hebrew was a precondition for becoming even a reader of Haskalah literature. Those who had learned basic Hebrew, but did not go far beyond the education of the *ḥeder*, were unable to understand the rich and sophisticated Hebrew texts of the Haskalah; this privilege was reserved to those who continued their studies in the yeshiva. As a result, the readership was limited to the narrow elitist social stratum of the *lomedim* circles, the 'young men who devote their youth to the study of Torah, and mature professional scholars'.[3]

The biographies of Haslakah writers provide evidence of the scholarly elitism that distinguished the society from which they were drawn. They all attended a *ḥeder* and studied for many years in a yeshiva before turning away from traditional Orthodoxy to embrace the notions and ideals of the Haskalah.[4] Most maskilim came from families which had been rooted in *lomedim* circles for several generations.[5] Beyond its other cultural and literary ramifications,[6] this elitism is significant for the present discussion because *lomedim* circles excluded women. In the eighteenth and nineteenth centuries, just as in previous generations, the majority of Jewish women were not familiar with Hebrew. Traditional middle-class women did learn the Hebrew alphabet (usually at home[7]), but only for the purpose of reciting the

[3] The concept and its definition derive from Immanuel Etkes, 'Marriage and Torah Study among the *Lomdim* in Lithuania in the Nineteenth Century', in Kraemer (ed.), *The Jewish Family*, 153–78. My description of the typical division of roles in the family in the *lomedim* circles is based on the conclusion of this chapter.

[4] This pattern is true of the majority of Haskalah writers, as emerges, for instance, from Klausner's biographical introductions: see Klausner (ed.), *History of Modern Hebrew Literature* (Heb.), 6 vols. (Jerusalem, 1952–4), for example Joseph Perl (ii. 285–6), Adam Hakohen (iii. 174–5), Abraham Mapu (iii. 272–4), Moses Leib Lilienblum (iv. 193), and Judah Leib Gordon (iv. 305–7).

[5] This applies, for instance, to Shneur Sachs, Isaac Baer Levinsohn, Mordecai Aaron Guenzburg, Adam Hakohen (the pen-name of Abraham Dov Lebensohn), and Abraham Mapu.

[6] On this point see Tova Cohen, 'The Scholarly Technique: A Code of Haskalah Literature' (Heb.), *Jerusalem Studies in Hebrew Literature*, 13 (1992), 137–69.

[7] See Z. Scharfstein, 'The *Ḥeder* in the Life of Our People', in *Shilo* (Heb.) (n.p., 1943), 120. However, there were also special *ḥeders* for girls (where they were taught to read Yiddish), especially towards

prayers or reading Yiddish texts. Beyond this limited knowledge, Hebrew remained an unknown language. They were never introduced to any Hebrew canonical texts (the Bible, the Mishnah, the Talmud, the later halakhic literature) since it was accepted that women should not study Torah.[8] This gave rise to a division among the recipients of traditional Jewish culture: Hebrew texts (halakhic and scholarly) were addressed to men, while Yiddish texts (like *teḥinot* or *Tse'enah ure'enah*) were addressed to women (and uneducated men).

The ability to read and understand a Hebrew text made the male member of the scholarly class a potential maskil; conversely, the inability to do so automatically excluded women from Haskalah circles. Thus the Jewish Enlightenment was governed by the same language-based and male-oriented elitism[9] that characterized the *lomedim* circles. This holds true even for women who underwent European acculturation and acquired a general education, a trend that began at the end of the eighteenth century among the German Jewish bourgeoisie and which, by the middle of the nineteenth century, had become popular in eastern Europe as well. These well-educated women, just like their uneducated predecessors, had no knowledge of Hebrew; in most cases, Hebrew and Torah study remained strictly male preserves.[10] Consequently the traditional division along gender–language lines carried over to the Haskalah: writing in Hebrew meant the renunciation of a female readership. The few maskilim who wanted to address women did so in Yiddish.[11]

the end of the 19th cent.: see Shaul Stampfer, 'Gender Differentiation and Education of the Jewish Woman in Nineteenth-Century Eastern Europe', *Polin*, 7 (1992), 63–87. Stampfer underlines the fact that although many women acquired formal education, they were barred from Hebrew education.

[8] R. Eleazar's saying as cited in the Mishnah (*Sotah* 3: 4)—'Whoever teaches his daughter Torah, it is as though he teaches her lewdness'—became the basis for extensive halakhic rulings that restricted or even banned the teaching of Torah to women. For details see E. G. Eilinson, *Between Woman and her Maker* (Heb.) (Jerusalem, 1984), 143–65.

[9] This is similar to European male-oriented cultural elitism, which was based on knowledge of Latin, a language that was learned almost exclusively by men. Since Latin was considered a necessary basis for literary writing, culture became inaccessible to women. See J. Donnovan, 'The Silence is Broken', in A. McConnell, R. Borker, and N. Forman (eds.), *Women and Language in Literature and Society* (New York, 1980), 205–18.

[10] Thus, for instance, Isaac Euchel translated the prayer-book into German for his student Rivka Friedlaender, who was unable to understand the Hebrew prayers. In his preface he quotes her complaint that in spite of her sound educational background she knows no Hebrew: 'How unfortunate, my dear friend, that nearly all women and most of the men are unable to experience this happiness [the Hebrew prayers]'. The translation was published in Königsberg in 1786. See Shmuel Feiner, 'The Modern Jewish Woman: A Test-Case in the Relationship between the Haskalah and Modernity' (Heb.; Eng. abstract), *Zion*, 58 (1993), 455.

[11] An early example of a maskil addressing women in Yiddish is Naphtali Herz Homberg's 1817 commentary on Jacob b. Isaac Ashkenazi of Janow's *Tse'enah ure'enah* [Go Out and See, *c.*1590] which is written in a Hebrew transcription of German and aims 'to reach out to those women who want to draw from the fountain of Torah'. On this book, and excerpts from it, see Chava Turniansky, 'A Haskalah Interpretation of the *Tse'enah ure'enah*' (Heb.; Eng. abstract), *Hasifrut*, 2/4 (1971), 835–41. By the middle of the 19th cent. there were many more examples. For instance, women were the main audience for the Yiddish translations of Mapu's works: see Shmuel Werses, *The Yiddish Translations*

While it is true that after the 1860s a few women formed part of the Haskalah readership, the rarity of this phenomenon, along with the astonishment which it generated among male maskilim, prove that these women were an exception. Men still constituted the vast majority of readers of Hebrew.[12] Even Miriam Markel-Mosessohn (formerly Wirszblowski; 1841–1920), whose education and fluency in Hebrew and German[13] gained the esteem of Mapu, Judah Leib Gordon, and Lilienblum, was treated as an exceptional phenomenon that might not repeat itself in the future.[14]

Hebrew women writers were even rarer. The Italian Jewish poet Rachel Morpurgo (1790–1871) stands out as a unique phenomenon of female Hebrew literary writing in the midst of the male-oriented Hebrew Enlightenment. Indeed, her contemporaries viewed her as an exception, and even as 'unfeminine'.[15] Other women did write letters and essays in Hebrew at the end of the Haskalah period. But although this pursuit had social significance, it cannot be viewed as a literary phenomenon.[16] The maskilim's amazement at any woman writing in Hebrew, even at that late stage, shows how strongly they were convinced of the male character of the Haskalah.

of 'Ahavat Zion' by Abraham Mapu (Heb.) (Jerusalem, 1989). The first Russian weekly in Yiddish, *Kol mevaser* (1st pub. 1862), included women among its staff, and its journalists regarded it as a primary vehicle for expressing women's views: R. Adler, *Women of the Shtetl through the Eyes of I. L. Peretz* (Cranbury, NJ, 1980), 120 n. 5. In this period too, Yiddish maskil fiction was written for the first time, by Israel Axenfeld (1787–1866), Isaac Meir Dick (1814–93), and Hayyim Lenski (1839–1915), on the assumption that these narratives were addressed to women as well. (In his introduction to *Maḥazeh mul maḥazeh* (1861) Dick explicitly states that the desire to reach Jewish female readers is what motivated him to write in Yiddish.) However, these were marginal phenomena before the emergence of the three Yiddish classics: Mendele Mokher Seforim, Shalom Aleichem, and I. L. Peretz.

[12] Thus, for instance, *Hamagid*, the Haskalah journal, published Devorah Ha'ephrati's Hebrew letter to Mapu on *Ahavat tsiyon*, introducing it as follows: 'Behold, this is new, what our eyes have seen—in the Hebrew language, handwritten by a Hebrew woman' (*Hamagid*, 3/12 (1858), 46). Judah Leib Gordon too, who in the 1870s received a number of Hebrew letters from young girls, observed in every one of his responses how rare the phenomenon was and how much it pleased him. For instance, see his letters to Sheina Wolf in Gordon, *Letters* (Heb.), comp. and ed. Y. Y. Weisberg, vol. ii (Warsaw, 1894), 5, and his letter to Nehamah Feinstein (ibid. 158).

[13] Women's knowledge of these languages is proved by the Hebrew edition of Isaak Aschev Francolm's *The Jews in England; or the Jews and the Crusaders in the Reign of Richard the Lionheart*, translated from the German by Miriam Markel (Warsaw, 1869).

[14] Smolenskin wrote to her: 'You are the first Hebrew woman to write a book . . . perhaps the last one too.' This letter, dated 1869, was published in *Ketuvim*, 3 (Nov. 1927), 5.

[15] On the responses of contemporary maskilim to the poems of Rachel Morpurgo see Y. Berlowitz, 'Rachel Morpurgo: Passion for Death, Passion for Poetry: On the First Modern Hebrew Woman Poet', in *Sadan: Studies in Hebrew Literature* (Heb.), vol. ii (Tel Aviv, 1996), 11–40.

[16] See Shifra Alchin, 'A Letter to My Father's Friends' (Heb.), *Hamelits*, 3 (1863), 119, which demands that the teaching of Hebrew to girls should not be neglected; Berta Kreidman's letter in *Hamagid*, supplement to no. 7 (1870), who makes the claim that she is an enthusiastic reader of Hebrew journals; Toybe Segal, 'The Question of Women' (Heb.), *Ha'ivri* (1879), 69, 78–9, 85, 94, 101–2, a feminist paper which impressed the editorial board as it was written in Hebrew. On these writings see Feiner, 'The Modern Jewish Woman'.

This maleness can also be attributed to social factors. According to David Biale,[17] the maskilim, just like contemporary hasidic Jews, formed closed societies, preferring to spend their leisure time in exclusively male company as a reaction to the enforced early marriage customary among the scholarly elite. Biale speculates that the traumatic experience of being married at the age of 13 or 14 made young husbands hostile to women. This explains the desire of hasidim, *lamdanim*, and maskilim alike to spend their time in a strictly male environment. Other reasons for this preference were the segregation between the sexes characteristic of traditional Jewish society and the male-oriented framework within which all Jewish intellectual activity—beginning in the *ḥeder*—was conducted. The all-male character of maskilic circles was therefore the continuation of the accepted situation in traditional Jewish society. The male character of Haskalah literature is as much a social phenomenon as a cultural-linguistic one.

The maskilim were aware of the 'masculinity' of the circle; they recognized that they did not have to make allowances for the sensibilities of female readers. In a letter to Miriam Markel-Mosessohn, who had reprimanded him for using obscene language in his writings, Lilienblum dwells on this point: 'You should bear in mind that you are the only woman who reads my book. Do I have to guard my mouth and tongue that speak our holy language (which is not alien to such expressions, forged in this spirit of the ancient land) in a book read by no gentle woman but you?'[18] This male orientation exerted a decisive influence on the portrayal of women, and gave rise to an exaggerated and biased characterization of them; in many cases descriptions are blatantly hostile to an extent possible only in a single-sex circle. The conventional trends of European androcentric literature, which typically creates an exaggerated distinction between women who are idealized ('angels') and those who are demonized ('monsters'), are reinforced in Haskalah literature.[19] Such depictions in non-Jewish European literature were somewhat moderated during the nineteenth century, when female readership increased. But Haskalah literature did not experience the same process. Aware of the male composition of their audience, Haskalah authors took the licence either to denigrate women through satirical criticism or to place them on a pedestal through idealized descriptions. These two stereotypes—the ridiculed women and the worshipped heroine—are so recurrent

[17] *Eros and the Jews* (New York, 1992), 158.

[18] Moses Leib Lilienblum's letter to Anshel Markel Mosessohn and his wife Miriam Markel, Odessa, 1870, in *Ketuvim* (1926), 3–4. It is noteworthy that five years later Smolenskin noticed the slight infiltration of women into the readership and realized that Hebrew writing was no more 'an exclusive club': in a letter to Judah Leib Levin dated 1875, he warns him to avoid writing obscenities, out of consideration for the readers of *Hashaḥar*, some of whom were women. See the catalogue edited by Rivkah Maoz entitled *Peretz Smolenskin Exhibition: On the 150th Anniversary of his Birth* (Jerusalem, 1992), 24.

[19] This dichotomy was described in detail in Simone de Beauvoir, *Le Deuxième Sexe* (Paris, 1949); trans. H. M. Parshley as *The Second Sex* (New York, 1972). The impact of this phenomenon on depictions of women in European literature is described in S. M. Gilbert and S. Gubar, *The Madwoman in the Attic* (New Haven, 1979).

in Haskalah literature that they can be categorized as the governing models for the portrayal of its female protagonists. Evidently, these models form part of the literary conventions that run through European and earlier Hebrew literature (such as the *makama*). Nonetheless, their persistence in Haskalah literature derives directly from the fact that it was written by and for men. As in all androcentric literature, but in a particularly marked way, the male-oriented descriptions are far removed from real women, being mere projections of their authors' fears and fantasies.

To this must be added the way in which the attitude towards women—whether critical or worshipful—united the writers and readers of male literature: both perceived the woman as the 'other'. While this tendency is characteristic of European patriarchal culture in general,[20] its prevalence in Haskalah literature is of particular importance. By characterizing women as 'other', the maskil author, whether consciously or unconsciously, created a bond of understanding with his male readers which was especially valuable in view of the fact that some of them were not yet fully convinced of the movement's principles.[21] In the satirical descriptions the female protagonist becomes a scapegoat for the evils of traditional society; personifying a whole range of social ills, she exonerates the male reader from responsibility and makes him receptive to the author's criticisms. A similar function of bonding between writer and reader is fulfilled by the image of the woman on a pedestal, representing as she does a shared yearning for the ideal.

Through its male orientation, Haskalah literature reinforced the tendency to produce male-biased descriptions of women. A well-balanced and thorough examination of how women were portrayed in Haskalah literature must therefore take into account its male orientation.

THE EXTRA-LITERARY BASIS FOR THE PORTRAYAL OF WOMEN

The real-life woman whose character infuses the portrait of female characters in Haskalah fiction is the traditional wife, as found among the *lomedim* circles of

[20] Cf. de Beauvoir's definition: 'She [the woman] is defined and differentiated with reference to man and not he with reference to her; she is the incidental, the inessential as opposed to the essential. He is the Subject, he is the Absolute—she is the Other': *The Second Sex*, 16.

[21] In view of its didactic, extra-literary objectives as the organ of a revolutionary social movement, Haskalah literature addressed whoever was willing to open a Haskalah book. The writer had to do his best to make the reader sympathize with the ideas he expressed in order to effect the desired change in the reader's thinking and way of life. For this reason, it was advisable to create the broadest common denominator that could bring together reader and writer despite their differences of ideological opinion. This must be one of the reasons why the maskil maintained a considerable number of traditional Jewish techniques: he addressed the reader in a familiar language, he made references to texts that were known to the reader, and he suggested that the reader should apply the reading strategies customary in traditional scholarly pursuits. On this point see Tova Cohen, 'Simultaneous Reading: A Key Technique in Understanding the Confrontation with the Bible in the Poetry of Adam Hakohen' (Heb.), *Jerusalem Studies in Hebrew Literature*, 7 (1985), 71–89; Cohen, 'The Scholarly Technique'.

eastern and central Europe.[22] Her model is first and foremost the women with whom the maskil was familiar during his formative years. Since the basis for one's emotional perception of the world is formed at a very young age, early experiences and acquaintances with members of the opposite sex affect the way one subsequently treats them: long after the maskil had severed ties with his society of origin, he continued to relate to women in conformity with the attitude prevalent in that society.[23] Such was the case even with regard to the women he met as an adult and who turned out to be completely different from the traditional women he had known as a boy, either because, just like him, they had experienced European acculturation, or because they had learned to demand equality in the spirit of the Russian revolutionary ideologies. They too were cast into the bipolar female moulds that were imprinted on his consciousness.

The women portrayed in the literature of the Haskalah mostly belonged to the Jewish community of central and eastern Europe. In the earlier works of the Haskalah, which originated in Germany at the end of the eighteenth century, female characterization is negligible. Satires such as *Ketav yosher* (The Book of Righteousness) by Saul Levin-Berlin, *Siḥah be'erets haḥayim* (A Dialogue in the Land of the Living) by Aaron Wolfsson, and *Ḥerev nokemet nekam berit* (A Sword Avenging the Covenant) by Meir Israel Breslau contain hardly any descriptions of women.[24] These and other works dealt with the essence of Judaism and criticized Jewish society in an abstract way, with virtually no reference to actual figures or to the writer's emotional attitude. When the maskilim of Germany wanted to treat the

[22] No full account is available of the status and characteristics of women in traditional European Jewish society in the 18th and 19th cents. It is particularly difficult to discover sources on the history of the Jewish woman, since most of the texts that serve as historical materials are not concerned with the world of women, which in Jewish society was relegated to the margins of social, and totally excluded from intellectual activity. Those few and partial descriptions of Jewish women in the 19th cent. that do exist are placed in the framework of a general discussion on the Jewish family in the period, and are mainly drawn from subjective and biased sources. Some studies rely on childhood memories of people who left the shtetl and emigrated to another country: see M. Zborowski and E. Herzog, *Life is with People: The Culture of the Shtetl* (New York, 1952); S. Stahl-Weinberg, *The World of Our Mothers* (Chapel Hill, NC and London, 1988). Other studies rely on autobiographical descriptions of the maskilim, or on literary descriptions of autobiographical nature: see David Knaani, *Studies in the History of the Jewish Family* (Heb.) (Tel Aviv, 1986); Biale, *Eros and the Jews*. These descriptions tend not to reflect reality, both because of the critical attitude of the maskilim and the nostalgic approach of the memoirs. Of special note is Etkes, 'Marriage and Torah Study', which describes the *lomedim* family with the help of internal sources.

[23] See e.g. the confession of the hero of *Urva parah* by Berdyczewski: 'I am not the one who is to blame for not being able to find the love I seek. It is my ancestors, along with their way of thinking and their books, who depressed our spirit': 'Miḥuts lateḥum', in *The Works of M. Y. Bin-Gorion [Berdyczewski]: Stories* (Heb.), vol. ii (Tel Aviv, 1936), pt. 1, p. 132.

[24] Incidentally, *Nezed hadema* by Israel of Zamosc, the only early satire that fully portrays a female character, reflects the Jewish community of eastern Europe. Israel b. Moses Halevi of Zamosc (1700–72) was born in eastern Galicia, and was raised in Zamosc, Poland, where he later served as a rabbi in the local yeshiva.

realities of everyday life they did so in their Yiddish-German rather than in their Hebrew works (as was the case, for instance, in the comedies of Wolfsson and Euchel). Hebrew was reserved either for scholarly discussions or for sublime epic poetry, where the contemporary Jewish woman was marginalized.[25]

In Haskalah fiction, real concern with female characters began only in the second decade of the nineteenth century (in Perl's social satire) and gathered momentum from the 1850s. By that time, the centres of the Hebrew Enlightenment were located in east-central and eastern Europe, and it is from the Jewish communities of those regions that the characters of Haskalah literature are drawn. The role of the wife in the *lomedim* circles of these regions differed markedly from that of women in other social strata. These women served as the breadwinners of the family to enable their husbands to devote all their time to studying Torah. This unusual economic structure developed primarily in the eighteenth and nineteenth centuries,[26] and became most pronounced in Lithuania. In other sections of Jewish society the division of roles was similar to that found among non-Jews: in the families of the rich Jewish merchants, for example, as in those of the contemporary European bourgeoisie, the husband was the sole provider while the wife was the homemaker, while in the families of craftsmen and labourers, just as in the non-Jewish lower classes, husband and wife alike worked for the family livelihood.[27]

The economic power wielded by wives in the *lomedim* families did not grant them official authority over family matters, or even equality within the family.[28]

[25] The difference between the way women were described in Hebrew and in German texts can be demonstrated by comparing the Hebrew and German works of Isaac Euchel. In 'The Letters of Meshulam Ha'eshtemoi' (Heb.), a series of pseudepigraphic letters published in *Hame'asef* (1789–90), he discusses the place of women in society (the very concern with the subject is unusual for his generation). He does not describe specific characters, but provides a general utopian account of women's status which conveys his criticism of the segregation of the sexes. In contrast, in his Yiddish-German play *Rabbi Henoch, or: What To Do With It* (1792), he describes in detail female characters drawn from the reality of contemporary German Jewry.

[26] Though in earlier periods too some women were involved in commercial dealings or even supported their husbands, this was a rare phenomenon, and regarded as an ideal. See Jacob Katz, *Tradition and Crisis: Jewish Society at the End of the Middle Ages*, trans. Bernard Dov Cooperman (New York, 1993), 164 n. 2. See also Gershon David Hundert, 'Approaches to the History of the Jewish Family in Early Modern Poland–Lithuania', in S. M. Cohen and P. E. Hyman (eds.), *The Jewish Family: Myth and Reality* (New York and London, 1986), 22.

[27] See Knaani, *Studies in the History of the Jewish Family*, 80–6. On the division of roles in European bourgeois family see nn. 42–4 below. On the division of roles in non-Jewish lower-class families as continuing the medieval autarkic structure see J. W. Scott and L. A. Tilly, 'Women's Work and the Family in Nineteenth-Century Europe', *Comparative Studies in Society and History*, 17/1 (Jan. 1975), 36–64.

[28] Samuel Horodezky argues that hasidism displayed an egalitarian attitude towards women: 'The Woman in Hasidism', in his *The Hasidim and the Hasidic Jews* (Heb.), vol. iv (Tel Aviv, 1943), 68–71. However, Ada Rapoport-Albert has demonstrated that Horodezky's descriptions are anachronistic, since they are influenced by the pioneering Zionist insistence on the equality of women. In her opinion there was no egalitarian ideology in hasidism; see 'On Women in Hasidism: S. A. Horodezky and the Maid of Ludmir Tradition', in A. Rapoport-Albert and Steven J. Zipperstein (eds.), *Jewish History* (London, 1988), 495–525.

For both spouses, studying the Torah reigned supreme. Hence the husband was accorded the highest status, while the wife's role as the family breadwinner was secondary.[29] However, there may have been a marked discrepancy between theory and practice. Contemporary personal memoirs suggest that in many cases 'the woman's informal status [was] more demanding and more rewarding than that formally assigned to her'.[30] The concentration of economic power in the hands of the wife enabled her to make and implement decisions; moreover, there could have been an easy transition from running financial affairs to making decisions on other family matters: 'Although children were encouraged to view their father as the head of the family, the mothers often made the important decisions.'[31]

The wife's position in *lomedim* circles had other consequences: she was seen as materialistic and possessed of a 'merchant's mentality'; she also tended to be out of the home for hours at a time in order to make a living. This double burden as breadwinner and homemaker, coupled with her decision-making responsibility, took their toll. To her children and husband she could appear impatient and hard-hearted.[32]

For the husband, the contrast between his wife's formal, inferior, status and the power she in practice wielded constituted a potential source of frustration. In the traditional system of values, Torah and its study reigned supreme, overshadowing nearly all aspects of mundane life,[33] so that the husband could feel secure in his role as a scholar. The pursuit of 'enlightenment' called into question the fundamental assumptions of Judaism and the resultant norms that shaped the structure of Jewish society. Thus, while the traditional scholar acknowledged his wife's economic power to be subservient to his own (superior) role, the scholar turned maskil, who no longer believed Torah learning to be a supreme value, resented the actual power exercised by the woman in her role as a breadwinner, and his hostility to her increased. The misogyny thus engendered was supplemented by the influences simultaneously exerted on the maskil's attitude towards women in general by the way of life in which he had been reared.

29 On the secondary status of women in the Jewish family see M. Zimbalist Rosaldo, 'Women, Culture, and Society: A Theoretical Overview', in M. Z. Rosaldo and L. Lamphere (eds.), *Women, Culture, and Society* (Stanford, Calif., 1974), 20. See also Stahl-Weinberg, *The World of our Mothers*, 6; Zborowsky and Herzog, *Life is with People*, 132; and Knaani, *Studies in the History of the Jewish Family*, 81.

30 Zborowsky and Herzog, *Life is with People*, 131. See also 'Matriarchy in Patriarchy', in Knaani, *Studies in the History of the Jewish Family*, 85–91.

31 Stahl-Weinberg, *The World of our Mothers*, 24.

32 'In many families the father was viewed as having a softer character than the mother. Many women who were burdened by the necessity of making a living did not leave themselves time to express feelings' (ibid. 25; see also Knaani, *Studies in the History of the Jewish Family*, 87).

33 For example, according to the sons of Rabbi Elijah, the Gaon of Vilna, their father showed no interest in the affairs of the world and the concerns of his family. He applauded 'those who leave the ways of this world and its business to occupy themselves with the Torah and its Commandments'. Etkes, 'Marriage and Torah Study', 105.

Foremost among these influences was the segregation of the sexes. Indeed, in the traditional Jewish community, men and women led almost separate lives, within clearly defined boundaries of their respective spheres of activity.[34] This social segregation limited the range of women that the maskil (just like any other male member of the community) was exposed to during his formative years, restricting it to members of the immediate family: mother, wife, and mother-in-law; young girls were strictly out of bounds and continued to be remote and alien 'others' even in his adult years. Consequently the satirized wives, who are modelled on the familiar married women within the family, are vivid and convincing characters.[35] In contrast, the idealized heroines (as a rule unmarried young girls) are portrayed with such fidelity to the literary conventions that they frequently seem to be cardboard figures.[36] The maskil's failure to depict these characters convincingly stems from his lack of intimate acquaintance with girls in his formative years, for which he compensated by resorting to literary models and conventions.

Another salient influence on the portrayal of women was the typical phenomenon of a young boy's separation from his family and his early marriage. The Jewish boy spent most of the day apart from his family as soon as he turned 3 and began to attend the *ḥeder*. Then, in his early teens, he left home to attend yeshiva in some distant town. Yet the most extreme separation from his family took the form of early marriage, which was customary in *lomedim* circles until the second half of the nineteenth century.[37]

[34] The strict segregation between the sexes that was implemented in Jewish society originates in the halakhic concept of modesty which functioned as a 'fence' against transgression. For this purpose, the halakhah established rules of separation between men and women in all spheres of life. In prayer: 'At first women were inside and men were outside but they were led to frivolity . . . Therefore it was ruled that women should sit above and men below (BT *Sukkah* 51*b*). At public gatherings: 'It is the duty of the court . . . to make sure that men and women do not congregate there [in public places] to eat and drink together and thus be led to immorality': Maimonides, *Mishneh torah*, trans. S. Gandz and H. Klein as *The Code of Maimonides: The Book of Seasons*, vi. 21 (New Haven, 1961), 304; for a parallel see *Shulḥan arukh*: *Oraḥ ḥayim*, 589: 4). During meals at religious ceremonies: 'One should make sure that men and women do not eat in the same room' (*Kitsur shulḥan arukh*, 149: 1). Educating children: 'Do not mix boys and girls together lest they commit a sin' (*Sefer ḥasidim*, para. 168). For a systematic and chronological listing of all the relevant sources divided into topics, with emphasis on present-day rulings, see E. G. Eilinson, *Walking Modestly: Woman and the Commandments* (Heb.), vol. ii (Jerusalem, 1981), chs. 1 and 2.

[35] This is how they are described in literary criticism. See for instance Joseph Klausner's evaluation that the satirical figure of Sarah the Widow in Smolenskin's *Hato'eh bedarkhei haḥayim* 'demonstrates the descriptive talent of Smolenskin the realist': Klausner, *History of Modern Hebrew Literature*, v. 225.

[36] This point too was raised by the literary critics. See for instance Lilienblum's criticism of the figure of Elisheva, the heroine of Mapu's *Ayit tsavua*, in his article 'The World of Chaos' (Heb.), *Hashahar* (1873), and Yosef Hayim Brenner's criticism, in his essay 'In Memory of J. L. Gordon' (Heb.), in *Collected Works*, vol. iii (Tel Aviv, 1967), 11–34, on the figure of Bat-Shu'a in *Kotso shel yod* [The Point on Top of a *Yod*] by J. L. Gordon.

[37] See Shmuel Stampfer, 'The Social Meaning of Premature Marriage in Eastern Europe in the Nineteenth Century', in A. Mendelson and Chone Shmeruk (eds.), *P. Glickson Memorial Volume: A*

Early marriage characterizes the biographies of most maskilim who were originally affiliated with the *lomedim* circles. This must have influenced their attitude towards women, matchmaking, and traditional married life. On the one hand, this early separation produced the nostalgic yearning for childhood and the mother figure seen in some Haskalah literary descriptions. On the other hand, it inspired feelings of resentment towards the *ḥeder* and early marriage, the two institutions responsible for the separation.[38] Being uprooted from his family and going to live with his in-laws made the young husband resent them too, a feeling which only intensified as he experienced adolescent rebelliousness.[39]

Contemporary literature supplies several testimonies to the traumatic effect of premature marriage on young men who had grown up in a segregated society.[40] The experience often generated strong antagonisms not only to the institution of marriage and the matchmaking process which made it possible, but also to the women involved—the wife and her mother. For the maskil the traditional wife represented forced marriage, economic dependence on in-laws, and the burden of married life. Once he was drawn to the Enlightenment in rebellion against the traditional norms and in pursuit of a new way of life, his family and wife felt like millstones around his neck. In view of these circumstances, it is no wonder that the maskil writer used bitter satire to describe the wife as a representative of the restrictions of traditional society.[41]

What sharpened these descriptions of women and their place in society was the maskil's contrasting vision of the ideal family. That vision was motivated not merely by his rejection of the existing situation, but also by his adoption of contemporary European ideals, primarily the west European bourgeois ethos. Only towards the end of the nineteenth century is it possible to discern another influence—that of radical Russian ideologies.

Collection of Studies on the Jews of Poland (Heb.) (Jerusalem, 1987), 71. By this time, the practice of premature marriage was no longer widespread in European society (see J. Hajnal, 'European Marriage: Patterns in Perspective', in D. V. Glass and E. D. Eversley (eds.), *Population in History* (London, 1965), 101–43), but it persisted in the *lomedim* circles of eastern Europe. According to Stampfer, 'Gender Differentiation', 74, this practice was such a defining characteristic of the elite *lomedim* circles that people adopted it in order to affiliate themselves with them.

[38] Biale, *Eros and the Jews*, 151–8.

[39] This is Biale's view: ibid. 157.

[40] For examples see Knaani, *Studies in the History of the Jewish Family*, 19–29.

[41] The hostility towards the wife, to whom the boy was married at a young age, and towards the family which was formed as a result of this marriage, is clearly described by Mordecai Aaron Guenzburg in his autobiography, *Avi'ezer* (Vilna, 1864), and it found trenchant expression at the end of the Haskalah period in autobiographical works (e.g. Lilienblum, *Ḥatot ne'urim* [Sins of My Youth] and treatises (e.g. Isaac Kovner, *Hamatsref* [The Crucible]). On *Hamatsref* and its author see Shmuel Feiner, 'Jewish Society, Literature, and Haskalah in Russia as Represented in the Radical Criticism of I. E. Kovner' (Heb.; Eng. abstract), *Zion*, 55 (1990), 283–316. The descriptions of women in Kovner and Lilienblum demonstrate how resentment of premature marriage provoked such strong hostility towards traditional married women that it found its way even into the writings of radical maskilim who called for egalitarian relationships between the sexes.

The European bourgeois ethos posited the division of society into two spheres of action. One was the male-dominated public sphere: work and business, war and politics, and learning. The other was the domestic sphere of female activities: housework, child care, and homemaking, providing men with a peaceful haven into which they could retreat from the troubles of the outside world.[42] From this ethos emerged the literary stereotype of 'the angel in the house', an amalgamation of the Holy Virgin and the romantic heroine. Since the woman was removed from worldly affairs, she was perceived as weaker, but also purer, than the man. Undisturbed by the pressures of the coarse masculine world, she was free to adhere to her ideals without compromise, and was therefore attentive to the voice of conscience and responsive to the language of feelings. Her physical weakness required the man's protection while her emotional and moral strength served as his conscience and guided his conduct.[43] The woman's activity, according to this ethos, was confined to the fine arts of homemaking and elegant entertaining. She thus needed to become accomplished in piano-playing, needlework, and fluent conversation in French.[44]

The maskilim welcomed the west European ideal of femininity as an antidote to the uncouth and domineering working women of their traditional background. Filtering this ideal through their own notion of femininity, they portrayed a heroine who was passive and refined, a domestic creature content with trivial pastimes of no productive value. As a symbol of love and loyalty she was a nurturing figure, the source of warmth and comfort. Her carriage and personality made her the perfect match for her mate, the hero of Haskalah literature. This exponent of Haskalah values was, in the eyes of the maskilim, the exact opposite of the Jewish scholar. He was active, assertive, and in control of his own destiny. Moreover—and unlike the traditional scholar—he supported his family by undertaking productive work. This division of roles, according to which the wife is a full-time homemaker while the husband is a productive member of society, conforms to the dual targets incorporated into the ideology of the Jewish Enlightenment: confining women to the domestic sphere, and insisting on the need to make Jewish society economically productive.[45] An excerpt from *Imrei shefer* (1802) by Naphtali Herz Homberg (1749–1841) illustrates this attitude well. In the context of discussing the advantages of education segregated along gender lines, Homberg makes the following observations about the family:

> It is the husband's duty to love his wife . . . to honour her, to provide her with all the housekeeping necessities . . . And even though the husband is the master of the house, he should

[42] This division of spheres is characterisic of western Europe from the late 18th cent. onwards, as industry moved away from the home to the factory, and the economic role of the urban middle-class woman, who until the Industrial Revolution had played an active part in supporting the family financially, became increasingly restricted.

[43] J. N. Burstyn, *Victorian Education and the Ideal of Womanhood* (London, 1980), 31.

[44] V. L. Bullough, *The Subordinate Sex* (Urbana, Ill., 1973), 3.

[45] See Shmuel Ettinger, *The History of the Jewish People in Modern Times* (Heb.) (Tel Aviv, 1969), 73–4. See also Israel Bartal, *The Metamorphosis of the Idea of the Productivization of the Jews in the Eighteenth to Twentieth Centuries: Sources for MA Seminar* (Heb.) (Jerusalem, 1985).

not treat her as if she were a servant . . . and from time to time he ought to consult with her about his business affairs even when he does not need her advice, if only to show his affection and loyalty. It is the wife's duty to her husband to love and honour him, and to cater to all his needs . . . without keeping him away from his business . . . She has the duty to manage the household prudently, to look after her children lovingly . . . and to converse with her husband in a pleasant manner and in good taste, so that day by day his love for her shall grow . . . She ought to be chaste in words and deeds . . . and her eyes should always be fixed upon him, for he is her lot in life.[46]

Several decades later, Mordecai Aaron Guenzburg endorsed the same view. One of the letters compiled in *Kiryat sefer* postulates this ideal as antithetical to contemporary practice, which Guenzburg regarded as a striking deviation from the natural order of things.[47] The writer describes his beloved woman in terms of 'the angel in the house': 'While she was engaged in her needlework, I read to her fine discourses from her brother's books . . . All her gestures are levelled by the balance of morality and aligned according to the strict rules of etiquette. She does not fill her mouth with laughter as do the common girls . . . for morality is her measuring line.' For the Haskalah, the liberation of the woman thus involved her removal from the public domain and her reinstatement in the domestic sphere under the man's protection. The education of this woman was intended to make her a suitable mate by providing her with conversational skills and perfecting her 'feminine' virtues.

In the 1860s, towards the end of the Haskalah period, the influence of the bourgeois ethic on the maskilim's descriptions of women was supplemented by models taken from the social ideology of Russian radical movements. In keeping with its insistence on equality, Russian social ideology generated a new model of the ideal woman, epitomized in Russian literature by the figure of Vera Pavlona, the heroine of Chernyshevsky's novel *What Is To Be Done?* (1863). This model, known as the 'new woman', is anchored in the socio-economic notion of equality between the sexes, which holds that women should possess the same rights and privileges as men. Any form of subordination or exploitation is precluded, and women are afforded a chance to earn a living and gain economic independence and equal status. Hence the 'new woman', who has acquired the same kind of education as her male

[46] *Imrei shefer kolelim inyenei torah umusar leyaldei benei yisra'el, elem ve'almah* [Words of Wisdom, Including Matters of Torah and Morals for the Jewish Boy and Girl] (1802; repr. Vienna, 1816), 156–8. This book served as a textbook for teaching religion to Jewish children. It was printed as an educational project of the Haskalah under the aegis of the Austrian government.

[47] 'And in this respect, the way boys are raised in this country seems to me better than our own customs, for they follow nature . . . the young men develop their strength on the streets, while the young women prepare their strength at home, and the glory of a king's daughter is within . . . In our customs, on the other hand, nature is distorted, the wheel is turned upside-down. The young men are hidden in the schools as if they were gaoled . . . while the maidens, having been taught the art of bargaining, remove the veil of shame that Nature wrapped around them': *Kiryat sefer: Mikhtavim melukatim al tohorat leshon hakodesh* [The City of the Book: Selected Letters on the Purity of the Holy Tongue] (Warsaw, 1873), 72.

counterpart, is active, independent, and self-supporting. Her characteristics and qualifications are not gender-specific, and she is valued as an equal human being.[48]

Even in the 1860s, however, the model of the 'new woman' did not gain popularity, though it left its imprint on some of the works and programmatic essays written by Lilienblum, Judah Leib Levin, and Braudes. The strikingly small number of heroines modelled upon the 'new woman' in Haskalah literature, including the works that were clearly influenced by Russian radical ideology, is in itself proof of the pervasiveness of the earlier female stereotypes. In Judah Leib Gordon's later works, just as in Mendele Mokher Seforim's *Ha'avot vehabanim* and the stories of Braudes, the ideal of womanhood advocated by the west European bourgeois ethos overshadows the 'new woman' inspired by the Russian revolutionary literature.

THE INFLUENCE OF CONVENTIONAL LITERARY MODELS

In their effort to shape modern Hebrew fiction the maskilim emulated the formal structures of European literature. In its earliest period, Haskalah fiction was marked by two pervasive prose genres directly influenced by European literature: satire (as early as the end of the eighteenth century) and romance (from the middle of the nineteenth century). Much as these genres were 'Judaized', their major conventional contours were preserved in the Hebrew works.[49]

The characters populating the early fictional works of the Haskalah were fashioned in accordance with the conventions typical of satire and romance. However, the distinctive socio-cultural context of Hebrew literature caused the European models to be Judaized in content as well as in language. As I will clarify below, these changes involved both the extra-literary content that is refracted in the fictional description, and the literary medium, which was adapted to the particular mentality of the Haskalah readership.

In their Haskalah incarnations, these European models established themselves as fixed conventions governing the portrayal of women. At first, they appeared in the framework of the original genres. Over time they came to operate autonomously: female characters typical of west European satire or romance were also introduced into social novels, short stories, and poetry. The pervasiveness of these stock characters in Haskalah fiction created its own literary tradition of the depiction of women, and female protagonists were accordingly cast into two basic moulds: the satirized

[48] On the women's liberation movement in Russia in the 19th cent. and the 'new woman' in the teachings of radical thinkers such as Michaelov, Chernyshevsky, and Pisarev see R. Stites, *The Women's Liberation Movement in Russia* (Princeton, NJ, 1978).

[49] On the influence of European satire see e.g. Shmuel Werses, 'The Satirical Methods of Joseph Perl', in id., *Story and Source: Studies in the Development of Hebrew Prose* (Heb.) (Ramat Gan, 1971). On the influence of European romance see e.g. Dan Miron, *From Romance to the Novel: Studies in the Emergence of the Hebrew and Yiddish Novel in the Nineteenth Century* (Heb.) (Jerusalem, 1979), 112–18.

woman and the romantic heroine. As noted above, a third type, the 'new woman', was marginally adopted towards the end of the Haskalah period.

The Satirized Woman

Portraits of the satirized woman conform to the general (i.e. European) rules of satirical characterization. This character is a type—a representative of a social group which the author criticizes by means of irony.[50] For this purpose, it is presented as a flat character and viewed from a perspective that discourages sympathy. Since the satirical type represents an entire group of people, he or she becomes recognizable by use of a small cluster of fixed, stereotypical, and mostly negative traits, which are established on the basis of exaggeration, distortion, and vulgar reduction.

In addition to incorporating the satirical content of general social criticism, the convention of the satirized woman also betrays misogynistic attitudes typical of patriarchal societies. In European satires the woman is characterized by physical weakness (which she exploits to her advantage by controlling men), treachery and guile, and tattling. Cultivated by women as protective measures against their subordinate status in patriarchal society, these perceived traits posed a threat to male dominance and hence became the focus of satirical criticism directed at women.[51] Any other female trait that threatened to undermine male dominance could be added to round out the description. By exaggerating them, the satirist expressed his fear of, and hostility towards, women and his desire to destroy them with the weapon of his satire. By the eighteenth century this stock character had become a well-established literary model which was carried over into Hebrew literature.

In Haskalah satire the European model of the satirized woman was supplemented by other characteristics, derived from the social reality of the maskil's background, which added a distinctly Jewish dimension to the model of the satirized woman. Thus, the satirized Jewish woman is:

1. A businesswoman who turns away from domestic affairs to trade with the outside world. She is greedy, materialistic, and shrewd in her business dealings.
2. Domineering: she controls her environment and overshadows her husband.
3. A middle-aged wife who is described in terms of her relationship with her husband, rather than her interaction with her children (the maskil's satirical criticism derives from his hostility towards the woman in her role as a wife, not as a mother).

Once these traits had been assimilated, they became an inextricable part of the model and served as common denominators that invariably characterized all the satirized woman portrayed in Haskalah literature.

[50] My presentation of the characteristics of the satirical figure is based on the following sources: L. Feinberg, *Introduction to Satire* (Ames, Ia., 1967); D. C. Meuck, *The Compass of Irony* (London, 1969); O. M. Hodgart, 'Satire', in R. Paulson (ed.), *Satire: Modern Essays in Criticism* (London, 1971), 79–107.

[51] Hodgart, 'Satire'.

The integration of a European model into Hebrew Haskalah satire also brought about changes in descriptive techniques, since the satire was addressed to a different 'interpretative community'.[52] Haskalah fiction uses irony, a key tool of satire, is produced by juxtaposing two fundamentally incompatible frames of reference: in this case the traditional scholarly method of learning—the simultaneous reading of several texts[53]—is applied to the satirical depiction of the Jewish woman. This technique, known as 'bisociation',[54] works on the traditional biblical notion of the ideal woman the figure of *eshet ḥayil* (a woman of valour), the paragon of female virtue (Proverbs 31), or famous women such as Deborah the prophetess or Queen Esther. Placed in this context, the satirized woman is reduced to a vulgar imitation of the ideal. Thus the stylistic parody becomes an integral component of her portrait and a major feature of its Jewish essence.

Haskalah fiction provides numerous examples of female characters modelled upon its own version of the satirized woman. The recurrence of this ridiculed figure established a sort of convention or tradition manifest not only in social satires (such as the rabbi's virtuous wife in Perl's *Megaleh temirin*) but also in later works. This tradition yielded such characters as Sarah, Ephrayim's wife, and Hannah, the ritual bath attendant and servant, in Mendele Mokher Seforim's *Ha'avot vehabanim*; Deborah, wife of Zevulun the Melamed, in Smolenskin's *Kevurat ḥamor* (1874); the ridiculed landlady in *Simḥat ḥanef* (The Joy of the Godless), also by Smolenskin; the rabbi's wife in *Kaf regel egel* (The Calf's Foot) by Judah Leib Gordon; and Reicheli in *Bank lemisḥar uleḥaroshet hama'aseh* (A Bank for Commerce and Industry) by Brandstaedter.

The first solid character of this type is the satirized wife described in *Nezed hadema* (A Pottage of Tears) (1773) by Israel of Zamosc:

> She is noisy and ungovernable. She too is a woman of valour. Watchwoman, what of the night? She lies in wait from morning till evening. She rises while it is yet night so that she shall have no lack of gain. As a bride she adorns herself with her jewels. Her feet do not remain in her house; like a restive young camel, she runs and returns. On the street she raises her voice to pursue her own business and speak with everyone who passes by. And she profusely greets those who are far and near.[55]

This passage is a parody of Proverbs 31. The negative qualifiers 'noisy and ungovernable' deflate the exalted portrait of the 'woman of valour', the ideal mistress of the house. The description then proceeds along the same lines by copying

[52] This is the term coined by Stanley Fish, who defines interpretative strategies as 'the shape or reading' shared by members of specific interpretative communities: 'These strategies exist prior to the act of reading and therefore determine the shape of what is read': *Is There a Text in this Class?* (Cambridge, Mass., 1980), 171.

[53] See Cohen, 'The Scholarly Technique'.

[54] 'The effect produced by perceiving an idea or event simultaneously in two habitually incompatible frames of reference': Hodgart, 'Satire'. See also Yehuda Friedlander's use of the term in *Studies in Hebrew Satire*, i: *Hebrew Satire in Germany* (Heb.) (Tel Aviv, 1979).

[55] Y. Friedlander, *Hebrew Satire in Europe*, ii: *The Eighteenth and Nineteenth Centuries* (Heb.) (Ramat Gan, 1989), 75–6.

the biblical text almost verbatim ('She rises while it is yet night'; 'so that she shall have no lack of gain'). But the biblical allusions produce a 'bisociation': the original meaning—praising the housewife's industry—is transformed into a strong denunciation of the working wife, who deserts her domestic territory for commercial dealings. In using the text of *eshet ḥayil* as a frame of reference for this parody, the denunciation of her modern counterpart is reinforced, as the satirized woman is contrasted with the very ideal she is supposed to epitomize.

The thrust of the satire in this description is the tradeswoman's conduct: her greed drives her from home in pursuit of commercial activities that involve frivolous and immodest intercourse with strangers. The extra-literary reality of the female breadwinner becomes an integral part of the literary figure. Nonetheless, this description does not accurately reflect extra-literary reality; the satirical intent gives rise to a deliberately distorted and exaggerated description. For example, the reiteration of the woman's bustling activity conveys purposeless movement, typical of satirical descriptions and in particular those addressing female conduct, conventionally recognized as 'much ado about nothing'. This hyperactivity perfectly fits the character of the tradeswoman and marks her out as a ridiculous and contemptible figure, driven by eccentricity rather than by a desperate struggle to survive. This description underlines the maskil's resentment of female dominance and role-reversal.

The Romance Heroine

It was in the mid-nineteenth century that the model of the romance heroine began to strike root alongside the satirical genre and influence the development of Haskalah literature. Specifically, the appearance of the prose romance can be dated to the publication of Mapu's *Ahavat tsiyon* in 1853, later followed by his other works: *Ayit tsavua* (1857–64) and *Ashmat shomron* (1865). The romance does not describe reality in the same way as the novel: 'The romance is an heroic fable which treats fabulous persons and things . . . The romance in lofty and elevated language describes what never happened nor is likely to happen.'[56] Romance heroes are deliberately presented as exalted and heroic figures, and the reality they reflect is universal and supra-temporal.

The romance heroine represents the author's vision of the ideal woman. This vision incorporates his criticism of female reality and the ideals he strives to attain. Accordingly, through the romance heroine, reality is refracted in two ways: whereas it stands out as the exact opposite of those aspects of female reality that the author finds unacceptable, it also conveys his inner reality, his fantasies and ideals. The heroine of the romance literature[57] is generally portrayed in accordance with a

[56] The definition follows Clara Reeve's well-known book *The Progress of Romance* (London, 1785). This genre originated in medieval courtly romance, but found its way into fiction.

[57] For a detailed account of the characteristics of the romance heroine and how they were formed see R. M. Brownstein, *Becoming a Heroine* (New York, 1982); Bullough, *The Subordinate Sex*; J. M. Ferrante, *Women as Image in Medieval Literature* (New York, 1973).

conventional model that is anchored in the medieval concept of courtly love. She is well born (usually either a noblewoman or a member of the upper class), perfect, chaste, and beautiful. As the object of the hero's devoted love and passionate yearnings, she motivates him to seek bold adventures in order to win her heart. Fixed in her remote position on a pedestal of perfection, she leads no significant life of her own. Her essential role lies in her passive existence as the personification of pure love that can be attained only through the hero's sustained efforts and persistent devotion.

The model of the romance heroine was a major source of inspiration to Mapu and the maskilim who followed him. The ideal heroines populating the literature of the Haskalah are beautiful, noble (the nobility of class is replaced in the Haskalah narratives by the nobility of wealth), perfect, and passive, serving as the exalted object of the hero's love. Certain departures from utter passivity are discernible in some of Mapu's heroines (such as Tamar, the heroine of *Ahavat tsiyon*), but they do not amount to a consistent trait: by the end of the story, even these heroines resume their passive role.

The romance heroines of the Haskalah are diametrically opposed to the satirized 'real' women that dominate the maskil's background. They are never married;[58] most are young unmarried girls, but even the older ones (for example Na'amah in *Ahavat tsiyon*, or Yehosheba in *Ashmat shomron*) are unattached, being widows or deserted wives; they are usually sheltered from the pressures of the outside world; on the whole, they come from wealthy and respectable families and are not constrained to earn a living.[59] The removal of the idealized heroine from the world of action testifies to the influence of the European bourgeois ethos, as well as to the author's intention to portray her as the countertype of the 'real' wife in her role as the family provider. She is also distinguished by the excessive passivity which permeates her interactions with the members of her family. In this respect too, she is the opposite of the 'real' woman, who is both assertive and domineering. In fact, the heroine's passivity is frequently juxtaposed with her own mother's assertiveness.[60] Significantly, the unfolding of the plot clearly suggests that passivity is a

58 In early European romances the hero's beloved, whom he worships and idealizes, might be a married woman. This is not the case in Haskalah literature as it goes against the strict conventions of morality, from which the maskil never deviates.

59 Mapu's heroines, for instance, conspicuously belong to this category. When an idealized romantic heroine earns a living, as does Bat-Shu'a, the heroine of J. L. Gordon's *Kotso shel yod*, this is a matter of necessity. She regards her work as a temporary stage in her life and is looking forward to the day when she will retire and assume the delicate passivity of 'the angel in the house'.

60 For instance, in *Ahavat tsiyon* Tamar plays a much more passive role than her mother Tirza during the confrontations with Tamar's father. To give another example, the passive figure of Rachel in Mendele Mokher Seforim's *Ha'avot vehabanim* (Odessa, 1868) is in sharp contrast to the active, gregarious, and excessively fussy figure of her mother Sarah. It is precisely her passivity that leads Rachel to the idyllic conclusion of the love story: her beloved Ben-David, who is portrayed as an active and successful person, redeems her and the entire family.

virtue. In Haskalah literature assertiveness and dominance are relegated to portraits of satirized women.

Like the model of the satirized woman, that of the romance heroine is also appropriated by Haskalah literature and endowed with specifically maskilic characteristics. At the most basic level, this is achieved by the Judaization of her name, background, etc. More interesting, however, are two other devices. The first is the ambivalent formulation of the heroine as an educated woman; the second is the use of a distinctive biblical linguistic code to describe her. Each of these two devices warrants more detailed analysis.

The maskilim were ambivalent about women's education. Although pleased when female readers of Hebrew joined their ranks, they nevertheless remained committed to the traditional notion that learning was the exclusive domain of men. This ambivalence had a dual impact on their portrayal of the romance heroine. First, they created heroines who were uneducated but nonetheless successful in life. This is true not only of the heroines of Mapu's biblical romances, but also of those placed in a nineteenth-century setting, such as Shifra and Ruhama in *Ayit tsavua*. Second, the kind of education acquired by the heroine is described in terms that make it seem merely decorative, with no actual bearing on her life. Rachel in *Ha'avot vehabanim*, Elisheva in *Ayit tsavua*, and Sarah in *Aḥarit simḥah tugah* by Judah Leib Gordon carry the banner of women's education. Yet the way their story unfolds suggests that their education has no real influence on their lives; they still depend on the hero to redeem them. The opposite holds true of the romance hero, who takes advantage of his education to change the course of his life.

To elaborate this point, I will discuss the case of Elisheva in some detail. Her presentation as the idealized heroine, as well as the emphasis on her talents, her education (she is versed in Hebrew and European culture), and her ability to discourse with men[61] undoubtedly express the author's approval of women's education. In effect, her struggle to exercise her right to acquire an education is reminiscent of the struggle of the maskilim to transcend the constraints of their society. Addressing this issue in a letter to her grandfather, Elisheva writes:

> You condemn learning as folly because of many people who tell me that my wisdom and my knowledge have led me astray. Why do they consider me wayward? My graceful speech is my crime, and my wisdom—the sin of my soul. I was schooled in learning, I studied books and languages, but you, my father, pronounced judgement upon them, saying that they corrupt the soul and will bring shame upon me.[62]

However, Elisheva's education has no impact on her choices in life. *Ayit tsavua* ends with her predictable marriage to Na'aman, with whom she made an alliance in her childhood. At the same time, however, Na'aman does benefit from his education: he travels to study agronomy and chooses a new way of life.

[61] See the chapter 'Ḥitsei lashon' [Arrows of the Tongue], in *Ayit tsavua*, in *The Works of A. Mapu* (Heb.) (Tel Aviv, 1964), 333–7.

[62] Ibid. 247.

Before getting married, Na'aman writes a letter to Elisheva in which he describes their future married life:

Now I'll tell you how I imagine my own house. For it is not good that man should live alone. And she who is to be the mistress of the house, the one I shall choose, will love what is precious to my soul and together with me shall lie down in green pastures and among the plants of Eden, planted with my own hands. And my desire will be to delight the soul of my beautiful wife. She too will make an effort to be a woman of valour, the crown of her husband, who looks well to the ways of her household and loves my beloved ones just as I do . . . I will also prepare a selection of books in my study, which we shall read in the autumn and winter nights, when no work is done in the fields. Not so during the working days. Then I shall ride my horse to awaken my brethren who cultivate the land. And my wife will rejoice over her good life . . . for under my shadow she will enjoy the pleasures of love and the treasures of life.[63]

This vision of married life accords with the bourgeois notion of separate spheres. For Elisheva, education is merely decorative: it enables her to help brighten the long autumn and winter nights she spends with her husband in the intimacy of shared reading. Otherwise it has nothing to do with her life and her role as a wife: she is confined to the domestic sphere, where she takes her proper place in the shadow of her loving and generous husband. The idyllic ending of the romance suggests that the author approves of this marriage and shares Na'aman's vision of married life.

It is important to note, however, that some of the late Haskalah works express a significant change of attitude towards women's education. This was inspired by the Russian radical movement, which advocated women's education as a means of granting them independence and equality.[64] In the 1870s it gave rise to a new type of heroine, who stands half-way between the romance heroine and the 'new woman'. This heroine's education actually influences her life and grants her more equality with men.[65]

Thus extra-literary social ideals exert some influence on the formulation of the

[63] Ibid. 253.

[64] This new ideology was articulated, for example, in Moses Leib Lilienblum, *Mishnat elisha ben avoyah* [The Doctrine of Elisha b. Abuyah], 1st pub. as a series in *Asefat hakhamim* (1878) and *Hame'asef* (1879). See Yehuda Friedlander, *Hebrew Satire in Europe*, iii: *The Nineteenth Century* (Heb.) (Ramat Gan, 1994), 206.

[65] Thus, for instance, in Reuven Asher Braudes, *Hadat vehaḥayim* [Religion and Life] (1876–9), Rachel's education influences her relationship with Samuel and to some extent affects her decisions and the course of her life. Another example of the heroine's education as shaping her destiny is found in the description of Loira, the heroine of *Kefar mezagegim* [The Glaziers' Village] (1894) by Mordecai David Brandstaedter. These heroines are still modelled upon the conventional romantic heroine, but their education serves as a guiding factor in their life. A more extreme example of how education affects the destiny and personality of the idealized heroine is to be found in 'Elḥanan', the unfinished poem by Judah Leib Levin, pub. in *Hashaḥar*, 9 (1878–9) and 10 (1880–1). For Miriam, the protagonist of this work, education becomes such a dominant factor that it transforms her into an active and independent person—a 'new woman'.

literary character. Nevertheless, the ideal heroine is much less convincing than the satirized woman. Haskalah ideal heroines are described in accordance with the contours and formulas of the romance convention; indeed, they frequently seem to be carbon copies of previous romance heroines. Such fidelity to the convention of the romance heroine becomes particularly ridiculous in the realistic social novels that emerged at the end of the period. The hero of *Ha'avot vehabanim* even makes fun of this practice.[66] However, it transpires that in this work too, the character of Rachel the heroine and the unfolding of the plot conform to the same model that is ridiculed by the hero. The maskil's inability to provide a convincing description of the young beloved heroine may be explained by his upbringing: the social segregation of the sexes in traditional Jewish society meant he had no close acquaintance with young unmarried women. Any description of such a woman is thus more likely to be a figment of his literary imagination than a realistic portrait, and it comes as no surprise to find that the unmarried girls described in Haskalah literature carry no conviction.

The singularity of the Haskalah romance heroine also finds expression in the linguistic formulation of her depiction. Adopting a neoclassical approach to canonical texts, the Haskalah writers embedded biblical allusions in their descriptions, expanding the meaning of their text by alluding to a multiplicity of voices. Their preferred topos in depicting the romance heroine is that of the beloved woman in the Songs of Songs. It was initially employed by Mapu and later adopted by Smolenskin, Judah Leib Gordon, and Brandstaedter. It was used with such consistency that any female character described in terms of the beloved of Song of Songs was duly recognized as a romance heroine; even a single detail derived from this topos ('her stature was like a palm tree') sufficed to evoke the entire picture in the mind of the reader.

The model of the romance heroine governed the portrait of the ideal heroine in Haskalah fiction to the very end of this period and permeated genres other than the romance. This is apparent, for instance, in *Aḥarit simḥah tugah* by Judah Leib Gordon. Though far removed from Mapu's romance style, this story still revolves around a typical romance heroine. Young Sarah comes from a wealthy family and is blessed with a host of feminine virtues. She is good-looking, noble-hearted, and pure. Her identity as a romance heroine is established as soon as she makes her first appearance (in the chapter 'A Lily among the Thorns'). The very title of this chapter, as well as other typical details from the Song of Songs, provide the reader with sufficient clues:

[66] 'If you manage to betroth Rachel, then a fine writer can use your story to produce a wonderful love story. He will find in it all the materials he needs: a good-looking maiden, shining like the sun; her lips are like a thread of scarlet and her eyes and her hair are as black as a raven; her neck is polished ivory, her head is wrapped in curls, her hands are filled-up silver rolls. She is an only daughter to her father, a wealthy man who conserves vanities' (Mendele Mokher Seforim, *Complete Works* (Heb.) (Tel Aviv, 1952)), 28.

A good-looking woman, young in age and youthful in spirit . . . she walks with an upright carriage and her fine and delicate head is raised majestically above her ivory neck ['Thy neck is like a tower of ivory', S. of S. 7: 5] . . . For a few moments the gentle woman planted herself [*ra'atah*] in the garden like a lily ['my beloved is mine and I am his, he feeds [*ro'eh*] among the lilies', S. of S. 2: 16].[67]

Indeed, as the scene progresses, other features of the model of the ideal woman round out the description of the heroine. Sarah is not only beautiful, young, and of a wealthy family; she is also well educated and courted by Albert, a respectable member of the medical profession—the perfect maskil. Thus, even in a story of a satirical-realistic character, the heroine is cast in the romance mould, demonstrating the strength of persistence of this convention.

*

The case of Haskalah descriptions of the nineteenth-century east European Jewish woman illustrates the manner whereby reality is reflected in literature. In this chapter I have attempted to analyse the dual roots of such descriptions. On the one hand, I have shown the formulation of the literary character to be influenced by extra-literary social realities. These influences on descriptions of women were complex. The portraits integrate realistic elements of the dominant female character known in Haskalah literature to the maskil from his own family with the author's male bias and his European/Enlightenment ideology. At the same time it has been possible to discern the degree to which the depiction of women also constitutes part of a literary and linguistic tradition. Literary conventions played a crucial role in the formulation of female characters in Haskalah literature; indeed, the use of literary models and of specific linguistic techniques was typical of the Jewish Enlightenment fashioning the two dominant female types to be found in this corpus: the satirized wife and the romanticized maiden.

The blending of these two streams of influence created the female figures which are characteristic of Hebrew Haskalah literature. Indeed, the central models are so powerful and dominant that they hardly altered throughout the period—even when the maskil consciously attempted to liberate himself from them. Admittedly, alternative models (such as that of the 'new woman' or the 'suffering woman') do begin to appear towards the end of the Haskalah, and even become more evident in the period categorized as *hateḥiyah* (the Hebrew revival). Nevertheless, during the Haskalah era itself, the two models analysed here are those which typify the formulation of literary portraits of women.

[67] *Collected Works: Prose* (Heb.) (Tel Aviv, 1960), 29.

TEN

Enlightened Rabbis as Reformers in Russian Jewish Society

JOSEPH SALMON

HISTORICAL research has paid little attention to the 'enlightened rabbi' type in eastern Europe in the 1860s and 1870s. Such rabbis combined tradition and enlightenment, a trait that made them potentially and practically social reformers in the sense that they took a stand on social issues and were willing to examine them anew in the light of their intellectual commitments.[1] The different combinations of enlightenment and tradition explain the various rabbinical positions taken in regard to the proposed reforms of Jewish society. Advocating nationalism was only one of the options suggested by this group, and it was not their first choice.

There is a prevalent distinction in the literature between traditional and enlightened Jews in Russian Jewish society in the second half of the nineteenth century, as well as one between the moderate or conservative members of the Haskalah and those who were more radical. Nineteenth-century writers coined the terms *ḥaredim maskilim* (enlightened religious Jews) and *maskilim yesharim* (moderate maskilim),[2] and in the past few decades the expressions 'enlightened rabbi' and 'enlightened Torah scholar' have been used; attention has also been paid to the expressions used by enlightened Jews themselves, such as *haskalah datit* (religious Haskalah) and *maskilim min hatorah* (Jews whose Haskalah is based on the Torah).[3] But all these expressions are meant to denote more or less the same type of east European Jew, one who up to now has been deprived of his rightful place in the historiography of east European Jewry. Binary thinking has made it difficult for scholars to envisage a pluralist social structure with a broad range of positions and human types.

[1] David Fishman, *Science, Enlightenment and Rabbinic Culture in Belorussian Jewry: 1772–1840* (Cambridge, Mass., 1985), 195–6, 208.

[2] Jacob Lipschitz, *Zikhron ya'akov* [A Memorial for Jacob] (Jerusalem, 1968), pt. II, p. 95.

[3] Shmuel Feiner, 'Jewish Society, Literature, and Haskalah in Russia as Represented in the Radical Criticism of I. E. Kovner' (Heb.; English abstract), *Zion*, 55 (1990), 283–316. See also Immanuel Etkes, 'On the Question of the Precursors of the Haslakah in Eastern Europe', in id (ed.), *Religion and Life: The Jewish Enlightenment in Eastern Europe* (Heb.) (Jerusalem, 1993), 33. For the variety of terms used see Ze'ev Yavetz, 'The Tower of the Century' (Heb.), *Keneset yisra'el*, 1 (1886), 124. Yavetz claims that Moses Mendelssohn was the first 'enlightened religious Jew', followed by R. Yitzhak Bernays. A

ENLIGHTENMENT AND TRADITION

The many studies of the Haskalah in Lithuania have repeatedly shown that the maskilim were traditional Jews whose education included not only Hebrew grammar and medieval Jewish thought but also knowledge of other languages, as well as of the philosophical and aesthetic literature of their times. This education was carried out through the initiative of parents or other available teachers. A lively description appears in Solomon Maimon's autobiography, which provides a picture of the 1760s and 1770s: he lists the books belonging to his father, who was a merchant in the city of Königsberg, as well as the books he borrowed from Rabbi Shimshon of Slonim. Without embarking on a discussion of the Vilna Gaon's position on the Haskalah, it is enough to note that the first enlightened books, written by people such as Rabbi Baruch Schick of Shklov, Menahem Mendel Lefin, Manasseh of Ilya, Isaac Baer Levinsohn, and others were endorsed by famous rabbis of their time. Even if this society objected to the sort of Enlightenment that was imposed by the government, which they saw as a secularizing force, they considered it advantageous to acquire a general education in private, autodidactic ways,[4] and did not consider secularization would be a necessary outcome of this. Although a few isolated maskilim actually left the fold, even going so far as to convert to Christianity, this only lowered the threshold of sensitivity without creating an anti-Haskalah stance among traditional Jews.[5]

Only in the 1840s, when the Russian government tried to force general education on the Jewish community, did Jews begin to consolidate their opposition to the Haskalah. This opposition strengthened as, from the 1860s, the maskilim in Russia became more radicalized;[6] it was expressed in polemics in the press, and was especially opposed to any reform in the educational system that was in the spirit of the Haskalah.

At the same time, a sizeable group of rabbis and writers tried to withstand the trend among traditional Jewry of avoiding the Haskalah. This group, which will be

wide variety of terms may also be found in Immanuel Etkes, 'The Enlightenment of Eastern Europe: An Introduction', in id. (ed.), *Religion and Life*, 9–24. For the use of the phrase 'Jews whose enlightenment is based on the Torah' see Mendel Piekarz, *The Early Development of Hasidism* (Heb.), (Jerusalem, 1978), 33–4, and Zevia Nardi, 'Transformations in the Enlightenment Movement in Russia', in Etkes (ed.), *Religion and Life*, 301–2. The use of the term 'enlightened rabbi', is discussed in Fishman, *Science, Enlightenment and Rabbinic Culture*.

4 See Saul Ginsburg, 'Individuals and Generations', in Etkes (ed.), *Religion and Life*, 383. See also Michael Stanislawski, 'The Beginnings of Russian Enlightenment', 127, 129; Nardi, 'Transformations in the Enlightenment Movement in Russia'; Isaac Barzilay, 'Acceptance or Rejection: Manasseh of Ilya's (1767–1831) Ambivalent Attitude Toward Hasidism', *Jewish Quarterly Review*, 74 (1983–4), 3. Jacob Raisin, in *The Haskalah Movement in Russia* (Philadelphia, Pa., 1913), 119–23, went too far in his theories, claiming that the Haskalah was the mainstream way of thinking in Russian Jewish society.

5 Louis Greenberg, *The Jews in Russia*, vol. i (New Haven, 1944), 24–8. Greenberg's summary of this issue is too general and not satisfactory. See also Raisin, *The Haskalah Movement in Russia*, 131.

6 Gideon Katznelson, *The Literary War between the Orthodox and the Enlightened Jews* (Heb.) (Tel Aviv, 1954), 15–19.

the focus of attention in this chapter, made considerable efforts to argue against the radicalizing trends in both of the opposing camps. It did not comprise just a few activists working sporadically, but was made up of individuals who had a conscious commitment to their views and were searching for ways to express and actualize them. These people also looked for allies in the more moderate enlightened camp. As Immanuel Etkes has said, 'most of the maskilim in Russia in the first half of the nineteenth century did not see themselves as transgressors who were abandoning Judaism. On the contrary, they considered themselves as people who were renewing and revitalizing Judaism in its pure form.'[7]

TYPES OF MASKILIM

The moderate enlightened camp included people such as Abraham Baer Gottlober, Eliezer Zweifel, Samuel Joseph Fuenn, Hayim Leib Markon, Matthias Strashun, and Mordecai Flungian. Among the members of the radical enlightened camp were writers such as the brothers Abraham Uri and Isaac Kovner, Shalom Jacob Abramowitz (Mendele Mokher Seforim), Judah Leib Levin, Moses Leib Lilienblum, Judah Leib Gordon, and Peretz Smolenskin. The enlightened traditional camp included rabbis and writers such as Yehiel Michael Pines, Yitshak Margoliot, Mordecai Eliasberg, Joseph Zechariah Stern, Mordecai-Gimpel Jaffe, Samuel Mohilewer, Alexander Moses Lapidot, Jacob Lipschitz, and Isaac Jacob Reines. Isaac Barzilay calls the last group the 'enlightened Orthodox',[8] while David Fishman calls them '*rabanim maskilim*'.[9]

I should like to indicate a number of points of encounter between these groups and discuss their public positions. I shall focus on the enlightened traditional camp, and mention the others only in so far as they served to evoke responses from this camp. As long as the discussion within the enlightened camp was confined to literary values and the authority of the older maskilim, the traditional maskilim had nothing to argue about. It was only when the radical maskilim began to express rage against the rabbis, halakhah, and the moderate maskilim that intense controversies broke out.[10]

The Reading Material of the Traditional Maskil

To describe the type of education acquired by the enlightened rabbi is difficult because information is scanty. The evidence of the Vilna Gaon's children and students, however, implies that he studied all sorts of secular knowledge, only forbidding the

[7] Etkes, 'Precursors of the Haskalah', 42–3.

[8] 'The Life of Manasseh of Ilya (1767–1831)', *Proceedings of the American Academy for Jewish Research*, 5 (1983), 16.

[9] *Science, Enlightenment and Rabbinic Culture*, 195–6, 208.

[10] See Shmuel Feiner, 'Eliezer Zweifel and the Moderate Russian Enlightenment', in Etkes (ed.), *Religion and Life*, 343; Nardi, 'Transformations in the Enlightenment Movement in Russia', 302–5, 314–15; Lipschitz, *Zikhron ya'akov*, pt. II, pp. 65–7.

study of philosophy. Although he considered secular knowledge subordinate to Torah study, he did not reject it. The writings of Baruch of Shklov, who was close to the Vilna Gaon, imply that he himself studied astronomy, physiology, geometry, pharmacology, medicine, and other disciplines. Moreover, the Gaon knew about Baruch's studies and even encouraged him to translate scientific literature into Hebrew.[11] It is known that some of the Vilna Gaon's students who became maskilim, such as Manasseh of Ilya, even studied the social philosophy of their time,[12] since they apparently understood the Gaon's restriction on the study of philosophy to encompass only theology and theosophy. In addition, the testimony of Lithuanian rabbis in the mid-nineteenth century implies that the knowledge of languages—generally German—as well as of astronomy, geometry, geography, and Hebrew grammar were all part of their secular education.[13]

In his book *Zikhron ya'akov* (A Memorial for Jacob), which historians have not yet fully explored, Jacob Lipschitz describes the situation:

> There were some rabbis and Torah students who were wonderfully knowledgeable about the Bible, understanding the text, and well versed in Hebrew grammar, who were also writers, using wonderful figures of speech in the style of those days. They were called 'perfect', and these 'perfect' people, who observed the Torah and respected those who were even more observant, were loved by everyone and praised by everyone.[14]

The figure Lipschitz apparently had in mind was Rabbi Jacob Barit of Vilna (1797–1883), an industrialist who was also a Torah scholar and the head of a yeshiva, 'who was one of the great men of his generation in Torah knowledge and observance, a man with great knowledge in many academic areas as well, and respected among Jews and gentiles alike'.[15] Lipschitz distinguished between having a secular education and becoming a secular—that is, non-religious—person, something that the historical literature has not yet succeeded in doing.

THE BACKGROUND

My discussion will focus on a group of enlightened rabbis from Lithuania, some of whom were personally related to one another by family connections. The path of

[11] Immanuel Etkes, 'The Vilna Gaon and the Haskalah: Image and Reality', in I. Etkes and Joseph Salmon (eds.), *Chapters in the History of Jewish Society in the Middle Ages and the Modern Period* (Heb.) (Jerusalem, 1980), 204.

[12] Manasseh's book, *Shekel hakodesh* [The Holy Shekel] (Kapust, 1823), is based on theoretical assumptions of Jeremy Bentham's utilitarian school, namely the principle of greatest happiness. Manasseh made use of the extensive library of R. Joseph Mazal of Vyasin. See Barzilay, 'The Life of Manasseh of Ilya', 14–15; the books in Mazal's library are described on pp. 16 and 19.

[13] Lipschitz, *Zikhron ya'akov*, pt. II, p. 46. He attests to the secular education of R. Ze'ev Troib, the father-in-law of Abraham Simon Troib of Kaidan.

[14] Ibid. 143. Interestingly, Lipschitz himself, who was at the strictly observant end of the range of enlightened rabbis and writers, found it appropriate to mention the good traits of those with more extensive secular education in the memoirs he wrote many years later (ibid. 15).

[15] Ibid. 205.

religious reform taken by these rabbis began with criticism of the unproductive nature of the occupations followed by members of the Jewish communities; this was extended to criticism of traditional education on the one hand and the demand for reforms in the halakhah on the other, and finally issued in membership in the Zionist movement known as Hovevei Zion. They appear to have seen a logical connection between their Enlightenment demands and joining the Zionist movement, an interesting example of the confluence of a social stream in the Haskalah and Enlightenment motifs in the Jewish national movement. The members of this group wrote in Hebrew, publishing their writings in the Hebrew press. The first such Hebrew journal was *Halevanon*, which was later joined by *Hamagid*; even the less traditional *Hamelits* accepted their writings. They included people born between the 1820s and 1840s. Educated at Lithuanian yeshivas, they were among the elite Lithuanian rabbis. Despite the views they held in common, there were also differences and even principled controversies between them, and the group ultimately gave rise to two types of east European Orthodoxy: ultra-Orthodoxy and religious Zionism ('Orthodoxy' is used here in the sense of a reaction to modernity, a clinging to the traditional world).

To illustrate how the group's thinking developed, and examine how far its members were prepared to compromise with modernity, I will discuss their involvement in public life from the 1860s until the outbreak of the First World War, focusing on five key issues: the debate about the suggestions for religious change in 1868–71; the reaction to the famine in Russia, especially in the districts of Lithuania and White Russia, following the floods and drought there in 1867–9; the debate about the *etrogim* from Corfu from 1874 on; the establishment of the Hovevei Zion movement; the debate following the attempt to establish a rabbinical seminary in Russia in 1882.

The oldest members of the group were rabbis Mordecai Eliasberg (b. 1817), Samuel Mohilewer (b. 1824), and Mordecai-Gimpel Jaffe (b. 1820). Somewhat younger was Joseph Zechariah Stern (b. 1831).[16] Some of them studied at the Volozhin yeshiva. In the 1840s and early 1850s these older members of the group witnessed the unsuccessful efforts of the government to bring about its own sort of enlightenment. In contrast, the younger members, including Isaac Jacob Reines (b. 1839), Yitshak Margoliot (b. 1842), and Yehiel Michael Pines (b. 1843), grew up at the time of the social crisis in Russia just before the religious debate of 1868–71. All of them were aware of the government's efforts to further the Jews' secular education and economic productivity, but past experiences made the older rabbis suspicious:

[16] Eliahu Yaffe, *The Book of Memoirs of Mordechai* (Warsaw, 1913), contains letters, sermons, and a eulogy of R. Mordecai-Gimpel Jaffe. These include moral letters to his sons, a letter of 1846 to Moses Montefiore, a eulogy of Montefiore from 1885, a sermon on the rise to power of Alexander II in 1856, a letter to the Barons von Ginsburg opposing the establishment of the rabbinical seminary in Russia, and a eulogy of Mordecai-Gimpel Jaffe by Yeruham Fishel Pines. On Stern see Binyamin Yaffe, 'Rabbi Joseph Zechariah Stern', in id., *Yavneh* (Jerusalem, 1942), 154–5.

unlike the secular maskilim, who justified the authorities' efforts, they raised doubts about their intentions, seeing them as a threat to the Jewish community. By the 1860s the medium of public debate was the press, and the struggle between the various Jewish factions that took place has therefore been called the 'literary war', or the 'press war'.[17]

THE 1860s

Historians tend to see the period of crisis that led to the crossroads in Russian Jewish history as having begun in the 1880s, with the outbreak of the pogroms in Russia. The 1860s and 1870s, seem to them, by contrast, an optimistic period of emancipation in western Europe, with a regime favourable to the Jews of Russia. These were the years in which there was considerable Jewish influence on European politics due to the political and economic activity of Jewish magnates and politicians in both western and eastern Europe: Crémieux and Fuld in France, Montefiore and Rothschild in England, Lasker and Bleichröder in Germany, and Baron von Ginsburg and Polyakov in Russia. A sense of optimism was also found among various sectors of Russian Jewry.

A thorough examination of the weekly press reveals a rather different picture: a political crisis in Romania and the Balkans, a severe economic crisis in Russia, and a growing polarization of the Jews in Germany, Hungary, and Russia (the centres of European Jewry). Traditional circles actually feared that the optimism of the 1860s and the acculturation of the Jews of western Europe, which also touched the border of the Russian Pale, were liable to be followed by a hostile atmosphere that would lead to social disintegration.[18]

This period witnessed the greatest number of attempts at reforming Judaism in Europe and America: the Reform synods in Germany (1868 and 1871), the Congress in Hungary (late 1868), the Congress of Reform Rabbis in Philadelphia (1869), and the public discussion of religious reform in Russia (1868–70). The cumulative impression is that the Reform movement was succeeding and that its increasingly radical nature posed a serious threat to traditional Jewish society.[19]

In Russia this was a period of profound economic and moral crisis, following the cholera epidemic that claimed many victims during 1866–7 and the famine from summer 1867 to the summer of 1869, which resulted from the floods and the drought that occurred primarily in Lithuania.[20]

[17] The 'literary war' is a phrase of Jacob Lipschitz's; see *Zikhron ya'akov*, pt. I, p. 234, pt. II, pp. 5, 13–19; Gideon Katznelson, a historian of the period, calls it 'the press war' in his *Literary War*, 98.

[18] Katznelson, *Literary War*, 20–1.

[19] See Jacob Katz, *The Unhealed Rift* (Heb.) (Jerusalem, 1995), 151–78; Michael A. Meyer, *Tradition and Progress* (Heb.) (Jerusalem, 1989), 210–21, 295–9.

[20] Lipschitz, *Zikhron ya'akov*, pt. II, pp. 69–70; Katznelson, *Literary War*, 69.

THE CONTROVERSY OVER RELIGIOUS REFORM

The controversy over religious reform, which reached its peak in a series of articles by Lilienblum in *Hamelits* called 'The Ways of the Talmud', starting from the April 1868 issue,[21] actually began with a call by the enlightened rabbis for an alliance with the moderate maskilim against the radicalization of the Haskalah. Radical positions of this sort were expressed in articles by Abraham Uri Kovner, in which he was joined by his brother Isaac, the propagandist articles and early novels of Mendele Mokher Seforim, the poems of Judah Leib Gordon, and the propagandist articles of Joshua Heschel Schorr. The first person to write an article in *Hamelits* calling for moderation was Rabbi Abraham Simon Troib of Kaidan,[22] who found an attentive listener in Abraham Baer Gottlober, a veteran maskil who believed that an alliance between the enlightened rabbis and the moderate maskilim would serve to fend off the radical wing of the Haskalah, which he called 'hedonistic'. Interestingly, although *Hamelits* supported the Haskalah and even stood behind its more radical aspects, as the debate progressed it permitted the enlightened rabbis to express their opinions on its pages. This was not due to either inattention or a spirit of tolerance, but out of a sense that there was potential for agreement between the two sides; however, this was to dissipate a year later.[23] Lilienblum himself thought that he could persuade the enlightened rabbis to support a certain number of reforms in the halakhah, citing Mordecai-Gimpel Jaffe and his follower Pines. He did not have anything good to say about Troib—the rabbi of Kaidan, Lilienblum's own birthplace—since he had already come into conflict with him earlier.[24]

In this process of polarization it was precisely those whose views were most similar who became the leaders of the opposing camps. Rabbis Abraham Troib and Joseph Stern became the objects of the verbal assault of the radical maskilim, Troib because he did not permit the use of legumes on Passover (a practice forbidden by Ashkenazi custom), and Stern because he did not permit a woman who had been abandoned by her husband to remarry without a prior divorce.

What led Lilienblum to believe that Jaffe and Pines would support him? During 1867 Pines had published a series of articles called 'Jewry's Place among the Nations',[25] in which he made two major claims: first, that it was Jewish nationalism rather than religion that defined Judaism. This was intended as an argument against the Reform Jews, who were trying to separate religion from nationality and encourage Jews to attach themselves to the nations in which they were living. Second, that it was no longer appropriate for Jews to express hatred of non-Jews at a

[21] i.e. issue 8/13 onwards. The entire series is reprinted in *The Complete Works of Moses Leib Lilienblum* (Heb.), vol. i (Krakow, 1910), 7–138.

[22] 'Hark! My beloved Lord knocketh' (Heb.), *Hamelits*, 7/6 (1867), 44–6; see also Katznelson, *Literary War*, 53 ff.

[23] When Lipschitz, *Zikhron ya'akov*, pt. II, p. 26 called the literature of the 1860s and 1870s 'the religious reform literature', this was obviously a retrospective view from the standpoint of an Orthodox activist struggling against the Haskalah.

[24] Ibid. 60.

[25] *Hamelits*, 7/16–18 (1867).

time when the latter respected Jews. Pines argued that one could make use of halakhic categories such as 'avoiding the desecration of God's name' and 'living in peace with the non-Jew' to abrogate all the talmudic expressions denigrating non-Jews. He believed that these categories were not intended for the formulation of halakhic rulings but rather to make distinctions among the attitudes of non-Jews and that, when these attitudes changed for the better, especially at a time when non-Jews need no longer be considered idol-worshippers, then Jews must likewise change their attitude towards non-Jews.[26] These claims led people to suspect Pines of intending to reform the halakhah, since he asserted that it contained elements that were not relevant to the present. Since he refused to repudiate these claims he was subjected to criticism by members of his own camp.

The first to respond to Pines was his own teacher, Mordecai-Gimpel Jaffe, the rabbi of Ruzhany, who later emigrated to Palestine, settled in Yehud, and served as rabbi in the area until his death in 1891. Jaffe himself had much secular knowledge. Even prior to the religious reform controversy, in 1846, he had been involved in discussions with Moses Montefiore about reforming Judaism in Russia, and in 1856 he wrote an enthusiastic address for the accession of Alexander II. In his response to Pines he made two points: first, he rejected the claim that Maimonides accepted the idea of the Messiah only in order to ground a sense of nationalism; second, he rejected the claim that the halakhah always expressed a hostile attitude to non-Jews. On the contrary, he argued, the halakhah was more concerned with ethical issues between Jews and non-Jews than was any other legal system. It was, for example, wrong to claim that it condoned cheating non-Jews: as Pines was well aware, Jaffe himself was always very careful to tell his own congregants to avoid this, and Christians often came to him in their disputes with Jews because they knew that he would not discriminate in the latter's favour.[27] It was this article of Jaffe's that Lilienblum alluded to in 'The Ways of the Talmud'.

Pines responded with two counter-arguments. First, that although the idea of the Messiah was intended to perfect the world by creating a Kingdom of God, it was difficult for a people to continue to exist purely on the basis of a spiritual idea, so God also promised that were they to be overcome by despair and would 'try to assimilate, and abandon Judaism; then the Messiah would be revealed'. Second, most rabbis were quite indifferent to their congregants' cheating non-Jews; Jaffe was simply an exception to the rule.[28]

We can already see that there were two types of enlightened rabbi. Pines was an exponent of the left wing, which accepted the Haskalah's criticism of traditional society and was open to moderate halakhic reform. His teacher Jaffe, by contrast, took a middle path: he denied the pertinence of Haskalah criticism while espousing it in principle, and rejected the idea of halakhic reform without denying the need for changes in areas not covered by halakhah.[29]

[26] *Hamelits*, 7/17 (1867).
[27] Jaffe, in *Hamelits*, 7/24 (1867).
[28] Pines, in *Hamelits*, 7/24 (1867).
[29] Katznelson, *Literary War*, 60.

In a further series of articles in *Hamelits*[30] Pines severely criticized traditional Jewish education. He defined his audience as 'average people' who were searching for a synthesis between tradition and enlightenment—'the ones who want to go forward in the spirit of the times in all areas of knowledge, without going astray even one whit from the path of faith'.[31] The mistake was not to prescribe the proper dosage of Torah studies to balance secular education: the traditional education of both boys and girls was inadequate. Pines had no doubt that the mingling of tradition and modernity must have a moral underpinning rather than being a merely technical combination: 'If we want to educate Jews in the ways of the Haskalah, we must give it a sacred form . . . We must show that a secular education is a most secure means of strengthening religion.'[32] He also suggested a properly graded education in which various subjects were taught according to modern educational methods.

It was this article by Pines that attracted Lilienblum's attention and allowed him to conclude that Pines might support his position. But even before Lilienblum began presenting his own claims, Pines published a call to the Russian people to allow Jews to devote themselves to farming in Russia and even hinted that they might be willing to serve in the Russian army: 'If you sincerely want to give us land among you, and recognize us as loyal citizens . . . give us permission simply and naturally to occupy ourselves in our own handiwork.'[33]

In his series entitled 'The Ways of the Talmud', Lilienblum had apparently taken upon himself the task of refuting all denigrators of the Talmud, both Jews and non-Jews. The discussion demonstrates his extensive knowledge of the hidden corners of Torah literature. At this stage he went along with the positions of the circle of enlightened rabbis whose support he was seeking. Even his programmatic declaration passed this test: 'But our faith is the source of the life of our people. . . . We can only live with our faith in these times, and if its light fades the Jewish people will be lost.'[34] He attacked those Jews who abandoned their tradition, 'the laws of our spiritual realm'. Towards the end of the article he refers to Pines in his call to the rabbis to take the initiative and use their authority to change the traditional ways wherever possible according to the needs of the period: 'Good days are coming and we want to live like other people. This will require many changes in our lives, yet you are just standing there as if nothing is happening! . . . Why not remove many of the restrictions that were imposed by the rabbis of the last few centuries, which are an immeasurable burden for us?'[35] He ends by citing the arguments of Jaffe, quoted above, which he considered an example of rabbinic courage in matters that were halakhically permissible. This did not particularly disturb traditional Jews, perhaps because Lilienblum pretended that he was actually defending the

30 'The Ways of Educating Our Children, and What the People Want from their Rabbis' (Heb.), *Hamelits*, 7/35–43 (1867).

31 *Hamelits*, 7/35 (1867), 369–70.

32 *Hamelits*, 7/36 (1867), 376–9.

33 'Dear Advocate' (Heb.), *Hamelits*, 8/1 (1868), 6–7.

34 *Hamelits*, 8/13 (1868), 99–100; see also Joseph Klausner, *History of Modern Hebrew Literature* (Heb.), 6 vols. (Jerusalem 1952–4), iv. 198 ff.

35 *Hamelits*, 8/29 (1868).

tradition from its denigrators, or perhaps because his demands seemed to be close to those of Pines, and even Jaffe was likely to agree to them.[36]

Some time after his first series of articles was published Lilienblum began writing a second series, called 'Supplements to "The Ways of the Talmud"', which stirred genuine controversy. Was this because the first series had been accepted without real opposition, or because of the quarrels he had with the members of his community in Vilkomir around the time that he was writing the second series?[37]

At any rate, in the second series of articles Lilienblum questioned the traditional methods of deciding the halakhah, from the Talmud to the *Shulḥan arukh*: 'The Talmud is more of a guide than a source of halakhic decisions, and one should not decide the halakhah on the basis of the Talmud.' The halakhic authorities who came after the Talmud 'created new laws that had been unknown before . . . and since there are no longer any prophets among us we lost the right to create new laws once the Talmud was completed'.[38] He also denied the divine origin of the Talmud: 'In general, except for a few early laws and accepted interpretations, the Talmud . . . is the work of intelligent people who understood human nature. . . . [It] is a collection of different opinions, and since people's opinions differ from one another . . . we find contrasting views about faith as well as halakhah there.'[39] At the end of this series Lilienblum addressed the rabbis, asking for their support. He listed Isaac Elhanan Spektor, Israel Salanter, Mordecai-Gimpel Jaffe, Joseph Stern, and Alexander Moses Lapidot.[40] Not all the rabbis in this list belong to our category of 'enlightened rabbis'. Did Lilienblum really think that they would be likely to support his position, which meant abolishing the tradition of rabbinical decision and paving the way for a general reform of halakhah?

This issue created a gap between the radical maskilim and the enlightened rabbis. The controversy also divided the leading Hebrew journals: *Hamelits* supported the radicals, while after this the rabbis wrote mainly for *Halevanon*.

The first rabbi to reply to Lilienblum was Jaffe. He responded to Lilienblum's assertion that all his criticism was directed at the halakhic decision-making process by arguing that Lilienblum was trying to abolish the talmudic discussions as well, 'for his bow is aimed at the author of the *Shulḥan arukh*, but the arrows he shot have also penetrated the chest of the Talmud'.[41] The next angry reply came from Pines. Although he accepted the principle of development in the halakhah, he insisted that it must be a natural, internal process without external intervention. He claimed that demands such as Lilienblum's were attempts to sterilize what was still

[36] See Mordecai-Gimpel Jaffe, 'Concerning the Supplements to "The Ways of the Talmud"' (Heb.), *Halevanon*, 6/20 (1869), 154; see also Katznelson, *Literary War*, 82–3.

[37] The second explanation is offered by Joseph Klausner in his introduction to the first edition of Lilienblum, *Complete Works*, i. 11.

[38] Lilienblum, 'Supplements to "The Ways of the Talmud"' (Heb.), *Hamelits*, 9/8 (1869). Klausner, *History of Modern Hebrew Literature*, iv. 199–202.

[39] *Hamelits*, 9/9 (1869). See also Katznelson, *Literary War*, 89–92.

[40] *Hamelits*, 9/12 (1869).

[41] Jaffe, 'Supplements to "The Ways of the Talmud"', 153.

living, and would therefore not be accepted: 'All the halakhic restrictions are planted in the soil of Judaism, and as long as they are still fresh the Jewish people draws nourishment from them. We cannot uproot them from the ground without drying up the source of their freshness and weakening both the religious ground and the plants growing from it.'[42] The halakhah did indeed develop, but only through those authorized to implement it, and not through people who did not have such authority: 'Let us not be hasty in our changes before we know what to plant and what to uproot, and let us leave Judaism alone, as it will develop by itself according to the needs of the religion and the time.'[43]

In July 1869 Joseph Stern, the rabbi of Shavli in Lithuania, entered the picture. In a series of articles called 'A Time to Build the Walls of Religion', published in *Halevanon* over the course of many months, he countered one by one each of Lilienblum's claims about possible amendments to the halakhah. Stern, who was on the right wing of the camp of enlightened rabbis, asserted: 'If someone does not recognize the *Shulḥan arukh* as the direct continuation of the Talmud, his Judaism is worthless. The *Shulḥan arukh* and the Talmud embody all the modernization of Jewish society.'[44]

Alexander Moses Lapidot, the rabbi of Rossiyeny in Lithuania, expressed a more complex position. In a series of articles in *Halevanon* called 'Open Reproof'[45] he argued against any possible amendment to halakhah:

> Every custom in the halakhah has a source. The *Magen avraham* [a well-known commentary on the *Shulḥan arukh*] clarified the issue of customs and found that all of them have some support in the Talmud or in the early commentators on the Talmud [prior to the *Shulḥan arukh*], and they knew the source of each custom they listed. . . . Lilienblum claims that he does not believe in the special properties of magical formulas because they do not accord with the laws of nature, but why should we rely on him to be acquainted with the entire system of nature? . . . Lilienblum wants to change things in accordance with the needs of the times, that is, according to people's desires. These desires were determined by God and He set their limits.

Lapidot's responses are typically Orthodox, and in fact express a position even more extreme than his usual one, in order to pre-empt attacks from outsiders. The possibility that the enlightened rabbis would support changes in religion by forming a committee to make decisions of this sort was taken off the agenda. All demands for amendments to the halakhah that came from 'freethinkers' were rejected, even if they actually represented a reasonable compromise. Even magical formulas were given the status of truths. The true position of the early enlightened rabbis was the one defended by Pines—the awareness that the halakhah is dynamic and that it develops through *ad hoc* rabbinical decisions. Now, however, all declarations propos-

[42] Pines, 'Concerning the Supplements to "The Ways of the Talmud"' (Heb.), *Halevanon*, 6/21 (1869), 164.

[43] *Halevanon*, 6/22 (1869), 171.

[44] 'A Time to Build the Walls of Religion' (Heb.), *Halevanon*, 6/31–6 and 39–40 (1869).

[45] *Halevanon*, 6/41–3 (1869).

ing changes in the halakhah to fit the needs of the time were summarily rejected. Pines himself was reproved by Stern, who was Jaffe's son-in-law.[46] Stern claimed that when Pines admitted, in the course of his debate with Lilienblum, that there were some customs that had become entrenched without being authorized by any halakhic authorities, he was paving the way for abrogating the halakhah entirely. He insisted that Jews who are not God-fearing and who demanded the abolition of customs that are prevalent among traditional Jews would end up abolishing important halakhic principles as well. Stern drew a line between the enlightened rabbis and the 'freethinking' maskilim: the quarrel of traditional Judaism was not, he argued, with the Haskalah as such, but only with the freethinkers. It was the devotion to God which differentiated the two groups and constituted the basis for the Orthodoxy that was taking shape.

THE YEARS OF FAMINE

At the same time as the controversy about amending the halakhah was taking place, another bitter debate began in the journal *Hamagid* concerning ways of improving the Russian Jews' material state in the wake of the famine of 1867–9. In this debate the enlightened rabbis also made their opinions known, this time in a series of articles entitled 'How to Improve the Situation of Our Brethren in Russia'. *Hamagid* also played a leading role in forming the organization Tomkhei Dalim (Helpers of the Poor), which attempted to obtain assistance in western Europe for the Russian Jews; the Russian Jews considered this organization a means of entry to the West.

Pines's article in this series suggested improving the Russian Jews' productivity by settling the land in central Russia, America, and Palestine: 'The land is the basis on which to establish a political society and a national home.'[47] This was meant to continue an earlier idea of Samuel Joseph Fuenn, the editor and publisher of another journal, *Hakarmel*.

Jacob Lipschitz contributed an article countering the accusation that the rabbis had been too passive in responding to the economic crisis and praising the initiatives for productivity coming from the 'enlightened' group and the editor of *Hamagid*.[48] These analysts of the economic crisis were then joined by Mordecai Eliasberg, who deemed Fuenn's position on this issue to be realistic. Like the others, Eliasberg believed in the good intentions of the Russian government in helping relieve the Jews' economic problems. He also suggested setting up a central organization in St Petersburg to enhance the productivity of the Russian Jews.[49]

46 Joseph Zechariah Stern, 'Wise Men, Be Careful What You Say' (Heb.), *Halevanon*, 7/3 (1870), 17–21.

47 Pines, 'How to Improve the Situation of Our Brethren in Russia' (Heb.), *Hamagid*, 13 (1869), 98–9.

48 Lipschitz, 'How to Improve the Situation of Our Brethren in Russia' (Heb.), *Hamagid*, 13 (1869), 106–7.

49 Eliasberg, 'How to Improve the Situation of Our Brethren in Russia' (Heb.), *Hamagid*, 13 (1869), 129–30.

We can thus see that the enlightened rabbis were willing to go quite far to encourage the productivity of the Russian Jews in co-operation with the authorities. It seems clear that the Zionist idea of solving the problems of Russian Jewry through immigration to Palestine was not yet taken seriously by the Jewish public, even in those circles which were to advocate it strongly only a few years later.

While the enlightened rabbis in Russia were lining up to advocate the productivity of Jews within Russia itself, Rabbi Tsevi Hirsch Kalischer in Prussia was grappling with the concept of 'redemption' in the pages of *Hamagid*,[50] and the editor of this journal, David Gordon, published a series of articles of his own under the title 'The Time has Come: On the National Mission of the Jewish People'.[51] Gordon severely criticized the enlightened rabbis' advocacy of Jewish productivity within Russia. These rabbis' attitude towards the nationalist issue of emigrating to Erets Yisrael was expressed by Lapidot towards the end of 1869. Totally ignoring the nationalistic aspect of the initiative, he said: 'We will not force people to emigrate to Erets Yisrael. Only hasidim and kabbalists will emigrate there in order to worship God and pray for the welfare of their brothers in the Diaspora and for the entire world.'[52]

The 1869–70 discussions about the Russian Jews' productivity did not have any positive results. No public organization was formed to take the initiative in this area. Even the Russian government did not show any interest. The debate among the enlightened rabbis on the issue of religious reform ceased in 1871. The Franco-Prussian War stopped the publication of *Halevanon* until it was transferred to Germany and began publication again in Mainz, financed by the German Orthodox Jewish community. *Hamelits* moved to St Petersburg in 1871 and its editor refused to continue the debate. Isaac Elhanan Spektor tried to calm people's emotions. The pogrom in Odessa in 1871 raised doubts about the possibility of solutions in Russia. It seems that the wind was taken from their sails. The group of enlightened rabbis set out the far-reaching demand that the rabbinical seminaries and the journals should be placed under their control.

REFORMING JEWISH EDUCATION

When *Halevanon* began to appear once again, Samuel Mohilewer contributed two series of articles, the first entitled 'Religious Observance and the Enlightenment',[53] the second, 'Human Happiness'.[54] He also made a rather bold appearance at the Society for the Promotion of Culture among the Jews in April 1873, suggesting that the society ask the authorities to support the establishment of Jewish schools that would combine a Torah-based education with a secular one. This was originally the initiative of a number of rabbis, who requested the support of Baron Yosel

[50] Kalischer, 'The Righteous Person Will Live in his Faith' (Heb.), *Hamagid*, 13 (1869), 128.

[51] *Hamagid*, 13/27–34 (1869).

[52] Lapidot, 'Rossiyeny' (Heb.), *Halevanon*, 6/40 (1869), 638.

[53] *Halevanon*, 9/15–16 (1872).

[54] *Halevanon*, 9/27 and 29 (1872).

Ginsburg in abolishing the 'teachers' law', which imposed general education on the Jewish *melamedim*, and which was to become operative in 1875. Mohilewer, however, took an independent position on this issue and continued even when his colleagues decided to break off contact with Baron Ginsburg and the society.[55] The impression Mohilewer made on this group should not be underestimated. He was rabbi of an important community in Radom, Poland, who was speaking about a bold plan at a forum of public activists and writers which was considered hostile to traditional society.[56] In his speech to this forum, as well as in the series of articles mentioned above, Mohilewer asserted that 'we must join these two children of God, faith and Enlightenment'.[57] This was a far-reaching suggestion to put before a forum that supported the acculturation of the Jews to the Russia of the day, and whose activists included people who were demanding halakhic reforms.

THE CONTROVERSY OVER *ETROGIM*

The issue of settling Erets Yisrael became relevant in 1874, when Moses Montefiore visited the land of Israel for the seventh and last time and the decision was made to establish a Montefiore Memorial Foundation in his honour. A delegation was sent to Palestine by the Foundation's committee, headed by Samuel Montague and Asher Asher, to investigate what was being done in the old Yishuv—the existing Jewish settlement in Palestine. The harsh report that resulted from this investigation made the problems of the Yishuv more concrete and demonstrated the need to find ways to help it become more self-sufficient.

Again it was Pines who led the discussion, with *Halevanon* serving as the platform.[58] He explained that Jewish society had two approaches to the future of Erets Yisrael: the ascetic and the modern. The advocates of the ascetic approach were 'entirely devoted to making Jerusalem a refuge for ascetics who separate themselves from daily life and devote themselves to eternal life'; in contrast, the advocates of the modern approach wanted 'to see Jerusalem in its beauty as one of the glorious daughters of Europe'. He himself supported the modern approach. He aspired 'to see the pleasantness of the Holy Land when it would once more bloom like the Garden of Eden and produce fruitful vines and wheatfields, not for those Arabs, but for her hopeful sons who will stream from the ends of the earth to work and guard the land'.[59]

Here Pines made a practical suggestion: that Jewish residents of Palestine should be encouraged to grow *etrogim* for all the Jewish people to use on Sukot instead of the *etrogim* grown in Corfu that were being used at that time. He cast doubt on the

[55] Lipschitz, *Zikhron ya'akov*, pt. II, pp. 128–30.

[56] Leon (Judah Leib) Rosenthal, *The History of the Society for the Promotion of Culture among Russian Jews* (Heb.), pt. I (St Petersburg, 1886), 100–2 (the report is from 29 Apr. 1873).

[57] 'Religious Observance and the Enlightenment', *Halevanon*, 16 (1872), 123.

[58] Pines, 'On the Settlement of Erets Yisrael' (Heb.), *Halevanon*, 11/35–6 (1875).

[59] *Halevanon*, 11/35 (1875), 273.

halakhic acceptability of the Corfu *etrogim*, as they were grafted on to lemon trees, and also complained about their high price. The problem of the Corfu *etrogim* had already been much discussed, not only because of the connection with Erets Yisrael, but also because of the question of their halakhic acceptability. Pines combined the two issues. He was supported by his friend Stern and the editorial board of *Halevanon*.[60] This issue is interesting in and of itself, and deserves separate discussion. Here I will only mention that the enlightened rabbis were at the forefront of the attempt to ban the use of the Corfu *etrogim*.

Pines's article drew fire from two directions: from Joseph Rivlin, the secretary of the Committee of Jewish Communities, who was also a relative of Pines, and from Jacob Lipschitz. They were joined by Moses Montefiore and Yehiel Brill, who was the editor of *Halevanon*. All of them opposed Pines's criticism of the 'old Yishuv' in Palestine, which had already been expressed at length in the Montague–Asher report. Although they were willing to support the idea that the Yishuv should be productive, and thus also supported the ban on the Corfu *etrogim*, they were not prepared to support Pines's nationalist views.

Indeed, when the Hebrew press published advertisements to appoint a representative to the Montefiore Memorial Foundation in 1876 it was clear that the moderate maskilim, including radicals like Lilienblum and Gordon, supported Pines, since their views were already nationalistic and they liked Pines's criticism of the 'old Yishuv'. On the other hand, he was also supported by the rabbinical leaders of Russian Jewry, who did not have a consolidated nationalist view.[61] Pines was chosen even though he was not favoured by most of the English Jewish establishment, which had set up the Foundation, including Montefiore himself, as they did not support the nationalist view and stood behind the 'old Yishuv'. He did, however, fit all the requirements. He came from eastern Europe, was accepted by both traditional and enlightened Jews, and was close to the leaders of the Committee of Jewish Communities. In a letter he wrote to Rivlin in March 1878 Pines stated, 'I am the person who is favoured by every Torah observer and lover of the Haskalah, so why would I be an obstacle to any group in Jerusalem?'[62] In the end the community leaders accepted the appointment and Pines arrived in Palestine in September 1878.

Pines's activities in Jerusalem from the time of his arrival until his death in 1913 form a separate chapter that cannot be detailed here. We can say, however, that the Jewish settlement in Palestine during this period cannot be described without mentioning Pines. He had a hand in everything: establishing neighbourhoods outside the Jerusalem city wall, setting up collective villages, founding organizations of the new Yishuv, such as Tehiyat Yisrael and Benei Moshe, as well as institutions in which the old and new Yishuv co-operated, such as B'nai B'rith, Safah Berurah, Beit Midrash Abravanel, and Va'ad Halashon.

The fact that Pines was an enlightened rabbi who had already expressed a prin-

[60] Yaffe, 'Rabbi Joseph Zechariah Stern', 157; Lipschitz, *Zikhron ya'akov*, pt. II, pp. 174–6.

[61] Lipschitz, *Zikhron ya'akov*, pt. II, p. 181.

[62] Jerusalem: Central Zionist Archive, A109/50.

cipled position, which he would not abandon, in his book *Yaldei ruḥi* (My Spiritual Children, 1872), was an obstacle in his dealings with the old Yishuv and his attempts to persuade them to adopt the goals of the Montefiore Memorial Foundation. Rabbi Judah Leib Diskin and his followers from among the ultra-Orthodox Jews in Jerusalem at that time took advantage of Pines's vulnerability to the claim that he approved of halakhic reform. Pines was that rare combination—a philosopher who tried to actualize his ideas. While he was more capable of expressing ideas than of actualizing them, his practical achievements should not be underestimated. He constructed the bridges by which the people of the old Yishuv could cross over into the new one. The subject of the mobility from the old to the new Yishuv still awaits its historian.

THE HOVEVEI ZION MOVEMENT

Among the first people to react to the pogroms in Russia that began in 1881 was Samuel Mohilewer. He was also one of the first to suggest that the wave of Russian Jewish emigrants should be directed to Palestine. He expressed this opinion at a meeting of the representatives of the English Emissary Committee and the Mansion House Foundation in Lvov in April 1882. Mohilewer differed from the representatives of the large Jewish organizations of western Europe, who recommended emigration to America. It was only to be expected that Mohilewer, who had supported Kalischer's idea of redemption in stages even before the pogroms, should see the emigration of the Russian Jews as an opportunity to actualize the first stage of the redemption—the natural stage, as opposed to the later supernatural one.

In June 1882 Mohilewer persuaded two of the most important east European rabbis to sign a manifesto in favour of emigration to Erets Yisrael—Joseph Dov Soloveitchik of Brisk and Rabbi Elijah Hayim Meisel of Lodz. He managed to get their support only by increasing their fear that the Jews would emigrate to the United States, which they considered a *treif* country—a place in which Jewry became secularized. The achievements of the Reform movement in organizing American Jewry were already well known in Russia, and they were afraid that the Russian Jews would be easy prey. When the movement of emigration to Erets Yisrael started to be organized, however, it became clear that it was led by some of the eastern European maskilim, and rumours about the emigration of the Bilu movement reached the Russian Jews. It was therefore only natural that these two leaders of traditional Jewry in Russia should oppose it. Only someone with a solid nationalist view could have overcome the fear that this movement would be detrimental to traditional Judaism.[63]

This is not the place to detail the activities of Mohilewer and his colleagues—Eliasberg, Jaffe, Stern, Pines, Berlin, and others—in establishing and running the

[63] Joseph Salmon, 'Samuel Mohilewer: The Rabbi of Hovevei Zion' (Heb.), *Zion*, 56 (1991), 51–2.

Hovevei Zion movement, but it must be said that this movement could not be described without including the roles these rabbis played.

THE RABBINICAL SEMINARY CONTROVERSY

In 1881 a book called *Ḥotam tokhnit* (Seal of the Programme) was published in the areas of eastern Europe which had large Jewish populations. This book sharply criticized the teaching methods of the traditional or so called 'Lithuanian' yeshivas, and suggested a new methodology for studying the Torah literature, including halakhah, Midrash, and aggadah. The end of the book contains a critique of traditional Jewish society, a suggestion for reorganizing its institutions, and a blueprint for its relations with the state. The book's criticism echoes the ideas of the Haskalah, even though it rejects the Haskalah's basic values. Isaac Reines, who was serving as rabbi of Sventsyany in the Vilna district at the time and later became the leader of the Mizrahi movement, agreed with the value of the 'individual' celebrated by the Haskalah, but claimed that the Jewish individual needed the Torah and its commandments, since a Jew who abandons the Torah sins not only against his Jewishness but also against his humanity.[64]

Reines's plan, which was formulated just before the pogroms began, suggested that Jews should become part of Russian society in a civic sense, as a co-operative group. His discussion of the issue manifests a great optimism about the future of Russian Jewry, which he saw as conditional on their willingness to become part of the state. His practical plan for attaining this goal was the establishment of a 'reformed' yeshiva which would combine religious and secular studies, thus making it possible for its graduates to become state-approved rabbis.

The responses to Reines's analysis are quite interesting. An 'enlightened' response was that the cause of the weaknesses in Jewish society was not the rabbinate. Reines's biographers claim that he presented his plan at a rabbinical conference in 1882 at which many of the most important rabbis of the time were present—Isaac Elhanan Spektor of Kovno, Joseph Dov Soloveitchik of Brisk, Elijah Hayim Meisel of Lodz, and Naphtali Tsevi Judah Berlin of Volozhin. His basic claim was that if the yeshivas would teach the knowledge 'necessary for the time', if only to a limited extent, then the students would be satisfied with the secular knowledge gained in the yeshiva and would not seek it elsewhere. Reines's plan was rejected and his book was sharply criticized by the ultra-Orthodox, the *ḥaredim*.

Reines was not deterred, however, and he established his yeshiva without the approval of the other rabbis.[65] The yeshiva and its supporters were persecuted, and Reines himself was thrown into gaol after his opponents informed the authorities. The yeshiva thus lasted only a few years, but Reines remained convinced that his educational plan was in the spirit of the great Torah scholars of the past, who

[64] Joseph Salmon, 'The Beginning of the Reform in the Eastern European Yeshivas' (Heb.), *Molad*, 4 (1971), 161–72.

[65] Ibid.

had combined religious and secular wisdom. He also believed that this was the only formula that would preserve traditional Judaism. Without entering into the details of Reines's plan, it is clear that it was an original educational programme that tried to fulfil the expectations of the state, the maskilim, and of traditional Jews. More of an ideal world-view than a practical plan for obtaining academic degrees and the worldly goods they might bring, it was a strategy for shaping a new Jew who would fit the social, educational, and moral norms of the period. It was opposed by ultra-Orthodox activists, who had begun to organize in the 1870s in response to the controversy about religious reform. These activists, who were supported by the important Torah scholars of the time, believed that they were protecting traditional society from disintegration by preventing changes and modernization.

Twenty years after Reines's yeshiva in Sventsyany was closed, he established another along similar lines. This was the well-known Lida Yeshiva, founded in 1905,[66] which was very successful. During the intervening twenty years a group of traditional maskilim, many of whom had links with the Zionist movement in general and the Mizrahi movement in particular, had consolidated. These people were willing to offer public support for such a modern institution. The Lida Yeshiva was closed only in the aftermath of the First World War. The teachers went in different directions: some to the United States, such as Rabbi Solomon Polachik, who taught at Yeshivat Rabbi Isaac Elhanan in New York, and others to Palestine, such as Pinhas Schiffman, who taught in the Mizrahi (religious Zionist) educational system.

Modern Orthodoxy in the United States and the Mizrahi movement in Israel are both faithful followers of the enlightened east European rabbis of the second half of the nineteenth century. These movements believe that secular knowledge and tradition are not contradictory. The secularization that accompanied the Haskalah put the enlightened rabbis in a defensive position, confronting the secular modernists on the one hand and the ultra-Orthodox on the other.

[66] Joseph Salmon, 'The Yeshiva of Lida: A Unique Institution of Higher Learning' (Heb.), *YIVO Annual*, 15 (1974), 106–25.

ELEVEN

Towards a Historical Definition of the Haskalah

SHMUEL FEINER

EVEN though the Haskalah movement ended a century ago it remains exceptionally difficult to define it precisely. Unlike other agents of change in modern Jewish history, the Haskalah had no ideological and institutional coherence, comprehensive organization, constitution, generally agreed programme, principles, or allegiance to a specific defined ideology. Although the term 'Haskalah' was so continuously used that it was at the epicentre of bitter polemics and on everyone's lips, it remains ambiguous and elusive since every modern Jew was identified as a maskil and every change in traditional religious patterns was dubbed Haskalah.

The European Enlightenment met a similar fate, and until recently many scholars were totally frustrated by attempts to find a common denominator for what appeared to be a motley collection of national, religious, and local Enlightenments, *philosophes*, and *Aufklärer* of different and even contradictory kinds.[1] 'Within limits', writes the English historian Norman Hampson, 'the Enlightenment was what one thinks it was . . . There does not seem to me much point in attempting any general definition of the movement. Such a definition would have to include so many qualifications and contradictions as to be virtually meaningless.'[2]

Despite these difficulties, we should not abandon all systematic attempts at arriving at a historical definition of 'Haskalah'. On the contrary, the fact that the Haskalah eludes efforts to place it within an ideological and chronological framework, a locality, and defined institutions makes it all the more imperative to grapple with the question of definition. In addition, the new research that enriches our knowledge of the movement's history, personalities, and ideas, as well as advancing new interpretations, compels us to come to grips with the fundamental question: how is the term 'Haskalah' to be understood? What were the affinities between Haskalah and Enlightenment? What were its geographical boundaries, local centres, and chronological limits, its basic assumptions, thought patterns, programmes, and methods of activity? Finally, in what ways was the Haskalah connected to the pro-

[1] Roy Porter, *The Enlightenment* (London, 1990); Roy Porter and Mikulas Teich (eds.), *The Enlightenment in National Context* (Cambridge, 1981).

[2] *The Enlightenment* (Harmondsworth, 1968).

cesses of modernization and secularization? The absence of dictionaries and lexicons of Jewish historical terms does not absolve students of Jewish history from the attempt to delineate the context and chronology of the Haskalah.[3]

More easily defined movements and trends existed before, after, and at the same time as the Haskalah movement: hasidism, the mitnagedim of the Lithuanian yeshivas, the *musar* movement, the first Zionist movement Hibbat Zion, the early Jewish socialist movement in eastern Europe, the Reform movement, Positive-Historical or Conservative Judaism, Orthodoxy, and Wissenschaft des Judentums in central and western Europe. While there is general agreement over the ideological and programmatic content, principal figures, and coherent social frameworks of these movements, in all these respects the Haskalah is rather blurred. It is usually causally lumped together with the other historical processes of emancipation, religious reform, assimilation, nationalism, and the development of modern Hebrew literature. Hence a historical definition of Haskalah would liberate it by rendering it an independent concept. Only after the Haskalah has achieved this 'emancipation' and 'autonomy' will it be possible properly to place it within the wider historical context, and revitalize the crucial and intriguing question of its role in the process of historical change, secularization, and modernization that affected central and east European Jewish society in the eighteenth and nineteenth centuries. A definition of Haskalah would enable us to arrive at a more precise differentiation of Jewish modernization, be more faithful to historical truth, and highlight the historical meaning of the movement.[4]

REDEMPTIVE HASKALAH: SELF-DEFINITIONS

More important than the overdue and detached analyses of historians are the perceptions of contemporaries, especially those who considered themselves members of the Haskalah movement and who explicitly defined themselves as maskilim. As we shall see, their approaches varied widely, and the self-understanding of the Haskalah underwent a number of changes.[5] The maskilim's own distinction between 'true' and 'false' Haskalah, for example, was used as a rhetorical and ideological device to define the boundaries of the movement, and thus offers one way of

[3] See e.g. Horst Stuke's definition of 'Aufklärung' in his *Geschichtliche Grundbegriffe* (Stuttgart, 1977), and a brief article by Dominique Bourel on the Haskalah in Germany, 'Haskalah: Jüdische Aufklärung', in Werner Schneiders (ed.), *Lexikon der Aufklärung* (Munich, 1995), 174–5.

[4] For new views and directions in the research on Jewish modernization see Jonathan Frankel, 'Assimilation and the Jews in Nineteenth-Century Europe: Towards a New Historiography?', in Jonathan Frankel and Steven J. Zipperstein (eds.), *Assimilation and Community: The Jews in Nineteenth-Century Europe* (Cambridge, 1992), 1–37.

[5] Only in 1990 was the first attempt made to clarify the concept 'Haskalah'. See Uzi Shavit, 'An Examination of the Term Haskalah in Hebrew Literature' (Heb.), *Meḥkarei yerushalayim besifrut ivrit*, 12 (1990), 51–83.

arriving at a more precise definition; it also illustrates the ambivalent relationship between the Haskalah and modernity.

In order to understand the meaning of Haskalah we must therefore consider a whole spectrum of definitions, not only of Haskalah itself, but of other related terms, such as the frequently used *Aufklärung*. The 140-year history of the changing self-definition of the movement is more than a lexicographical or philological exercise; it is a fascinating journey into the minds and lives of its followers.

Haskalah as Philosophy

The early maskilim in Germany, Naphtali Herz Wessely, Moses Mendelssohn, Isaac Satanow, and others, began their literary careers between the 1750s and 1770s before forming defined circles and a movement, and before the first Haskalah forays into education (the Berlin *Freyschule*) and literature (the Torah translation and commentary called *Biur*). The dominant activities at this stage of early Haskalah were the renewal of the Jewish scientific tradition, Hebrew grammar, and to a lesser extent the Jewish philosophical tradition.[6] As Uzi Shavit has shown, the term Haskalah appeared a number of times in essays such as Maimonides' *Biur milot hahigayon*, which was published with Mendelssohn's commentary (1762, 1765), and Wessely's *Yein levanon* (1775).[7] Here, however, 'Haskalah' meant philosophy and almost nothing else.

Two contradictory trends were prominent in the early Haskalah. One considered philosophy to be a significant contribution to scholarship and belief, while another rejected philosophy out of fear that it would undermine religious faith. This is especially true of early Haskalah devotees in Poland and Lithuania, who focused on the natural sciences and had serious reservations about the study of philosophy.[8] The basic question was whether rationalist enquiry and the adoption of the rules and basic concepts of philosophy was legitimate, or whether they contradicted perfect faith, kabbalah, and divine wisdom originating in revelation. Wessely, for example, who was among those who were apprehensive of potentially negative influences, argued that one should go no further than harnessing 'rational proofs' to strengthen 'beliefs and opinions'.[9] Mendelssohn, on the other hand, as early as the publication of his first Hebrew work *Kohelet musar*, believed that philosophy (i.e. Haskalah) was eminently compatible with the sources of Judaism.[10] In the preface to *Biur milot hahigayon* he praised Haskalah and recommended that

[6] See David Sorkin, 'From Context to Comparison: The German Haskalah and Reform Catholicism', *Tel Aviver Jahrbuch für deutsche Geschichte*, 20 (1991), 23–41; id., 'The Case for Comparison: Moses Mendelssohn and the Religious Enlightenment', *Modern Judaism*, 14 (1994), 121–38.

[7] Shavit, 'The Term Haskalah', 62–70.

[8] See Immanuel Etkes, 'On the Question of the Precursors of the Haskalah in East Europe', in id. (ed.), *Religion and Life: The Jewish Enlightenment in Eastern Europe* (Heb.) (Jerusalem, 1993), 25–44 and Shmuel Feiner, 'The Early Haskalah in the Eighteenth Century' (Heb.), *Tarbiz*, 62/2 (1998), 189–240.

[9] Shavit, 'The Term Haskalah', 62–3; Wessely's letter to Mendelssohn (1768), in Mendelssohn, *Ketavim ivriyim* [Hebrew Writings], in id., *Gesammelte Schriften Jubiläumsausgabe*, vol. xix (Stuttgart, n.d.), 120–3.

[10] Mordecai Gilon, *Mendelssohn's 'Kohelet musar' in its Historical Context* (Heb.) (Jerusalem, 1979).

every maskil and scholar should apply philosophy in general, and logic in particular, to his search for truth. The methods and paths of Haskalah, he wrote, were not alien to Jews. On the contrary, 'there is no doubt that He who gave man knowledge also implanted within his heart the inclination to Haskalah and established virtuous laws and rules so that he might understand intricate matters and grasp subtleties'.[11] Thus the maskil is the philosopher who 'with scholarly methods seeks truth through Haskalah'.[12]

The early Haskalah represented the start of the transformation of traditional Jewish scholarship that sought to revive what was believed already to exist in the Jewish literature of the Middle Ages and Renaissance, and it can only partly be considered as precursor of the Haskalah movement. Its fields of study were limited to seeking truth in the world of thought, strengthening faith, and, at most, upholding the standing of the Jewish community in the eyes of the world. This underwent a drastic change in the late 1770s when the Haskalah developed into a world-view associated with a comprehensive programme of social and cultural transformation. The translation of the Pentateuch into German was more than a literary project; it was an attempt to draw Jews into European culture. Philanthropic motives stemming from an identification with the absolutist and mercantilist ethos were the driving force behind the establishment of the modern Jewish school in Berlin in 1778, and its founders consciously sought to educate Jews to be of service to the state in their occupations and social life. In 1782 Wessely's *Divrei shalom ve'emet* espoused an ideology and programme based on the belief that a new Europe was dawning, and along with it the vision of the Jew who was also a man and a citizen.[13] The first organized maskil group, Hevrat Dorshei Leshon Ever (Society for the Promotion of the Hebrew Language) founded in Königsberg in 1782, cultivated a distinct self-consciousness of pioneers paving the way for others. Its public declarations had a manifesto-like and revolutionary character which combined great enthusiasm with the promise of a new kind of secular redemption: 'The time of science has arrived for all peoples . . . Why should we be so lazy and do nothing? Please, O brothers, rise up and rescue the [previous] stones from heaps of rubble! . . . Men of truth will illuminate the path and the sun of justice will shine upon us from above and be the light of eternity.'[14]

[11] *Biur milot hahigayon leharav heḥakham beyisra'el . . . moreinu verabeinu moshe ben rabi maimon, im peirush mehatorani morenu harav rav moshe midesau* [Logical Terms . . .] (Berlin, 1765), preface.

[12] *Biur mendelssohn lemegilat kohelet* [Mendelssohn's commentary on Ecclesiastes] (1770), in Mendelssohn, *Ketavim ivriyim*, vol. i, p. vii; Shavit, 'The Term Haskalah', 10.

[13] Naphtali Herz Wessely, *Divrei shalom ve'emet* [Words of Peace and Truth] (Berlin, 1782). See also Mordecai Eliav, *Jewish Education in Germany during the Haskalah and Emancipation* (Heb.) (Jerusalem, 1960), and Shmuel Feiner, 'Educational Agendas and Social Ideals: Jüdische Freischule in Berlin, 1778–1825', in Rivka Feldhay and Immanuel Etkes (eds.), *Education and History: Cultural and Political Contexts* (Heb.) (Jerusalem, 1999), 247–84.

[14] Hevrat Dorshei Lashon Ever, *Naḥal habesor* [Announcement] (Königsberg, 1783). See also Shmuel Feiner, 'Isaac Euchel: Entrepreneur of the Haskalah Movement in Germany' (Heb.), *Zion*, 52 (1987), 427–69.

What Is Enlightenment?

It was precisely during the years when the Haskalah movement in Germany was shaped that the question 'Was ist Aufklärung?' was being debated in Germany. Even before the discussion was officially opened by the editor of the *Berlinische Monatsschrift* in 1784, a variety of definitions had been offered,[15] but now it became the crucial question for the future of the movement in Germany, and for its sense of identity.[16] The answers Immanuel Kant and Moses Mendelssohn offered are the most important and best known. Typically, Mendelssohn treated the question in a philosophical manner. He defined *Aufklärung* as rational thought, the theoretical aspect of the broader term *Bildung*,[17] which also included *Kultur*, the practical component related to crafts and cultural life. To all intents and purposes Mendelssohn maintained what he had already argued in his early Hebrew works: *Aufklärung* was understood as enlightenment in the sense of rational philosophy. It pertained, Mendelssohn stressed, to the human being as human being and was a universal value. The exaggerated use of *Aufklärung*, or its enlistment for harsh criticism, would be an abuse of the term and lead to moral lassitude and egotism, atheism, and anarchy, and should therefore be avoided.[18]

In Kant's eyes, by contrast, *Aufklärung* was not a relatively abstract category but a historical process, moving from a condition of immaturity, ignorance, and blind obedience to past and present authorities towards maturity. The sign of this intellectual and historical maturity was the slogan of the *Aufklärung*: free and independent rational thought. This transition, indeed the entire process, was an act of self-liberation, the acquisition of freedom, of individual autonomy. Even if Kant was excessively cautious in drawing the boundaries of freedom in order to avoid conflicting with the laws of Frederick the Great's Prussia (reason as much as you like and on any subject you like—but obey!), one cannot deny the revolutionary potential implied by Kant's definition: acquire knowledge, use reason, be critical and free of conventions so that you become a mature autonomous person! More than just individual and theoretical categories is implied, but an evolving, comprehensive historical process: we are not yet living in an enlightened age, but in an Age of Enlightenment.[19]

It seems that, with regard to the Haskalah, Mendelssohn's definitions more aptly

[15] See n. 3 above.

[16] See Ehrhard Bahr (ed.), *Was ist Aufklärung? Thesen und Definitionen* (Stuttgart, 1974); Natan Rotenstreich, 'Enlightenment: Between Mendelssohn and Kant', in S. Stein and R. Loewe (eds.), *Studies in Jewish Religion and Intellectual History* (Tuscaloosa, Ala., 1979), 279–363; J. Schmidt, 'The Question of Enlightenment: Kant, Mendelssohn and the *Mittwochgesellschaft*', *Journal of the History of Ideas*, 50 (1989), 269–91.

[17] See George L. Mosse, *German Jews Beyond Judaism* (Bloomington, Ind., 1985); David Sorkin, *The Transformation of German Jewry, 1780–1840* (New York, 1987).

[18] Moses Mendelssohn, 'Über die Frage, Was heisst Aufklärung?', *Berlinische Montatsschrift*, 4 (1784), 193–200. See also Shavit, 'The Term Haskalah', 58–9.

[19] Immanuel Kant, 'Beantwortung der Frage, Was ist Aufklärung', *Berlinische Monatsschrift*, 4 (1784), 481–94.

characterize the stage of 'early Haskalah', whereas the maskilim who understood their Haskalah in Kantian terms properly defined what developed in the 1770s and 1780s.

Guiding the Public

Even if the ideological meaning of the term 'Haskalah' was not yet explicit in the Hebrew sources, the maskilim used a rhetoric that assigned to themselves the historic task of leading their brethren in the transition from the epoch of immaturity to the epoch of maturity. They were the 'society' or 'fraternity' of maskilim, and their call for the mobilization of members and supporters was directed as 'young maskilim who love morality and knowledge'.[20] The call to leadership was already evident in 1783–8, the primary stage of the evolving Haskalah movement. More than anything, maskilim felt a sense of responsibility to the general public: 'know that we are your brothers who love you and are not seeking material benefit or making a name for ourselves, but work for your sake alone, dear brothers! Your benefit is our only objective.'[21] From the start, the maskilim assumed the position of a socially critical minority, a new intellectual class of teachers and writers who were waging all-out war against ignorance and were convinced that their victory would greatly benefit the Jewish community. The maskilim in Germany at the end of the eighteenth century were interested in something more than Mendelssohn's theoretical guidance. Some even proclaimed that government intervention was not needed to rid Jewish society of flaws in its education, culture, and leadership. Isaac Euchel, who has lately been regarded as the key figure of the Haskalah movement, insisted that Jews should transcend ignorance through their own efforts. A reformed education and the evolution of a new class of future leaders would be initiated by the maskilim alone, and they would foster Jewish regeneration. The maskilim saw themselves as 'moral physicians'—a common self-image, explaining to themselves and others that more than anyone else they had the right to prescribe the bitter pill which must be swallowed.[22]

The atmosphere of Hevrat Dorshei Lashon Ever in Königsberg was that of a reading club, a Jewish *Lesegesellschaft* of those seeking security and solace in the company of maskilim against 'the complacent and arrogant'. The circle preached the same transformation demanded by Kant, and was profoundly influenced by the programme for Jewish improvement proposed by the Prussian intellectual Christian Wilhelm Dohm. In the words of the Hebrew poet Shimon Baraz,

> Then they will be ready to improve those like them
> Sow seeds of reason where chaos reigns,
> Imbue dolts with comprehension

[20] *Takanot ḥevrat shoḥarei hatov vehatushiyah* [Regulations of the Society for the Propagation of Goodness and Virtue] (Berlin and Königsberg, 1787): 'it should be printed at the beginning of the book that maskilim have examined and found that the book is honest and correct'.

[21] *Naḥal habesor.*

[22] See Feiner, 'Isaac Euchel', 446–8.

Youths with shrewdness
Teach wisdom [*hokhmah*] to impetuous blunderers
And reason and intelligence that will fill the earth with knowledge![23]

This poem expresses the essence of the Haskalah experience for the next hundred years: a group of young people with a traditional education and family and social expectations of persevering in the study of Talmud, who had internalized some *Aufklärung* concepts, were exposed to European literature, met on the basis of common belief, youthful ideological exuberance, consciousness of entertaining not-quite-legitimate ideas, and a deep sense of their worthiness to preach to and rebuke a society that had lost its way. Above all, their mission was to herald a new historical age in Europe—the 'modern age'.[24] From then on the maskilim were those who identified with the Haskalah experience, took part in it, and were participants in the new consciousness of historical change and a programme of reform which, to their minds, stemmed from that change.

Distinctions between the terms Haskalah, enquiry (*hakirah*), and knowledge or wisdom (*hokhmah*) were virtually non-existent at the end of the eighteenth century. Moreover, use of 'Haskalah' in the sense of philosophy was maintained by maskilim such as Wessely and Satanow, who made the transition from the early to the ideological stage of the Haskalah. As has been noted, Wessely was one of the founders of the evolving Haskalah ideology. This was evident in his manifesto-like response to Joseph II of Austria's Edict of Tolerance and his efforts to convince the Jewish public of the need for basic, revolutionary changes in educational curricula. For Wessely, however, the term 'Haskalah' only meant rational philosophy and, like his predecessors, he believed it posed a threat to religious belief. Therefore, in *Sefer hamidot* he recommends that 'Haskalah and enquiry' should be restricted and made subordinate to 'morality and fear of the Lord'.[25] Satanow, the most prolific Hebrew writer of the period, had no such fears. He too interpreted Haskalah as rational philosophy, but found no better moral edification for his generation than 'Haskalah deeds'. Continuing in Mendelssohn's path, Satanow maintained that philosophical enquiry was imperative for a believing Jew: 'For wonderment [*peliah*] is the reason for Haskalah in God's verities. For he who does not wonder will not enquire, and he who does not enquire will not gain knowledge [*yaskil*].' In *Mishlei asaf* (The Proverbs of Asaf, 1788) 'Haskalah' still means philosophy ('enquiry which leads to truth is called Haskalah'), but now there appear ideological implications such as that of the metaphorical opposition of reason (*sekhel*) as light and sun, to ignorance and darkness. 'Haskalah' is now an opposing option with a transformative purpose.[26]

23 Shimon Baraz, *Ma'arakhei lev* [Workings of the Heart] (Königsberg, 1784).

24 See Shmuel Feiner, *Haskalah and History: The Emergence of a Modern Jewish Historical Consciousness* (Heb.) (Jerusalem, 1995).

25 Naphtali Herz Wessely *Sefer hamidot, vehu sefer musar haskel* [The Book of Ethics, a Book of Morals] (Berlin *c.*1785/7), 37. See also Shavit, 'The Term Haskalah', 66.

26 Isaac Satanow, *Sefer hamidot* [Book of Ethics] (Berlin, 1784), 7*a*; Shavit, 'The Term Haskalah', 72. Cf. the definition in Christoph M. Wieland, 'Sechs Fragen zur Aufklärung', *Der Teutsche Merkur*, 66 (Apr. 1789), 97–105.

Achieving Wisdom

In 1788, the peak organizational year of the Haskalah movement, *Hame'asef*, which had recently been moved from Königsberg to Berlin, published a discussion of basic concepts. The term used to denote the true outlook of the Haskalah is *ḥokhmah*, and is given a very broad definition: 'All labour and study and every kind of activity and leadership that brings a person closer to the goal of perfection'. Perfection is an individual's goal, and as the pinnacle of the creation he has a mind capable of enlightenment (*nefesh maskelet*). Solomon Maimon, in his 1791 book *Givat hamoreh*, had already explicitly used the term 'Haskalah' in this connection: 'everything has within it the potentiality of perfection; for the tree, for instance, it is the production of fruit, for man it is Haskalah'.[27] It is his duty to explore the environment and the world of humanity as much as he can, and along with knowledge and rational thought he must also adopt moral philosophy. Neglect of *ḥokhmah* is condemned as one of the most serious failures of traditional Jewish culture: 'There are so few maskilim' (i.e. people who create and foster *ḥokhmah*), and 'a proliferation of ignoramuses'. Euchel, the editor of *Hame'asef* and the man who penned these thoughts, henceforth placed his maskilic journal at the service of *ḥohkmah* against those who 'are afraid', 'belittle', and 'fight against' reason. Maskilim, who struggle to entrench *ḥokhmah* in society, are vilified and misunderstood, the social price of adopting a stance considered suspicious from the standpoint of faithfulness to religion: 'And they will attack him and say that he has lost all sense, his breath has gone bitter, he can no longer see what is holy, he has turned towards falsehood and cast faith behind his back.'[28]

The organized circle of maskilim and the editors of *Hame'asef* considered themselves the protectors of 'the young men of Israel marching towards' *ḥokhmah*, but who were fearful and hesitant. They saw the battle as the war of progress and light against backwardness and darkness; the consciousness of God was no longer conditioned only by tradition and Holy Writ, but also by knowledge and rational understanding of the world. Indeed, this was, in Kant's words, a process demanding courage and even audacity. As *Hame'asef* pleaded in 1788: 'Therefore, brothers, fear no one, seek justice, acquire knowledge from the wise and morals from those who understand. Now you are suffering, but you will be rewarded. Seek the great and awesome God from the depths of the *ḥokhmah* of His creation. *Ḥokhmah* will be your staff to guide you successfully to all its hidden knowledge.'[29]

27 Solomon Maimon, *Givat hamoreh* [The Hill of the Guide], ed. S. H. Bergman and Nathan Rotenstreich (Jerusalem, 1966), 1.

28 [Isaac Euchel], Preface (Heb.), *Hame'asef*, 4 (1788), unpaginated. On the connection between *ḥokhmah* and the Greek ideal of wisdom see Ya'akov Shavit, *Judaism in the Mirror of Hellenism and the Appearance of the Modern Hellenistic Jew* (Heb.) (Tel Aviv, 1992), ch. 5.

29 [Euchel], Preface. Moshe Hirschel of Breslau in 1788 defined *Aufklärung* in a similar vein, as liberation from superstition, the development of friendly relations between nations and religions, an attempt to fulfil civic and social duties, and an expression of the desire to attain human rights such as freedom of conscience and religion. Contemporary Jewish society, Hirschel claimed, did not match up

Indeed, in its self-image the Haskalah in Prussia in the 1780s was first of all a rebellion of young maskilim in the name of *ḥokhmah* and universal knowledge. The terms were rather abstract, but could nonetheless serve as the slogans of a programme of reform, especially in education. The maskilim had no intention of damaging religious faith and practice. Religious morality (*musar torati*) stood alongside moral philosophy, as did knowledge of man (*torat ha'adam*) alongside God's laws (*torat hashem*). The ideal maskil was also required to fear God.[30] Their objective was to restore the balance that they believed had been upset in recent generations, especially in Ashkenazi Jewry, between Jewish culture and universal culture, but their picture of the future still included religious scholars, rabbis, religious observance, and Torah study.[31] 'Acts of Haskalah' (*ma'asei haskalah*) were presented as a divinely orchestrated historical transformation even as the movement advocated the liberation of the autonomous human being: 'For the Lord has enjoined His people to liberate their enchained minds'.[32]

Enlightenment as Natural Religion

As I have outlined, in its early stage the Haskalah was understood in terms of rationalist philosophy but by the late eighteenth century the Kantian definition of a process of self-liberation through reason came to dominate. The reforms proposed to bring this about depended to a certain extent on the development of Hebrew language and literature, the translation of the Bible and prayer-book into German, the publication of sermons in both Hebrew and German and of a Hebrew–German journal, *Hame'asef*, a critique of customs and superstitions, and the establishment of schools with secular curricula to supplement traditional education. By the 1790s, however, even before it had become sufficiently entrenched, the first mutations in the meaning of the Haskalah and of its social and cultural roles began to appear. The accelerated processes of acculturation, the struggle of the wealthy Jewish elite for political equality, and the appearance of groups of Jewish Deists—processes that were especially marked in Berlin—led to the fragmentation and eventual dissolution of the Haskalah movement.[33] As a result, the problem of defining who was a Jew in religious terms became more compelling than the question of enlight-

to the conditions prevailing in the 18th cent., which to his mind was the 'aufgeklärte Jahrhundert': Moshe Hirschel, *Kampf der jüdischen Hierarchie mit der Vernunft* (Breslau, 1788), 68–9.

[30] See, among others, [Isaac Euchel], 'The Letters of Meshulam Ha'eshtemoi' (Heb.), *Hame'asef* (1789–90), repr. in Yehuda Friedlander, *Studies in Hebrew Satire*, i: *Hebrew Satire in Germany* (Heb.) (Tel Aviv, 1979), 41–58.

[31] See Feiner, 'Educational Agendas'.

[32] Isaac Euchel, *Toledot rabenu heḥakham moshe ben menaḥem* [Biography of our Wise Rabbi Moses Son of Menahem] (Berlin, 1789), 5. Cf. the opening sentence of Kant, 'Beantwortung', 452.

[33] See Steven M. Lowenstein, *The Berlin Jewish Community: Enlightenment, Family and Crisis 1770–1830* (New York and Oxford, 1994); id., 'Soziale Aspekte der Krise des berliner Judentums, 1780 bis 1830', in Marianne Awerbuch and Stefi Jersch-Wenzel (eds.), *Bild und Selbstbild der Juden Berlins zwischen Aufklärung und Romantik* (Berlin, 1992), 81–105.

enment, and the concept of *Aufklärung* assumed new overtones of a natural religion.

In 1793 the German philosopher and educator Lazarus Bendavid defined *Aufklärung* as a concept midway between the preservation of old-style Judaism and total religious apathy. In his eyes, the *Aufklärer* was an 'adherent of genuine natural religion'.[34] Seven years later Aaron Wolfssohn, a teacher in a modern school in Breslau, defined true enlighteners as devotees of natural religion, adherents of a new Jewish school of thought founded, according to him, by Mendelssohn and whose opponents belonged to the obscurantist camp.[35] In 1823 Leopold Zunz defined *Aufklärung* along similar lines as purified Jewish religion combined with European culture,[36] and about the same time Sabbatja Wolf claimed that only those who had formulated clear concepts about the true essence of the Jewish religion and who advocated religious reforms could be called truly enlightened. The members of this group believed in God and the immortality of the soul; they were moral and rationalist. Their failure to achieve reform led some of them to abandon religious life and the synagogue, but they rejected the option of conversion because it smacked of intellectual dishonesty.[37]

'To Guide the People in the Way of Light'

From the early nineteenth century the term 'Haskalah' became even more muddled. It had to be precisely defined, suggested an essay written in Prague in 1800, 'because encrustations had spread upon the word *Aufklärung* and every youth nowadays thinks he understands it without thoroughly knowing what it really means'. The broad definition, the essay stated, should reject a superficial understanding of the term and stress that it was primarily an intellectual category, a road sign of compass serving as a pathfinder in the search for the true, the good, and the moral: 'For this word teaches us to understand the difference between truth and falsehood, good and evil, knowledge and ignorance, and happy is he who chooses it.'[38]

The author of the essay was apparently Baruch Jeiteles, a key figure in the Prague Haskalah circle. Jeiteles may also have written the essay 'On Enlightenment', which appeared in 1802 in a short-lived Prague maskilic journal published by

[34] Bendavid, *Etwas zur Charackteristik der Juden* (Leipzig, 1793), 51.

[35] Aaron Wolfssohn, *Jeschurun, oder unparteyische Beleuchtung der dem Judenthume neuerdings gemachten Vorwürfe* (Breslau, 1804), 113.

[36] See Joseph Gutmann, 'Geschichte der Knabenschule der jüdischen Gemeinde in Berlin, 1826–1926', in *Festschrift zur Feier des hundertjährigen Bestehens der Knabenschule der jüdischen Gemeinde in Berlin* (Berlin, 1926), 16–17.

[37] Michael A. Meyer, 'The Orthodox and the Enlightened: An Unpublished Contemporary Analysis of Berlin Jewry's Spiritual Condition in the Early Nineteenth Century', *Leo Baeck Institute Year Book*, 25 (1980), 101–30.

[38] [Baruch Jeiteles], *Conversations Between the Year 1800 and the Year 1801, by a Lover of Truth* (Heb.) (Prague, 1800), 3. See also Shmuel Werses, *Haskalah and Shabbateanism: The Story of a Controversy* (Heb.) (Jerusalem, 1988), 79.

the Gesellschaft der Jungen Hebrär.[39] Here, too, the author complained about the abuse of the term and the confusion surrounding it. In his vicinity, he protested, every enlightened person was considered a destroyer of faith and morality, an anarchist living within, but corroding the life of society. *Aufklärung*, he pleaded, was 'to regard each matter from its true point of view'.[40] This was the first time an attempt had been made to delve into the semantics of the term, to clarify obscure concepts, and to set out the intellectual goals of the Haskalah: acquiring the ability to make moral distinctions, being liberated from error and prejudice, examining the capabilities and destinies of human beings, and applying these general rules in all areas of life, including physical health, education, and the behaviour appropriate to citizens of the state and members of human society.[41] Thirty years later, Judah Jeiteles, editor of the Austrian *Bikurei ha'itim*, recorded the gist of the definition explicitly using the term 'Haskalah'. Its goal, he declared, was to 'lead the people to where light dwells, to open the eyes of the blind, and enlighten those who lack understanding, to teach the knowledge of man, walk humbly with God, and treat others morally and with respect'. Examples of such behaviour, he continued, could be found among other nations to 'serve as our guides in Haskalah and Enlightenment', and to achieve its goal through literary means by publishing essays that 'bring light to our minds and purge them of nonsensical notions with neither fear of failure nor pursuit of misleading ideas, but for the love of truth and in order to do the right and honest [thing]'.[42]

Shalom Hacohen, who made a lone attempt to renew *Hame'asef* in the first decade of the nineteenth century when the Haskalah in Germany was already declining both as an ideology and as the focus of a social circle, warned against misrepresenting the term *Aufklärung* by identifying it with Deistic interpretations, rapprochement with Christians, or abrogation of Jewish law. According to Hacohen, the correct meaning of *Aufklärung* in the Jewish context was the cultivation of Hebrew language and literature, especially Hebrew poetry. It should be stressed that this 1807 definition was defensive: the preservation of the patriarchal religion; the encouragement of a romantic relationship with Hebrew as the original language of the people; the revival of Hebrew poetry as a treasure-house of the greatest talents of the Jewish people: all were attempts to protect the Jewish community and its traditions at a time when they seemed to be in great danger.[43]

[39] See Ruth Kestenberg-Gladstein, *Neuere Geschichte der Juden in böhmischen Ländern* (Tübingen, 1969); and also her 'A Voice from the Prague Enlightenment', *Leo Baeck Institute Year Book*, 9 (1964), 295–304.

[40] *Yiddish Deitsche Monatsschrift* (Prague and Brünn, 1802), 49.

[41] Ibid. 54–6.

[42] Judah Jeiteles, 'Announcement' (Heb.), *Bikurei ha'itim*, 12 (1831), 184; Shavit, 'The Term Haskalah', 77–9.

[43] Shalom Hacohen, *Mata'ei al admat tsafon* [Orchards of Yore on Northern Soil] (Rödelheim, 1807), pp. v–vi. Cf. Judah Leib Ben Ze'ev's critique, *Yesodei hadat* [Foundations of Religion] (Vienna, 1806), preface: 'they wanted to pull down the good old house because it was full of cracks and falling apart, but they didn't replace it with a new house . . . they razed the old house and didn't build another one in its stead'.

Living the Haskalah

None of the attempts at the beginning of the nineteenth century to retrieve the original definitions of Haskalah made much of an impression in Germany. A good example of this can be seen in a comparison of Hacohen's definition with that of the teacher and later Reform preacher Gotthold Salomon in his article 'On Enlightenment and Enlighteners', published in the German Jewish journal *Sulamith* in 1808.[44] On the one hand, Salomon's definition was similar to that of Judah Jeiteles: precise terminology and a distinction between the light of reason and the darkness of superstition. On the other hand, he also distinguished between two aspects of *Aufklärung*: 'scientific or learned' and 'religious'. The former consisted of the totality of scientific research in all fields; the latter—relevant and important for Jews—was the correct study of pure religious truths as a way towards perfection. The 'religious' *Aufklärung* was the future reformed religion of the Jews that would prevail over religion as a system of laws, precepts, and abstract reflection.

In Germany in the first decades of the nineteenth century young Jewish intellectuals were abandoning Haskalah in favour of religious reform, modern Jewish scholarship, and political, social, and cultural integration. In the process, *Aufklärung* assumed a content that had little to do with Haskalah. In eastern Europe at exactly the same time, however, the Haskalah movement was taking its first steps. More precisely, the maskilim in Galicia were self-consciously appropriating the outlook, ideas, and methods of their German predecessors. These maskilim saw themselves as the direct descendants of Haskalah activists of the past thirty to forty years. Meir Letteris, editor of the short-lived journal *Hatsefirah* published in Galicia in 1824, declared it to be the heir of *Hame'asef*. His image of the maskil left no room for doubt: he loved *ḥokhmah*, had experienced a kind of cultural conversion, a deep transformation of consciousness and outlook, and struggled against 'the anger of hard-hearted men', especially the hasidim.[45] The maskilim in Galicia experienced a sense of mission similar to that of their predecessors in Germany ('the great desire to be of benefit to our brethren and environment'), and their manifesto—'To the Maskilim of My People'—was also reminiscent of Germany.[46] According to the elderly Menahem Mendel Lefin in his address to Nahman Krochmal, the recognized leader of the Haskalah in Galicia in the first half of the nineteenth century, the maskil's primary goal was to spread rays of light among the people, especially in times of crisis when so many deviated from the path of reason.[47]

The maskilim defined themselves as a minority in a Jewish society that was divided into at least three main groups: the simple and ignorant who blindly followed tradition out of force of habit; fanatical militant hasidim: and *gebildeten Aufklärer*, the maskilim. Joseph Perl of Tarnopol in eastern Galicia, who fought against hasidism,

44 'Über Aufklärung und Aufklärer', *Sulamith*, 2/1 (1808), 217–32.

45 Letteris, 'A Word to the Reader' (Heb.), *Hatsefirah* (Zolkiew, 1824), unpaginated [pp. 1–6].

46 Jacob Samuel Bick, 'To the Maskilim of My People', ibid. 71–7.

47 *Kerem ḥemed*, 1 (1833), 74–5.

defined the maskilim as 'men whose sole desire was that the Jews should not be a mockery in the eyes of other nations, [who wished] to learn various languages and disciplines, but without—perish the thought—abandoning the ways of our ancestors and in accordance with the faith and fear of God'.[48] Despite this moderate self-image as faithful adherents of tradition rather than revolutionaries—as people assuming leadership out of a sense of responsibility and whose modest educational demands included the study of foreign languages, science, and the pursuit of productive occupations—they locked horns with the hasidim in an all-out battle of cultures. In their attempt to mobilize allies they appealed to 'Fair youths with unbent necks . . . whose delicate souls have not been warped by the malicious evil-hearted destroyers among us',[49] and they saw themselves as martyrs for their cause. Their acceptance of suffering and pain in this cultural war was seen as an integral part of the maskilic experience. We see this, for example, in a letter from the scholar Shneur Sachs (1815–92) to the physician and satirist Isaac Erter:

> I certainly knew that you, too, would also have to run the gauntlet through the devil's minions stationed along the path to *hokhmah*. For there isn't a single God-seeking maskil beckoned by truth who ascends the spiral staircase of the wondrously built temple of *hokhmah* who doesn't have to struggle with a thousand on one side and ten thousand on the other grabbing his nape and throwing him down the stairs—that's the reward awaiting seekers of knowledge, the prize awaiting every maskil who wants truth![50]

The experience of cultural 'conversion' appears repeatedly as an integral part of the making of a maskil. It was seen as a kind of rebirth and unshackling of the spirit, or even as divine inspiration and the descent of the spirit of prophecy upon the maskil. It was said of Erter, who became a maskil under the influence of Joseph Tarler, that he was given 'a life of spirit and contemplation and liberation of soul that enabled him to follow the road of reason'.[51] This personal experience was also expressed collectively by the group of young Galician men which formed spontaneously and informally in the area of Lvov and Zolkiew under the revered Nahman Krochmal in the 1820s and 1830s. As Jacob Bodek testified, they saw themselves as a band of prophets engulfed by the holy spirit: 'one spirit, the spirit of *hokhmah* and understanding and truth-seeking Haskalah, animated them and bound their hearts!'[52] Like the groups of maskilim in eighteenth-century Königsberg and Berlin, they experienced 'the association of comrades, shepherds of reason whose zeal inspired

[48] Joseph Perl, *Bohen tsadik* [Who Tries the Righteous] (Prague, 1838), 47; N. M. Gelber, *Zu Vorgeschichte des Zionismus* (Vienna, 1927), 259–61.

[49] Joseph Perl, 'Oil for the Lamp' (Heb.), *Kerem hemed*, 2 (1836), 38–9.

[50] In *Kanfei yonah*, supplement to *Hayonah* [The Dove], 1st booklet (Berlin, 1848), 33.

[51] Meir Letteris, 'Biography of the Author' (Heb.), introduction to Isaac Erter, *Hatsofeh leveit yisra'el* [The Watchman of the House of Israel] (Warsaw, 1883), p. xv.

[52] Bodek, 'Additional Details' (Heb.), additional section for the year 1824 in Abraham Triebesch, *Korot ha'itim* [History] (Lemberg, 1851), unpaginated.

them', and cultivated an avant-garde consciousness and missionary desire to generate a maskilic revolution: 'Our blood will purify our hearts . . . we will go from darkness to light, put an end to conventions and carry the torch of reason through a dark land; [we will be] a lamp unto the feet of those who walk in darkness to illuminate their paths.'[53]

The Metaphysical Essence of Haskalah

At this point there should no longer be any doubt about the meaning of the Hebrew term 'Haskalah'. A precise translation and definition can be found in *Te'udah beyisra'el* by Isaac Baer Levinsohn, for instance, who studied with the Galician maskilim and later returned to his native Kremenetz in Russia. Levinsohn wrote in 1823 (the book itself was published in 1828) about 'the sun of *ḥokhmah* and Haskalah [*die Aufklärung*]', and in his later book, *Efes damim* (1837), explained: 'One cannot imagine how much Haskalah [*die Aufklärung*] has spread among the Jews, and in all countries Jews, as in the past, are learning the languages of the country because they know it will help them earn a decent living, as doctors, professors, or the like.'[54]

Thus the term 'Haskalah' was the precise translation of the German version of the European term. Because Germany was the dominant cultural region throughout most of the Enlightenment movement, the German version encompassed both the general Enlightenment and the particular Jewish phenomenon. But what exactly was understood to be the content of the Haskalah in Russia, the greatest centre of the Jewish Enlightenment in the second half of the nineteenth century? As the maskilim's pathos-filled rhetoric attests, Haskalah was conceived as a process of secular revelation and redemption through the acquisition of knowledge. In the eyes of Levinsohn, for instance, it was the light of the sun dispersing the darkness of stupidity that had covered medieval Europe, a light that had even penetrated the masses and was generating a radical mental transformation: 'Even the masses among the gentiles who lived in darkness have seen a great light, and have become caught up in the fire of Haskalah that has brought *ḥokhmah* to their hearts and morality and knowledge and the Torah of man into their dwellings.' The secular development of religious toleration, political rights, human morality, and progressive education, which were taking Jews to the threshold of a spiritual resurrection, inspired Levinsohn to quote the prophecies of the end of days. 'Open your eyes, my people', he pleaded, 'and understand that the bountiful waters of Eden are flowing about you by the grace of our king.'[55] In this secular, messianic vision, the maskilim performed the function of seers of modernity mobilized 'for the swelling of Haskalah throughout Russia'.

[53] Samson Halevi Bloch, *Shevilei olam* [Ways of the World], vol. i (Zolkiew, 1822), unpaginated.

[54] *Te'udah beyisra'el* [Testimony in Israel] (Vilna and Horodno, 1828), 182; id., *Efes damim* [No Blood; against blood libel] (1837; Warsaw, 1879), 47.

[55] Levinsohn, *Te'udah beyisra'el*, 182.

This self-consciousness appears to have been more forcefully expressed during the period of the government-sponsored Haskalah project (*haskalah mita'am*) in the 1840s, than at any other time. Haskalah rhetoric in public and private letters soared to dizzying new heights and was laden with images borrowed from the physics of transformation and modernization: ice-thawing, earthquakes, electrical charges, erupting volcanos, and so on. Nonetheless, it was the secularized theological concepts that were especially prominent. Maskilim spoke of the 'footsteps of Haskalah' drawing nigh; of the 'Haskalah sun' appearing as a divine revelation ('the revelation of Haskalah in our city of Vilna', for example); of maskilim as labourers in the 'temple of *ḥokhmah*' and at the 'altar of Haskalah'. Samuel Joseph Fuenn, in an emotional oath of faith, declared: 'The Haskalah is more dear to me than all the vanities and pleasures of the world, and the truth for me is *ḥokhmah*, the pillar of light illuminating the darkness of my life.'[56] The maskilim were the apostles of this new message, the 'soldiers of Haskalah' honing their weapons for the imminent battle to persuade the Jewish public to accept the new education. They had sworn allegiance to Haskalah until the goal of 'the spiritual emancipation of the Jewish people' had been accomplished.[57]

An especially metaphysical and mystical vision of a redeeming Haskalah was penned by Mordecai Aaron Guenzburg of Vilna, a leading maskil in the 1830s and 1840s:

> Haskalah is the spring whence the old hero renews the strength of his youth, imbibes rejuvenation in his old age, [retrieves] *ḥokhmah* and the light that has dimmed; [it is] a place of refuge for persecuted truth, consolation for the bereaved; it makes order out of the laws of life that have gone astray and annuls the laws of falsehood that stem from corruption of desire; it retrieves the truth of justice in matters of the heart; defends what society had thoughtlessly banned; breaks down barriers between people; strips away fancy clothes from a body without a soul; weighs heart against heart in the scales of justice, spirit against spirit and strength against strength; gives preference to the person deserving honour; judges the tree by its fruit—not by the ground upon which it grows and the person who planted it; wields the tiller in its hand to steer the ship of life safely into port through stormy seas.[58]

Haskalah was now much more than a programme of reform or a body of useful knowledge and learning; it was a redemptive formula. Guenzburg endowed it with the quality of holy, sin-purifying water, a fountain of youth, where those who bathed were reborn without blemish. Bathing in the waters of Haskalah purged impurities and brought about a total transformation. Haskalah served as a kind of supreme court of morality and truth. Guenzburg essentially maintained the char-

[56] *From Militant Haskalah to Conservative Maskil: A Selection of S. J. Fuenn's Writings* (Heb.), ed. Shmuel Feiner (Jerusalem, 1993), 186.

[57] Anonymous article written in Lublin, published in *Algemeine Zeitung des Judenthums*, 2 (Dec. 1841), 18–21.

[58] Guenzburg, 'The Wisdom of Toilers' (Heb.), in id., *Devir*, 2 vols. (1844 and 1862; Warsaw, 1883), i. 22–41.

acterization of Haskalah as a marvellous, organic entity that could not be broken down into component parts. The maskil who did not grasp the Haskalah's message for the present and future, and insisted on seeking its roots or legitimization in tradition, drained it of content and consigned it to oblivion. This was a thinly veiled criticism by a future-oriented maskil of the Russian maskilim, for whom Haskalah was the study of history which sought to justify enlightenment as a restoration of Judaism by uncovering what already existed in Jewish tradition. The belief in Haskalah burned in the hearts of the maskil prophets, and they yearned to put it into practice. However, the maskil who

> seeks to crack Haskalah open to see its innards—nothing can stop him. He'll grab a knife, cut Haskalah open and analyse it bit by bit, pick at its tendons and arteries, gaze at them, count them, and keep going until he gets to the heart, uncovers every little bit and has overlooked nothing. In reality what he has seen is nothing but a body without a soul, dead, lifeless bones. Perhaps he located the well, but there was no water inside . . .[59]

The Cultural 'Conversion'

By the second half of the nineteenth century the term 'Haskalah' was common coin. It was the Hebrew translation of *Aufklärung*,[60] and implied a world-view disseminated through literature and newspapers by maskilim,[61] the 'enlightened or people for whom reason lit the way, *die Aufgeklärten*'.[62] The period was perceived as utterly new and unprecedented—the 'modern age'—'unsere neie gantz oifgeklerte zeit' ('our new and completely enlightened age'),[63] fully dominated by the laws of nature, which had displaced superstition, mysticism, and all kinds of devils, demons, and ghosts.

As in Galicia, the personal cultural conversion that each and every maskil underwent from darkness to light, from slavery to freedom, was a fundamental experience perceived as parallel to the larger historical transformation from the old to the new. In retrospect, the decision to join the maskil camp was an act of awakening or of the revelation of the Haskalah spirit as the spirit of prophecy. As Abraham Baer Gottlober wrote in his autobiography, 'for my eyes were opened and I saw new vistas that I had never before imagined'.[64] The Hebrew lexicographer Eliezer Ben-Yehuda, who became a maskil in Lithuania in the 1870s, recalled the clandestine,

59 Ibid. 23.

60 See e.g. Samuel Resser, 'The Work of the Enlightenment and Education in Modern Times', in *A Concise History of the World* (Yiddish) (Vilna, 1864), 219–21.

61 An example of a headline from *Hamelits*, edited by Alexander Zederbaum, that began publication in Odessa in 1860: '*Hamelits*, a publication that will spread the spirit of knowledge and Haskalah among the nations'. See also Shavit, 'The Term Haskalah', 79–80.

62 Abraham Baer Gottlober, *Bikoret toledot hakara'im* [A Critique of Karaite History] (Vilna, 1864), 126 n.

63 Isaac Meir Dick, *Alte idishen zogen* [Old Jewish Sayings] (Vilna, 1876), 2.

64 'Zikhronot miyemei ne'urai' [Memoirs of My Youth] ([Warsaw], 1886), in id., *Zikhronot umasaot*, ed. R. Goldberg, vol. i (Jerusalem, 1976), 81–2.

forbidden, illegitimate process that had the nature of a conversion, that worked its way through young men for whom traditional talmudic Jewish scholarship had been their entire world. For them Haskalah meant first of all an expansion of the library that provided inspiration and taught about life. One sought refuge, was drawn towards Haskalah, bit into the fruit of the tree of knowledge, encountered a new taste, opened once blind eyes, and went out into a new world:

That was the onset of my Haskalah. But I do not know if I would actually have been caught up by the spirit of Haskalah . . . [if not for] the head of the yeshiva, Yossi Bloiker, who opened my eyes and let the light of the Haskalah in; I was drawn towards this pleasant heresy . . . Torah, Gemara, Rashi, and the Tosafists, the *posekim*, *Guide of the Perplexed*, [Albo's] *Principles of the Faith*, *Fundamentals of Ḥokhmat hashi'ur*, [Slonimsky's] *Kokhva deshavit*, *Treasury of Wisdom* by Tsvi Rabinowitsch, were the books I secretly studied at night, and I believed with a perfect faith that they really contained all the *ḥokhmah* the human mind was capable of, and that through them I would reach the highest level of human science and the attainment of the perfect happiness discussed in the *Guide of the Perplexed* . . .[65]

The Movement Divides

Differences of opinion and the proliferation of sub-groups in Russia, at its height in the 1860s and 1870s, led to a constant battle over the meaning of 'Haskalah':

The term 'Haskalah' has not yet been properly defined and understood because so many people, depending on their education and knowledge, use it for different purposes. Some say that knowledge of Scripture and the Holy Tongue is Haskalah; [others that] he who studies traditional texts and can write elaborate letters is considered a maskil; others exalt and esteem as Haskalah the knowledge of Russian or German or one of sciences everyone needs such as mathematics, geography, or history. There are even those who say that, more than anything, [Haskalah is] the desire to relax, to a greater or lesser extent, time-hallowed customs and ways of life because they are not compatible with the needs of the present generation . . . and because of the confusion over Haskalah there are those who praise and others who condemn it, some who revere and sanctify and others who curse it, and many who wonder where it can be found, who laid its cornerstone, set its boundaries, defined its rules and regulations, and what it is that requires us to abide by it and follow its path.[66]

'The meaning of Haskalah has not been sufficiently established . . . and how is it possible to spread Haskalah without yet knowing its nature in the world?'[67] Moses Leib Lilienblum, who asked this question, had a liberal, pluralist outlook, and suggested that everyone should approach Haskalah as they saw fit. However, under the influence of Russian radicalism he had taken a stronger line, demanding change from the elitism of the pantheon of Haskalah authors to a more populist approach:

[65] Eliezer Ben-Yehuda, *Dream and Awakening: A Selection of Letters on Language Issues* (Heb.), ed. R. Sivan (Jerusalem, 1986), 60–2.

[66] Samuel Joseph Fuenn, 'Haskalah and Halakah' (Heb.), *Hakarmel*, 7/14 (1868), 105–6.

[67] Lilienblum's letter from Odessa to Gordon, 21 July 1872, in *Letters of M. L. Lilienblum to J. L. Gordon* (Heb.), ed. S. Breiman (Jerusalem, 1968), 133.

'We need mass Haskalah, a Haskalah where all Jews learn to recognize the value of life in this world, citizenship and civilization and work towards breaking the chains binding us to the Dark Ages, the spirit of the Talmud, and the Asiatic wilderness.'[68] Lilienblum was so bitter that he referred to the old kind of Haskalah as the 'empty chaos our writers call Haskalah'.[69] Another time, in a special article written in 1878, he lashed out again: 'And what is Haskalah as understood by young men and by most writers? A puff of wind, a vacuous, vain concoction! A person who can write Hebrew is only a person who can write . . . a person who has read many different books and still has no clear knowledge is only someone who has collected a handful of wind.'[70] As an alternative to this 'useless' Haskalah Lilienblum advised exchanging *belles-lettres* and historical research for the sciences, 'absolute *ḥokhmah*', that would at least be of benefit in the real world.

Other radical maskilim similarly demanded that the Haskalah should focus on the masses and on real-life situations. 'Natural Haskalah should always take precedence over spiritual Haskalah', declared Isaac Kovner, who also insisted on well-formulated and precise definitions. 'Individual Haskalah' meant 'each person reckoning with his soul, cognizant of his duties in relation to society; 'general Haskalah' aimed to transform the people and the quality of leadership: 'ameliorating the state of the people, its unity, the wholehearted, willing guidance of its leaders, the willingness of the people to follow honest leaders'.[71]

The moderate maskilim against whom this criticism was directed became increasingly defensive, and emphasized the conservative and theoretical components of Haskalah. Now, like Perl in the struggle between the hasidim and maskilim, they took pains to add oaths of loyalty to faith and Torah every time they mentioned their own definition of Haskalah and their reformist goals. According to Eliezer Zweifel, for instance, Mendelssohn 'illuminated the Haskalah with the lamp of religion',[72] and Yehiel Michael Pines proclaimed that Haskalah was not only the sister of religion, but also its daughter: 'the Haskalah and the need to understand worldly issues, which until now has been inimical to religion, will actually enhance religious feelings and guard the mitzvot'.[73] Fuenn on the other hand reconstructed the development of Haskalah as pattern embedded in Jewish history that had been blurred by European influence. On one occasion he described it as 'religious Haskalah', whose pillars were the Hebrew language, love of the Jewish people, belief in

[68] Ibid. 132.

[69] *Ḥatot ne'urim* [Sins of My Youth] (1876), in *Autobiographical Writings* (Heb.), ed. S. Breiman (Jerusalem, 1970), 129.

[70] 'What is Haskalah?' (Heb.), 1st pub. in *Hatsefirah* (1878); repr. in *The Complete Works of Moses Leib Lilienblum* (Heb.), vol. ii (Kraków, 1912), 113–16.

[71] See Shmuel Feiner, 'Jewish Society, Literature, and Haskalah in Russia as Represented in the Radical Criticism of I. E. Kovner' (Heb.; Eng. abstract), *Zion*, 55 (1990), 310–11.

[72] *Shalom al yisra'el* [Peace Upon Israel], vol. i (Zhitomir, 1868), 20–2. The quotation is from S. J. Fuenn, *Kiryah ne'emanah* [Faithful City] (Vilna, 1860), 141–3.

[73] *Yaldei ruḥi* [My Spiritual Children], vol. i (Jerusalem, 1934), 63.

God, and faithfulness to Torah; elsewhere, he described it as a general compass and method of rational thought—'It illuminates the mind in everything: study of Torah, *ḥokhmah*, morality, way of life and vocation'—and fostered a proper understanding of all of life's needs.[74]

As opposed to the 'mass' and 'natural' versions of the Haskalah advocated by the radicals and the 'religious Haskalah' of the moderates, a 'national Haskalah' evolved in the 1860s. Its main spokesman was Peretz Smolenskin, whose essays appeared in the journal *Hashaḥar*. Like the radical Haskalah, it was motivated by revision: after the destruction of the Mendelssohn myth, it raised concerns about the movement's future, and cast doubt on its optimistic and reformist outlook.[75] In the 1870s more and more of its central beliefs, such as the hopes pinned on benevolent absolutist regimes and faith in history's progress towards a brighter future, were being destroyed by radical and nationalist maskilim.[76] In an attempt to rewrite Jewish history for the modern age, Smolenskin called upon maskilim to change their order of priorities and give preference to the struggle against all forms of anti-nationalist assimilation. The image of Haskalah until now, he asserted, had not provided a suitable blueprint for the future of the Jewish community. On the contrary, it had seriously jeopardized the Jews' collective existence and national consciousness. 'Won't everyone finally understand that it was all a pack of lies and Haskalah couldn't possibly have improved our lot?'[77] Smolenskin dislodged the concept of Haskalah from its ideological moorings, and, very much like Fuenn, left it neutral and in the individual realm:

> What is Haskalah? For people to learn what is to their benefit. Everyone who seeks the right way to live is a maskil because he thinks about what is beneficial and is wary of what is harmful. Haskalah is meant to stimulate each person's natural intelligence so that they don't blunder about uselessly, but do their work just like the organ of the body . . . Everyone needs Haskalah to the extent their intelligence and bodily strength allows . . . That is the theory of Haskalah, to enlighten [*lehaskil*] and fill a person with intelligence so that he does what he can to bring benefit to his spirit or body and not waste his strength and time in vain pursuits.[78]

'HASKALAH-HATING MASKILIM': THE END OF THE HASKALAH

It was statements like Smolenskin's that probably led to the dissolution of the Haskalah as separate movement with a clearly defined world-view. The question

[74] Fuenn, *From Militant Haskalah to Conservative Maskil: Letters*, 145–6.

[75] See Shmuel Feiner, 'Smolenskin's Haskalah Heresy and the Roots of Jewish National Historiography' (Heb.), *Hatsiyonut*, 16 (1992), 19–31.

[76] See e.g. Judah Leib Levin's poem 'The Issue at Hand', in id., *Memoirs and Pensées* (Heb.), ed. Y. Slutzki (Jerusalem, 1968), 140–3.

[77] Peretz Smolenskin, *Derekh la'avor ge'ulim* [To Pass Through Redemptions] (1881); pt. 2, *Ma'amarim* [Articles] (Jerusalem, 1925), 174.

[78] Ibid. 172.

whether the Haskalah had indeed reached a dead end was raised subsequently and even more forcefully after the pogroms in Russia in the 1880s and the establishment of Hibbat Zion, which greatly affected the relative strength of the different camps. Lilienblum demanded that the question of Haskalah—in reality the struggle for religious reform—should be deferred because of the need for the maskilim and Orthodox to co-operate to further the idea of Hibbat Zion. Judah Leib Gordon sought a formula that would allow continued adherence to 'Europe' and Haskalah, even when the trend towards 'Asia' and nationalism was gaining the upper hand. For Gordon the historical task of the Haskalah was to resolve the cultural conflict within Jewish society; this was an absolute precondition for the success of the nationalist movement. Mendele Mokher Seforim, a radical maskil of the 1860s, reflected on events in the camp of the maskilim with astonishment:

> How the generations and people's spirit have changed! . . . It used to be that men your age, with shortened sidelocks and shortened clothes, boasted about Haskalah and considered it to be the Jews' dew of revival, source of life, and redemption of their souls. They defended it against all comers, and many a spirited argument was then heard in these parts; they underwent physical deprivation for its sake and were thrown out of their homes; sons ran away from their fathers' houses, students from yeshivas, and bridegrooms from their father-in-laws' homes and took to the roads to find a place where they could become enlightened—even in abject poverty. And there were those who, though they did not run away, hid in cellars and attics and other hideaways . . . and now . . . now . . . everything has gone topsy-turvy and I see—Haskalah-hating maskilim![79]

Even as this rearguard battle over Haskalah was in progress, its great stalwarts such as Gordon seemed to realize that the Haskalah was drawing its last breath. Especially in the 1890s, the first histories of the Haskalah were written with the sense that it was a phenomenon of the past.[80]

The maskilim gave the struggle among themselves a public airing in the journals of the 1880s and 1890s. What had brought about the dissolution of the maskil camp, asked Zalman Epstein on the pages of *Hamelits*: had the 'forty-year war' come to an end? Had they abandoned the battle on the threshold of victory? Was the Erets Yisrael solution dependent on being liberated from 'European civilization'?[81] Hebrew literature spoke of a new era, a 'new move', and novels such as

[79] 'The Academy in Heaven and the Academy on Earth', in Mendele Mokher Seforim, *Complete Works* (Heb.) (Tel Aviv, 1952), 435. Cf. Ehud Luz, *Parallels Meet: Religion and Nationality in the Early Zionist Movement in East Europe (1882–1904)* (Heb.) (Tel Aviv, 1985), 64–9. Shavit, *Judaism in the Mirror of Hellenism*, 147–9. A particularly incisive critique of the maskilic concept of progress and security in Europe can be found in a poem by Abraham Jacob Paperna, 'Animal and Bird Talk' (1893), in *Collected Writings* (Heb.), ed. Y. Zmora (Tel Aviv, 1952), 344–6.

[80] See, among others, Ze'ev Yavetz, 'The Tower of the Century' (Heb.), *Keneset yisra'el*, 1 (1886), 89–152; Judah Leib Kantor, 'The *Me'asef* Generation', in *The 'Me'asef' Book: Addendum* (Heb.) (Warsaw, 1886) 1–34; A. H. Weiss, 'The Beginning of the Haskalah in Russia' (Heb.), *Mimizraḥ umima'arav*, 1 (1894), 9–16.

[81] Zalman Epstein, 'The Division of our Maskilim' (Heb.), *Hamelits*, 24 (1882), 475–80.

Al haperek (On the Agenda, 1887), by A. Z. Rabinovich made a final reckoning with Haskalah and the maskil who had come to a bitter end.[82] The Orthodox were well aware of this turn of events and made maximum use of the opportunity to lash out at their opponents. So, they mocked, even some maskilim have come to the conclusion we proclaimed long ago—that the message of the Haskalah was nothing but a lie![83] Gordon, then the main defender of the Haskalah, took on all comers, whether Orthodox or breast-beating erstwhile maskilim. Nevertheless, even in that rearguard battle the concept of Haskalah underwent a transformation that blunted its ideological barbs:

> Haskalah, known among the nations as culture, is the spiritual property of all peoples, the light of life that illuminates all people, the catalytic element in the world. There is no Berlin or Volozhin Haskalah, no Greek Haskalah, and no Israelite Haskalah—there is only one Haskalah for anyone with a mind. Haskalah is not something that stands on its own, but is a description of other things. Each one has an address and distinctive features.[84]

Of the nationalist maskilim who followed Smolenskin, Ahad Ha'am was the most prominent, and he further abandoned the Haskalah. He defined it in retrospect as a 'movement of the negative-minded' which endangered the continued existence of the Jewish people and undermined its unity.[85] In an article entitled 'The Man in the Tent' he said its outlook was summed up in Gordon's slogan, 'Be a man in the street and a Jew at home.' Indeed, Ahad Ha'am argued, this 'man' was no more than a camouflage for the imitation of other nationalities, while the 'Jew' was totally neglected. The pogroms, however, had led to a rude awakening: 'He came to his senses and understood that he had been fed a pack of lies decked out in alien garb that hardly suited his spirit.' Haskalah lost all influence in one fell swoop. The new national option repudiated Haskalah, denouncing it as an ideology promoting assimilation and imitation of alien cultures, and called for the development of an authentic, home-bred national culture. Now, Ahad Ha'am wrote, be a Jew in the street, and only then 'a man in your home'.[86]

Fearful of a return to the situation prior to the Haskalah, Moses Reines (the son of Rabbi Isaac Jacob Reines) adopted a more balanced stance: 'Have the dark dreary clouds truly shut out the light of day, darkened the sun of Haskalah . . . and set the clock back to the dismal days of yore? . . . Are we witnessing the spirit of

[82] See Ben-Ami Feingold, 'A. Z. Rabinovich's *Al haperek* and the Haskalah's Soul-Searching' (Heb.), *Mozna'im*, 49 (1979), 119–26.

[83] Jacob Lipschitz, 'A Generation and its Writers' (Heb.), *Hakerem* (1888), 165–91.

[84] Judah Leib Gordon, 'Mehi Kavel' (Heb.), *Hamelits*, 10–15 (1888). See also Gedalia Alkoshi, 'Judah Leib Gordon the Critic' (Heb.), *Metsadah*, 7 (1954), 481–4; Michael Stanislawski, 'Haskalah and Zionism: A Re-examination', *Vision Confronts Reality: The Herzl Yearbook*, 9 (1989), 56–67.

[85] Ahad Ha'am, 'On the History of Positive and Negative' (1891), in *Collected Writings* (Heb.) (Jerusalem, 1947), 77–8.

[86] 'The Man in the Tent' (Heb., 1891), in *Collected Writings*, 50–1; 'A Small Briefcase' (Heb.), *Hashiloah*, 2 (1897), 279–80. Cf. Micha Joseph Berdyczewski, 'On Hasidism' (Heb.), *Hamagid le-yisra'el*, 33 (1897), 264.

reaction?' Reines thought that it was too early to bury and eulogize the Haskalah, because in the final analysis, at least in Russia, it had been a resounding success. With caution, and with respect for the Jewish heritage, Haskalah, Reines wrote, had prevailed over 'the sons of darkness'. The crisis after the 1880 pogroms had created a false impression of failure; critics had claimed that the Haskalah had failed to reach its goal of improving the Jews' lot, and that nationalism had taken its place. However, from the standpoint of 'pure Haskalah'—the type of Haskalah that even maskilim devoid of belief had not managed to distort—there was actually no cause for disappointment. Haskalah had instead:

turned us into civilized people and members of general human society . . . We are the wiser, more knowledgeable, and understanding for it . . . It got rid of the chaotic lack of order in our inner lives; weakened the phoney hasidism; did much to improve the material lot of our people; put an end to immature marriages; and in general enhanced our respect in the eyes of the nations. All this, however, is nothing when compared to its greatest benefit: the revival of the Hebrew language![87]

As late as 1900 an article was published defending the 'Haskalah's honour', condemning the ingratitude of critics who had forgotten its contribution to literature and art, and, finally, begging 'forgiveness for the maskilim because their Haskalah was inadequate for the twentieth century'.[88] But this, too, was an apologetic response to harsh criticism, more specifically that of Mordecai Ehrenpreis (1869–1951):

When a century ago a group of enthusiastic young men gathered in Berlin and Königsberg to found a kind of literary congregation, they did not create a literary movement that echoed the sound of the people, but fashioned something disfigured and inferior instead, called Haskalah. The major characteristics of this 'Haskalah' . . . the literary efforts of dilettantes . . . did not come from within the nation, neither did it nourish the nation . . . [and] it had no relation to the culture of the time. It was not part of the general spiritual movement of a period, but stood outside the general spiritual trend.[89]

In this *fin-de-siècle* atmosphere Mordecai Ze'ev Feierberg sent his anguished hero Nahman out into the Russian Jewish Hebrew-reading public sphere to express his unease at the 'new literature'. Indeed, there was no denying the Haskalah's historical function, 'for many have toiled to bind the nation's wounds . . . fight death and petrifaction wherever they were'. Now, however, writers and maskilim were like 'fish swimming in a vessel of murky water' and 'this new literature was the throes and sighs of the nineteenth century'.[90] Only in 1909 did Shai Ish Horowitz's

87 Moses Reines, 'Spirit of the Time' (Heb.), *Otsar hasifrut*, 2 (1888), 45–69 (the quotation is on p. 56). Samuel Leib Zitron, 'Literature and Life' (Heb.), *Pardes*, 1 (1892), 173–204, also thought that it was too early to say that the Haskalah was over: 'Many say and believe that this transitional period from ignorance to Haskalah is passing on (in truth it is not so!)' (p. 185). Unlike Reines, however, Zitron had doubts about the Haskalah's success.

88 Y. A. Trivetsch, 'In Honour of the Haskalah' (Heb.), *Aḥi'asaf*, 8 (1900), 225–39.

89 'Where To?' (Heb.), *Hashiloaḥ*, 1 (1897), 489–503.

90 Feierberg, *Writings* (Heb.), ed. A. Steiman (Tel Aviv, n.d.), 97–8.

summation come to terms with the historical end of the Haskalah movement, the fact that its picture of the future had not been fully realized and that it had to make room for new experiments:

Years have passed. After momentous events and the well-known 'propaganda' that came hard on their heels, Haskalah has come to an end in midstream . . . What it did manage to do was instil in many hearts the feeling of being human beings, to demand respect as human beings, and crave liberty and a normal life as human beings, but it has not managed to take the Jew out of exile and the ghetto, and liberate him from the yoke of the oppressive traditions of exile . . . The Jewish heart halah era as not rid itself of all its rot. And now we are at the *fin de siècle* that marks the end of our Haskand many other sound movements in general human culture . . .[91]

A MODERATE OPTION FOR MODERNIZATION

Unity and Continuity of the Haskalah

This survey of self-definitions of the Haskalah confirms the basic assumption of this chapter: the Haskalah movement, like the Enlightenment in general, was a complex and multifaceted phenomenon. There is no doubt, however, that maskilim, even when struggling with an exact definition and trying to prevent misinterpretations from the right (the Orthodox) and the left (Deists, libertines, and assimilationists), believed that there was only one Haskalah: a historical phenomenon that had a clear and recognizable identity.

Beginning with the Prussian Haskalah and continuing for almost 120 years maskilim, whether in Prague, Amsterdam, Posen, Vienna, Lvov, Brody, Jaroslav, Tarnopol, Bolichov, Vilna, Kovno, Kremenetz, Berdichev, Odessa, or elsewhere, considered themselves members of a single continuous movement founded in Berlin by the revered Moses Mendelssohn and his associate Naphtali Herz Wessely. The figures, models, concepts, slogans, and institutions of that formative Prussian period remained a continuous source of reference. The history of the movement was portrayed as a passing of the torch of Haskalah from one generation to the next and from one Haskalah centre to another. One expression of the movement's vertical unity was its literary continuity: Haskalah books first published in Berlin were reprinted time and again in Vienna, Prague, and Brünn, and some of them in Russia, especially Vilna and Warsaw, in the nineteenth century. The essays of Mendelssohn and Wessely were translated into French in Alsace, into Dutch in Amsterdam, and into Italian in Austrian Italy. From the 1820s onwards, the pan-Austrian journal *Bikurei ha'itim* reprinted entire sections of *Hame'asef*. Members of Hevrat To'elet in Amsterdam in the 1810s and 1820s gathered to read portions of *Hame'asef*, and both they and Galician maskilim read Ben Ze'ev's influential grammar, *Talmud leshon ivri*. Among the 'heretical' works confiscated in 1869 from the lending library

[91] Shai Ish Horowitz, 'Hasidism and Haskalah' (Heb.), *He'atid*, 2 (1909), 29–99.

established in Vilkomir, Lithuania by Lilienblum, and for which he was persecuted and forced to flee, was Wessely's *Shirei tiferet*, first published in Berlin in 1788. The libraries established by east European maskilim in Jerusalem in the 1870s and 1880s contained selections of works by Galician and Russian maskilim. The discovery of works by Isaac Baer Levinsohn, Joseph Fuenn, and Kalman Schulman in the libraries of Jerusalem incensed the Orthodox and the libraries were closed.[92] Indeed, Orthodox opposition only strengthened the movement's sense of identity. Orthodox opponents considered maskilim members of the 'cult of Moshe Dessauer', that is, Mendelssohn, and referred to them as 'Deitchen' and 'Berliners'. In their eyes, the maskil camp was united, powerful, and full of intrigues. All this contributed to the definition of the Haskalah as a distinct and recognizable movement in Jewish society.[93]

These images and the movement's high degree of self-awareness were promoted by the international connections of its leading figures: Mendel Lefin—Berlin to Galicia; Shalom Hacohen—Berlin to Vienna via Amsterdam, Hamburg, and London; David Friedrichsfeld—Berlin and Amsterdam; Isaac Baer Levinsohn—Galicia and Russia; Bezalel Stern—from Odessa to Brody and Tarnopol; and there were many others. A ramified system of correspondence created literary networks: in the nineteenth century a network was established that linked Poland, Lithuania, Galicia, Germany, Holland, Bohemia, Moravia, and Hungary, and by the end of the century extended to communities such as Salonika, Mogador, Tunis, Algiers, and Jerusalem. This functioned alongside the internal networks of correspondence of each country. In the absence of a single organizational framework (the idea had been raised at various times as a vital necessity), and where only few formal organizations and permanent circles existed, correspondence was a crucial means of communication. Journals provided another ideological and literary forum and were the focus of intense debate and discussion; it can be argued that they were the

[92] For book printing, journals, reading clubs, and libraries see, among others, Peter Beer, 'Über Literatur der Israeliten in den kaiser österreichischen Staaten im lezten Decenio des achtzehnten Jahrhunderts', *Sulamith*, 2/1 (1808), 342–457: 421–6; 2/2 (1809), 42–61; Michael Silber, 'The Historical Experience of German Jewry and the Impact of Haskalah and Reform in Hungary', in Jacob Katz (ed.), *Toward Modernity: The European Jewish Model* (New Brunswick, NJ and Oxford, 1987), 107–8; Menucha Gilboa, *Hebrew Periodicals in the Eighteenth and Nineteenth Centuries* (Heb.) (Jerusalem, 1992), 57–76; Joshua Heschel Schorr, 'Prophecy on Rabbis' (Heb.), *Heḥaluts*, 3 (1857), 71; Lilienblum, *Ḥatot ne'urim*, 138 ff; Joseph Michman, *Studies in the History and Literature of Dutch Jewry*, Jubilee volume (Heb.) (Jerusalem, 1994), 207–28; P. Tuinhout-Keuning, 'The Writings of Hevrat To'elet in Amsterdam and the Haskalah in Germany', in Joseph Michman (ed.), *Studies in the History of Dutch Jewry* (Heb.) (Jerusalem, 1988), 217–71; Dov Sidorsky, *Libraries and Books in Late Ottoman Palestine* (Heb.) (Jerusalem, 1990), 113–53, and appendices 4–5; Mordechai Zalkin, *A New Dawn. The Jewish Enlightenment in the Russian Empire: Social Aspects* (Heb.) (Jerusalem, 2000), chs. 4 and 7.

[93] See e.g. Lilienblum's testimony, *Ḥatot ne'urim*, 146–7. Cf. Israel Bartal, 'Simon the Heretic: a Chapter in Orthodox Historiography', in Israel Bartal, Ezra Mendelsohn, and Chava Turniansky (eds.), *'According to the Custom of Ashkenaz and Poland': Studies in Jewish Culture in Honour of Chone Shmeruk* (Heb.) (Jerusalem, 1993), 243–68.

real meeting-ground of the Haskalah as a movement. Alongside the journals there were, of course, the books that were distributed first among those most involved—the maskilim themselves—but also to circles relatively far removed from the inner movement and its ideological ferment: those with moderate Haskalah interests, and readers and benefactors who subscribed to the maskilim's publications. Not infrequently the establishment of a library with a collection of traditional and modern 'Haskalah culture' books turned into a 'readers' club', in actuality a cell of maskilim. Some of these were kept secret for fear of hostile reactions. Together they constituted a satellite ring around the Haskalah 'literary republic'. Linking the inner and outer rings were printers and proof-readers, such as the printing house of Hevrat Hinukh Ne'arim (Society for the Education of Youth) in Berlin under Isaac Satanow, that of Anton Schmid in Vienna where Judah Leib Ben Ze'ev and Shlomo Levisohn worked as proof-readers, the presses adjacent to Perl's school in Tarnopol, Fuenn's in Vilna, Smolenskin's in Vienna, and others, all of vital importance to the Haskalah.[94]

The Characteristic Maskil Type and the Maskilic Experience

The Haskalah movement was fostered by what could be called the 'maskil type', a distinctive figure both in his own eyes and in the eyes of those around him. The biographies of many maskilim are identical in terms of their experience and sociocultural background: they typically shared the same attitudes, moved in the same conceptual world, and were characterized by the same rhetoric, slogans, and allusions; despite some recognizable differences, they generally shared the same world-view and ideology. The maskil had no precedent in Jewish history. As in the parallel process taking place in eighteenth-century European society, a secular Jewish intelligentsia was emerging powerful enough to challenge the traditional authorities such as Talmud scholars, preachers, homileticists, and rabbis.[95] For the first time, from a traditional society and religious culture came modern writers, sharp-witted publicists, and secular preachers who exposed the flaws that they believed had entered Jewish life. They also professed a new teaching that contained a detailed, comprehensive programme of modernization. They offered this alternative in the belief that, if realized, it would normalize Jewish existence and integrate Jews into the modern, progressive European world. Out of an avant-garde self-awareness, the maskil presumed to be a guide to an entire society, claiming to know better than anyone else how to read the map of history. With the call 'Follow me' he

[94] For printing houses see Moritz Steinschneider, 'Hebraeische Buchdruckerei in Deutschland', *Zeitschrift für die Geschichte der Juden in Deutschland*, 5 (1892), 166–82; A. M. Haberman, 'The Hebrew Press in Tarnopol', in *Pages in Bibliography and Jewish History*, year 2, pamphlet 1 (Vienna, 1935), 24–31; Mordecai Letteris, 'Some Issues Matter' (Heb.), *Bikurim*, 2 (1866), 20–38; Hayim D. Friedberg, *History of the Jewish Press* (Heb.) (Antwerp, 1937), 94–101.

[95] See Porter, *The Enlightenment*, 70–5.

sought to lead the people into a new era of critical historical change.[96] The journal, the textbook translated into German, and biting satire were his literary weapons and propaganda tools.

The maskil was a transitional type. It was uncommon to find a 'born' maskil; in most cases Haskalah was not passed from father to son. Each generation experienced the transition to Haskalah, a distinct process usually occurring in a person's late twenties. Euchel became a maskil in 1775, Perl in 1810, Baer Levinsohn in 1820, Fuenn in 1830, Lilienblum in about 1860, and Ben-Yehuda in the 1870s. Sons and daughters of maskilim did not have to grapple with this transitional process, were hardly concerned with Haskalah struggles, and generally entered other modern occupations such as banking, business, the universities, and other professions. The 'maskil experience' was inseparable from the maskil image. The transition in consciousness from the old to the new, which had the force of a conversion or an eye-opening sense of discovery, left a deep mark. Since becoming a maskil was a personal and individual experience, due at times to the influence of another maskil or to independent study, the maskil sought solace among other maskilim.

These groups were united on the basis of an extremely ambitious programme to create the new Jew and a new Jewish society. The spirit of modernism pulsated within them. In their self-awareness they believed that they had discovered a new continent in time, a 'New Age'. This was what fuelled the maskilim and was the basis of their politics, their demand to lead the Jews into the brave new world. Everything they did derived from this consciousness. Just as they underwent a personal transition, they became harbingers of change for all Jews—an intelligentsia whose chief desire was to lead Jewish society from one epoch to another.[97] The maskilim were critics of the old age, and the nursemaids, heralds, preachers, and guides of the new. They proclaimed the Jewish renaissance and were the prophets of modernity.

All this, however, was in the domain of wishful thinking. The actual experience of most maskilim was quite different. With few exceptions their socio-economic status was low to middling, and in order to survive, publish their books, and find work as private tutors or clerks, they needed the patronage of the wealthy. The maskil's status in society, especially in eastern Europe, was that of a despised and even threatened minority. Most of society and the spokesmen of the traditional scholarly or hasidic elite considered the maskilim a menace. Isolation, sometimes even persecution, was the price they paid for Haskalah, and slander and excommu-

[96] Gillon, *Mendelssohn's 'Kohelet musar'*, ch. 10; Shavit, *Judaism in the Mirror of Hellenism*, 95–6, defines the maskilim as follows: 'A socio-culturally new type of Jew appearing in Europe during the eighteenth century, before what was later called "intelligentsia". This group had its own socio-cultural consciousness. It was aware of the change it wanted to generate and worked for its own ends in different ways . . . This is a new social group that did not bow to the traditional spiritual-social authority . . . It was interested in the vision of "modernization", in other words a "Europeanization" of the Jews.'

[97] See Anthony D. Smith, *Theories of Nationalism* (London, 1971), 133–8.

nication were often part of that experience. They lived in tension and felt persecuted and illegitimate, like people who had secretly tasted forbidden fruit ('death in the pot of Haskalah') and drunk stolen water, but they were fortified by the desire for victory and to show everyone that light, justice, and truth were on their side. When and where the cultural climate was fairly open there was no need for Haskalah. The consciousness of mission felt by pioneers, the self-image of elite soldiers of modernity and captains of the ship, were particularly relevant and perhaps only valid in historical situations where the maskil lived in a hostile atmosphere.

Nor is there any doubt that an added motivation for the Haskalah was aroused by the rulers of the centralized states and spokesmen of the non-Jewish intelligentsia. These were Dohm, Lessing, and Nicolai in Germany, Joseph II in Austria, and Alexander I, Nicholas I, Serge Uvarov, his minister of education, and Alexander II in Russia. The confidence of maskilim in the modern age depended on belief in political change in Europe, identification with the centralized state, and reliance on 'angels of grace' who sought to reform and improve the circumstances of the Jewish community. Even in North Africa, where Europe's image was that of a colonial power threatening cultural conquest, there were similar expectations, even if the few maskilim there saw their mission mainly as deterring French influence.[98]

A Dualistic World-View

These experiences and the maskilim's self-image as healers of the world's afflictions led to a unique rhetoric. A certain pathos sharpened the consciousness of the avant-garde, reflected the maskil mentality, and sometimes went far beyond the realities of the 'war for Haskalah'. The rhetoric of the Haskalah was black and white. Even moderates did not distinguish intermediate shades, but generally adopted their own single-minded approach that negated both left and right. Few, indeed, were ready to accept ideological pluralism. Everything moved between truth and lies, 'morning light' and dark clouds, lofty idealism and defamation, perception and blindness, wisdom and stupidity, goddesses (adulation) and she-devils (idolatry), youth and old age, common sense and superstition, and a magnificent temple of wisdom versus a decrepit edifice of ignorance.

The 'war for Haskalah', or the image of the sons of light fighting the sons of darkness, was indeed meaningful for small groups with consummate faith in their view. The Haskalah's ideology, however, did not propose a total abrogation of tradition; it did not seek to build a new world on the ruins of the old. The Haskalah was the

[98] See Joseph Shitrit, 'New Awareness of Anomalies and Language: Beginnings of the Hebrew Haskalah Movement in Morocco at the End of the Nineteenth Century' (Heb.), *Mikedem umiyam*, 2 (1986), 129–68; id., 'Hebrew Nationalist Modernism as Opposed to French Modernism: The Hebrew Haskalah in North Africa at the End of the Nineteenth Century' (Heb.), *Mikedem umiyam*, 3 (1990), 11–76; Yaron Tsur, 'Tunisian Jewry at the End of the Pre-Colonial Period' (Heb.), *Mikedem umiyam*, 3 (1990), 77–113; id., 'Jewish Sectional Societies in France and Algeria on the Eve of the Colonial Encounter', *Journal of Mediterranean Studies*, 4 (1994), 263–76.

first ideology to advocate Jewish modernization. Yet its revolution was to introduce a dualism into Jewish society and offer itself as a cure for Judaism's ills. The personal transformation to Haskalah did not demand a burning of bridges; it was not assimilation or baptism. Conversion to Haskalah was actually a transposition from a world depicted as one-dimensional to a more complex world, but in no case was there a total abandonment of the community, Jewish society, or Judaism. Just as the maskil did not reject the Bible, Mishnah, Talmud, and other halakhic works, but sought to redress an imbalance by adding to his library new works in Hebrew and other languages, so he adopted new ideas without rejecting more traditional ones. Haskalah spoke and preached with a dual tongue, demanding that balance be restored in all areas: study the Torah of God together with that of man; be a Jew but also a man and a citizen; practise Torah and *mitsvot* but also learn European languages and read their literature; cultivate the Hebrew language (but get rid of Yiddish unless it can be of tactical and propagandistic use!) but also improve your knowledge of the language of the state and the language of European culture; cultivate a deep attachment to the new Europe—but do not abandon your Asiatic heritage. As Israel Bartal has shown, the language issue is a good example of the movement's transformation:

> The future vision of the Haskalah Movement in Eastern Europe was not aimed at an abrogation of bilingualism, but at a replacement of its two components: Yiddish by the language of the state or a major European language (usually German), and the 'holy tongue' by biblical Hebrew. Perhaps more than anything else the new bilingualism . . . reflected the dual nature of Haskalah: the corporative pre-modern society that was to be displaced by identification with the modern state, and the religious language and spiritual creativity that was to be purified and cut off from its supposedly corrupt and defective parts.[99]

The same was true for the Haskalah's image of the future. The Haskalah never sought to take the Jews beyond Judaism and Jewish society, but to effect a transformation that would repair rather than destroy what was 'antiquated'. The rabbi as maskil was the highest aspiration of the maskilim. Other 'traditional' aspects of their programme included: a non-coercive community in matters of faith; a *Shulkḥan arukh* winnowed by the rabbis themselves of customs that made life difficult for Jews; a rabbinical academy training a modern, Torah-educated elite unsullied by the mystical and magical; a grammatically correct Hebrew; the thorough study of Torah with the aid of the clarifying terms of an advanced European language; rationalist *musar* books; a reliance on universalist rational truths and the belief in revelation and historical tradition; and a Jew who, like his ancestors, earned his daily bread from farming or a craft rather than petty business—a Jewish farmer who studied Torah in his spare time (Perl's *Boḥen tsadik*), enrolled his daughters in a Russian gymnasium, but hired a tutor to teach them Hebrew and Judaism. Thus the Haskalah offered a variety of solutions, transitional and permanent, for Jewish

[99] 'From Traditional Bilingualism to National Monolingualism', in Lewis Glinert (ed.), *Hebrew in Ashkenaz: A Language in Exile* (New York and Oxford, 1993), 141–50.

life in the modern world, all of which encompassed a duality of internal and external, sacred and profane, old and new.

For more than a century all ideological shadings of the Haskalah were variations on this basic dualism. The difference in emphasis between one maskil, Haskalah centre, or period and another was a difference of degree. The spectrum created by a dualistic approach left much leeway for variety, and for secondary Haskalah types —radical and moderate, Deist and socialist, materialist and nationalist. So long as this duality was maintained—Judaism and the Jews, Europe and its culture—one could still speak of Haskalah. Only when it was abandoned, as in David Friedländer's attempt to become a Christian on his own terms, or Solomon Maimon's journey from Haskalah to philosophy, or Abraham Uri Kovner's abandonment of Hebrew literary criticism, or Samuel Jacob Bick's condemnation of Haskalah and endorsement of hasidism, do we see paths out of Haskalah.

Boundaries and Branches

The Haskalah's boundaries can be drawn on the basis of chronology, geography, and the ways in which different groups approached the modern, non-Jewish world. As I have outlined, the eighteenth-century Haskalah movement was preceded by the 'early Haskalah',[100] but its beginnings as an ideological movement lay in Prussia in the late 1770s. The *Biur* project began in 1778, the year the first modern Jewish school, the *Freyschule*, was established by Hevrat Hinukh Ne'arim with great expectations for the realization of the maskil programme. Until the end of the eighteenth century, the Haskalah's centre was in the Prussian cities of Berlin, Königsberg, and Breslau, with minor branches in such cities as Hamburg, Cassel, and Frankfurt am Main, as well as in Prague, Amsterdam, Trieste, Metz, and Shklov, with readers and subscribers to Haskalah literature elsewhere. With the exception of Breslau, and the Polish districts annexed by Prussia, such as Posen, where a group of maskilim coalesced under David Caro, the Prussian phase came to an end at the turn of the eighteenth century. However, centres of Haskalah in Germany (Dessau and Cassel) and the Austrian empire (Bohemia, Moravia, Galicia, and Hungary) consciously brought the 'Berlin Haskalah' into the beginning of the nineteenth century, as did groups and individual maskilim in Holland and England.[101]

From the 1820s onwards, the movement was almost exclusively located in eastern

[100] Etkes, 'On the Question of the Precursors of Haskalah'; Sorkin, 'From Context to Comparison'. On the early Enlightenment in Germany see John G. Gagliardo, *Germany under the Old Regime, 1600–1790* (London and New York, 1991), ch. 15; Feiner, 'The Early Haskalah'.

[101] See Silber, 'The Historical Experience of German Jewry', and also the following chapters in Katz (ed.), *Toward Modernity*: Israel Bartal, 'The Heavenly City of Germany and Absolutism *à la mode d'Autriche*: The Rise of the Haskalah in Galicia' (pp. 33–42); Hillel Kieval, 'Caution's Progress: The Modernization of Jewish Life in Prague, 1780–1830' (pp. 71–105); Joseph Michman, 'The Impact of German Jewish Modernization on Dutch Jewry' (pp. 171–88); Lois C. Dubin, 'Trieste and Berlin: The Italian Role in the Cultural Politics of the Haskalah' (pp. 189–224); and Todd Endelman, 'The Englishness of Jewish Modernity in England' (pp. 225–46).

Europe. Especially intense in Galicia until 1848 and in Russia from the 1840s, it won supporters and members until it peaked in the 1860s and 1870s. Nonetheless, the 'German' character of the Haskalah was preserved even among maskilim who had a strong affinity with Russian culture and language. German was the maskil's second language even after the Russian romance; the Haskalah was rooted in its hero, Mendelssohn, and Berlin remained a focal point long after it ceased to be an active centre.

The branches of the east European Haskalah in some major North African communities are now being examined for the first time. The travels of European maskilim in the Islamic countries, the importation of Hebrew Haskalah literature (by Abraham Mapu, Peretz Smolenskin, Kalman Schulman, and others) led a number of teachers, printers, and booksellers to encounter the Haskalah. Individual maskilim lived in different parts of the Ottoman empire throughout the nineteenth century. Among the most prominent was Jacob Judah Nehama of Salonika, who can be considered a full member of the mid-nineteenth-century 'literary republic'.[102] However, intensive activity on the part of individual maskilim and in Haskalah circles with a strong reformist motivation in Tunis, Algiers, Mogador, and elsewhere began only in the last two decades of the century. These maskilim not only subscribed to such publications as *Hamagid*, *Hakarmel*, *Hatsefirah*, and *Hashaḥar*, the 'brothers from afar' also contributed articles, bought Haskalah books, published Arabic–Hebrew newspapers, and translated essays and books by east European maskilim: for example, Schulman's *Ḥarisot beitar* (The Ruins of Betar) and his Hebrew translation of Eugène Sue's *Mystères de Paris*, and Mapu's *Ahavat tsiyon*. They internalized the rhetoric, values, concepts, and criticism of society characteristic of the east European Haskalah. Isaac Ben-Ya'ish of Mogador, for one, fought the superstition prevalent among Jews and Muslims, and Shalom Flah of Tunis declared that the 'light of civilization' shining throughout Europe, that had reached 'some of the cities of Africa and Asia to illuminate the dark night of ignorance, is spreading its wings over the entire breadth of the lands of the savages'.[103]

The colonial circumstances of these countries influenced the special character of their Haskalah. The fact that the main agent of secularization was the Alliance Israélite Universelle placed the maskilim in a defensive position almost from the beginning. The Haskalah in Tunis, Morocco, and Algeria was in most cases a disillusioned opposition to the Alliance. The maskilim were wary of what they considered an exchange of the *talmud torah* that the French organization had promised to cultivate in its schools for *talmud tsarfat*, the study of French culture, and warned that the Alliance schools might ring the death knell of Hebrew and Judaism: 'The

[102] Jacob Judah Nehama, *Mikhtavei dodim miyayin* [Letters More Delightful than Wine] (Salonika, 1893). See David Benvenisti, 'Rabbi Jacob Judah Nehama, Precursor of the Haskalah Period in Salonika', in M. Zohory, A. Tartakover, M. Zand, and A. Hains (eds.), *Studies on Jewish Themes by Contemporary Jewish Scholars from Islamic Countries* (Heb.) (Jerusalem, 1981), 144–66.

[103] Flah, 'Our Distant Brethren' (Heb.), *Hatsefirah*, 15/45–6 (1888), 45–6.

chief desire of the Hebrew maskilim in North Africa was to propose a Hebrew national track to compete with the general French modernization track.'[104] In the moderate Haskalah of eastern Europe that position was a dialectical product and articulated a change in the maskilim's thought; it was the starting-point of the North African Haskalah which fought for 'the true Haskalah whose foundations are high up in the mountains of pure religion', and a reformed Hebrew education to counter that of the Alliance. 'The French Haskalah,' Shalom Flah wrote in *Hatsefirah*, printed in Warsaw, 'that reigns supreme and unlimited over the children in the Alliance general school, was a source of destruction for Jewish life . . . The Age of Enlightenment might be illuminating the night of ignorance and chasing bats out of human habitations, but it is replacing them with beasts of prey.'[105]

The Jerusalem branch of the east European Haskalah was much more militant and determined. After Yisrael Frumkin became editor of *Haḥavatselet* in 1870, and especially after Eliezer Ben-Yehuda joined in 1881, it struggled against the opponents of educational reform, the leadership, the *ḥalukah* system of charity, and the occupations preferred by members of the old Yishuv: 'The rebels against the light will not prevail. Despite them, the sun of Haskalah will shine in Jerusalem, the clouds will disperse, shadows disappear and the light of knowledge will shine for all of Israel.'[106] The Jerusalem maskilim were a varied lot, and their educational and literary activity centred on the new schools, the Zionist Hovevei Zion, the new public libraries, and on journals. They had constant contact with Russian and Galician maskilim through correspondence and visits, and received encouragement and promises of support. Abraham Baer Gottlober of Zhitomir, Aaron Dornzweig of Lvov, Berish Goldberg of Tarnopol, Abraham Shapira of Warsaw, and others pinned great hopes on the new Jerusalem branch's success:

> The time has come for the Holy Land to shake off its dust, remove the garb of mourning, and become another of the enlightened countries that follow the light of *ḥokhmah* and science that now illuminates the earth . . . How good it is that you wise, reverent, and perfect men are the pioneers leading our people in their Holy Land towards straight paths in the eyes of God and man.[107]

The Haskalah movement's continuity can be seen on the shelves of the two public libraries set up by Jerusalem maskilim in 1874 and 1884. Visitors could read the works of Mendelssohn and volumes of *Hame'asef*, as well as many European-language journals and the works of Wessely, Ben Ze'ev, Baer Levinsohn, Perl,

[104] Shitrit, 'Hebrew Nationalist Modernism', 12. For the Alliance Israélite Universelle school system in the Islamic countries, see Aaron Rodrigue, *French Jews, Turkish Jews: The Alliance Israélite Universelle and the Politics of Jewish Schooling in Turkey, 1860–1925* (Bloomington, Ind., 1998).

[105] Flah, 'Pain of Love' (Heb.), *Hatsefirah*, 15/89 (1888), 3–4; id., 'Observer of Tunis' (Heb.), *He'asif*, 6 (1894), 78–94.

[106] Yisrael Frumkin, 'On Education' (Heb.), 1st pub. *Haḥavatselet*, 15–17 (1880); repr. in *The Collected Writings of Yisrael Dov Frumkin* (Heb.), ed. G. Kresel (Jerusalem, 1954), 93.

[107] Abraham Baer Gottlober, 'From Zhitomir' (Heb.), *Haḥavatselet*, 25 (1872), 196.

Abraham Uri Kovner, Mapu, Smolenskin, Zweifel, Fuenn, Guenzburg, and Schulman.[108]

The writings of Frumkin, Ben-Yehuda, Dov Steinhardt, and other teachers and journalists show that they had absorbed maskil rhetoric and slogans to argue that the conditions prevailing in the Yishuv showed the need for Haskalah and reforms. They provoked a cultural battle, demonstrating the same inner struggles typical of the transitional stage of Haskalah. But like the Haskalah in North Africa, the Jerusalem version was of the moderate east European type that was concerned about the future of the Hebrew language, national unity, and religious belief. In a manner reminiscent of maskilim such as Flah in Tunis, Frumkin and his Jerusalem colleagues rejected the French modernization of the Alliance in favour of the 'national Haskalah' advocated by Smolenskin, and rejected criticism of religion and religious laxity.

*

The first and formative German period of the Haskalah movement was short-lived, being over by about 1800. But the movement's final stage did not occur until the 1890s, simultaneous with the development of nationalism and the appearance of counter-Haskalah patterns. Whether or not nationalism was the alternative to Haskalah, it was clear that a fundamental change had taken place. The main spokesmen in eastern Europe died in the 1880s and 1890s[109] and were replaced by a new generation of writers, most of them nationalists who had not undergone the maskil experience. The basic Haskalah programme was simply accepted, a new and wide reading public had emerged that was not terribly interested in culture wars and ideology, and a modern education was considered to be important: 'Sons of the poor . . . leave their countries and towns . . . and penniless, travel to seek *ḥokhmah* and knowledge; societies for spreading Haskalah, modern schools and libraries are established all the time; even the religious and ultra-Orthodox expose their sons and daughters to Haskalah studies; [and] rabbis, rabbinical adjudicators and teachers encourage their sons to study the "Haskalah demanded by the time"'.[110] The culture war had passed on to another stage, and the Haskalah as an ideology of transition ended. Even the term maskil assumed a neutral meaning, and referred to someone with book learning, and an interest in literature, science, and the issues of

[108] For the Haskalah in Palestine see Yehoshua Kaniel, 'The Beginnings of the New Yishuv in Jerusalem', in M. Eliav (ed.), *The Book of the First Aliyah* (Heb.), vol. i (Jerusalem, 1982), 319–36; Joseph Salmon, 'Urban Ashkenazi Settlement in Erets Yisrael from the Time of the First Aliyah', in I. Kolatt (ed.), *History of the Jewish Yishuv in Erets Yisra'el from the Time of the First Aliyah* (Heb.) (Jerusalem, 1990), 580–605; Yisrael Hanani, 'The Haskalah Movement in Erets Yisrael' (Heb.) (Ph.D. diss., Jerusalem, 1959); Galia Yardeni, *Hebrew Journalism in Erets Yisrael, 1863–1904* (Heb.) (Tel Aviv, 1969), 55–81; Sidorsky, *Libraries and Books in Late Ottoman Palestine*, ch. 3.

[109] David Gordon, 1886; Eliezer Zweifel, 1888; Abraham Baer Gottlober, 1889; Samuel Joseph Fuenn, 1890; Judah Leib Gordon, 1892; Alexander Zederbaum, 1893; Joshua Heschel Schorr, 1895; Kalman Schulman, 1899; Moses Leib Lilienblum, 1910.

[110] Reines, 'Spirit of the Time', 66.

the day. The ideological, contentious party connection grew dim and gave way to new polemics. In North Africa the maskilim failed in their attempt to weaken the European cultural influence of the Alliance schools, and the maskilim in Palestine retreated to such an extent that when some of them realized with disappointment that the Zionist, partly secular, new Yishuv was gaining the upper hand, they even adopted an Orthodox anti-Haskalah stance.

Haskalah and Modernity

The Haskalah movement played a crucial role in the modernization of the Jews. Yet the limitations it set itself as a controlled and limited option for change were characteristic. The relationship between Haskalah and modernization was not clear-cut but ambivalent: support and enthusiasm on the one hand, constraint and control on the other.[111] At every point and in almost every Haskalah centre, the position of the maskil was somewhere between right and left. Despite conventional opinion, the Haskalah can be held responsible neither for the entire process of modernization and secularization, nor for the full extent of Jewish acculturation that preceded it. Likewise the Haskalah did not in itself produce either assimilation, conversion, and religious reform, or the struggle for emancipation. Militant Orthodoxy, especially hasidism, stood to its right, while at the left was what the maskilim referred to as 'false Haskalah', the religiously indifferent, Deists, libertines, assimilationists, and others whose acculturation was rather shallow, but who nevertheless boasted about 'their' Haskalah. Maskilim repudiated these phenomena time and again, blaming them on the inflexible rejection of Haskalah by their opponents on the right. Here Haskalah was actually seen as a bulwark against heresy, apostasy, and moral corruption.[112] Suffice it to say that the frequent distinctions made by the maskilim between legitimate, 'real' Haskalah and 'counterfeit' Haskalah were an important component of their self-definition and identity. That was the borderline. Everything beyond an 'inner Haskalah deriving from introspection and study',[113] everything alienating and damaging to Jews and Judaism, was beyond the Haskalah.

Their secularism was also limited, moderate, and controlled. The writers and teachers were indeed a secular intelligentsia who constituted an alternative to the traditional scholars and rabbis. The maskil associations represented a secularization of the traditional house of study and charity associations; they introduced the

[111] See Israel Bartal, 'Mordecai Aaron Guenzburg: A Lithuanian Maskil Faces Modernity', in F. Malino and D. Sorkin (eds.), *From East and West: Jews in a Changing Europe 1750–1870* (Oxford, 1990), 126–47; Shmuel Feiner, 'The Modern Jewish Woman: A Test-Case in the Relationship between the Haskalah and Modernity' (Heb.; Eng. abstract), *Zion*, 58 (1993), 453–99; Fuenn, *From Militant Haskalah to Conservative Maskil*, ed. Feiner.

[112] See Shmuel Feiner, 'The Pseudo-Enlightenment and the Question of Jewish Modernization', *Jewish Social Studies*, 3/a (1996), 62–88; Dan Miron, *Between Vision and Reality* (Heb.) (Jerusalem, 1979), 277–9.

[113] *Letters of M. L. Lilienblum to J. L. Gordon*, 79.

modern school and rabbinical academy, a secularized *ḥeder* and yeshiva; they pioneered grammatically correct aesthetic Hebrew and the new Hebrew literature and poetry, and they secularized *lashon hakodesh*, the Holy Language.[114] Yet there was good reason for maskilim, at a certain point in their lives, to consider themselves no less a bulwark against radical innovation than critics of the obsolete. The world of the maskilim was broad: they believed in the power of knowledge to improve people and society; they took universal morality and reason as their guides, and believed that there was a crucial need to change the outdated social, economic, political, and cultural patterns that were no longer relevant in the 'modern age'. The cultural war was directed at religious issues, rabbis, and hasidic leaders, but not against Torah or religion itself. The Haskalah opposed the dominant sociocultural function fulfilled by Talmud, but in the main (with some exceptions such as *Heḥaluts* publisher Joshua Heschel Schorr in Galicia) it was not against the Talmud itself, even if it may be safely assumed that the maskilim were not unaware that their cultural programme meant modifying the influence of the Talmud. A clear religious and theological orientation was characteristic of the post-Haskalah stage in Germany, but only after the issues concerning the legitimacy of sciences (*ḥokhmot*) and European languages had already been resolved. Even the polemic associated with religious reform in Russia at the end of the 1860s had nothing to do with theology, but was concerned rather with certain *halakhot* (such as eating legumes on Passover) versus the exigencies of 'life', that is, the dire poverty of the Jews in Russia.[115]

Haskalah and Enlightenment

Recent research which recognizes the national variations in the period of the Enlightenment[116] helps us see the Haskalah as one of them. There is no doubt, for instance, that the Haskalah was far from the French Enlightenment's political radicalism and anti-clericalism. Even the closest example, the German Protestant *Aufklärung*, with which the Prussian maskilim had direct contact, was unlike the Haskalah. The *Aufklärer* consisted of government officials, clergy, and university lecturers; none of these professional groups existed in the Jewish community.[117] There were only isolated cases of Enlightenments aside from the Haskalah that lasted throughout the nineteenth century. Moreover, it cannot be said that the maskilim were part of the great family of *philosophes* in Peter Gay's sense.[118] It would also

[114] Bartal, 'Traditional Bilingualism'.

[115] See Gideon Katznelson, *The Literary War between the Orthodox and the Maskilim* (Heb.) (Tel Aviv, 1954); Michael Stanislawski, *For Whom Do I Toil? Judah Leib Gordon and the Crisis of Russian Jewry* (New York, 1988), chs. 5 and 6.

[116] Porter, *The Enlightenment*.

[117] Horst H. Möller, *Vernunft und Kritik. Deutsche Aufklärung im 17. und 18. Jahrhundert* (Frankfurt am Main, 1986); Franklin Kopitzsch, *Aufklärung, Absolutismus und Bürgertum in Deutschland* (Munich, 1976).

[118] Gay, *The Enlightenment: An Interpretation. The Rise of Modern Paganism* (New York, 1966).

appear that the famous case of Moses Mendelssohn, and to a lesser extent Marcus Herz and David Friedländer, were exceptions that prove the rule. Other characteristics of the maskil type, such as self-consciousness, a modernist mentality, a sense of prophecy, activism, discovery of the 'modern era', rhetoric, and so on do have similarities with other versions of the Enlightenment.[119] Nonetheless, it is also necessary to emphasize that the maskilim hardly attempted to underscore their Enlightenment connection. Thus surprisingly little was done to make the Enlightenment's main literary works available in Hebrew. Maskil translators mainly translated educational textbooks, travelogues for young men, or the plays by Lessing or satires by Wieland that had relevance for Jews, while the works of Voltaire, Locke, Montesquieu, Hume, Kant, and other major European thinkers were left untranslated.

CONCLUSION

The Definition

Having examined the self-definitions of the maskilim and the results of historical research on the general Enlightenment and its major tenets it is possible to offer a historical characterization and delineation of the movement.

The Haskalah was one of the European Enlightenments that existed between the 1770s and the 1890s in western, central, and eastern Europe (the Berlin Haskalah existed only in the last quarter of the eighteenth century, in Galicia and Russia throughout the entire nineteenth century), with branches at the end of the nineteenth century in Palestine and North Africa. It brought the Jews' ideology of transition into the 'modern age'. The maskilim were mainly writers and members of a new secular intelligentsia who had themselves gone through the experience of transition from a world of 'old' knowledge and values to the 'new' world of Haskalah. This intellectual, variegated elite was the carrier of the first modern ideology in Jewish history with a general liberal rationalist orientation. The maskilim were not organized on a formal basis but maintained a kind of literary republic of writers and journals, reading clubs and libraries, circles of maskilim and supporters of Haskalah.

Haskalah was one form of modernization available to Jews. The Haskalah's version was characterized primarily by its ideological nature and its awareness of modernity. Its major feature was dualism: an attempt to maintain a balance between the inner and the outer, between the 'Torah of God' and 'knowledge of man'; between the cultural patterns, religion, and customs of the Jewish heritage and European culture and its civic ethos. The policy of the centralized European state to ameliorate the Jews' condition was generally enthusiastically and actively fostered by the maskilim. It served as the Haskalah's main catalyst and helped it elicit the patronage and support of wealthy Jews. Haskalah advocacy involved a critique of

[119] 'The Enlightenment was the era which saw the emergence of a secular intelligentsia large enough for the first time to challenge the clergy': Porter, *The Enlightenment*, 72–3.

institutions, thought, and behaviour, past and present, that was meant to bring about a fundamental regeneration and transformation and which included independent and autonomous thought, humanism and tolerance, a change of values to new social, economic, and cultural ideals, and the normalization of Jewish existence. However, the Haskalah set limits to these aspirations for renewal in order to prevent the annihilation of Jewish culture. Because the maskilim were intimately involved in Jewish ethnicity, religion, and culture, they were acutely aware of the destructive influence of a superficial and external modernism. They often altered their stance from a straightforward struggle against the 'old' to conserving and protecting the 'old' against the 'new'. They sought some form of golden modernizing mean.

In its conscious and reasoned critique of Jewish tradition, the Haskalah provoked Orthodox reaction, the Jewish *Kulturkampf* that has lasted more than 200 years. Yet the Haskalah built its support for Jewish renewal on Jewish tradition, especially the Hebrew language, Bible, and national history. In comparison with other options for modernization, the Haskalah seems relatively conservative and moderate. Although its programmes pointed to a comprehensive reformation of the life of the Jewish community, in practice the maskilim were mainly active in the fields of *belles-lettres*, journalistic writings, and education and only occasionally assumed the new political role of liaison between Jews and government authorities, or launched organizations and projects to reform Jewish life. The Haskalah played a crucial but not exclusive role in the process of Jewish secularization, and it was fundamental to the development of the culture, mentality, and state of mind characteristic of the liberal modern Jew.

Glossary

aggadah Story; non-halakhic material in the Talmud.

ba'al shem 'master of the divine name'; title given from the Middle Ages onwards to one who possessed the secret knowledge of the Tetragrammaton and other holy names, and who knew how to work miracles by the power of these names.

Ba'al Shem Tov Popular title of Israel ben Eliezer (*c.*1700–60), charismatic founder and first leader of hasidism (q.v.) in eastern Europe.

derush (pl. ***derashot***) Homily or sermon. The public oral exposition of Scripture is a continuous tradition dating from Ezra and the return from exile in Babylonia. Medieval Jewish exegesis recognized four levels of interpretation, of which the homiletical was the third. The homiletical method of exposition is often contrasted with *peshat*, the plain or literal meaning of the text.

Edict of Tolerance Edict issued by Emperor Joseph II in 1782 for Vienna and Lower Austria. It was one of a series of patents granted to the major non-Catholic denominations of Austria, guaranteeing existing rights and obligations and laying down additional ones.

etrog (pl. ***etrogim***) A type of citrus fruit used in the ritual of Sukot (q.v.).

Four Year Sejm The extended session of the Polish parliament in Warsaw in 1788–92 that, most notably, adopted the Constitution of 3 May 1791 which reformed the government of the Polish state.

Frankists Followers of Jacob Frank (1726–91), the head of a mystical antinomian sect among Polish Jews.

halakhah The legal or prescriptive part of Jewish tradition which defines the norms of behaviour and religious observance. Based on the legislation in the Bible, it was expanded by the rabbis in the Talmud and in a varied body of later literature, including codes, commentaries, and responsa.

hasidism A mystically inclined movement of religious revival consisting of distinct groups with charismatic leadership. It arose in the borderlands of the Polish–Lithuanian Commonwealth in the second half of the eighteenth century and quickly spread through eastern Europe. The hasidim emphasized joy in the service of God, whose presence they sought everywhere. Though their opponents, the mitnagedim (q.v.), pronounced a series of bans against them beginning in 1772, in the nineteenth century the movement became identified with religious orthodoxy.

ḥeder Colloquial name for a traditional Jewish elementary school.

ḥokhmah Wisdom. In the Pentateuch and Prophets all wisdom is seen to be of divine origin; a group of later books (Job, Ecclesiastes, Proverbs, Song of Songs) was known as the wisdom literature. Rabbinic and medieval literature debated whether *ḥokhmah* encompassed only Jewish sources and knowledge or external ones as well. The Haskalah generally advocated a broad definition of the term to incorporate secular knowledge such as languages, science, and mathematics, but there was disagreement over whether it should include such a controversial subject as philosophy.

lomedim Male students in eastern Europe who were supported by relatives so that they could devote themselves full-time to studies favoured by the Haskalah.

masoretic text The traditionally accepted text of the Bible.

me'asfim Hebrew writers associated with the journal of the Berlin Haskalah, *Hame'asef* (The Messenger) (1784–1811).

melamed Teacher in a *ḥeder* (q.v.).

Midrash Body of rabbinic literature from the mishnaic and talmudic periods, containing homiletical expositions of biblical texts, sermons, and halakhic analyses of biblical texts; 'midrash' can by extension be used to mean the rabbinic interpretation rather than the plain meaning of a biblical text.

mitnagedim The rabbinic opponents of hasidism (q.v.).

Mizrahi Party of religious Zionists.

***musar* movement** A movement for the establishment of strict ethical behaviour in the spirit of halakhah (q.v.), which arose in the nineteenth century among the mitnagedim (q.v.) of Lithuania.

Oral Law The authoritative interpretation of the Written Law (Pentateuch), regarded as given to Moses on Sinai, and therefore coexistent with the Written Law.

peshat The plain or literal meaning of Scripture. Among the four levels of interpretation recognized by medieval Jewish exegesis, *peshat* was the most basic. The commentators and commentaries devoted to the plain meaning comprise the *pashtanit* tradition.

Philanthropin movement An educational movement of the eighteenth century which, under the influence of Rousseau and the German Enlightenment, advocated a natural education that aimed to develop the full range of a child's abilities. Subjects to be taught included crafts, vernacular language, science, mathematics, and physical education, while the method of instruction was play and discovery. The major figures of the movement were Johann Bernhard Basedow (1724–90), who founded the Philanthropin School in Dessau (1774), and Johann Heinrich Campe (1746–1818), who founded schools and revised curricula.

pilpul The traditional method of discussing the Talmud; by extension it can also mean a form of hair-splitting argument.

Pirkei avot Tractate of the Mishnah, consisting largely of ethical maxims.

posekim Halakhic authorities.

Prague school A group of rabbis and scholars, most of whom studied with or were influenced by the rabbi of Prague, Judah Loew Bezalel (the Maharal, 1525–1609). Loew criticized the curriculum of Ashkenazi Jewry for neglecting central internal disciplines such as the study of the Bible, Mishnah, and the Hebrew language, as well as excluding such external subjects as science and mathematics.

Sages Collective term used of the rabbis of the talmudic period.

Shabbateanism Seventeenth-century messianic movement, named after Shabbetai Zevi (1626–76), the largest and most influential such movement in Jewish history.

Shekhinah The Divine Presence of God.

Sukot Feast of Tabernacles, observed for eight days in the month of Tishrei (autumn).

teḥinot Type of prayer; many were written in Yiddish for use by women.

tsadik (pl. ***tsadikim***) The leader of a hasidic group, often credited with miraculous powers by his followers.

Tse'enah ure'enah A popular late sixteenth-century miscellany of tales and exegetical comments woven around a Yiddish version of the Pentateuch, the *haftarot*, and the *megilot*, and read largely by women.

yeshiva A rabbinical college; the highest institution in the traditional Jewish system of education.

Notes on Contributors

HARRIS BOR received his doctorate in Jewish history from the University of Cambridge. Following postdoctoral research he is currently pursuing a career in law.

EDWARD BREUER teaches at the Department of Theology, Loyola University, Chicago.

TOVA COHEN is Associate Professor of Hebrew Literature, and head of the Center for the Study of Women in Judaism at Bar Ilan University.

IMMANUEL ETKES is Professor of Modern Jewish History, and the head of the Department of Jewish History at the Hebrew University of Jerusalem.

SHMUEL FEINER is Associate Professor of Modern Jewish History and Director of the Samuel Braun Chair for the History of the Jews in Prussia at Bar Ilan University.

YEHUDA FRIEDLANDER is Professor of Hebrew Literature at Bar Ilan University, and former Rector of the University.

DAVID B. RUDERMAN is Meyerhoff Professor and Director of the Center for Advanced Judaic Studies at the University of Pennsylvania.

JOSEPH SALMON is Professor of Modern Jewish History, and head of the Department of History at Ben-Gurion University of the Negev, Be'er Sheva.

NANCY SINKOFF is Assistant Professor of History at Rutgers University.

DAVID SORKIN is Frances and Laurence Weinstein Professor of Jewish Studies and Senior Fellow at the Institute for Research in the Humanities, University of Wisconsin-Madison.

SHMUEL WERSES is Emeritus Professor of Hebrew Literature at the Hebrew University of Jerusalem.

Bibliography

ABRAHAM B. SAMUEL ZACUTO, *Sefer yuḥasin* [Book of Pedigrees] (Constantinople, 1566); ed. Abraham Hayim Freimann as *Sefer yuḥasin hashalem* (Frankfurt am Main, 1925); ed. Tsevi Filipowski (London and Edinburgh, 1857).

ABRAHAMS, ABRAHAM. *See* TANG

ABRAMOWITZ, S. Y. *See* MENDELE MOKHER SEFORIM

ADLER, R., *Women of the Shtetl through the Eyes of I. L. Peretz* (Cranbury, NJ, 1980).

AGNON, SHMUEL YOSEF, *Hakhnasat kalah*, trans. I. M. Lask as *The Bridal Canopy* (New York, 1987).

AHAD HA'AM, 'On the History of Positive and Negative' (1891), in *Collected Writings* (Heb.) (Jerusalem, 1947), 75–8.

——'The Man in the Tent' (1891), in *Collected Writings* (Heb.) (Jerusalem, 1947), 48–51.

——'A Small Briefcase' (Heb.), *Hashiloaḥ*, 2 (1897), 278–80.

ALCHIN, SHIFRA, 'A Letter to my Father's Friend' (Heb.), *Hamelits*, 3 (1863), 119–21.

ALKOSHI, GEDLIA, 'Judah Leib Gordon the Critic' (Heb.), *Metsadah*, 7 (1954), 481–4.

ALTER, ROBERT, 'Literary Reflections of the Jewish Family', in D. Kraemer (ed.), *The Jewish Family: Metaphor and Memory* (New York and Oxford, 1989), 225–41.

ALTMANN, ALEXANDER, *Moses Mendelssohn: A Biographical Study* (Tuscaloosa, Ala., 1973).

ANON. ['by one of the unfortunate officers'], *The Shipwreck of the Antelope East India Packet, H. Wilson, Esq. Commander, on the Pelew Islands, situate in the West Part of the Pacific Ocean; in August 1783* (London, 1788).

ARKUSH, A., 'Voltaire on Judaism and Christianity', *Association of Jewish Studies Review*, 18 (1993), 223–43.

ASAF, SIMCHA, *Sources for the History of Jewish Education* (Heb.), 4 vols. (Tel Aviv, 1954).

ASCHHEIM, STEVEN E., *Brothers and Strangers: The East European Jew in German and German Jewish Consciousness, 1800–1823* (Madison, Wis., 1982).

ASHKENAZI, ASHER HAKOHEN, *Keter rosh: Oreḥot hayim* [The Crown of the Head: Ways of Life] (Warsaw, 1914).

ASSAF, DAVID, *The Regal Way: The Life and Times of Rabbi Israel of Ruzhin* (Heb.) (Jerusalem, 1997).

BAHR, ERHARD (ed.), *Was ist Aufklärung? Thesen und Definitionen* (Stuttgart, 1974).

BARAZ, SHIMON, *Ma'arakhei lev* [Workings of the Heart] (Königsberg, 1784).

BARNETT, A., and BRODETSKY, S., 'Eliakim ben Abraham (Jacob Hart): An Anglo-Jewish Scholar of the Eighteenth Century', *Transactions of the Jewish Historical Society of England*, 14 (1940), 207–23.

BARTAL, ISRAEL, 'From Distorted Reflection to Historical Fact: Haskalah Literature and the Study of the Hasidic Movement' (Heb.), *Mada'ei hayahadut*, 32 (1992), 7–17.

——'From Traditional Bilingualism to National Monolingualism', in Lewis Glinert (ed.), *Hebrew in Ashkenaz: A Language in Exile* (New York and Oxford, 1993), 141–50.

——'Gentiles and Gentile Society in Hebrew and Yiddish Literature in Eastern Europe, 1856–1914' (Heb.) (Ph.D. diss., Jerusalem, 1981).

——'The Heavenly City of Germany and Absolutism *à la mode d'Autriche*: The Rise of the Haskalah in Galicia', in Jacob Katz (ed.), *Toward Modernity: The European Jewish Model* (New Brunswick, NJ, 1987), 33–42.

——*The Metamorphosis of the Idea of the Productivization of the Jews in the Eighteenth to Twentieth Centuries: Sources for MA Seminar* (Heb.) (Jerusalem, 1985).

——'Mordecai Aaron Guenzburg: A Lithuanian Maskil Faces Modernity', in Frances Malino and David Sorkin (eds.), *From East and West: Jews in a Changing Europe, 1750–1870* (Oxford, 1990), 126–47.

——'Simon the Heretic: A Chapter in Orthodox Historiography', in Israel Bartal, Ezra Mendelsohn, and Chava Turniansky (eds.), *'According to the Custom of Ashkenaz and Poland': Studies in Jewish Culture in Honour of Chone Shmeruk* (Heb.) (Jerusalem, 1993), 243–68.

BARZILAY, ISAAC, 'Acceptance or Rejection: Manasseh of Ilya's (1767–1831) Ambivalent Attitude Toward Hasidism', *Jewish Quarterly Review*, 74 (1983–4), 1–20.

——'The Life of Manasseh of Ilya (1767–1831)', *Proceedings of the American Academy for Jewish Research*, 5 (1983), 1–35.

BASEDOW, JOHANN BERNHARD, *Elementarwerk*, vol. i (Berlin and Dessau, 1774).

BEER, PETER, 'Über Literatur der Israeliten in den kaiser österreichischen Staaten im lezten Decenio des achtzehnten Jahrhunderts', *Sulamith*, 2/1 (1808), 342–457; 2/2 (1809), 42–61.

BEN ZE'EV, JUDAH LEIB, *Yesodei hadat* [Foundations of Religion] (Vienna, 1806).

BENDAVID, LAZARUS, *Etwas zur Charackteristick der Juden* (Leipzig, 1793).

BEN-SASSON, H. H., 'Concepts and Reality in Jewish History in the Late Middle Ages' (Heb.), *Tarbiz*, 29 (1960), 297–312.

BENVENISTI, DAVID, 'Rabbi Jacob Judah Nehama, Precursor of the Haskalah Period in Salonika', in M. Zohory, A. Tartakover, M. Zand, and A. Hains (eds.), *Studies on Jewish Themes by Contemporary Jewish Scholars from Islamic Countries* (Heb.) (Jerusalem, 1981), 144–66.

BEN-YEHUDA, ELIEZER, *Dream and Awakening: A Selection of Letters on Language Issues* (Heb.), ed. R. Sivan (Jerusalem, 1986).

——*Zikaron basefer* [Memoirs] (Warsaw, 1889).

BERDYCZEWSKI, MICHA JOSEPH, 'On Hasidism' (Heb.), *Hamagid leyisra'el*, 33 (1897), 264.

——*The Works of M. Y. Bin-Gorion* [Berdyczewski]: *Stories* (Heb.), vol. ii (Tel Aviv, 1936).

[BERLIN, SAUL], review of Raphael Cohen, *Marpe Lashon* (Berlin, 1790) (Heb.), *Hame'asef*, 6 (1790), 362–80.

BERLOWITZ, Y., 'Rachel Morpurgo, Passion for Death, Passion for Poetry: On the First Modern Hebrew Woman Poet', in *Sadan: Studies in Hebrew Literature* (Heb.), vol. ii (Tel Aviv, 1996), 11–40.

BERSOHN, N. R., 'Isaac Satanov, the Man and his Work: A Study in the Berlin Haskalah' (Ph.D. diss. Columbia University, 1975).

BIALE, D., *Eros and the Jews* (New York, 1992).

BICK, ABRAHAM [Shauli], *Rabbi Jacob Emden* (Heb.) (Jerusalem, 1975).

BICK, JACOB SAMUEL, 'To the Maskilim of My People' (Heb.), *Hatsefirah* (Zolkiew, 1824), 71–7.

BLANNING, T. C. W., *Reform and Revolution in Mainz, 1743–1803* (London, 1974).

BLOCH, SAMSON HALEVI, *Shevilei olam* [Ways of the World], vol. i (Zolkiew, 1822).

BOCK, MOSES BEN ZVI, *Moda'ah leyaldei benei yisra'el uleda'at beḥokhmah umusar vehu reshit halimud belashon ivri, ashkenazit vesefardit* [Announcement to Jewish Children for the Knowledge of Wisdom and Ethics, which is the Beginning of the Study of the Hebrew Tongue, Ashkenazi and Sephardi] (Berlin, 1812).

BODEK, JACOB, 'Additional Details' (Heb.), additional section for the year 1824 in Abraham Triebesch, *Korot ha'itim* [History] (Lemberg, 1851), unpaginated.

BÖHME, H., and BÖHME, G., 'The Battle of Reason with the Imagination', in J. Schmidt (ed.), *What is Enlightenment? Eighteenth-Century Answers and Twentieth-Century Questions* (Berkeley, Calif., 1996), 426–53.

BOUREL, DOMINIQUE, 'Haskalah: Jüdische Aufklärung', in Werner Schneiders (ed.), *Lexikon der Aufklärung* (Munich, 1995), 174–5.

BRANDSTAEDTER, MORDECAI DAVID, *Kefar mezagegim* [The Glaziers' Village] (1894).

—— *Sipurim* [Stories], ed. B. E. Feingold (Jerusalem, 1974).

BRAUDES, REUVEN ASHER, *Hadat vehaḥayim* [Religion and Life] (1876–9; Warsaw, 1885); ed. G. Shaked, 2 vols. (Jerusalem, 1974).

BRENNER, YOSEF HAYIM, 'In Memory of J. L. Gordon' (Heb.), in id., *Collected Works*, vol. iii (Tel Aviv, 1967), 11–34.

BREUER, EDWARD, *The Limits of Enlightenment: Jews, Germans and the Eighteenth-Century Study of Scripture* (Cambridge, Mass., 1996).

BREUER, MORDECHAI, 'The Early Modern Period', in Michael Meyer (ed.), *German-Jewish History in Modern Times*, 4 vols. (New York, 1996–8), i. 79–260.

—— 'Keep your Sons Away from *Higayon*', in Y. Gilat and A. Stern (eds.), *Mikhtam ledavid: Memorial Book for Rabbi David Oks* (Heb.) (Ramat Gan, 1977), 242–61.

BROWNSTEIN, RACHEL M., *Becoming a Heroine* (New York, 1982).

BULLOUGH, V. L., *The Subordinate Sex* (Urbana, Ill., 1973).

BURSTYN, J. N., *Victorian Education and the Ideal of Womanhood* (London, 1980).

BYNUM, W. F., and PORTER, R. (eds.), *William Hunter and the Eighteenth-Century Medical World* (Cambridge, 1985).

CAMPE, JOACHIM HEINRICH, *Kleine Seelenlehre für Kinder* (Berlin, 1783); trans. as *Elementary Dialogues for the Improvement of Youth* (London, 1792).

——*Sammlung interessanter und durchgängiger zweckmässig abgefasster Reisebeschreibungen für die Jugend* (Reutlingen, 1786–93).

——*Theophron* (Hamburg, 1783).

CASSIRER, ERNST, *The Philosophy of the Enlightenment*, trans. Fritz L. A. Koelln and James P. Pettegrave (Princeton, NJ, 1951).

CHARTIER, ROGER, *The Cultural Origins of the French Revolution* (Durham, NC, 1991).

COHEN, TOVA, 'The Scholarly Technique: A Code of Haskalah Literature' (Heb.), *Jerusalem Studies in Hebrew Literature*, 13 (1992), 137–69.

——'Simultaneous Reading: A Key Technique in Understanding the Confrontation with the Bible in the Poetry of Adam Hakohen' (Heb.), *Jerusalem Studies in Hebrew Literature*, 7 (1985), 71–89.

COLLINS, K. E., 'Jewish Medical Students and Graduates of Scotland, 1739–1862', *Transactions of the Jewish Historical Society of England*, 27 (1978–80).

DAN, JOSEPH, *Ethical and Exegetical Literature* (Heb.) (Jerusalem, 1975).

——'Ethical Literature', *Encyclopedia Judaica*, vi. 922–31.

——*The Hasidic Story* (Heb.) (Jerusalem, 1975).

——*Jewish Mysticism and Jewish Ethics* (Washington, DC, 1996).

DARNTON, ROBERT, 'George Washington's False Teeth', *New York Review of Books*, 27 Mar. 1997, pp. 34–8.

DAVIES, J. M., 'The Cultural and Intellectual History of Ashkenazi Jews 1500–1750', *Leo Baeck Institute Yearbook*, 38 (1993), 343–91.

DAVIES, M. M., *Identity or History? Marcus Herz and the End of the Enlightenment* (Detroit, 1995).

DE BEAUVOIR, S., *Le Deuxième Sexe* (Paris, 1949); trans. H. M. Parshley as *The Second Sex* (New York, 1972).

DEI ROSSI, AZARIAH, *Me'or einayim* [Enlightenment of the Eyes] (Mantua, 1574).

DICK, ISAAC MEIR, *Alte idishen zogen* [Old Jewish Sayings] (Vilna, 1876).

——*Pilei hashem* [Wonders of the Lord] (Vilna, 1856).

DINUR, BENZION, *At the Turn of the Generations* (Heb.) (Jerusalem, 1954).

——*Historical Writings* (Heb.), vol. i (Jerusalem, 1955).

DONNOVAN, J., 'The Silence is Broken', in A. McConnell, R. Borker, and N. Forman (eds.), *Women and Language in Literature and Society* (New York, 1980), 205–18.

DOV BER B. SHMUEL OF LINITS, *Shivḥei habesht* [Praises of the Ba'al Shem Tov] (Kopys, 1814–15); ed. Abraham Rubinstein (Jerusalem, 1992).

DUBIN, LOIS C., 'Trieste and Berlin: The Italian Role in the Cultural Politics of the Haskalah', in Jacob Katz (ed.), *Toward Modernity: The European Jewish Model* (New Brunswick, NJ, 1987), 189–224.

DUBNOW, SIMON, *A History of Hasidism* (Heb.) (1931; Tel Aviv, 1960).

——*History of the Jews*, 5 vols. (1925–9; South Brunswick, NJ, 1967–73).

DUCKESZ, YEHEZKEL, *Ḥakhmei A H V* [Sages of A[ltona], H[amburg], and W[andsbeck]] (Hamburg, 1905).

——'Zur Genealogie Samson Raphael Hirschs', *Jahrbuch der Jüdisch-Literarischen Gesellschaft*, 17 (1926), 113–31.

EHRENPREIS, MORDECAI, 'Where To?' (Heb.), *Hashiloaḥ*, 1 (1897), 489–503.

EILBERG-SCHWARTZ, HOWARD, *The Savage in Judaism* (Bloomington, Ind., 1990).

EILINSON, E. G., *Between Woman and her Maker* (Heb.) (Jerusalem, 1984).

——*Walking Modestly: Woman and the Commandments* (Heb.), vol. ii (Jerusalem, 1981).

EISENBACH, ARTUR, *The Emancipation of the Jews of Poland, 1780–1870*, ed. Antony Polonsky, trans. Janina Dorosz (London, 1991).

EISENSTEIN, JUDAH DAVID (ed.), *A Jewish Treasury* (Heb.), vol. iii (New York, 1951).

EISENSTEIN-BARZILAY, ISAAC, 'The Background of the Berlin Haskalah', in Joseph Blau (ed.), *Essays on Jewish Life and Thought* (New York, 1959), 183–97.

——'The Enlightenment and the Jews: A Study in Haskalah and Nationalism' (Ph.D. diss., Columbia University, 1955).

——'National and Anti-National Trends in the Berlin Haskalah', *Jewish Social Studies*, 21/3 (July 1959), 165–92.

ELIAKIM B. ABRAHAM. *See* HART, JACOB

ELIASBERG, MORDECAI, 'How to Improve the Situation of Our Brethren in Russia' (Heb.), *Hamagid*, 13 (1869), 129–30.

ELIAV, MORDECAI, *Jewish Education in Germany during the Haskalah and Emancipation* (Heb.) (Jerusalem, 1960).

ELIOR, RACHEL, 'Nathan Adler and the Frankfurt Pietists: Pietist Groups in Eastern and Central Europe during the Eighteenth Century' (Heb.), *Zion*, 59 (1994), 31–64.

EMDEN, JACOB, *Beit ya'akov* [House of Jacob] (Altona, 1745–7; Lemberg, 1904).

——*Ḥali ketem* [Ornament of Fine Gold], in id., *Tefilat yesharim*, 22*b*–28*a*.

——*Luaḥ eresh* [Tablet of Expression] (Altona, 1769).

——*Megilat sefer* [Scroll of the Book] (Altona, 1740; new edn., based on MS at the Bodleian Library, Oxford: Warsaw, 1896).

——*Mitpaḥat sefarim* [A Scroll Wrapper] (Altona, 1768; 2nd edn. Lvov, 1871).

——*Shevet legav kesilim: Kuntres shelishi mitokh sefer shimush* [A Rod for the Fool's Back: A Chapter from the Book of Service] (Amsterdam, 1758–62).

——'Sulam beit el mutsav artsah verosho magia ashamaimah' [The Ladder of Bethel is set up on earth and the top of it reaches to heaven], introduction to id., *Beit ya'akov*.

——*Tefilat yesharim* [Prayer of the Upright] (Altona, 1775).

——*Torat hakenaot* [Law of Jealousies] (Amsterdam, 1752; 3rd edn. Lvov, 1870).

ENDELMAN, TODD, 'The Englishness of Jewish Modernity in England', in Jacob Katz (ed.), *Toward Modernity: The European Jewish Model* (New Brunswick, NJ, 1987), 225–46.

ENDELMAN, TODD, *The Jews of Georgian England 1714–1830* (Philadelphia, Pa., 1979).

——*Radical Assimilation in English Jewish History 1656–1945* (Bloomington, Ind., 1990).

EPSTEIN, ZALMAN, 'The Division of our Maskilim' (Heb.), *Hamelits*, 24 (1882), 475–80.

ERIK, MAX, *Studies in the History of the Haskalah* (Yiddish) (Minsk, 1934).

ERTER, ISAAC, *Hatsofeh leveit yisra'el* [The Watchman of the House of Israel] (Warsaw, 1883); ed. Yehuda Friedlander (Jerusalem, 1996).

——*Ḥasidut veḥokhmah* [Hasidism and Wisdom] (n.p., 1836).

ESCHELBACHER, J., 'Die Anfänge allgemeiner Bildung unter den deutschen Juden vor Mendelssohn', in *Festschrift zum siebzigsten Geburtstage Martin Philippsons* (Leipzig, 1916), 168–77.

ETKES, IMMANUEL, 'The Enlightenment in Eastern Europe: An Introduction', in id. (ed.), *Religion and Life: The Jewish Enlightenment in Eastern Europe*, 9–24.

——'Marriage and Torah Study among the *Lomdim* in Lithuania in the Nineteenth Century', in D. Kraemer (ed.), *The Jewish Family: Metaphor and Memory* (New York and Oxford, 1989), 153–78.

——'On the Question of the Precursors of the Haskalah in Eastern Europe', in id. (ed.), *Religion and Life: The Jewish Enlightenment in Eastern Europe*, 25–44.

——'R. Shneur Zalman of Lyady's Style of Hasidic Leadership' (Heb.), *Zion*, 50 (1985), 323–31.

——'The Role of Magic and *Ba'alei Shem* in Ashkenazi Society in the Late Seventeenth and Early Eighteenth Centuries' (Heb.), *Zion*, 60 (1995), 69–104.

——'The Vilna Gaon and the Haskalah: Image and Reality', in I. Etkes and Joseph Salmon (eds.), *Chapters in the History of Jewish Society in the Middle Ages and the Modern Period: Essays in Honour of Jacob Katz* (Heb.) (Jerusalem, 1980), 192–217.

——(ed.), *Religion and Life: The Jewish Enlightenment in Eastern Europe* (Heb.) (Jerusalem, 1993).

ETTINGER, S., *The History of the Jewish People in Modern Times* (Heb.) (Tel Aviv, 1969).

EUCHEL, ISAAC, 'The Letters of Meshulam Ha'eshtemoi' (Heb.), *Hame'asef*, 6 (1789–90) [series of pseudepigraphic letters].

——Preface (Heb.), *Hame'asef*, 4 (1788).

——*Rabbi Henoch, or: What To Do With It* (Yiddish–German) (1792).

——*Toledot rabenu heḥakham moshe ben menaḥem* [Biography of our Wise Rabbi Moses Son of Menahem] (Berlin, 1789).

FAGAN, BRIAN, *Clash of Cultures* (New York, 1983).

FEIERBERG, MORDECAI ZE'EV, *Writings* (Heb.), ed. A. Steiman (Tel Aviv, n.d.).

FEINBERG, L., *Introduction to Satire* (Ames, Ia., 1967).

FEINER, SHMUEL, 'The Dragon in the Beehive: Yitshak Margoliot and the Paradox of the Early Haskalah' (Heb.), *Zion*, 63 (1998), 39–74.

——'The Early Haskalah in Eighteenth-Century Judaism' (Heb.), *Tarbiz*, 62/2 (1998), 189–240.

——'Educational Agendas and Social Ideals: Jüdische Freischule in Berlin, 1778–1825', in R. Feldhay and Immanuel Etkes (eds.), *Education and History: Cultural and Political Contexts* (Heb.) (Jerusalem, 1999), 247–84.

——'Eliezer Zweifel and the Moderate Russian Enlightenment', in Immanuel Etkes (ed.), *Religion and Life: The Jewish Enlightenment in Eastern Europe* (Jerusalem, 1993), 336–79.

——*Haskalah and History: The Emergence of a Modern Jewish Historical Consciousness* (Heb.) (Jerusalem, 1995). (English translation forthcoming)

——'Isaac Euchel: Entrepreneur of the Haskalah Movement in Germany' (Heb.), *Zion*, 52 (1987), 427–69.

——'Jewish Society, Literature, and Haskalah in Russia as Represented in the Radical Criticism of I. E. Kovner' (Heb.; Eng. abstract), *Zion*, 55 (1990), 283–316.

——'Mendelssohn and Mendelssohn's Disciples: A Re-examination', *Leo Baeck Institute Yearbook*, 40 (1995), 133–67.

——'The Modern Jewish Woman: A Test-Case in the Relationship between the Haskalah and Modernity' (Heb.; Eng. abstract), *Zion*, 58 (1993), 453–99.

——'The Pseudo-Enlightenment and the Question of Jewish Modernization', *Jewish Social Studies*, 3/a (1996), 62–88.

——'"The Rebellion of the French and the Freedom of the Jews": The French Revolution in the Image of the Past of the East European Jewish Enlightenment', in Richard Cohen (ed.), *The French Revolution and its Historiography* (Heb.) (Jerusalem, 1991), 215–47.

——'Smolenskin's Haskalah Heresy and the Roots of Jewish National Historiography' (Heb.), *Hatsiyonut*, 16 (1992), 19–31.

——'The Turning-Point in the Evaluation of Hasidism: Eliezer Zweifel and the Moderate Haskalah in Russia' (Heb.), *Zion*, 51 (1986), 167–210.

FEINGOLD, BEN-AMI, 'A. Z. Rabinovich's *Al haperek* and the Haskalah's Soul-Searching' (Heb.), *Mozna'im*, 49 (1979), 119–26.

——'Books and Literature as a Subject in Maskilic Literature', in *Testimony: Research on Hebrew Literature* (Heb.), vol. v (Tel Aviv, 1986), 85–100.

FERRANTE, J. M., *Women as Image in Medieval Literature* (New York, 1973).

FINGER, O., *Von der Materialität der Seele. Beitrag zur Geschichte des Materialismus im Deutschland der 2. Hälfte des XVIII. Jahrhunderts* (Berlin, 1961).

FISH, S., *Is There a Text in this Class?* (Cambridge, Mass., 1980).

FISHMAN, DAVID E., *Russia's First Modern Jews: The Jews of Shklov* (New York, 1995).

——*Science, Enlightenment and Rabbinic Culture in Belorussian Jewry: 1772–1840* (Cambridge, Mass., 1985).

FLAH, SHALOM, 'Observer of Tunis' (Heb.), *He'asif*, 6 (1894), 78–94.

——'Our Distant Brethren' (Heb.), *Hatsefirah*, 15/45–6 (1888), 45–6.

——'Pain of Love' (Heb.), *Hatsefirah*, 15/89 (1888), 3–4.

FLECKELES, ELEAZAR, *Ahavat david* [The Love of David], pt. 4 of *Olat haḥodesh* [The Sacrifice of the New Month] (Prague, 1800).

FORCE, J., *William Whiston, Honest Newtonian* (Cambridge and New York, 1985).

FRANCOLM, ISAAK ASCHER, *The Jews in England; or the Jews and the Crusaders in the Reign of Richard the Lionheart*, trans. into Heb. from German by Miriam Markel-Mosessohn [Wirszblowski] (Warsaw, 1869).

FRANKEL, JONATHAN, 'Assimilation and the Jews in Nineteenth-Century Europe: Towards a New Historiography?', in Jonathan Frankel and Steven J. Zipperstein (eds.), *Assimilation and Community: The Jews in Nineteenth-Century Europe* (Cambridge, 1992), 1–37.

FRANKFURT, MOSES MENDELSOHN [Moses b. Mendel Frankfurt], *Metsi'at ha'arets haḥadashah* [Discovery of the New Land] (Altona, 1807).

——*Penei tevel* [Face of the World] (Amsterdam, 1872).

FRIEDBERG, ABRAHAM SHALOM, *Sefer hazikhronot* [Book of Memoirs] (Warsaw, 1899).

FRIEDBERG, HAYIM D., *History of the Jewish Press* (Heb.) (Antwerp, 1937).

FRIEDLANDER, YEHUDA, 'Hasidism as the Image of Demonism: The Satiric Writings of Judah Leib Mises', in Jacob Neusner, Ernst S. Frerichs, and Nahum N. Sarna (eds.), *From Ancient Israel to Modern Judaism: Intellect in Quest of Understanding, in Honor of Marvin Fox*, vol. iii (Atlanta, Ga., 1989), 159–77.

——*Hebrew Satire in Europe*, vol. ii: *The Eighteenth and Nineteenth Centuries* (Heb.) (Ramat Gan, 1989).

——*Hebrew Satire in Europe*, vol. iii: *The Nineteenth Century* (Heb.) (Ramat Gan, 1994).

——'The Place of Halakhah in Haskalah Literature: The Attitude to Maimonides as a Halakhic Authority' (Heb.), *Meḥkarei yerushalayim bemaḥshevet yisra'el*, 5 (1986), 349–62.

——'The Revolt against "Traditional Authority of the Sages" in Hebrew Satire of the Nineteenth Century' (Heb.), in Avigdor Shinan (ed.), *Proceedings of the Sixth World Congress of Jewish Studies*, vol. iii (Jerusalem, 1977), 363–76.

——*Studies in Hebrew Satire*, vol. i: *Hebrew Satire in Germany* (Heb.) (Tel Aviv, 1979).

——'Tuviah Gutman Feder: *Kol meḥatsetsim* (Voice of the Archers)' (Heb.), *Zehut* (May 1981), 275–303.

FRIEDRICHSFELD, DAVID, *Zekher tsadik* [In Memory of a Righteous Individual; biography of Naphtali Herz Wessely] (Amsterdam, 1808).

FRUMKIN, YISRAEL, 'On Education' (Heb.), *Haḥavatselet*, 15–17 (1880) [series of articles]; repr. in *The Collected Writings of Yisrael Dov Frumkin* (Heb.), ed. G. Kresel (Jerusalem, 1954).

FUENN, SAMUEL JOSEPH, *From Militant Haskalah to Conservative Maskil: A Selection of S. J. Fuenn's Writings* (Heb.), ed. Shmuel Feiner (Jerusalem, 1993).

——'Haskalah and Halakhah' (Heb.), *Hakarmel*, 7/14 (1868), 105–6.

——*Kiryah ne'emanah* [Faithful City] (Vilna, 1860).

FÜRST, JULIUS, *Bibliotheca Judaica*, vol. ii (Leipzig, 1863).

GAGLIARDO, JOHN G., *Germany under the Old Regime, 1600–1790* (London and New York, 1991).

GASCOIGNE, J., *Cambridge in the Age of Enlightenment: Science, Religion, and Politics from the Restoration to the French Revolution* (Cambridge, 1989).

GAY, PETER, *The Enlightenment: An Interpretation. The Rise of Modern Paganism* (New York, 1966).

GELBER, N. M., *Arim ve'imahot beyisra'el* ['Cities and Mothers of Israel'], vol. vi: *Brody*, ed. Y. L. Maimon (Jerusalem, 1955).

——*Zu Vorgeschichte des Zionismus* (Vienna, 1927).

GILBERT, S. M., and GUBAR, S., *The Madwoman in the Attic* (New Haven, 1979).

GILBOA, MENUCHA, *Hebrew Periodicals in the Eighteenth and Nineteenth Centuries* (Heb.) (Jerusalem, 1992).

GILON, MORDECAI, *Mendelssohn's 'Kohelet musar' in its Historical Context* (Heb.) (Jerusalem, 1979).

GINSBURG, SAUL, 'Individuals and Generations', in Immanuel Etkes (ed.), *Religion and Life: The Jewish Enlightenment in Eastern Europe* (Heb.) (Jerusalem, 1993), 380–404.

GLOGAU, TSEVI HIRSH, 'Ethical Rebuke' (Heb.), *Hame'asef*, 8 (1809), 195–200.

GOLDBLUM, YAFAZ A., 'Jubilee: On the Seventieth Anniversary of the Life of Shneur Sachs' (Heb.), *Keneset yisra'el*, 1 (1886), cols. 883–6.

GOLDISH, M., 'Newtonian, Converso, and Deist: The Lives of Jacob (Henrique) de Castro Sarmento', *Science in Context*, 10 (1997), 651–75.

GORDON, DAVID, 'The Time has Come: On the National Mission of the Jewish People' (Heb.), *Hamagid*, 13/27–34 (1869) [series of articles].

GORDON, JUDAH LEIB, *Collected Works: Prose* (Heb.) (Tel Aviv, 1960).

——*Letters* (Heb.), ed. Y. Y. Weisberg, vol. ii (Warsaw, 1894).

——'Mehi Kabel' (Heb.), *Hamelits*, 10–15 (1888).

GOTTLOBER, ABRAHAM BAER, *Bikoret toledot hakara'im* [A Critique of Karaite History] (Vilna, 1864).

——'From Zhitomir' (Heb.), *Haḥavatselet*, 25 (1872), 196–7.

——*Hizaharu bivenei aniyim* [Take Care of the Children of the Poor] (Warsaw, 1877).

——'Memoirs' (Heb.), *Hamagid*, 39 (1873).

——'Zikhronot miyemei ne'urai' [Memoirs of my Youth] ([Warsaw], 1886), in id., *Zikhronot umasaot*, ed. R. Goldberg, vol. i (Jerusalem, 1976).

GRAETZ, HEINRICH, *Geschichte der Juden* (1853–75); repr. in 6 vols. (Munich, 1985); trans. as *The History of the Jews* (Philadelphia, Pa., 1956).

GRAETZ, MICHAEL, 'The Jewish Enlightenment', in Michael Meyer (ed.), *German Jewish History in Modern Times*, trans. William Templer, 4 vols. (New York, 1996–8), i. 261–380.

GRAUPE, H. M., 'Mordechai Gumpel (Levison)', *Bulletin des Leo Baeck Instituts*, 5 (1962), 1–12.

GREENBERG, LOUIS, *The Jews in Russia*, vol. i (New Haven, 1944).

GREENBLATT, STEPHEN, *Marvelous Possessions: The Wonder of the New World* (Oxford, 1991).

GUENZBURG, MORDECAI AARON, *Avi'ezer* (Vilna, 1864).

——*Kiryat sefer: Mikhtavim melukatim al tohorat leshon hakodesh* [The City of the Book: Selected Letters on the Purity of the Holy Tongue] (Warsaw, 1873).

——'The Wisdom of Toilers' (Heb.), in id., *Devir*, 2 vols. (1844 and 1862; Warsaw, 1883), i. 22–41.

GUMPERTZ, AARON SOLOMON, *Megaleh sod* [Revealer of Secrets] (1765; Lemberg, 1910).

GUTERMAN, ALEXANDER, 'The Suggestions of the Jews of Poland for the Reforms of their Legal, Economic, Social and Cultural Status' (Heb.) (MA thesis, Jerusalem, 1975).

GUTMANN, JOSEPH, 'Geschichte der Knabenschule der jüdischen Gemeinde in Berlin, 1826–1926', in *Festschrift zur Feier des hundertjährigen Bestehens der Knabenschule der jüdischen Gemeinde in Berlin* (Berlin, 1926), 7–17.

HABERMAN, A. M., 'The Hebrew Press in Tarnopol', in *Pages in Bibliography and Jewish History*, year 2, pamphlet 1 (Vienna, 1935), 24–31.

HACOHEN, SHALOM, *Mata'ei kedem al admat tsafon* [Orchards of Yore on Northern Soil] (Rödelheim, 1807).

HA'EPHRATI, DEVORAH, letter to Abraham Mapu on *Ahavat tsiyon* (Heb.), *Hamagid*, 3/12 (1858), 46.

HAJNAL, J., 'European Marriage: Patterns in Perspective', in D. V. Glass and E. D. Eversley (eds.), *Population in History* (London, 1965), 101–43.

HALEVI, JUDAH, *Sefer hakuzari* [Book of the Kuzari] (11th cent.).

HALKIN, SIMON, *Modern Hebrew Literature: From the Enlightenment to the Birth of the State of Israel. Trends and Values* (New York, 1950).

——*Trends and Forms in Modern Hebrew Literature* (Heb.) (Jerusalem, 1984).

HAMPSON, NORMAN, *The Enlightenment* (Harmondsworth, 1968).

HANANI, YISRAEL, 'The Haskalah Movement in Erets Yisrael' (Heb.) (Ph.D. diss., Jerusalem, 1959).

HANAU, SOLOMON ZALMAN B. JUDAH LOEB HAKOHEN, *Binyan shelomo* [Solomon's Building] (Frankfurt, 1708).

——*Sha'arei tefilah* [Gates of Prayer] (Jessnitz, 1725).

——*Sha'arei torah* [Gates of Torah] (Hamburg, 1718).

——*Tsohar hateivah* [Window of the Word/Ark] (Berlin, 1733).

——*Yesod hanikud* [Foundation of Vocalization] (Amsterdam, 1730).

HARRIS, JAY, *How Do We Know This? Midrash and the Fragmentation of Modern Judaism* (Albany, NY, 1995).

HART, JACOB [Eliakim b. Abraham], *Sefer milḥamot adonai* [Book of the Wars of the Lord] (London, 1794).

HAZARD, PAUL, *La Crise de la conscience européenne* (Paris, 1935); trans. as *The European Mind 1680–1715* (Harmondsworth, 1964).

HEINROTH, J. C. A., *Erziehung und Selbstbildung* (1837); trans. A. Schloss as *On Education and Self-Formation* (London, 1838).

HERTZBERG, ARTHUR, *The French Enlightenment and the Jews* (New York and Philadelphia, Pa., 1968).

Hevrat Dorshei Lashon Ever [Society for the Promotion of the Hebrew Language], *Naḥal habesor* [Announcement] (Königsberg, 1783).

HIRSCHEL, MOSHE, *Kampf der jüdischen Hierarchie mit der Vernunft* (Breslau, 1788).

HODGART, O. M., 'Satire', in R. Paulson (ed.), *Satire: Modern Essays in Criticism* (London, 1971), 79–107.

HOMBERG, NAPHTALI HERZ, *Imrei shefer kolelim inyenei torah umusar leyaldei benei yisra'el, elem ve'almah* [Words of Wisdom, Including Matters of Torah and Morals for the Jewish Boy and Girl] (1802; repr. Vienna, 1816).

—— commentary on Jacob b. Isaac Ashkenazi of Janow's *Tse'enah ure'enah* [Go Out and See, *c.*1590] (1817).

HORODEZKY, SAMUEL ABBA, 'Rabbi Yisrael Besht' (Heb.), *He'atid*, bk. 2, 2nd edn. (Berlin and Vienna, 1923).

—— *The Hasidim and the Hasidic Jews* (Heb.), vol. iv (Tel Aviv, 1943).

HOROWITZ, ISAIAH ABRAHAM HALEVI, *Shenei luḥot haberit* [Two Tablets of the Law], abridged edn. (Frankfurt, 1717).

HOROWITZ, SHAI ISH, 'Hasidism and Haskalah' (Heb.), *He'atid*, 2 (1909), 29–99.

HUNDERT, GERSHON DAVID, 'Approaches to the History of the Jewish Family in Early Modern Poland–Lithuania', in S. M. Cohen and P. E. Hyman (eds.), *The Jewish Family: Myth and Reality* (New York and London, 1986).

HURWITZ, ELIJAH PINHAS B. MEIR, *Sefer haberit* [Book of the Covenant] (1797).

HURWITZ, SAUL ISRAEL, 'Hasidism and the Haskalah' (Heb.), *He'atid*, bk. 2, 2nd edn. (Berlin and Vienna, 1923).

IBN EZRA, ABRAHAM, *Sefer torat elohim: Ḥumash* [Book of the Law of God: Pentateuch], 5 vols. (Warsaw, 1879–80).

—— *Yesod mora* [Foundation of Awe] (Hamburg, 1770).

ISRAEL B. MOSES HALEVI OF ZAMOSC, *Sefer netsaḥ yisra'el* [Book of the Eternal Israel] (Frankfurt an der Oder, 1741; repr. Brooklyn, NY, 1991).

ISRAEL B. MOSES HALEVI OF ZAMOSC, *Sefer ruaḥ ḥen* [Book of the Spirit of Grace] (1744; Warsaw, 1826; repr. Jerusalem, 1969).

ITTAMARI, ELIJAH HAKOHEN, *Shevet musar* [The Rod of Chastisement] (Smyrna, 1712; Jerusalem, 1989).

JAFFE, MORDECAI-GIMPEL, 'Concerning the Supplements to "The Ways of the Talmud"' (Heb.), *Halevanon*, 6/20 (1869), 153–6.

JANSEN, M. *Religionsunterricht und Sittenlehre philanthropischer Pädagogen als Konsequenz ihrer theologisch-anthropologischen Standorte* (Duisburg, 1978).

JAYNES, J., and WOODWARD, W., 'In the Shadow of the Enlightenment, I: Reimarus against the Epicurians', *Journal of the History of the Behavioural Sciences*, 10/1 (1974), 3–16.

[JEITELES, BARUCH], *Conversations between the Year 1800 and the Year 1801, by a Lover of Truth* (Heb.) (Prague, 1800).

[——] 'On Enlightenment' (German–Heb. letters), *Yiddish Deitsche Monatsschrift* (Prague and Brünn, 1802).

JEITELES, JUDAH, 'Announcement' (Heb.), *Bikurei ha'itim*, 12 (1831), 184–95.

KALISCHER, TSEVI HIRSCH, 'The Righteous Person Will Live in his Faith' (Heb.), *Hamagid*, 13 (1869).

KANIEL, YEHOSHUA, 'The Beginnings of the New Yishuv in Jerusalem', in M. Eliav (ed.), *The Book of the First Aliyah* (Heb.), vol. i (Jerusalem, 1982), 319–36.

KANT, IMMANUEL, *Anthropologie in pragmatischer Hinsicht* (1798), trans. Victor Lyle Dowdell as *Anthropology from a Pragmatic Point of View* (Carbondale, Ill., 1978).

——'Beantwortung der Frage, Was ist Aufklärung?', *Berlinische Monatsschrift*, 4 (1784), 481–94.

KANTOR, JUDAH LEIB, 'The *Me'asef* Generation', in *The 'Me'asef' Book: Addendum* (Heb.) (Warsaw, 1886), 1–34.

KATZ, BEN ZION, *Rabbinate, Hasidism, and Haskalah* (Heb.), vol. i (Tel Aviv, 1956).

KATZ, DAVID, *Jews in the History of England, 1485–1850* (Oxford, 1994).

KATZ, JACOB, 'On the Relationship between Shabbateanism and the Haskalah and Reform', in id., *Halakhah in Straits* (Heb.) (Jerusalem, 1992), 261–78.

——*Out of the Ghetto* (Cambridge, Mass., 1973).

——*Tradition and Crisis: Jewish Society at the End of the Middle Ages*, trans. Bernard Dov Cooperman (New York, 1993).

——*The Unhealed Rift* (Heb.) (Jerusalem, 1995).

——(ed.), *Toward Modernity: The European Jewish Model* (New Brunswick, NJ, 1987).

KATZNELSON, GIDEON, *The Literary War between the Orthodox and the Maskilim* (Heb.) (Tel Aviv, 1954).

KAUFMANN, D., and FREUDENTHAL, MAX, *Die Familie Gumperz* (Frankfurt am Main, 1907).

KERSTIG, C., *Die Genese der Pädagogik im 18. Jahrhundert. Campes 'Algemeine Revision' im Kontext der neuzeitlichen Wissenschaft* (Weinheim, 1992).

KESTENBERG-GLADSTEIN, RUTH, *Neuere Geschichte der Juden in böhmischen Ländern* (Tübingen, 1969).

——'A Voice from the Prague Enlightenment', *Leo Baeck Institute Year Book*, 9 (1964), 295–304.

KIEVAL, HILLEL, 'Caution's Progress: The Modernization of Jewish Life in Prague, 1780–1830', in Jacob Katz (ed.), *Toward Modernity: The European Jewish Model* (New Brunswick, NJ, 1987), 71–105.

KLAUSNER, JOSEPH, *History of Modern Hebrew Literature* (Heb.), 6 vols. (Jerusalem, 1952–4).

KLEMPERER, W., *Voltaire und die Juden* (Berlin, 1894).

KNAANI, DAVID, *Studies in the History of the Jewish Family* (Heb.) (Tel Aviv, 1986).

KOIDONOVER, TSEVI HIRSH, *Kav hayashar* [The Straight Measure] (Frankfurt, 1795; Jerusalem, 1993).

KOPITZSCH, FRANKLIN, *Aufklärung, Absolutismus und Bürgertum in Deutschland* (Munich, 1976).

KREIDMAN, BERTA, letter (Heb.), *Hamagid*, supplement to no. 7 (1870) [pages unnumbered].

KRESSEL, G., *Lexicon of Modern Hebrew Literature in Recent Times* (Heb.), vol. i (Merhavia, 1967).

KROCHMAL, NAHMAN, *Collected Writings*, ed. Shimon Ravidovitz (Berlin, 1924).

KUEHN, M., *Scottish Common Sense in Germany 1768–1800* (Montreal, 1987).

LAPIDOT, ALEXANDER MOSES, 'Open Reproof' (Heb.), *Halevanon*, 6/41–3 (1869) [series of articles].

——'Rossiyeny' (Heb.), *Halevanon*, 6/40 (1869), 637–9.

LEAHY, T. H., *A History of Psychology* (London, 1987).

LEDERHENDLER, ELI, *The Road to Modern Jewish Politics* (New York, 1989).

LEFIN, MENAHEM MENDEL, address to Nahman Krochmal, *Kerem ḥemed*, 1 (1833), 74–5.

——*Essai d'un plan de réforme ayant pour objet d'éclairer la Nation Juive en Pologne et de redresser par là ses mœurs* (Warsaw [1791]), in Artur Eisenbach, Jerzy Michalski, Emanuel Rostworowski, and Janusz Woliński (eds.), *Materialy do Dziejów Sejmu Czteroletniego* [Material on the History of the Four Year Sejm], vol. vi (Wroclaw, Warsaw, and Krakow, 1969), 409–21.

——*Ḥeshbon hanefesh* [Moral Accounting] (Lvov, 1809).

——*Likutei kelalim* [Collections of Rules], pub. as appendix 2 of N. M. Gelber, 'Mendel Lefin of Satanow's Proposals for the Improvement of Jewish Community Life Presented to the Great Polish Sejm (1788–1792)', in *The Abraham Weiss Jubilee Volume* (New York, 1964).

——*Masaot hayam* [Sea Journeys] (Zolkiew, 1818; 2nd edn. Vilna, 1823; 3rd edn., including pp. 37–52, Lemberg, 1859).

LEFIN, MENAHEM MENDEL, *Refuat ha'am* [Book of Popular Healing] (Zolkiew, 1794).

LEFIN, MENAHEM MENDEL, *Teshuvah* [Responsum]. Joseph Perl Archive, Jewish National University Library, Jerusalem, folder 72.

LEHMAN, Y. M., 'Maimonides, Mendelssohn and the *Me'asfim*', *Leo Baeck Institute Yearbook*, 20 (1975), 87–108.

LEPERER, S. B., 'Abraham ben Naphtali Tang: A Precursor of the Anglo-Jewish Haskalah', *Transactions of the Jewish Historical Society of England*, 24 (1974), 82–8.

LETTERIS, MEIR, 'Biography of the Author' (Heb.), introduction to Isaac Erter, *Hatsofeh leveit yisra'el* [The Watchman of the House of Israel] (Warsaw, 1883).

——'A Word to the Reader' (Heb.), *Hatsefirah* (Zolkiew, 1824), unpaginated [pp. 1–6].

——*Zikaron basefer* [Memoirs] (Vienna, 1868).

——(ed.), *Mikhtavim* [Letters] (Lemberg, 1827).

——(ed.), *Mikhtavim* [Letters] (Zolkiew, 1827).

LETTERIS, MORDECAI, 'Some Issues Matter' (Heb.), *Bikurim*, 2 (1866), 20–38.

LEVI, DAVID, *Letters to Dr Priestley in Answer to his Letters to the Jews* (London, 1794).

——*A Succinct Account of the Rites and Ceremonies of the Jews* (London, 1782).

LEVIN, JUDAH LEIB, 'Elḥanan' [unfinished poem], *Hashaḥar*, 9 (1878–9); 10 (1880–1).

——'The Issue at Hand', in id., *Memoirs and Pensées* (Heb.), ed. Y. Slutzki (Jerusalem, 1968), 140–3.

——*Sefer hazikhronot* [Memoirs] (Zhitomir, 1910).

LEVINE, HILLEL, 'Between Hasidism and Haskalah: On a Disguised Anti-Hasidic Polemic', in Immanuel Etkes and Joseph Salmon (eds.), *Chapters in the History of Jewish Society in the Middle Ages and the Modern Period* (Heb.) (Jerusalem, 1980), 182–91.

——'Menachem Mendel Lefin: A Case Study of Judaism and Modernization' (Ph.D. diss., Harvard University, 1974).

LEVINSOHN, ISAAC BAER, *Beit yehudah* [The House of Judah] (Vilna, 1858).

——*Efes damim* [No Blood; against blood libel] (1837; Warsaw, 1879).

——*Emek refa'im* [Valley of the Spirits] (Vilna, 1830), pub. in id., *Yalkut ribal*.

——*Te'udah beyisra'el* [Testimony in Israel] (Vilna and Horodno, 1828).

——*Yalkut ribal* [anthology of Levinsohn's works] (Warsaw, 1878).

LEVISON, MORDECHAI GUMPEL SCHNABER, *Ma'amar hatorah vehaḥokhmah* [On the Torah and Wisdom] (London, 1771).

——*Shelosh-esreh yesodei hatorah* [Foundations of the Torah] (Altona, 1792).

LEVITA, ELIJAH BAHUR B. ASHER HALEVI ASHKENAZI, *Mesoret hamasoret* [The Tradition of the Tradition] (Venice, 1538).

LIEBERMAN, HAYIM, *The Tent of Rachel* (Heb.), vol. i (New York, 1980).

LIEBERMAN, SAUL, *Hellenism in Jewish Palestine* (New York, 1962).

LILIENBLUM, MOSES LEIB, *Complete Works* (Heb.) (Krakow, 1910–13).

——*Ḥatot ne'urim* [Sins of My Youth], in *Autobiographical Writings* (Heb.), ed. S. Breiman (Jerusalem, 1970).

——letter to Anshel Markel and Miriam Markel-Mosessohn (Odessa, 1870), *Ketuvim* (1926), 3–4.

——*Letters of M. L. Lilienblum to J. L. Gordon* (Heb.), ed. S. Breiman (Jerusalem, 1968).

——*Mishnat elisha ben avoyah* [The Doctrine of Elisha b. Abuyah], 1st pub. as a series in *Asefat hakhamim* (1878) and *Hame'asef* (1879).

——'Supplements to "The Ways of the Talmud"' (Heb.), *Hamelits*, 9/18– (1869) [series of articles].

——'The Ways of the Talmud' (Heb.), *Hamelits*, 8/13– (1868) [series of articles].

——'What is Haskalah?' (Heb.), 1st pub. in *Hatsefirah* (1878); in Lilienblum, *Complete Works* (Heb.), vol. ii (Krakow, 1912), 113–16.

——'The World of Chaos' (Heb.), *Hashaḥar* (1873).

——*Writings* (Heb.) (1926).

LIPSCHITZ, JACOB, 'A Generation and its Writers' (Heb.), *Hakerem* (Warsaw, 1888), 165–91.

——'How to Improve the Situation of Our Brethren in Russia' (Heb.), *Hamagid*, 13 (1869), 106–7.

——*Zikhron ya'akov* [A Memorial for Jacob] (Jerusalem, 1968).

LOCKE, J., *An Essay Concerning Human Understanding*, ed. P. H. Nidditch (Oxford, 1975).

LOWENSTEIN, STEVEN M., *The Berlin Jewish Community: Enlightenment, Family and Crisis, 1770–1830* (New York and Oxford, 1994).

——'Soziale Aspekte der Krise des berliner Judentums, 1780 bis 1830', in Marianne Awerbuch and Stefi Jersch-Wenzel (eds.), *Bild und Selbstbild der Juden Berlins zwischen Aufklärung und Romantik* (Berlin, 1992), 81–105.

LUZ, EHUD, *Parallels Meet: Religion and Nationality in the Early Zionist Movement in East Europe (1882–1904)* (Heb.) (Tel Aviv, 1985).

LUZZATTO, SAMUEL DAVID, 'Letter 24' (Heb.), *Kerem ḥemed*, 2 (1836), 149–50.

MAHLER, RAPHAEL, *Chronicles of Jewish History* (Heb.), vol. i, bk. 4 (Rehavia, 1956); trans. as *A History of Modern Jewry* (London, 1971).

——*Hasidism and the Jewish Enlightenment: Their Confrontation in Galicia and Poland in the First Half of the Nineteenth Century* (New York and Philadelphia, Pa., 1985).

MAIMON, SOLOMON, *Givat hamoreh* [The Hill of the Guide], ed. S. H. Bergman and Nathan Rotenstreich (Jerusalem, 1966).

——*Ḥayai* (1792; Tel Aviv, 1953); trans. I. L. Baruch as *My Life* (Jerusalem, 1942).

MAIMONIDES, MOSES, *Mishneh torah*, trans. S. Gandz and H. Klein as *The Code of Maimonides: The Book of Seasons* (New Haven, 1961).

——*Shemoneh perakim* [Eight Chapters] (1168).

MALINO, FRANCES, *A Jew in the French Revolution: The Life of Zalkind Hourwitz* (Oxford, 1996).

MANASSEH B. JOSEPH OF ILYA, *Shekel hakodesh* [The Holy Shekel] (Kapust, 1823).

MANUEL, FRANK E., *The Broken Staff: Judaism through Christian Eyes* (Cambridge, Mass., 1992).

—— *The Eighteenth Century Confronts the Gods* (Cambridge, Mass., 1959).

MAOZ, RIVKAH (ed.), *Peretz Smolenskin Exhibition: On the 150th Anniversary of his Birth*, exhibition catalogue (Jerusalem, 1992).

MAPU, ABRAHAM, *Ahavat tsiyon* [The Love of Zion] (n.p., 1853).

—— *Ashmat shomron* [The Guilt of Samaria] (Vilna, 1865–6).

—— *Ayit tsavua* [The Hypocrite] (1857–64), in *Collected Works* (Heb.) (Tel Aviv, 1939).

MARCUSE, MOSES, *Ezer yisra'el* [The Help of Israel] (Paritzk, 1790).

MEDALIA, H. A., 'Biography of Abraham Mapu' (Heb.), *Hamelits*, 11 (1869), 23–4.

MEISEL, WOLF ALOYS, *Leben und Wirken Naphtali Hartwig Wesselys* (Breslau, 1841).

MELER, Y., 'Biography of Rabbi Samson Bloch' (Heb.), *Kochavei yitshak*, 7 (1846), 44–5.

MENAHEM AZARIAH OF FANO, *She'elot uteshuvot harama* [collection of responsa] (Venice, 1600; Jerusalem, 1963).

MENDELE MOKHER SEFORIM, *Complete Works* (Heb.) (Tel Aviv, 1952).

—— *Ha'avot vehabanim* [Fathers and Sons] (Odessa, 1868).

MENDELSSOHN, MOSES, *Biur mendelsohn lemegilat kohelet* [commentary on Ecclesiastes] (1770), in id., *Ketavim ivriyim*, vol. i.

—— *Biur milot hahigayon leharav hehakham beyisra'el . . . morenu verabenu moshe ben rabi maimon, im peirush mehatorani morenu harav rav moshe midesau* [Logical Terms, by the Rabbi and Scholar in Israel . . . our Teacher and Rabbi Moses the Son of Rabbi Maimon, with the Commentary of the Torah Scholar, our Teacher and Rabbi Moses of Dessau] (Berlin, 1765).

—— *Gesammelte Schriften Jubiläumsausgabe*, vols. i–iii(1), vii, xi, xiv, xvi, ed. F. Bamberger *et al.* (Berlin, 1929–38); repr. and continued under the editorship of Alexander Altmann (Stuttgart, 1971–).

—— *Phädon oder über die Unsterblichkeit der Seele in drey Gesprächen* (Berlin, 1767); trans. into Heb. by Isaiah Beer of Metz as *Pha'edon: Hu sefer hasharat hanefesh* [*Phaedon*; or On the Immortality of the Soul] (Berlin, 1787).

—— 'Über die Frage, Was heisst Aufklärung?', *Berlinische Monatsschrift*, 4 (1784), 193–200.

MEUCK, D. C., *The Compass of Irony* (London, 1969).

MEYER, MICHAEL A., *The Origins of the Modern Jew* (Detroit, 1967).

—— 'The Orthodox and the Enlightened: An Unpublished Contemporary Analysis of Berlin Jewry's Spiritual Condition in the Early Nineteenth Century', *Leo Baeck Institute Year Book*, 25 (1980), 101–30.

—— *Response to Modernity: A History of the Reform Movement in Judaism* (New York, 1988; Heb. edn. Jerusalem, 1989).

—— *Tradition and Progress* (Heb.) (Jerusalem, 1995).

—— (ed.), *German-Jewish History in Modern Times*, trans. William Templer, 4 vols. (New York, 1996–8).

MICHMAN, JOSEPH, *Studies in the History and Literature of Dutch Jewry*, jubilee volume (Heb.) (Jerusalem, 1994).

——'The Impact of German-Jewish Modernization on Dutch Jewry', in Jacob Katz (ed.), *Toward Modernity: The European Jewish Model* (New Brunswick, NJ, 1987), 171–88.

MIESES, JUDAH LEIB, *Kinat ha'emet* [The Zeal for Truth] (Vienna, 1828).

MINSK, MOSES, *Sefer even shoham* [Book of the Shoham Stone] (London, 1772).

MIRON, DAN, *Between Vision and Reality* (Heb.) (Jerusalem, 1979).

——*From Romance to the Novel: Studies in the Emergence of the Hebrew and Yiddish Novel in the Nineteenth Century* (Heb.) (Jerusalem, 1979).

MOHILEWER, SAMUEL, 'Human Happiness' (Heb.), *Halevanon*, 9/27 and 29 (1872) [series of articles].

——'Religious Observance and the Enlightenment' (Heb.), *Halevanon*, 9/15–16 (1872) [series of articles].

MÖLLER, HORST H., *Vernunft und Kritik. Deutsche Aufklärung im 17. und 18. Jahrhundert* (Frankfurt am Main, 1986).

MOSES B. MENDEL FRANKFURT. *See* FRANKFURT, MOSES MENDELSOHN

MOSES MENDELSON OF HAMBURG. *See* FRANKFURT, MOSES MENDELSOHN

MOSSE, GEORGE L., *German Jews Beyond Judaism* (Bloomington, Ind., 1985).

MOSSNER, E. C., 'Deism', *Encyclopedia of Philosophy*, 8 vols. (New York and London, 1967), ii. 326–35.

NAHMAN OF BRATSLAV, *Sipurei ma'asiyot* (Berdichev, 1815); pub. as *The Tales*, ed. Arnold J. Band (New York, 1978).

NARDI, ZEVIA, 'Transformations in the Enlightenment Movement in Russia', in Immanuel Etkes (ed.), *Religion and Life: The Jewish Enlightenment in Eastern Europe* (Heb.) (Jerusalem, 1993), 300–27.

NEHAMA, JACOB JUDAH, *Mikhtavei dodim miyayin* [Letters More Delightful than Wine] (Salonika, 1893).

NIGAL, GEDALIAH, *Dibuk Stories* (Heb.) (Jerusalem, 1983).

O'NEIL, E., 'Influxus Physicus', in S. Nadler (ed.), *Causation in Early Modern Philosophy: Cartesianism, Occasionalism, and Pre-established Harmony* (University Park, Pa., 1993), 27–55.

OPHEK, URIEL, *Hebrew Children's Literature: Beginnings* (Heb.) (Tel Aviv, 1979).

ORON, MICHAL, 'Dr Samuel Falk and the Eibeschütz–Emden Controversy', in K. E. Grözinger and Joseph Dan (eds.), *Mysticism, Magic, and Kabbalah in Ashkenazi Judaism* (Berlin, 1995), 243–56.

——'Mysticism and Magic in London in the Eighteenth Century: Samuel Falk, the Ba'al Shem Tov of London', in R. Tzur and T. Rozen (eds.), *The Book of Israel Levine* (Heb.) (Tel Aviv, 1995), 7–20.

PAPERNA, ABRAHAM JACOB, *Collected Writings* (Heb.), ed. Y. Zmora (Tel Aviv, 1952).

PELLI, MOSHE, *The Age of Haskalah: Studies in Hebrew Literature of the Enlightenment in Germany* (Leiden, 1979).

——'The Literary Genre of the Travelogue in Hebrew Haskalah Literature: Shmuel Romanelli's *Masa be'arav*', *Modern Judaism*, 11 (1991), 241–60.

PERL, JOSEPH, *Boḥen tsadik* [Who Tries the Righteous] (Prague, 1838).

——*Megaleh temirin* [Revealer of Secrets] (Vienna, 1819); Eng. edn. *Revealer of Secrets*, ed. Dov Taylor (New York, 1997).

——'Oil for the Lamp' (Heb.), *Kerem ḥemed*, 2 (1836), 16–39.

PIEKARZ, MENDEL, *The Early Development of Hasidism* (Heb.) (Jerusalem, 1978).

PINES, YEHIEL MICHAEL, 'Concerning the Supplements to "The Ways of the Talmud"' (Heb.), *Halevanon*, 6/21–2 (1869) [series of articles].

——'Dear Advocate' (Heb.), *Hamelits*, 8/1 (1868), 6–7.

——'How to Improve the Situation of Our Brethren in Russia' (Heb.), *Hamagid*, 13 (1869), 98–9.

——'Jewry's Place among the Nations' (Heb.), *Hamelits*, 7/16–18 (1867) [series of articles].

——'On the Settlement of Erets Yisrael' (Heb.), *Halevanon*, 11/35–6 (1875) [series of articles].

——'The Ways of Educating Our Children, and What the People Want from their Rabbis' (Heb.), *Hamelits*, 7/35–43 (1867) [series of articles].

——*Yaldei ruḥi* [My Spiritual Children], 2 vols. (1872); vol. i (Jerusalem, 1934).

POLIAKOV, LÉON, *Histoire de l'antisémitisme de Voltaire à Wagner* (Paris, 1968).

POPKIN, RICHARD H., 'David Levi: Anglo-Jewish Theologian', *Jewish Quarterly Review*, NS 87 (1996), 79–101.

——'Scepticism, Theology and the Scientific Revolution in the Seventeenth Century', in Imre Lakatos and Alan Musgrave (eds.), *Problems in the Philosophy of Science* (Amsterdam, 1968), 1–28.

PORTER, ROY, *The Enlightenment* (London, 1990).

——and TEICH, MIKULAS (eds.), *The Enlightenment in National Context* (Cambridge, 1981).

RAISIN, JACOB ZALMAN, *The Haskalah Movement in Russia* (Philadelphia, Pa., 1913).

RAMBAM. *See* MAIMONIDES, MOSES

RAPOPORT, SOLOMON JUDAH LEIB, 'Ner mitsvah' [Lamp of the Commandment], in *Naḥalat yehudah* [The Inheritance of Judah] (Krakow, 1868), 1–26.

RAPOPORT-ALBERT, ADA, 'On Women in Hasidism: S. A. Horodezky and the Maid of Ludmir Tradition', in Ada Rapoport-Albert and Steven J. Zipperstein (eds.), *Jewish History* (London, 1988), 495–525.

REEVE, CLARA, *The Progress of Romance* (London, 1785).

REHLE, B., *Aufklärung und Moral in der Kinder- und Jugendliteratur des 18. Jahrhunderts* (Frankfurt am Main, 1989).

REINES, MOSES, 'Spirit of the Time' (Heb.), *Otsar hasifrut*, 2 (1888), 45–69.

REIZEN, ZALMAN, 'Campe's "Entdeckung von Amerike" in Yiddish', *YIVO Bleter*, 5/1 (1933), 29–40.

RESSER, SAMUEL, 'The Work of the Enlightenment and Education in Modern Times', in *A Concise History of the World* (Yiddish) (Vilna, 1864), 219–21.

RIVLIN, ELIEZER, *The Tsadik Rabbi Joseph Sundel of Salant and his Masters* (Heb.) (Jerusalem, 1927).

RODRIGUE, AARON, *French Jews, Turkish Jews: The Alliance Israélite Universelle and the Politics of Jewish Schooling in Turkey, 1860–1925* (Bloomington, Ind., 1998).

ROMANELLI, SAMUEL AARON, *Masa be'arav* [Journey in Arab Lands] (Berlin, 1792).

ROSALDO, M. ZIMBALIST, 'Women, Culture, and Society: A Theoretical Overview', in M. Z. Rosaldo and L. Lamphere (eds.), *Women, Culture, and Society* (Stanford, Calif., 1974), 17–42.

ROSENBLUM, N., 'The First Hebrew Encyclopedia: Its Author and its Development' (Heb.), *Proceedings of the American Academy for Jewish Research*, 55 (1988), 15–65.

ROSENTHAL, LEON (JUDAH LEIB), *The History of the Society for the Promotion of Culture among Russian Jews* (Heb.), pt. 1 (St Petersburg, 1886).

ROSKIES, DAVID, 'The Medium and the Message of the Maskilic Chapbook', *Jewish Social Studies*, 41 (1979), 275–90.

ROSMAN, MOSHE, *Founder of Hasidism: The Quest for the Historical Ba'al Shem Tov* (Berkeley, Calif., 1996).

ROTENSTREICH, NATAN, 'Enlightenment: Between Mendelssohn and Kant', in S. Stein and R. Loewe (eds.), *Studies in Jewish Religion and Intellectual History* (Tuscaloosa, Ala., 1979), 279–363.

——*Jewish Philosophy in Modern Times: From Mendelssohn to Rosenzweig* (New York, 1968).

ROTH, CECIL, *Essays and Portraits of Anglo-Jewish History* (London, 1962).

——'The Haskalah in England', in H. J. Zimmels, J. Rabbinowitz, and I. Finestein (eds.), *Essays Presented to Chief Rabbi Israel Brodie on the Occasion of his Seventieth Birthday* (London, 1967), 365–76.

——'The Lesser London Synagogues of the Eighteenth Century', *Miscellanies of the Jewish Historical Society of England*, 3 (1937), 1–7.

RUBINSTEIN, AVRAHAM (ed.), *Chapters in the Doctrine and History of Hasidism* (Heb.) (Jerusalem, 1977).

RUDERMAN, DAVID B., *Jewish Enlightenment in an English Key: Anglo-Jewry's Construction of Modern Jewish Thought* (Princeton, NJ, 2000).

——*Jewish Thought and Scientific Discovery in Early Modern Europe* (New Haven, 1995).

——'Newtonianism and Jewish Thought in England: The Case of Eliakim ben Abraham Hart', *Science in Context*, 10 (1997), 677–92.

RUTHERFORD, D., 'Metaphysics: The Late Period', in N. Jolley (ed.), *The Cambridge Companion to Leibniz* (Cambridge, 1995), 124–75.

SA'ADYA GAON, *Sefer ha'emunot vehade'ot* [Book of Doctrines and Beliefs] (10th cent.; Berlin, 1789).

SACHS, SHNEUR, letter to Isaac Erter in *Kanfei yonah*, supplement to *Hayonah*, 1st booklet (Berlin, 1848), 33.

SADAN, DOV, *Avnei bedek* [Test Stones] (1947; Tel Aviv, 1962).

SALMON, JOSEPH, 'The Beginning of the Reform in the Eastern European Yeshivas' (Heb.), *Molad*, 4 (1971), 161–72.

——'Samuel Mohilewer: The Rabbi of Hovevei Zion' (Heb.), *Zion*, 56 (1991), 17–78.

——'Urban Ashkenazi Settlement in Erets Yisrael from the Time of the First Aliyah', in I. Kolatt (ed.), *History of the Jewish Yishuv in Erets Yisrael from the Time of the First Aliyah* (Heb.) (Jerusalem, 1990), 580–605.

——'The Yeshiva of Lida: A Unique Institution of Higher Learning' (Heb.), *YIVO Annual*, 15 (1974), 106–25.

SALOMON, GOTTHOLD, 'Über Aufklärung und Aufklärer', *Sulamith*, 2/1 (1808), 217–32.

SALZMANN, C. S., *Moralisches Elementarbuch* (Leipzig, 1785); trans. as *Elements of Morality for the Use of Young Persons* (Boston, Mass., 1850).

SAMET, MOSHE, 'M. Mendelson, N. H. Wessely, and the Rabbis of their Generation', in A. Gilboa, B. Mevorach, *et al.* (eds.), *Research into the History of the Jewish People and the Land of Israel* (Heb.), vol. i (Haifa, 1970), 244–53.

SATANOW, ISAAC, commentary on Judah Halevi, *Sefer hakuzari* (Berlin, 1795).

——*Mishlei asaf* [The Proverbs of Asaf] (Berlin, 1788).

——*Sefer hamidot* [Book of Ethics] (Berlin, 1784).

SCHARFSTEIN, Z., 'The *Ḥeder* in the Life of our People', in *Shiloh* (Heb.) (n.p., 1943).

SCHATZ-UFFENHEIMER, RIVKA, *Hasidism as Mysticism: Quietistic Elements in Eighteenth-century Hasidic Thought* (Jerusalem, 1993).

SCHIRMANN, J., 'The First Hebrew Translation from English Literature: Congreve's *Mourning Bride*', *Scripta Hierosolymitana*, 19 (1967), 3–15.

SCHMIDT, J., 'The Question of Enlightenment: Kant, Mendelssohn and the *Mittwochgesellschaft*', *Journal of the History of Ideas*, 50 (1989), 269–91.

SCHNABER, MORDECHAI GUMPEL. *See* LEVISON, MORDECHAI GUMPEL SCHNABER

SCHOEPS, H. J., 'Gumpertz Levison. Leben und Werk eines gelehrten Abenteurers des 18. Jahrhunderts', *Zeitschrift für Religions- und Geistesgeschichte*, 4 (1952), 150–61; repr. in id., *Studien zur unbekannten Religions- und Geistesgeschichte* (Berlin, 1963), 216–27; trans. into French as 'La Vie et l'œuvre de Gumpertz Levison', *Revue d'histoire de la médicine hébraïque*, 27 (1955), 133–43.

SCHOLEM, GERSHOM, '*Devekut*, or Communion with God', in (id.), *The Messianic Idea in Judaism* (New York, 1971), 203–27.

——'The First Emergence of the Hasidic Way' (Heb.), *Zion*, 15 (1951).

——'The First Two Testimonies on the Relation between Hasidic Groups and the Ba'al Shem Tov' (Heb.), *Tarbiz*, 20 (1949), 228–40.

——'The Historical Figure of R. Israel Ba'al Shem Tov', in id., *Explications and Implications* (Heb.) (Tel Aviv, 1975).

SCHORR, JOSHUA HESCHEL, 'Prophecy on Rabbis' (Heb.), *Heḥaluts*, 3 (1857), 42–74.

SCHUCHARD, MARSHA KEITH, 'Yeats and the "Unknown Superiors": Swedenborg, Falk and Cagliostro', in M. M. Roberts and H. Ormsby-Lennon (eds.), *Secret Texts: The Literature of Secret Societies* (New York, 1995), 114–68.

SCOTT, J. W., and TILLY, L. A., 'Women's Work and the Family in Nineteenth-Century Europe', *Comparative Studies in Society and History*, 17/1 (Jan. 1975), 36–64.

SEGAL, TOYBE, 'The Question of Women' (Heb.), *Ha'ivri* (1879), 69, 78–9, 85, 94, 101–2.

SEPTIMUS, BERNARD, *Hispano-Jewish Culture in Transition: The Career and Controversies of Ramah* (Cambridge, Mass., 1982).

SHAVIT, UZI, 'An Examination of the Term Haskalah in Hebrew Literature' (Heb.), *Meḥkarei yerushalayim besifrut ivrit*, 12 (1990), 51–83.

SHAVIT, YA'AKOV, *Judaism in the Mirror of Hellenism and the Appearance of the Modern Hellenistic Jew* (Heb.) (Tel Aviv, 1992); trans. Chaya Naor and Niki Werner as *Athens in Jerusalem: Classical Antiquity and Hellenism in the Making of the Modern Secular Jew* (London and Portland, Ore., 1997).

SHAVIT, ZOHAR, *Deutsch-jüdische kinder- und Jugendliteratur von der Haskala bis 1945*, 2 vols. (Stuttgart, 1996).

——'From Friedländer's *Lesebuch* to the Jewish Campe: The Beginning of Hebrew Children's Literature in Germany', *Leo Baeck Institute Yearbook*, 33 (1988), 385–415.

——'Literary Interference between German and Jewish Hebrew Children's Literature during the Enlightenment: The Case of Campe', *Poetics Today*, 13/1 (1992), 41–61.

SHERWIN, BYRON L., *Mystical Theology and Social Dissent: The Life and Works of Judah Loew of Prague* (Rutherford, NJ, 1982).

SHITRIT, JOSEPH, 'Hebrew Nationalist Modernism as Opposed to French Modernism: The Hebrew Haskalah in North Africa at the End of the Nineteenth Century' (Heb.), *Mikedem umiyam*, 3 (1990), 11–76.

——'New Awareness of Anomalies and Language: Beginnings of the Hebrew Haskalah Movement in Morocco at the End of the Nineteenth Century' (Heb.), *Mikedem umiyam*, 2 (1986), 129–68.

Shivḥei habesht. See DOV BER B. SHMUEL OF LINITS

SHMERUK, CHONE, 'Regarding Several Principles of Mendel Lefin's Translation of Proverbs', in id., *Yiddish Literature in Poland: Historical Research and Insights* (Heb.) (Jerusalem, 1981), 165–83.

——'The Stories about R. Adam Ba'al Shem and their Formulations in the Versions of the Book *Shivḥei habesht*' (Heb.), *Zion*, 28 (1963), 86–105.

——*Yiddish Literature: Chapters in its History* (Heb.) (Tel Aviv, 1978).

——*Yiddish Literature in Poland: Historical Research and Insights* (Heb.) (Jerusalem, 1981).

SHOHAT, AZRIEL, *Changing Eras: The Beginning of the Haskalah among German Jewry* (Heb.) (Jerusalem, 1960).

SIDORSKY, DOV, *Libraries and Books in Late Ottoman Palestine* (Heb.) (Jerusalem, 1990).

SILBER, MICHAEL, 'The Historical Experience of German Jewry and the Impact of Haskalah and Reform in Hungary', in Jacob Katz (ed.), *Toward Modernity* (New Brunswick, NJ and Oxford, 1987), 107–58.

SIMON, ERNST A., 'Pedagogic Philanthropism and Jewish Education', in Moshe Davis (ed.), *Jubilee Volume in Honor of Mordecai Kaplan* (Heb. section) (New York, 1953), 149–87.

SINGER, SIMEON, 'Early Translations and Translators of the Jewish Liturgy in England', *Transactions of the Jewish Historical Society of England*, 3 (1896–8), 36–71.

SMITH, ANTHONY D., *Theories of Nationalism* (London, 1971).

SMOLENSKIN, PERETZ, *Derekh la'avor ge'ulim* [To Pass Through Redemptions] (1881); pt. 2, *Ma'amarim* [Articles] (Jerusalem, 1925).

——*Hato'eh bedarkhei haḥayim* [The Wanderer in the Paths of Life], 4 vols. (1869–71; Warsaw, 1910).

——letter to Miriam Markel-Mosessohn (1869), *Ketuvim*, 3 (Nov. 1927), 5.

SOKOLOV, NAHUM, *Sefer zikaron lesofrei yisra'el haḥayim itanu hayom* [Memorial Book for Jewish Sages Alive Today] (Warsaw, 1888; 3rd edn. Tel Aviv, 1940).

SOLOMON B. MOSES OF CHELM, *Sefer mirkevet hamishneh* [Chariot of the Second-in-Command], 3 pts. (1: Frankfurt an der Oder, 1751; 2–3: Salonika, 1782).

SORKIN, DAVID, 'The Case for Comparison: Moses Mendelssohn and the Religious Enlightenment', *Modern Judaism*, 14 (1994), 121–38.

——'From Context to Comparison: The German Haskalah and Reform Catholicism', *Tel Aviver Jahrbuch für deutsche Geschichte*, 20 (1991), 23–58.

——*Moses Mendelssohn and the Religious Enlightenment* (Berkeley and Los Angeles, 1996).

——*The Transformation of German Jewry, 1780–1840* (New York, 1987).

STAHL-WEINBERG, S., *The World of Our Mothers* (Chapel Hill, NC and London, 1988).

STAMPFER, S., 'Gender Differentiation and Education of the Jewish Woman in Nineteenth-Century Eastern Europe', *Polin*, 7 (1992), 63–87.

——'The Social Meaning of Premature Marriage in Eastern Europe in the Nineteenth Century', in A. Mendelson and Chone Shmeruk (eds.), *P. Glickson Memorial Volume: A Collection of Studies on the Jews of Poland* (Heb.) (Jerusalem, 1987).

STANISLAWSKI, MICHAEL, 'The Beginnings of Russian Enlightenment', in Immanuel Etkes (ed.), *Religion and Life: The Jewish Enlightenment in Eastern Europe* (Heb.) (Jerusalem, 1993), 126–66.

——*For Whom Do I Toil? Judah Leib Gordon and the Crisis of Russian Jewry* (New York, 1988).

——'Haskalah and Zionism: A Re-examination', *Vision Confronts Reality: The Herzl Yearbook*, 9 (1989), 56–67.

——*Tsar Nicholas I and the Jews: The Transformation of Jewish Society in Russia, 1825–1855* (Philadelphia, Pa., 1983).

STEINSCHNEIDER, MORITZ, 'Hebraeische Buchdruckerei in Deutschland', *Zeitschrift für die Geschichte der Juden in Deutschland*, 5 (1892), 166–82.

STEPHAN, L., *History of English Thought in the Eighteenth Century*, 2 vols. (New York, 1962).

STERN, JOSEPH ZECHARIAH, 'A Time to Build the Walls of Religion' (Heb.), *Halevanon*, 6/31–6 and 39–40 (1869) [series of articles].

——'Wise Men, Be Careful What You Say' (Heb.), *Halevanon*, 7/3 (1870), 17–21.

STITES, R., *The Women's Liberation Movement in Russia* (Princeton, NJ, 1978).

STUKE, HORST, 'Aufklärung', *Geschichtliche Grundbegriffe* (Stuttgart, 1977).

Takanot ḥevrat shoḥarei hatov vehatushiyah [Regulations of the Society for the Propagation of Goodness and Virtue] (Berlin and Königsberg, 1787).

TANG [ABRAHAM ABRAHAMS], *Beḥinat ha'adam* [Examination of Man]. Extant manuscripts: St Petersburg RNL Heb. II A22 (Institute for Microfilmed Manuscripts, University and National Library, Jerusalem, no. 63945); Frankfurt am Main 8*59, cat. no. 63 (Jerusalem, no. 25906) (both contain pt. 1 only); Cincinnati Hebrew Union College 728/1 (Jerusalem, no. 35913) (also contains the beginning of pt. 2).

——commentary on Ecclesiastes. MS Jews College 7 (Institute for Microfilmed Manuscripts, University and National Library, Jerusalem, no. 4676) (1773).

——*Kol sinai*. MS Cincinnati Hebrew Union College 728/2.

——['A Primitive Ebrew'], *A Discourse Addressed to the Minority* (London, 1770).

——'Sabei debei atunah' [The Sages of the Athens Academy]. MS Jews College 35 (Institute for Microfilmed Manuscripts, University and National Library, Jerusalem, no. 4698).

——*The Sentences and Proverbs of the Ancient Fathers . . . Written originally in Ebrew . . . by . . . R. Jehudah the Holy . . . now translated into the English Language . . . By a primitive Ebrew* [commentary on *Pirkei avot*] (London, 1772).

TEETER DOBBS, B. J., and JACOB, M. C., *Newton and the Culture of Newtonianism* (Atlantic Highlands, NJ, 1995).

TISHBY, ISAIAH, *The Wisdom of the Zohar*, 3 vols. (Oxford, 1989).

——and DAN, JOSEPH, 'Hasidic Thought and Literature', in Avraham Rubinstein (ed.), *Chapters in the Doctrine and History of Hasidism* (Heb.) (Jerusalem, 1977), 250–315.

————*Selected Ethical Literature* (Heb.) (Jerusalem, 1970).

TRIEBESCH, ABRAHAM, *Korot ha'itim* [History] (Lemberg, 1851).

TRIVETSCH, Y. A., 'In Honour of the Haskalah' (Heb.), *Aḥi'asaf*, 8 (1900), 225–39.

TROIB, ABRAHAM SIMON, OF KAIDAN, 'Hark! My beloved Lord knocketh' (Heb.), *Hamelits*, 7/6 (1867), 44–6.

TSAMRIYON, TSEMAH, '*Hame'asef*': *The First Modern Periodical in Hebrew* (Heb.) (Tel Aviv, 1988).

TSUR, YARON, 'Jewish Sectional Societies in France and Algeria on the Eve of the Colonial Encounter', *Journal of Mediterranean Studies*, 4 (1994), 263–76.

TSUR, YARON, 'Tunisian Jewry at the End of the Pre-Colonial Period' (Heb.), *Mikedem umiyam*, 3 (1990), 77–113.

TUINHOUT-KEUNING, P., 'The Writings of the Hevrat To'elet in Amsterdam and the Haskalah in Germany', in Joseph Michman (ed.), *Studies in the History of Dutch Jewry* (Heb.) (Jerusalem, 1988), 217–71.

TURNIANSKY, CHAVA, 'A Haskalah Interpretation of the *Tse'enah-ure'enah*' (Heb.; Eng. abstract), *Hasifrut*, 2/4 (1971), 835–41.

VIDAS, ELIJAH B. MOSES DE, *Reshit ḥokhmah* [Beginning of Wisdom] (Mantua, 1623).

WATKINS, ERIC, 'The Development of Physical Influx in Early Eighteenth-Century Germany: Gottsched, Knutzen, and Crusius', *Review of Metaphysics*, 49 (1995), 296–339.

WEINER, MEIR, *The History of Yiddish Literature in the Nineteenth Century* (Yiddish) (Kiev, 1940).

WEINLÖS, ISRAEL, 'Menachem Mendel Lefin of Satanow' (Heb.), *Ha'olam*, 13/39–42 (1925) [series of articles].

——'Mendel Lefin of Satanow: A Biographical Study from Manuscript Material' (Yiddish), *YIVO Bleter*, 1 (1931), 334–57.

WEISS, A. H., 'The Beginning of the Haskalah in Russia' (Heb.), *Mimizraḥ umima'arav*, 1 (1894), 9–16.

WEISS, JOSEPH, 'The First Emergence of the Hasidic Way' (Heb.), *Zion*, 15 (1951), 53–5.

WERSES, SHMUEL, 'The Development of Autobiography in the Haskalah', in id. (ed.), *Trends and Forms in Haskalah Literature*, 249–60.

——'Hasidism in the Eyes of Haskalah Literature: From the Polemic of Galician Maskilim', in Immanuel Etkes (ed.), *Trends and Forms in Haskalah Literature*, 91–109.

——*Haskalah and Shabbateanism: The Story of a Controversy* (Heb.) (Jerusalem, 1988).

——'The Joseph Perl Archives in Jerusalem and their Wanderings' (Heb.), *Ha'universitah*, 19/1 (Mar. 1974), 38–52.

——'On the Tracks of the Pamphlet, *Making Wise the Simple*', in id. (ed.), *Trends and Forms in Haskalah Literature*, 319–37.

——'The Satirical Methods of Joseph Perl', in id., *Story and Source: Studies in the Development of Hebrew Prose*, 21–8.

——*Story and Source: Studies in the Development of Hebrew Prose* (Heb.) (Ramat Gan, 1971).

——'The World of Folklore in Mendele's Works' (Heb.), *Dapim lemeḥkar basifrut*, 9 (1994), 7–27.

——*The Yiddish Translations of 'Ahavat Zion' by Abraham Mapu* (Heb.) (Jerusalem, 1989).

——(ed.), *Trends and Forms in Haskalah Literature* (Heb.) (Jerusalem, 1990).

WESSELY, NAPHTALI HERZ, *Divrei shalom ve'emet* [Words of Peace and Truth] (Berlin, 1782; 2nd edn. Vienna, 1826).

——*Ein mishpat* [The Fountain of Judgement] (Berlin, 1784).

——*Gan na'ul* [A Locked Garden], 2 vols. (Amsterdam, 1765–6).

——'Ḥikur din' [Discourse on Final Judgement], *Hame'asef*, 4 (1788), 97–111, 145–65.

——*Ḥokhmat shelomoh* [The Wisdom of Solomon] (Berlin, 1780).

——'Mehalel rea' [In Praise of a Friend] (written *c.*1778), in Moses Mendelssohn, *Gesammelte Schriften Jubiläumsausgabe*, ed. F. Bamberger *et al.* (Berlin, 1929–38) and Alexander Altmann (Stuttgart, 1971–), vol. xv(1).

——*Rav tuv leveit yisra'el* [Blessings on the House of Israel] (Berlin, 1782).

——*Reḥovot* (Berlin, 1785).

——*Sefer hamidot vehu sefer musar haskel* [The Book of Ethics, a Book of Morals] (Berlin, *c.*1785/7).

——*Shirei tiferet* [Songs of Glory] (Berlin, 1788).

——*Yein levanon* [Wine of Lebanon] (Berlin, 1775).

WETZLAR, ISAAC, *Libes briv*, ed. and trans. Morris M. Faierstein, Brown Judaic Studies 308 (Atlanta, Ga., 1996).

WIELAND, CHRISTOPH M., 'Sechs Fragen zur Aufklärung', *Der Teutsche Merkur*, 66 (Apr. 1789), 97–105.

WINTER, EDUARD, *Frühaufklärung* (Berlin, 1966).

WOLF, JOSEPH, 'Über das Wesen, der Charakter und die Nothwendigkeit der Religion', *Sulamith*, 1 (1806), 117–25, 207–14, 314–19, 441–54.

WOLF, LUCIEN, 'A Plea for Anglo-Jewish History', *Transactions of the Jewish Historical Society of England*, 1 (1893–4).

WOLFF, CHRISTIAN, *Vernunftige Gedancken von Gott, der Welt und der Seele des Menschen* (Frankfurt, 1733).

WOLFF, LARRY, *Inventing Eastern Europe: The Map of Civilization in the Mind of the Enlightenment* (Stanford, Calif., 1994).

WOLFSON, H. A. 'The Internal Senses in Latin, Arabic, and Hebrew Philosophical Texts', in id., *Studies in the History of Philosophy and Religion* (Cambridge, Mass., 1973), 250–315.

WOLFSSOHN, AARON, *Jeschurun, oder unparteyische Beleuchtung der dem Judenthume neuerdings gemachten Vorwürfe* (Breslau, 1804).

WORMS, ASHER ANSEL, *Mafte'aḥ he'algebrah heḥadashah* [Key to the New Algebra] (Offenbach, 1722).

——*Seyag letorah* [A Fence for the Torah] (Frankfurt am Main, 1766).

YAFFE, BINYAMIN, 'Rabbi Joseph Zechariah Stern' (Heb.), in id., *Yavneh* (Jerusalem, 1942).

YAFFE, ELIAHU, *The Book of Memoirs of Mordechai* (Warsaw, 1913).

YAMPOLSKI, P., 'Memoirs of my Youth' (Heb.), *Keneset yisra'el*, 1 (1886), col. 863.

YARDENI, GALIA, *Hebrew Journalism in Erets Yisrael, 1863–1904* (Heb.) (Tel Aviv, 1969).

YAVETZ, ZE'EV, 'The Tower of the Century' (Heb.), *Keneset yisra'el*, 1 (1886), 89–152.

YERUSHALMI, YOSEF HAYIM, *The Lisbon Massacre of 1506 and the Royal Image in the Shebet yehudah*, HUCA Supplements 1 (1976).

YUDELOW, YIZHAK, 'The Book *Ḥelkat re'uven*' (Heb.), *Alei sefer*, 14 (1987), 139–41.

——'The Portion of Reuben' (Heb.), *Alei sefer*, 14 (1987), 139–40.

ZALKIN, MORDECHAI, *A New Dawn. The Jewish Enlightenment in the Russian Empire: Social Aspects* (Heb.) (Jerusalem, 2000).

ZAWADZKI, W. H., *A Man of Honour: Adam Czartoryski as a Statesman of Russia and Poland, 1795–1831* (Oxford, 1993).

ZBOROWSKI, M., and HERZOG, E., *Life Is With People: The Culture of the Shtetl* (New York, 1952).

ZINBERG, ISRAEL, *A History of Jewish Literature*, vol. vi (New York, 1975).

ZIPPERSTEIN, STEVEN J., *The Jews of Odessa: A Cultural History, 1794–1881* (Stanford, Calif., 1986).

ZITRON, SAMUEL LEIB, 'Literature and Life' (Heb.), *Pardes*, 1 (1892), 173–204.

ZWEIFEL, ELIEZER TSEVI HAKOHEN, *Shalom al yisra'el* [Peace Upon Israel], 4 vols. (Zhitomir, 1868–73); ed. Abraham Rubinstein (Jerusalem, 1973).

Index

Printed and bound by CPI Group (UK) Ltd, Croydon, CR0 4YY

09/06/2025

14685793-0002